Sport, Policy and Politics

D0165750

Why is it that now most governments, whether democratic or authoritarian, accord sport a high status in central administration and spend considerable sums of public money on the development of sport in general, and elite sport in particular? *Sport, Policy and Politics* unravels both the processes involved in policy-making for sport, and what motives might lie behind investment by the governments of five countries: Australia, Canada, Ireland, the United Kingdom and the United States of America.

Barrie Houlihan examines the process by which sport policy is made and explores the administrative framework for sport, focusing on the respective responsibilities of central or federal governments, state governments and local authorities. The book explores the evolution of the division of responsibility between different levels of government and how the relationships are managed. Moreover, this book provides an analysis of the policy-making process for two important contemporary issues: drug abuse by athletes, and the provision of sport and physical education in schools.

Sport, Policy and Politics evaluates how different countries approach similar problems and the extent to which they produce similar policy solutions. One of the problematic conclusions of this study is an emerging concern with the future role of domestic governing bodies of sport, and the dangers for sports development of increasing dependence on government resources. This book will be an ideal textbook for those studying sport, leisure management or policy-making, as well as for political scientists.

Barrie Houlihan is Associate Dean and Professor of Public Policy in the School of Humanities and Social Sciences at Staffordshire University. He is highly respected in the field of sport and public policy. His many publications include *Sport and International Politics* (1994), and *The Government and Politics of Sport* (Routledge, 1991).

Sport, Policy and Politics

A comparative analysis

Barrie Houlihan

London and New York

First published 1997
Reprinted 2001 by Routledge
11 New Fetter Lane, London EC4P 4EE

Simultaneously published in the USA and Canada
by Routledge
29 West 35th Street, New York, NY 10001

Routledge is an imprint of the Taylor & Francis Group

British Library Cataloguing in Publication Data
A catalogue record for this book is available from the British Library

Library of Congress Cataloguing in Publication Data
Houlihan, Barrie.
Sport, policy and politics: a comparative analysis / Barrie Houlihan.
p. cm.
Includes bibliographical references and index.
1. Sports and state–Cross-cultural studies. 2. Sports–Political
aspects–Cross-cultural studies. I. Title.
GV706.35.H687 1997
796'.06'9–dc21

97–3355
CIP

ISBN 0–415–12918–4 (hbk)
ISBN 0–415–12919–2 (pbk)

Transferred to digital reprinting 2001

Printed in Great Britain by Antony Rowe Ltd, Eastbourne

To Maureen,

James, Matthew,

Maria and Erica

Contents

Tables

Preface

The origin of this book lies in an earlier study of politics and policy of British sport. In some respects the present work represents an updating of aspects of the earlier study, but it also represents an extension. The main policy issues examined in the British study concerned soccer hooliganism, drug abuse by athletes and sport for school-age children and it was quite apparent that with regard to drug abuse and hooliganism, the international dimension to policy-making was important both in terms of the significance of international governmental and non-governmental bodies and also in terms of the extent to which governments monitored policy development in other countries.

The book is intended to introduce students to some of the issues and problems associated with comparative study and to identify some of the potential insights to be gained from comparative study. It is also intended that the book should provide a stimulus to debate about the future direction of government involvement in sport.

Acknowledgements

In any piece of academic research authors soon realise how dependent they are upon the goodwill of others. In undertaking this study I have accumulated a very large number of debts and hope that the mention of their names here will go some way towards acknowledging the debt that I owe to those who provided information, their reflections on policy questions and who gave me the opportunity to test my analysis against their experience. Needless to say none of those mentioned is responsible for the interpretation reflected in this book.

Simon Broadley, Department of National Heritage; Phillip Brown, Irish Rugby Football Union; Mary Burns, City of San Francisco; Paul Butcher, Colorado Springs City Council; Jay Coakley, University of Colorado at Colorado Springs; Lawrence Chalip, Griffith University, Australia; Harold Cliff, Swimming Canada; Sue Consineau, Canadian Association for Health, Physical Education, Recreation and Dance; Pat Duffy, National Coaching and Training Centre, Ireland; Ray Essick, US Swimming; Wade Exum and Joan Price, US Olympic Committee; Graham Fredericks, Australian Cycling Federation; Alex Gardener, Athletics Canada; Roddy Gaynor, Institute of Leisure and Amenity Management, Ireland; Jan Grieve and colleagues, North Sydney Council; Garry Harding and Kevin Flynn, Sydney City Council; Richard Haslam, University College, Cork; Steve Haynes, Confederation of Australian Sport; Geraldine Herbert, Canadian Parks and Recreation Association; Natalie Howson, Australian Sports Drug Agency; Joan Hult, University of Maryland at College Park; Arthur Johnson, University of Maryland, Baltimore County; Lyn Jones, US Weightlifting; Steve Kalend, Australian School Sports Council; Michael Kennedy, Marc Howard, Sheila Hickey and Arthur Kelly, Ministry of Education; Angela Lumpkin, North Carolina State University; Gerry Macken, Dublin City Corporation; Vena Murray, Australian Swimming Inc.; Shay McDonald and Dermot Sherlock, Olympic Council of Ireland; Craig McLatchy, Australian Olympic Committee; Sue Neill, Sport Canada; Harvey Newton, National Strength and Conditioning Association; Grainne O'Donovan, Physical Education Association of Ireland; Mark Owens, Robyn Calder, Colin Lane and Robin Nielson, ACT Bureau of Sport, Recreation and Racing; Tim

Rose and Judy Young, National Association for Sport and Physical Education; Allan Russell, NSW Department of Sport and Recreation; Barry Tindall and Jodi Landry, National Recreation and Park Association, USA; Duffy Mahoney, USA Track and Field; Hans de Vaal and colleagues, Toronto City Council; Michelle Verroken, UK Sports Council; Casey Wade and Joseph de Pencier, Canadian Centre for Drug-free Sport; Wilf Wedman, Canadian Sport and Fitness Administration Centre; Cleve Williams, City of Oakland; and Leon Younger, City of Indianapolis.

Abbreviations

AAP	Athlete Assistance Programme
AAU	American Athletic Union
ACB	Australian Cricket Board
ACF	Australian Cycling Federation
ACHPER	Australian Council for Health, Physical Education and Recreation
ACT	Australian Capital Territory
ACTU	Australian Council of Trade Unions
AEC	Australian Educational Council
AHPERD	Association for Health, Physical Education, Recreation and Dance
AIS	Australian Institute of Sport
AOF	Australian Olympic Federation
ASC	Australian Sports Commission
ASDA	Australian Sports Drug Agency
ASI	Australian Swimming Inc.
ASSC	Australian School Sport Council
ASSIST	Assessment in Second Level Teaching
ATP	Association of Tennis Professionals
AWF	Australian Weightlifting Federation
BAAB	British Amateur Athletic Board
BAF	British Athletic Federation
BOA	British Olympic Association
CAHPER	Canadian Association for Health, Physical Education and Recreation
CAHPERD	Canadian Association for Health, Physical Education, Recreation and Dance
CAI	Confederation of Australian Industry
CCDS	Canadian Centre for Drug-free Sport
CCPR	Central Council of Physical Recreation
CCT	Compulsory Competitive Tendering
COA	Canadian Olympic Association
CONI	Italian National Olympic Committee

COSPÓIR	see NSC
CTFA	Canadian Track and Field Association
DfEE	Department for Education and Employment
DNH	Department of National Heritage
DoE	Department of the Environment
DES	Department of Education and Science
EPRUC	English Professional Rugby Union Clubs
EU	European Union
FASB	Fitness and Amateur Sport Branch
FASD	Fitness and Amateur Sport Directorate
FSA	Foundation for Sport and the Arts
GAA	Gaelic Athletic Association
GDR	German Democratic Republic (former East Germany)
HCRS	Heritage Conservation and Recreational Service
hGH	human growth hormone
HSC	Higher Sports Council
IAAA	Irish Amateur Athletic Association
IAAF	International Amateur Athletic Federation
ICC	International Cricket Conference
IF	international federation
ILAM	Institute of Leisure and Amenity Management
IOC	International Olympic Committee
IRA	Irish Republican Army
IRFU	Irish Rugby Football Union
KLA	key learning area
MHLG	Ministry of Housing and Local Government
MLBPA	Major League Baseball Players Association
MUC	Montreal Urban Community
NACA	National Athletic and Cycling Association
NASPE	National Association for Sport and Physical Education
NBA	National Basketball Association
NCAA	National Collegiate Athletic Association
NCCA	National Council for Curriculum and Assessment
NCPE	National Curriculum for Physical Education
NCTC	National Coaching and Training Centre
NDP	New Democratic Party
NFL	National Football League
NGO	non-governmental organisation
NHL	National Hockey League
NSC	National Sports Council (COSPÓIR)
NSO	National Sports Organisation
OCI	Olympic Council of Ireland
PCP	Progressive Conservative Party
PEAI	Physical Education Association of Ireland
QDPE	Quality Daily Physical Education

QPP	Quadrenniel Planning Process
RFU	Rugby Football Union
SCAA	School Curriculum and Assessment Authority
SFAF	Sports Funding and Accountability Framework
SMCC	Sports Medicine Council of Canada
TAC	The Athletic Congress
TD	Teachta Dála–member of parliament in the Irish Republic
USATF	United States of America Track and Field
USOC	United States Olympic Committee
WITA	Women's International Tennis Association
WPA	Works Progress Administration
WSC	World Series Cricket

1 Comparing policy for sport and recreation

In little over one hundred years sport has been transformed from a parochial activity arousing only passing interest among governments to a global phenomenon demanding the attention of presidents, prime ministers and monarchs. The opening of the 1992 Olympic Games in Barcelona took place in front of King Juan Carlos and the event was intertwined with a number of major political issues including Catalonian nationalism, European Union supra-nationalism and Yugoslavian disintegration. Four years later the fortunes of the national teams competing in the European soccer competition, Euro '96, were followed closely by political leaders at home, with victories prompting congratulatory messages and motorcades in capital cities upon the return of the team. Helmut Kohl of Germany, Vaclav Havel of the Czech Republic, and the UK Prime Minister and Queen were among those who attended matches.

Up until the late nineteenth century sporting pastimes were largely local and informal with government intervention, if indeed any interest was shown at all, largely limited to the maintenance of the social exclusivity of some sports, such as hunting, or the encouragement of particular, usually militaristic, sporting pastimes. As sport became more organised in the last quarter of the nineteenth century it was within a national framework constructed mainly through the establishment of a range of sport-specific voluntary governing bodies.

The development of national sports organisations was stimulated by the growth in regional and national competitions and by the consequent need for agreed rules and an effective organising capacity for events. The next stage in development was the growth in the significance of international competition during the 1930s and, due to the interruption of the Second World War, more strongly from the late 1940s. The most recent stage in the history of sport has been the development of global sport from the 1960s stimulated particularly by the advances in satellite broadcasting. Geostationary satellite transmission was available for the 1964 Olympic Games in Tokyo and although the impact was limited, due to the differences in time zones, the major television companies soon realised the opportunities that the live broadcast of major sports events offered. During the 1970s the Games ceased to be an adjunct to a television company's sports schedule and became the centre-piece. Real (1986) estimated that two-thirds of adults in developed countries watched some part of the 1984 Olympic Games contributing to a total global audience of 2.5bn.

Paralleling the development of sport into a global phenomenon was the growth in government awareness of, involvement in, and manipulation of, sport. While the expansion of government interest in sport has followed slightly different paths, most industrial countries have reached a position where sport and government are inextricably linked across a wide and diverse range of policy issues. The diversity and extent of governmental involvement is easily illustrated. In 1980 the US government orchestrated a boycott of the Moscow Olympic Games and more recently, in 1993, the US House of Representatives supported a proposal opposing Beijing as a possible location for the 2000 Olympic Games. The Canadian government, in October 1988, established an inquiry under Charles Dubin to investigate the circumstances surrounding Ben Johnson's positive drug test at the 1988 Olympics. In 1986 the Australian Sports Commission launched 'Aussie Sport', a federal government-funded sports education programme aimed at teachers and coaches and intended to integrate sport and PE more firmly into the school curriculum. In Britain the report of Lord Justice Taylor into the Hillsborough tragedy led the government to require soccer clubs in the two higher divisions to introduce seats in all parts of their stadiums.[1] For all governments, modern international sport presents both problems (spectator violence, defection of athletes and drug abuse, for example) and opportunities for achieving political objectives.

Yet it is not just governments that see sport as presenting political opportunities. Ted Turner's sponsorship of the Goodwill Games was motivated, at least in part, by a desire to improve relations between the United States and the then Soviet Union following the US boycott of the 1980 Moscow Olympic Games. Turner's ownership of one of America's major television broadcasting companies was an additional reason for the promotion of the Goodwill Games. Australia's Aborigine population saw Sydney's bid to host the 2000 Olympic Games as an opportunity to draw attention to their political and economic marginalisation. Finally, unionist terrorists in Northern Ireland used the World Cup soccer match between the Irish Republic and Italy as an opportunity to attack Catholics watching the match on television at a bar in Loughinisland, and as an opportunity to achieve global media coverage.

The increasing economic, cultural and political significance of sport over the past twenty years or so has also prompted considerable academic interest. There is currently a healthy, and growing, literature concerned with the history and sociology of sport. The literature that explores the interconnection between politics, policy and sport is smaller, but is also rapidly expanding. There is now a substantial number of single-country studies which include Canada (Macintosh *et al.* 1987), Australia (Cashman 1995; Lawrence and Rowe 1986), Soviet Union (Riordan 1977; 1978), Britain

(Coghlan 1990; Henry 1993; Houlihan 1991), and France (Andreff 1989; Andreff and Nys 1994; Chazaud 1989; Pigeassou 1991). There is also a significant literature that seeks to examine the overlap between domestic sports politics and international relations (see, for example, Allison 1986; 1993; Wilson 1988; Lowe *et al.* 1978; Houlihan 1994; Nafziger 1988; Macintosh and Hawes 1994; Landry *et al.* 1991; Peppard and Riordan 1993; Redmond 1986). While these studies provide a considerable amount of information and analysis of value, there are few examples of sustained comparative country studies of sport and leisure policy.

In contrast to the study of sport and leisure most other policy areas such as education, economic management and social welfare have an established body of comparative literature. It is easy to understand the appeal of the comparative study of policy. For academics there are a number of intriguing questions concerning the relationship between different political systems, policy processes, and policy outputs and outcomes. Superficially at least there is evidence to suggest that very different political systems have produced very similar policies towards sport, for example: in the areas of fostering elite talent; the promotion of sport and physical education in the school curriculum; and the diplomatic use of sport. For the practitioner comparison offers, among other things, an opportunity to avoid the policy mistakes of other countries and an opportunity to identify potentially successful policies which might be imported. As international sport has expanded, countries have been required to confront increasingly similar problems and issues such as drug abuse, violence in sport, and the exploitation of young athletes. In many of these areas there is the assumption that lessons may be learned from other countries and that policies are transferable across national boundaries.

PROBLEMS IN COMPARING PUBLIC POLICY

Despite the attractiveness and potential value of a comparative approach there are a number of significant theoretical and methodological problems that need to be overcome, or at least taken account of, before a credible strategy for the comparison of sport and recreation policy can be developed. An important initial problem concerns the ambiguity of the concept of 'policy'. While this is a general problem in policy studies, it is of particular significance in comparative policy analysis. For many, such as Heclo (1972), government activity is a defining attribute of policy. Similarly Smith refers to policy as 'bundles of government decisions based on issues' (T. A. Smith 1975: 1). Jenkins provides a useful definition of public policy as:

> a set of interrelated decisions taken by a political actor or group of actors concerning the selection of goals and the means of achieving them within a specified situation where these decisions should, in principle, be within the power of these actors to achieve.
>
> (Jenkins 1978: 15)

As Hill and Bramley (1986: 3) point out, this definition identifies a number of key attributes of public policy. First, the emphasis on the interrelatedness of decisions suggests that policies are not discrete but form part of a cluster or sequence of decisions. Second, the reference to 'political actors' draws attention to the relationship between power and policy influence, and implicitly alerts us to the assumptions of pluralist politics where power and resource control are not monopolised by holders of formal offices. Third, Jenkins's definition clearly indicates that policy is about setting objectives and their implementation. The final element in the definition is that policy should be achievable. This is more open to challenge as it is frequently suggested that policy actors will, on occasion, select policies for their symbolic properties and that a government, in particular, may select policies that it suspects, hopes or knows will be unsuccessful. Yet even this formulation is not clear cut, for policy may not simply be defined by government action but also as governmental aspiration (Hogwood 1987: 4) or government inaction, for as Heclo (1972: 85) observes: 'A policy, like a decision, can consist of what is not being done.' To complicate matters further Hofferbert (1974: 6) notes that private activities which are tolerated by government often have the appearance of being the product of public policy. Rose (1988: 220) illustrates the definitional ambiguity by highlighting the use of four definitions of policy in the United States: namely, policy as a synonym for a problem or issue area, as a statement of intentions, as a programme and finally, as programme impact. Arriving at a consensus within a country on the definition and use of the term policy is difficult enough but the problems are considerably greater when the intention is to compare because many countries have no equivalent in their language to the Anglo-American term 'policy' (Heidenheimer 1986). In Germany and France, for example, the distinction between politics and policy, which is familiar in Anglo-American political science, is much less distinct.

A second and related issue involves a sensitivity to the dangers of transposing the policy experience of one country to another uncritically and without qualification. Ravitch (1983) shows how analyses of developments in British junior school education were progressively distorted in the United States and used as the basis for a successful campaign for public funds. Part of the problem lies in a willingness to ignore differences in the historical and constitutional context of policy (Hansen 1983), the competence of administrative units, variations in policy objectives and general policy style (Freeman 1985), and part lies in an overconcentration on policy outputs. Of especial significance is the need for sensitivity to the language of political discourse in different countries. Different countries may generate distinctive responses to apparently similar problems because they situate the problem within different political discourses. In his examination of race relations in the United States, Britain and France, Freeman argued that each country located the policy issue within a different political discourse, equal rights, immigration policy and economic policy, respectively. The consequence was the development of distinctive policy responses to a similar problem. The development of policy towards football hooliganism in Britain was initially located within a discourse that defined the issue as primarily a private matter of crowd management for individual soccer clubs and the governing body. Later the problem was relocated within the discourse of law and order which resulted in the involvement of a new set of policy actors and a radically different set of policy options (Houlihan 1991).

According to Warwick and Osherson (1973), particular care needs to be taken with three aspects of comparative study. The first is to ensure that the concepts being compared, such as mass participation, leisure and even sport, correspond. As Bramham *et al.* note, there is little consensus concerning the definition of leisure among European countries. Most of the contributors found that 'their national language [did] not have a suitable translation for the word leisure and . . . that in many nation-states no coherent body of policy, defined as (national) leisure policy [existed]' (1993: 5). Second, care is needed when selecting indicators. For example, there is considerable variation between countries in defining what constitutes 'regular participation' in sport. The final aspect concerns the linguistic problems in ensuring agreement on the meaning of concepts that Heidenheimer (1986) identified in relation to the concept of 'policy'. Unfortunately, too often due caution in comparison is replaced by rash acceptance of ultimately superficial similarity (J. Higgins 1986: 223). This is particularly evident when attempts are made to build a comparative analysis on the basis of a series of independent case studies. Nevertheless, there is a strong tradition in western political science which incorporates assumptions of convergence into comparative analysis (Bell 1973; Nelson 1978; Kerr 1983). According to this view 'the role for political choice, innovation, and statecraft is seriously limited' (Freeman 1985: 468).

A third problem concerns the misinterpretation of results and the temptation to build elaborate analysis on the basis of weak or limited data. Anderson (1975) cites the example of Cutright's (1969) construction of an index of social welfare achievement covering seventy-six countries being interpreted by others (for example, Irish and Prothro 1973) as an indicator of 'democratic performance'. Such overextension of conclusions is not confined to the early phase of comparative research. Noah (1984) gives the example of the way data on comparative levels of educational achievement were used by one researcher to argue that achievement levels in the United States were relatively low and by another to suggest that American school children performed quite well when compared with children in other economically advanced countries. The temptation to overextend quantitative data is often the product of frustration at the difficulty of finding data sets that provide a secure basis for comparison. In the area of recreation there are a number of countries that have undertaken participation surveys, for example, where differences in survey design, such as age range covered and time period, make comparison all but impossible. For example, American surveys cover those aged 12 years and over, but similar UK surveys include those aged 16 and over, while Australian surveys include those aged 14 and above. US surveys ask about participation in a range of activities over a twelve-month period, UK surveys cover the previous four weeks and Australian surveys cover the previous seven days (Veal 1989).

Fourth, there is the problem of ethnocentrism which affects not only our definition of what constitutes a problem (what is worth comparing) and what is considered a satisfactory solution, but also the general frame of reference within which comparison takes place. Hancock has drawn attention to the popularity of comparative analysis among those, in the 1970s, who 'look(ed) with favour on the activist state and its twentieth century socio-economic achievements' (1983: 287). Until the 1980s the number of examples of neo-conservative comparisons of public policy, for example, remained overshadowed by those that displayed 'great enthusiasm for Scandinavian institutions and practices (but) relative neglect of Southern Europe and economically conservative regimes . . . ' (Anderson quoted in Hancock 1983: 287). An additional problem associated with ethnocentrism results from the assumption that the political motives underpinning a policy in one country also underpin the policy in other countries. For example, in the 1980s a number of countries had rigorous testing procedures for drug use by athletes. Yet to assume that the motive in all countries was to eliminate drug abuse would clearly be misleading as testing in the GDR, for example, was designed to ensure that drugs administered at state training centres had been flushed out of the body before the athlete went abroad to compete.

Finally, there is the problem of deciding whether the similarity of response by different governments to common problems is the result of the intrinsic characteristics and imperatives of a problem, the characteristics of the national political system or the consequence of a process of policy diffusion between countries. For example, a large number of totalitarian regimes responded to the perceived need to produce an elite international squad of sportsmen and women in very similar ways (Riordan 1978). The similarity of response is much more likely to be the result of the diffusion of the Soviet model of elite sport development than the outcome of either the imperatives of elite development (i.e. the argument that the elite could *only* be developed in this way) or the argument that totalitarian regimes could respond to this problem only in this particular way. However, the issue becomes more complicated and more intriguing when the policies of non-totalitarian regimes towards the same problem are included in the comparison. Australia, and to a lesser extent Canada, have both adopted policies of elite squad development which are very close to the Soviet model in a number of key respects including the systematic sifting of school-age children as a means of identifying the potential elite, the development of specialist training academies, the subordination of domestic governing bodies to government policy and the use of public money to support individual elite athletes. This pattern of policy similarity prompts a fresh set of hypotheses regarding the source of that similarity. For example, whether the Australian approach is the result of borrowing a successful communist model or is a largely unavoidable outcome of the nature of the objective, i.e. the objective can only be achieved in a very limited number of ways.

THE VALUE OF COMPARISON

Given that comparative policy analysis is so problematic, one could be excused for asking why bother to compare? The most obvious answer is that contextually sensitive comparison enables policy-makers to learn from other political systems facing similar problems. In recent years developed nations have faced a series of common problems including the oil price increases of the 1970s, the spread of AIDS and urban decline. Through careful comparison policy-makers may learn which policies it is probably wise to avoid and which are most likely to prove useful. At the very least policy-makers will be encouraged to view the problems they face from a broader perspective and hopefully avoid limiting the range of policy options considered because of national parochialism. As Heidenheimer *et al.* note: 'Even if there are no direct lessons, policy comparisons will often throw light on hidden assumptions operating within one's own country' (1990: 2; see also Antal *et al.* 1987: 15). Rose, reinforcing this observation, acknowledges that policy-makers may be attracted to comparative analysis owing to the 'prospect that their government will be able to borrow policies or institutions from another country for use in resolving domestic problems', but adds that comparison also helps to avoid 'culture-bound generalisations' (1973: 69). Thus during the 1970s Britain looked to the United States for policies designed to tackle inner-city decline (Deakin 1974; Higgins 1978) while the US looked to Britain for models of health care (Heidenheimer *et al.* 1976).

The current opportunities to examine sport and leisure policy options from other countries are limited as the comparative literature in the field of sport and leisure is scant (Aitchison 1993). There have been a few valuable comparative studies of the use of leisure time (Rodger 1978; Szalai 1972) and of physical education and sport in the school curriculum (Bennet *et al.* 1975; Simri 1979). However, these tend to be descriptive and focus on the identification, rather than on the explanation, of difference. Leisure policy also has only a small number of comparative and analytic studies. Arbena's study of sport in Latin America (1988), Wilson's analysis of sport in the UK, US and totalitarian regimes (1988), and Riordan's study of sport in five communist states (1978) are among the most valuable and revealing studies. The two volumes by Bramham *et al.* (1989; 1993) go some way to combining analysis, explanation and comparison. However, both books eschew comparative analysis as the explicit organising conceptual and theoretical framework for their case studies. In the study of leisure policy in a range of west European cities they admit that 'each [study] deals predominantly with aspects of policy development in a single nation-state' (Bramham *et al.* 1989: 4). The more recent volume gives greater prominence to policy comparison: it explores the motives for government involvement in leisure and particularly how international and transnational pressures, such as democratisation, economic retrenchment and privatisation, are 'experienced, presented and handled' at the state and local level (Bramham *et al.* 1993: 5). Consequently the emphasis of the case studies is largely on the identification of 'the variety of "local" features of . . . national leisure policy' (ibid.). The case studies, though containing a wealth of empirical data and insightful analysis, have not been written explicitly from within the comparative policy analysis literature.

Finally, comparison is of potential value to the student of politics for the insights it offers into the role of institutions, for example, interest groups, government departments, legislatures and the sub-national governments, in the policy process and in the broader political system. The defining concerns of politics are: who governs; how do they govern; and with what effect on citizens.

HOW AND WHAT TO COMPARE

Comparison is at the heart of much political science; comparison may be, for example, over time, between policy sectors, between responses to a range of issues or between countries. If the intention is to compare particular policy issues, problems or sectors between countries, the question of the criteria and rationale for country choice needs to be addressed. Comparative policy research developed in Europe and north America with the consequence that most comparative policy analysis studies the experiences of the industrialised world. It is important to note that the reasons for this focus are historical rather than methodological and highlight the important debate within comparative analysis concerning the merits of comparing similar or dissimilar political systems.

Przeworski and Teune (1970), and DeFelice (1986) argue for the selection of dissimilar cases on the basis that it is possible to identify more confidently the significance of issues/policy problems within political systems if the emphasis is placed on subsystem characteristics such as the growth and extent of education/literacy, for example. At the heart of this approach is the assumption that there are only a limited number of different types of political issue (distributive, redistributive and regulatory, for example) and that the nature of the issue prompts participation by particular interests and imposes constraints on the policy options available, consequently generating broadly similar policy. The comparative research design assumes that the political systems selected for study are as different from each other as possible except for the phenomenon to be explained. 'It is among these different systems that the search is made for general causes, that is, for variables that relate in a similar manner to the given phenomenon within each system' (DeFelice 1986: 423). For example, if one was concerned to study the phenomenon of the emergence of a sporting elite one might select the People's Republic of China, Canada and Argentina on the grounds that the three countries exhibit significant differences in the key areas of wealth, political system and sporting tradition. If the subsequent study found that all three countries had adopted similar policies then it would be possible to draw conclusions relating the capacity of particularly salient issues to prompt a similarity of response by government and other key actors in the policy process. This approach is particularly attractive to advocates of convergence theory with its assumption that 'policy determines politics' (Freeman 1985).

While this method is attractive there is a major problem, namely the ability to identify confidently significant differences between countries. It is also very difficult to claim that a similar policy response is the result of the intrinsic characteristics or imperatives of an issue rather than, for example, being the result of a poorly identified and an underexplored aspect of the political system. Although the 'most different systems' research design has its strengths most comparative studies are based on the selection of broadly similar countries. Lijphart suggests the selection of countries that are similar 'in a large number of important characteristics (variables) which one wants to treat as constants, but dissimilar as far as those variables are concerned which one wants to relate to each other. If such comparable cases can be found, they offer particularly good opportunities for the application of the comparative method because they allow the establishment of relationships among a few variables while many other variables are controlled' (Lijphart 1971: 687). The attractiveness of this approach is reflected in the large number of comparative studies that focus upon groups of Scandinavian, western European or Anglo-American countries, with their broadly common cultural, economic and legal background.

While the similar cases strategy proposed by Lijphart offers a more secure basis for drawing conclusions from comparison it is not without its critics (for example, DeFelice 1986). The primary danger is an undue degree of confidence that key variables have been identified. A secondary danger, though one not peculiar to this method, is the interpretation of correlation as causality. Consequently, although the similar cases method is preferred caution is still needed. The countries selected for this study (Australia, Canada, Ireland, UK, and USA) share the following characteristics: sport is a significant cultural element; democracy is well established and stable; interest group activity is a major feature of democratic politics; economies are relatively mature; and higher education is well established. Although each country has distinctive features these are considered to be outweighed by the degree of overall comparability.

A second issue relating to the process of comparison is deciding what to compare. For a number of researchers the choice is seen as being between structure, on the one hand, and process or strategy on the other. Those who give priority to structural factors in explaining policy outputs and outcomes would emphasise, for example, the significance of the institutional relationship between government and sports organisations, the administrative arrangements of government, the allocation of functions between central and local government, and whether particular functions of government are statutory or discretionary. Thus the frequent demands in the UK that sport be made a statutory responsibility of local government or that responsibility for sport be given to a Cabinet-level minister are often based on the perceived effectiveness of these arrangements in other countries. The assumption is made that there is a link between administrative arrangements and particular policy impact.

Although a small number of comparative studies do rely on the correlation between aspects of a country's political structure or system's performance and policy outcomes, most moderate any conclusions based solely on this approach with an appreciation of the significance of political processes. An emphasis on process directs attention to the perception of problems and the tactics and strategies adopted by policy actors in furthering interests and resolving problems. Particularly, a focus on process makes an overconcentration on the actions of the state less likely. In addition, the focus of study is often on the exploration of the impact of policy and the relationship between the intentions of actors and policy performance. However, the main problem with this approach is that it is open to the accusation that it relies on impressions and subjective interpretation. As Anderson observes, such an approach may be judged to be ' "insightful" or "revealing" but seldom completely "accurate" ' (1975: 234).

Bearing these warnings in mind the following study focuses on two issues common to all the selected countries namely, sport and physical education in the school curriculum and drug abuse by athletes. The analysis will concentrate on public policy programmes produced in response to these issues. Policy programmes are, in Rose's words, 'resources of law, money and personnel modified by government organisations and converted into outputs meant to realise more or less clearly identified political purposes' (1988: 222). The intention is to identify the particular response of government to these issues as reflected in the mix and application of law, money and human resources employed. An emphasis on government programmes, at least in the initial stage of research, ensures the availability of accessible empirical data: laws are codified, expenditure patterns recorded and policies documented. The basic hypothesis of the research is that there will be significant cross-national similarities in policy programmes related to both the issues identified. It is anticipated that programmes will be influenced as much by the characteristics intrinsic to the issue as by national particularity or policy diffusion. Further, the research will explore the extent to which the pace and direction of programme change is similar across the five countries. The study will also explore the hypothesis that a policy community for sport along with a series of policy networks is either in operation or is emerging.

More specifically the research will seek to identify the membership, interaction and processes that enable the community and networks to function. Finally, consideration will also be given to the extent to which policy in the areas identified has expanded beyond national boundaries, prompting the need to define the parameters and characteristics of an international policy process.

One problem with the proposed approach is that comparative studies generally produce a time-bound analysis and thus take no account of the differential rate at which issues might emerge and mature, nor of the variation in the period over which policy is determined and implemented. The value of longitudinal analysis is that 'it lends itself more readily to cause–effect interpretation' (Albritton 1994). Although there are few elaborated longitudinal and comparative studies, the analysis contained in this study will seek to incorporate an awareness of the temporal context of the issues and policies.

A third issue concerns the role of theory in comparison. It is a truism that while empirical case studies that eschew theoretical questions 'can be interesting in themselves the possibilities of explanation, generalisation and analysis are limited' (Higgins 1981: 16). Yet there is also a danger of an overambitious employment of theory. Much neo-Marxist, structural-functionalist and corporatist theorising aimed at providing generalisations about society as a whole is overextended and ultimately unsatisfying. These macro-level theories share not just an implicit or explicit developmental sequence, but also 'relegate political action to a minor and epi-phenomenal role and view the activities of the modern state as being essentially similar' (Castles 1988). The trend in recent comparative policy studies has been to move away from hypotheses derived from macro theorising and its broad reliance on mono-causal explanations to a greater degree of theoretical diversity and multi-causal models of the policy process (for example, see Flora and Heidenheimer 1981; Goldthorpe 1984; Vig and Schier 1985). Consequently there has been an increase in comparison grounded in middle-range theory, for example, relating to organisational behaviour, interest articulation and decision-making. However, shifting the emphasis from mono-causal macro theories to multi-causal middle-range theories does not resolve the problem of explaining the causal link between independent variables in the determination of policy.

The systems approach derived from Easton's work (see, for example, Easton 1953; 1965), is a valuable general framework for comparison, particularly in the emphasis it gives to the outputs of government and also to the conceptualisation of the policy process it suggests. The stress on inputs and outputs and their interrelationship is attractive because of the strong (and simple) subdivision of the policy process. But it also needs to be acknowledged that the systems framework sits more easily within a broadly pluralist view of the policy process than one that stresses class interests, circumscribed policy agendas and non-decisions. However, although approaches to the comparison of public policy may vary in detail, the majority accept, either explicitly or implicitly, a broad systems framework that 'considers variations in outputs as a function of variable inputs and then looks for other sources of explanation in policy structures or processes to account for further variation' (Albritton 1994: 166).

The most theoretically sophisticated body of comparative research is to be found in the area of social policy where an increasing number of substantiated generalisations have been produced. For example, the status of socio-economic development and political mobilisation as necessary conditions for the development of social welfare policies is now acknowledged (Heidenheimer *et al.* 1983). In addition, there is significant confirmation of the role of the historical context in explaining the pattern and pace of social policy development. Albritton (1994: 170) highlights three important aspects of the historical contextualisation of policy-making: first, that policy can be seen as moving through different phases, 'experimentation', 'consolidation', and 'expansion' (Heclo 1981); second, that policy development is the result of institutionalised incremental growth; and finally, the periodic tension between individualism of liberal democracies and the egalitarian values underpinning welfare policies. Although politicians have frequently perceived public policy towards sport as part of the repertoire of resources available in the pursuit of foreign policy objectives, sport and recreation policy is essentially an element of welfare policy within most western industrial countries. As such the accumulated body of comparative research into social policy may be accepted as a valid starting point for a comparative analysis of sport policy.

A fourth issue concerns the need to move beyond the boundaries of national political systems in order to appreciate the variety of interests involved in shaping the policy eventually implemented in a country. As Hechter noted, comparative research assumes that the 'causes of development were located within units defined by political boundaries, such as sovereign states' (1975: 217). Most recent comparative study of policy takes individual countries/political systems as the unit of analysis and assumes that these units are substantially closed systems. While this is appropriate for many aspects of individual policy areas, it is not wholly satisfactory. The main weakness is that an increasing number of issues are no longer tackled exclusively within national political systems but are 'strongly embedded in supra-national networks, especially economic and strategic' (Heidenheimer 1985: 459; see also Antal *et al.* 1987; Wellhofer 1989; Wallerstein 1979 and 1983). The emergence over the past twenty years of a growing number of regional and global issues has forced a reorientation of focus away from an analysis of domestic political systems and their comparison and towards an acknowledgement of an increasing level of interrelatedness in the world system and interdependence in the treatment of issues. The problem for the policy analyst is to determine whether actors external to the domestic political system are participants in a *national* policy process or whether the proper focus should be on the global policy arena to which national actors seek entry and influence. For Andersen and Eliassen, in their study of policy-making in the European Union, the answer is clear:

> Europeification of policy-making implies a need for a new way of delineating the policy context, where the European political system becomes the unit of analysis. The scope of national policy-making has to be widened, to include the central EC institutions, the European network of national political institutions and actors operating at both levels.
>
> (Andersen and Eliassen 1993: 12)

Similarly, Nagel argues strongly that greater attention needs to be paid to issues whose dimensions can only be appreciated and understood fully within an international context. He identifies three established types of global policy problem. The first type refers to trans-boundary problems which involve, for example, the movement of people, goods and pollution across national boundaries. The second type is common property problems and involves decisions about exploitation of the seas and space. Finally, there are simultaneous problems which, according to Nagel, include health, education and welfare and 'about which all countries can learn from each other' (Nagel 1990: xiii).

While some problems in sport and recreation, such as the content of the school curriculum, remain largely insulated from global political processes, an increasing number of issues – drug abuse by athletes, the location of major sports events, or the eligibility of athletes to participate in events for example – involve the interaction between domestic and international policy actors. Drug abuse by athletes, using Nagel's typology, is both a trans-boundary and a simultaneous problem. Yet there is a frequent reluctance to apply the concepts and methods of policy analysis beyond the nation-state. Part of the explanation for this is, according the Soroos, 'the common conception of a policy as being the product of a type of governmental structure that does not exist in the anarchic international political order' (1990: 3). Yet this reluctance clearly needs to be overcome. It would be a rashly limited analysis that examined the British or French commercial sports sector without acknowledging the impact of the European Union, or that considered the collapse of apartheid in South Africa without assessing the impact of a range of external policy actors including the United Nations and the International Olympic Committee. One possible solution to the problem of selecting the appropriate level of analysis is through the use of the concepts of policy community and policy network where, in part at least, the level of operation (international or national) of the community or network is defined by its membership.

POLICY COMMUNITIES AND POLICY NETWORKS

Scharpf argues that if comparative policy analysis is to progress beyond the anecdotal there is a 'need for a language to describe the relationship between substantive policy and the structural and environmental factors influencing policy processes' (1977: 336). For Scharpf such a language would aid the development of a typology 'of the structural and processional variables that influence the substance of the policy formation and implementation process' (ibid.). Unfortunately attempts to develop such a language have not been marked by a great degree of success. One of the more recent and rewarding attempts has centred on the use of the concepts of policy community and policy network.

Over the past ten years or so the concepts of the policy community and policy network have come to dominate analysis of policy-making processes not only in much of western Europe but also in Canada and Australia. Even where the descriptive language differs, as in the United States, many of the underlying assumptions are shared in common. Within the UK the notion of the policy community emerged as a result of the blending together of a number of research themes across the social sciences. The major contributions came from work in organisational sociology concerned to examine the implications of the tension experienced by organisation members between organisational maintenance and the attainment of the public goals of the organisation (Wilson 1973). There was also evidence that organisations often have an acute sense of those issues and decisions which are rightfully their property or which, to use Downs' phrase, fall within their 'policy space' (Downs 1967).

There is also a strong link between the current discussions of policy communities and the long-established tradition in political science related to group theory (Truman 1951; Olson 1971). For group theorists public policy is the product of the interaction between government and a cluster of interest groups which reflects the prevailing balance of influence (Richardson and Jordan 1979). A common assumption among group theorists is that clusters of interest groups can be identified with particular policy areas and exhibit a degree of stability over time.

The combination of the tendency for interest groups to cluster around particular governmental organisations responsible for specific services has led to the conceptualisation of the policy process as taking place within policy sectors or policy communities. As might be expected with any concept that is being applied to such a broad activity as policy-making, there is considerable variation in the precise way in which the concept is defined and used. For Rhodes (1986; 1988; 1990) and Marsh and Rhodes (1992), there is a variety of policy networks including policy communities, professional networks and issue networks. Within Rhodes' typology networks vary according to a range of characteristics including membership, patterns of interdependence and resource control. A key distinguishing feature between different types of policy network is the degree of integration. Thus, policy communities are tightly integrated whereas issue networks are relatively loosely integrated. Rhodes' typology is underpinned by a resource dependence model characterised by mutual dependencies among members. An alternative conceptualisation is provided by Wilks and Wright (1988). For them the term policy community refers to a general policy sector while a policy network has a more focused and limited membership and is concerned to link policy actors involved in resolving particular issues.

Although both the Marsh and Rhodes (1992) model and that proposed by Wilks and Wright (1988) have their strengths, they have been subject to considerable criticism primarily because the 'policy networks literature has been too descriptive and insufficiently explanatory' (Mills and Saward 1994: 87). The conceptualisation proposed by Rhodes has been subject to a number of particular criticisms. Mills and Saward (1994: 84) criticised Rhodes for failing to articulate more clearly the relationship between policy networks and their environment. For Atkinson and Coleman (1992) and Smith (1993) a key weakness lies in the failure to identify the source of change to the structure of networks and also the lack of attention paid to the process of the birth and demise of networks. Other criticisms include the imprecision of the notion of resources (Stones 1990) and the failure to contextualise policy communities beyond locating them in relation to the national- or central-level state institutions rather than situating the concepts within a theoretical context (Mills and Saward 1994). The definitions of policy community and network provided by Wilks and Wright have also been subject to similar criticism. In addition, Dowding claims that Wilks and Wright substitute definitional imposition for empirical investigation and are guilty of a degree of 'categorical proliferation [which] serves no useful purpose and stems from the attempt to force a disparate world into rigid natural categories which simply do not exist' (Dowding 1994: 64).

Given the strength of these criticisms there is a need to avoid the temptation of overstating the explanatory power and precision of the concepts. But it is important to note that the expression of forceful criticism of the concepts of policy community and policy network has rarely been accompanied by suggestions of plausible alternatives. Thus, while it is acknowledged that the concepts are vulnerable to criticism they none the less are capable of fulfilling an important function both as elements of a typology of policy-making and as a step towards a more theoretically informed explanation of the policy process. As regards the elaboration of the concepts of policy community and network to form a classificatory schema, it is intended to use the definitions offered by Wilks and Wright as a starting point. The continuum that they suggest ranges from policy universe, where direct involvement in the formulation of policy is negligible, through to the policy network where members are closely involved in shaping policy responses.

The policy universe refers to the large number of potential policy actors with a direct or indirect interest in a particular policy area and clearly includes a vast number of organisations (Wilks and Wright 1987: 296). However, it is important to acknowledge that on the fringe of every policy community there are a number of organisations that might, from time to time, become involved in a particular sports issue. The policy community exists within the policy universe. The concept of a policy community can best be explored in terms of the following aspects: the nature of the membership, the capacity of the community to exclude actors, the extent of organisation and structure, the issue scope of communities, and the sources of cohesion.

For some (Wright 1988), the key criterion for membership of a policy community is potential involvement: for others, the criterion is actual involvement. Laffin, for example, refers to a policy community as 'a relatively small group of participants in the policy process which has emerged to deal with some identifiable class of problems that have or could become the concern of central government' (1986: 110). Most policy communities consist 'not only of civil servants and ministers but of relevant "recognised" interest groups and other governmental bodies, both appointed and elected local authorities' (Hogwood 1987: 18). Hogwood's description of British policy communities is echoed in many of the discussions of the policy process in the United States. Ripley and Franklin refer to 'sub governments', which are typically composed of 'members of the House and/or Senate, members of congressional staffs, a few bureaucrats, and representatives of private groups interested in the policy area' (1976: 6; see also Thurber 1991; Petracca 1992). A key defining characteristic of policy communities, probably *the* defining characteristic, is the emergence of a core set of values that will inform the way in which problems are identified and defined, and also the way in which solutions are selected. If community values are sufficiently firmly established then membership of the specific policy network that deals with an issue is unnecessary in order to wield influence over outcomes.

In identifying the source of both the promotion and sustenance of value consensus professions are often given a significant role (Rhodes and Wistow 1988; Cox 1992; Sharpe 1985). The single profession community or, more commonly, multi-profession epistemic community, may operate substantially within a particular policy community or, as is more likely, may be represented across a range of policy communities. Doctors, as one of the influential professions, are clearly at the centre of the health service policy community but are also prominent in a number of others including the debate within sport about drug abuse, the safety of boxing and the training regimes for young athletes. For Haas an epistemic community establishes the capacity for authoritative intervention in the deliberations of policy communities because members:

> share intersubjective understandings; have a shared way of knowing; have shared patterns of reasoning; have a policy project drawing on shared

values, shared causal beliefs, and the use of shared discursive practices; and have a shared commitment to the application and production of knowledge.

(Haas 1992: 3, quoted in Richardson 1996)

While some professions are strongly established in the private sector a substantial number, including doctors, but also land-use planners and teachers, 'comprise governmental specialist functionaries who operate at the different levels of government, and share a common interest which is strengthened by membership of a professional association' (Sharpe 1985: 367). The strength of professions in government, even bearing in mind the vigour with which a number of governments during the 1980s sought to weaken their influence, has been such in the post-war years that Sharpe has referred to 'a general movement toward the development of a professionally dominated, technocratic policy process' (ibid.: 480). The significance of professionals is that they constitute one of the most organised, cohesive and influential lobbies within a policy community (see Laffin 1986; Anderson 1978). The capacity of professions to exert influence within policy communities raises a number of questions with regard to sport as strong professions are in short supply and professionalisation is at best slow and also sharply contested. Whereas in some countries PE teachers, coaches and sports development officers are organised into representative associations and a number have an established process for accreditation, few have acknowledged status and most are still expending considerable resources in attempting to promote their claims to professionalism.

One important aspect of an analysis of the membership of policy communities is not just who is a member but who is denied membership. The capacity to restrict entry is an important indicator of the strength of the community and creates a feudal pattern of policy-making. In the UK Rhodes suggests that the community is 'substantially closed to other communities and invariably to the general public (including Parliament)' (1986: 23) while in the United States Ripley and Franklin have argued that policy sub-governments remain 'normally closed' (1976: 6), creating a situation where 'each functional policy area tends to be governed as if it existed apart from the remainder of government' (Peters 1986: 22). The perception of policy communities as relatively stable was not universally persuasive, with Heclo arguing in the late 1970s that the 'iron triangle' of administrative agency, congressional sub-committee and pressure group had weakened and that policy processes were less exclusive (Heclo 1978). In Britain it is probable that any weakening of the exclusivity of policy communities has been the result of more authoritative interventions by the government during the Thatcher years than the ability of previously marginalised interests to force entry to relatively closed communities. As Richardson comments:

The Thatcherite revolution was not so much about excluding pressure groups in an attempt to govern without consensus, it was more about determining the new agenda for each policy sector. . . . Most of the radical policy change which took place did not emanate from policy communities or policy networks – they reacted to exogenous changes.

(Richardson 1996)

There has also been considerable discussion of the operation of policy communities with particular attention being paid to the identification of internal structural characteristics and the range of issues that they tackle. As regards the former question it is suggested that while internal structure will be loose, an 'implicit authority structure' (Jordan and Richardson 1982: 94) exists often reflecting patterns of resource dependency and as a result frequently focused on the government department or agency associated with the issue area. Policy communities will generally deal only with those routine issues that can be resolved effectively with the range of resources available. Consequently, there will be issues that bypass policy communities, possibly because of neglect or oversight, or those which are removed from its purview because of the successful assertion of interest by another more powerful community. For example, the issue of soccer hooliganism was defined as an issue of law and order rather than as one of crowd management with the result that the policy responses selected included legislation to define new public order offences, to ban the sale of alcohol, and to increase the level of penalty for existing offences committed at soccer grounds. Part of the reason for the loss of control was the unwillingness of the sports organisations to seek a leadership role in its resolution.

As regards the sources of cohesion of the policy community, greatest emphasis tends to be given to the development of shared perceptions of both problem definition and the identification of solutions often stimulated by the presence of a strong profession which can lead to the emergence of 'the acceptance or dominance of an effectively unified view of the world across different sectors and institutions' (Dunleavy 1981). An alternative or overlapping source of community values is the distinctive administrative cultures found in government departments.

Identifying the main features of policy communities helps in the process of identifying those policy areas that are more firmly established and organised but is of only limited value in helping to understand the dynamics of communities. If the concept of a policy community is to be of greater explanatory value, it needs to be set within a broader theory of power. One persuasive analysis locates policy communities within a view of society which emphasises the uneven distribution of power and the capacity of power-holders to manipulate value systems and agenda setting. Benson, for example, suggests that it is necessary to locate the pattern of relationships between organisations and actors within a 'deep structure' of power relations found in wider society (Benson 1979). In contradiction to pluralist explanations he argues that there are biases fundamental to the social structure that explain the nature and character of community configurations and the distribution of power is therefore not just the outcome of effective strategy development in the competition for resources. These biases are manifest not simply as power constellations (classes, interest groups, etc.) with vested interests in the stability or otherwise of the network or social structure, but also in the taken-for-granted rules of structure formation. In other words the acceptance within the community and network that solutions to problems must be consistent with the 'fundamental features of the total social formation' (ibid.). Although working from within a Marxist perspective his analysis has many echoes of Lindblom's (1977) neo-pluralist conceptualisation of the relationship between business and government.

Value consensus is derived from an acceptance of a 'deep structure' of power relations and is the foundation upon which both internal and external community relationships develop. In particular, the level of consensus determines the boundaries and nature of policy disagreement within the community. According to this view, professions and government departments are more the vehicles for articulating deep structural values than countervailing power centres as many liberal pluralists would suggest. If the manipulation of a value consensus is one significant resource in shaping the operation of policy communities, then it is augmented by the functioning of an elaborate pattern of resource dependence. Benson (1982), Rhodes (1985; 1986) and Dowding (1994) draw attention to the importance of resource dependence as the basis for the pattern and intensity of relations within a policy community. Resources may be of a variety of types and refer to any tangible or intangible product or activity that policy actors require in order to further successfully their interests. Resources may therefore include, *inter alia*, finance, control over legislation, specialist knowledge, legitimacy, manpower and equipment. Resource dependence occurs when resources required by one organisation are controlled by another. The result of resource dependence is a pattern of bargaining and negotiation. Normally there is a close correspondence between the deep structure of power relations and the distribution of organisational resources. But at any particular time within a community the degree of dependence and the extent of resource control exercised by individual actors will vary, thus allowing scope for outcomes of bargaining and negotiation to reflect genuine policy gain or, in Freeman's words, 'situational factors may permit or force at least temporary shifts in the "normal" policy-making mode' (1985: 478). In summary, while a value consensus may be a powerful spur to co-operation it is suggested that it is rarely sufficient to sustain a policy community through the tensions inherent in policy-making and that consequently it is frequently augmented by patterns of resource need and control.

Policy communities are frequently too large to deal effectively with the range of issues that impinge on their collective interests. As a result, a further concept, the policy network, is defined to describe those actors involved with specific issues, such as drug abuse by athletes and determining the school sport curriculum. In summary, a policy community contains those actors with a general concern for sport policy, while the policy network contains those actors involved in developing policy responses to a particular issue or problem. Distinguishing between the concepts of a policy community and a policy network has three important advantages (Wright 1988: 606). First, it enables a distinction to be drawn between those actors within the community who are none the less excluded from policy networks. Second, because not all members will be active across all community issues, the utilisation of policy networks enables us to distinguish those actors that are regularly involved across a number of policy networks from those whose involvement is more sporadic. More importantly it enables the identification of those members of policy networks who are normally members of other contiguous policy communities. For example, the question of safety in boxing involves actors from both the sport and the medical policy communities, and the determination of the future of school sport involves actors from the sport policy community and from the education policy community. Finally, one needs to acknowledge that while many policy sectors will generate a policy community, this is no guarantee that a policy network will emerge to deal with particular issues. Some communities may lack the necessary value consensus or strength of mutual interests to provide the basis for the formation of a network.

Part of the value of using the concept of a policy community, and the related concepts of policy universe and policy network, to study the process of policy-making is derived from its appeal as a descriptive device which takes account of the conventional wisdom concerning the negotiated nature of policy-making and avoids the rigidities of other, for example, corporatist, metaphors. More significantly it provides a set of concepts that enables 'detailed case studies and still [facilitates] the comparative analysis of several policy areas' (Wistow and Rhodes 1987). It enables a focus on the pattern of recurring relations between members, the nature, extent and source of value consensus and the degree to which issues are the property of identifiable groups of actors in the policy process. Within the context of a cross-country comparison, analysis of the concept of policy community also allows conclusions to be drawn regarding the relative influence of members, especially professionals and elected representatives, the salience of particular issues to government, and the nature and impact of the ideological context within which policy is formed.

There is much in the literature of policy-making to suggest that the development of a policy community, and a sub-set of policy networks, is a sign of a mature policy area where boundaries are acknowledged and the expertise of the community members is respected, thus providing a disincentive to intervention by (more powerful) outsiders. This description would seem more appropriate to policy areas such as housing, education and defence than to leisure and recreation. Indeed Wistow and Rhodes (1987: 8) describe leisure and recreation as an 'issue network' which, according to their use of the term, is less integrated and has a larger number of participants with a lower degree of interdependence, stability and continuity than a policy community. This assertion raises a number of important questions for the student of comparative public policy for sport and leisure: first, whether Wistow and Rhodes are accurate in their description and whether they are equally accurate across the countries contained in this survey; second, whether there are any signs of change and development in the sport and leisure policy area that would suggest that the characteristics associated with a policy community are emerging; and third, whether the prospects for the development of a mature policy community for sport and leisure are promising.

COMPARATIVE STUDY AND SPORT

Heidenheimer *et al.* (1990: 3) define comparative public policy as the study of 'how, why and to what effect different governments pursue particular courses of action or inaction'. Elaborating upon this definition they suggest that a consideration of 'how' governments choose to act directs attention to the institutional arrangements of government and the pattern of interaction between government and non-governmental policy actors such as interest groups, professions, etc. Asking 'why' governments act leads to a consideration of the cultural, ideological and historical context of policy formation. Heidenheimer *et al.*'s definition also directs attention to the outputs and more importantly the outcomes or impact of policy. For Antal *et al.* (1987) this is the feature of comparative policy research that distinguishes it from the related activities of comparative government or comparative political behaviour. Comparative policy analysis is seen to lie at the intersection of pure research and policy advice. As Teune remarks, 'The primary purpose of comparative policy research, however, is not to establish the universality of relationships. Rather it is to enhance the credibility of specific predictions about specific cases' (Teune 1978: 54 quoted in Dierkes *et al.* 1987).

2 Government, sport and policy-making

INTRODUCTION

In order to understand the range of policy responses adopted by different countries to sports issues it is necessary to have some appreciation of the structure of government, the development and organisation of sport and the dominant pattern of policy-making. In the discussions that follow it will become clear that while the five countries possess many similarities derived from a common cultural and political tradition they also vary significantly. For example, the federal systems of Canada, Australia and the United States obviously require a degree of policy bargaining between levels of government, but as will be seen each federal system is embedded in a different set of constitutional expectations, practices and experiences and is also affected by differences in history and political culture such that generalisations about federal systems and sport policy would need to be made with great care. In a similar fashion a review of the history of the emergence of organised sport in the five countries highlights that beneath a superficial correspondence there lies a unique pattern of influences drawn from, for example, educational structures, evolving national and regional identities, commercial development, and geographic and cultural isolation.

Finally, the chapter provides an overview of the patterns of policy-making evident in each country. As will become clear, while it is possible to make a number of generalisations about policy processes, it is much harder to generalise confidently about the policy styles of particular policy areas or to identify temporal continuities in policy-making. All five countries have stable and relatively open political systems which allow substantial access to organised interests at the various stages of the policy process. However, variation arises from, *inter alia*, differing constitutional arrangements, the extent of organisation of voluntary as opposed to commercial sports interests, the degree of unity of objectives among sports interests, and the salience of sport to the major parties and the public/electorate. Consequently, there is disagreement in some countries about the extent to which their policy-making procedures are better described as pluralist or corporatist. In all countries there is a debate over the most appropriate metaphor for the policy process, with policy network, policy community, sub-government and policy sector all having their advocates. This level of disagreement indicates first, the shifting character of policy-making processes and second, the contested nature of attempts at description and analysis.

The purpose of this chapter is to provide an initial context for the more detailed examination of the administrative arrangements and of the policy issues that follow. The chapter also provides a framework for the final chapter, in which the issues of administrative structure, policy process and the development of sport are reconsidered.

AUSTRALIA

The structure of government

Like the United States, Australia has a federal system of government. Power is shared between the states and the federal government based at Canberra. The rationale of Australian federalism is similar in many respects to that found in the US. The combination of a vast land mass (7.7m. sq km), a relatively small population (16m.), and the establishment by the original colonists of distinct forms of local administration provided fertile ground for federalism. Emy's observation that the 'point of federal politics is to maintain and explore the sense of "conditional union" ' (1978: 72, quoted in Stewart and Ward 1992) is especially appropriate to Australia. Many of the bitter disputes of the past twenty-five years over the interpretation of the constitution add weight to the remark that 'A federal system is one which is always in a state of becoming' (ibid.). The move to federation was long discussed and was stimulated as much by fear of external threat, a concern that other European imperial powers might see Australia as a target for expansion, as by a sense of common identity.

The 1901 Constitution is a clear compromise between two systems of government, namely, federalism and a model of responsible government derived from Britain. The reluctance of state politicians to dilute their power led them to establish a weak federal (Commonwealth) government. Commonwealth powers were limited largely to defence, foreign relations and customs, with only weak powers of taxation. Those favouring a weak federal system also argued that the executive need not comprise members of the legislature. However, those favouring a system of representative government carried the argument and it was agreed that members of the Cabinet would need to be members of Parliament. Within Parliament, the House of Representatives is the more powerful chamber and is elected every three years on the basis of population. The Prime Minister and government are drawn from the party that commands a majority in the House. The Senate is also an elected chamber with each of the original states returning the same number of Senators irrespective of population. The Constitution also insisted on equality between the two chambers.

In the period since the acceptance of federation the Constitution has, not surprisingly, evolved considerably, most notably in the extent to which the powers of the Commonwealth have increased, particularly in the field of taxation. However, the dominant feature of the modern Constitution is a high degree of complexity and ambiguity in the relationship between the states and the Commonwealth government, which is compounded by the deliberate equivalence of powers in many areas where powers are held concurrently. The status of the Senate also provides a basis for friction. Although the lower house alone can introduce money bills, the Constitution omitted to limit the power of the Senate to refuse the granting of supply. A number of devices have been introduced to attempt to overcome conflict including a provision for joint meetings of the two chambers and a double dissolution of Parliament. Unfortunately these devices and provisions are themselves ambiguous and the net effect is to displace conflict rather than resolve it (Coper 1987; Emy 1978; Aitkin *et al.* 1989). The ambiguities in the Constitution are best illustrated by the 1975 crisis, which highlighted the vagueness of the powers of the Senate and the Governor-General and also the vulnerability of some constitutional conventions to manipulation by political party and state interests (Emy and Hughes 1991; Coper 1987; Fletcher 1993).

The structure of Australian government is complemented by a political culture characterised by 'a rationalist, instrumental attitude towards the state' where the voices of radical ideologists are present but effectively 'assimilated in or drowned by the chorus of utilitarian consensus' (Collins 1989: 101 and 102). Collins suggests that Australian political culture is, by comparison with those found in Europe, narrowly based and uniform where '[l]ittle of the breadth and complexity of Europe's political ideas and experience will be found' with one consequence being that contemporary 'public policy debates reflect the exhaustion of the inherited ideas, practices and institutions in the face of a more heterogeneous society at home and a more subtly shifting pattern of conflict and co-operation abroad' (ibid.: 102 and 103).

As in many liberal democratic countries the organisation of the federal government is based on a functional principle. From a peak of thirty-seven federal departments in 1974 there were, in 1994, fifteen large departments many with a broad multi-service remit. The department which has formal responsibility for sport, Environment, Sport and Territories, is a good example of the multi-service department. The rationalisation of the federal bureaucracy was part of a broader tide of public sector reform that, in many ways, mirrored the efforts of the Thatcher governments in the UK to introduce a more market-oriented culture into the public sector (Mascarenhas 1993). Although there were more than 160,000 federal civil servants in 1990, they comprised only 9 per cent of the total public sector employment. The bulk of public sector employment, some 68 per cent, is at the state level.

The nature of Australian federalism is such that both federal and state governments are active across a similar range of policy areas. However the:

constitutional division becomes evident more in the content of their respective lawmaking than in their functional classification. Both make policy, but whereas the Commonwealth is biased towards measures that relate to financial resources and means, the states tend to be more concerned with rules and regulations, and organisational structures.

(Nelson 1989: 156)

Despite the differing concerns of the two levels of government, there still remains substantial overlap of policy interest that makes for considerable tension, for example, in relation to environmental protection, aboriginal land rights and health care (Chapman 1988; Nelson 1989). Policy areas of mutual interest are often characterised by the generation of a complex pattern of intergovernmental committees and ministerial councils.

Local authorities in Australia are the creations of states and their powers and responsibilities are defined by states rather than the Commonwealth government. Although local government units range in size from fewer than 1,000 to nearly 0.75m., the majority of the 800-plus councils have populations under 10,000. While local councils are able to levy taxes and pass bylaws, these powers are tightly prescribed. In the early years of the local government system the major responsibilities of councils were highways and sanitation. Although these functions are still prominent, the areas of service growth have been in recreation and culture, and personal welfare services.

The imposed limitations on the scope for the exercise of discretion by local government is compounded by their 'rather unambitious view of their responsibilities' (Painter 1989: 168). According to Painter the lack of ambition of local councils is due, *inter alia*, to the willingness of states to administer services, the lack of encouragement to councils to innovate and provide services given by states, and the electoral sensitivity of rates (the local property tax). Occasionally, disputes between local and state governments do emerge, most frequently over land use policy, but such disputes are comparatively rare.

Sport in Australia

Any discussion of sport in Australia faces serious problems of separating myth from reality. The intertwining of the symbolism of sport with notions of identity and the popularising of Australia as 'The Lucky Country' have produced a considerable number of largely self-congratulatory peons (Horne 1964; Australian Sports Institute Study Group 1975) and few critical analyses (Mercer 1977; Cumes 1979; Semotiuk 1986; Stratton 1986; and Cashman 1987, for example). In attempting to push aside the camouflage, particular attention needs to be paid to the significance of commercialism and nationalism (and racism) as distinctive elements in the development of sport and its current character.

At the time of the establishment of Australia in 1901 the population was

98 per cent British or of British descent, the economy was dominated by British capital and the Union flag was incorporated into the new Australian flag (Crowley 1974; Souter 1978). In the period leading up to independence and in the first fifty years of its life Australian links with Britain and the Empire were an essential element in the definition of its national identity and sport was an integral part of the process of self-definition. From the middle to the turn of the nineteenth century, sport, and particularly cricket, was an important mirror of the changing conception of Australian identity. Mandle traces the evolution of Australian cricketing nationalism through a series of phases from an initial period (in the 1860s) of 'humility and deference' towards English teams to a 'sense of cricketing confidence, even arrogance' by the 1890s (1976: 47 and 48). The mid-century insecurity was based on fears of racial inferiority owing to the convict origins of some of the settlers and fears of racial degeneration because of living south of the equator. Linked closely to this eugenic theme was a concern with the value of sport in instilling and demonstrating 'manliness' in the Australian character (Elford 1976). The importance of cricketing victories against England was such that Mandle was able to claim that 'Australian nationalism and self-confidence was first and most clearly manifested in the late 1870s because of the feats of its sportsmen and particularly its cricketers' (1976: 60). By the end of the century Australian cricketing nationalism had given way to a political nationalism capable of promoting and sustaining moves to independence.

Following independence, sport remained an integral and, according to some, a defining element in Australian national identity (Greenwood 1955; Jaques and Pavia 1976a; Dunstan 1973; Horne 1964). The rejection of the suggested British Empire team for the 1916 Olympics (Jobling 1986) and the reaction to the alleged intimidatory bowling tactics of the English cricket tourists in 1932/33 (Le Quesne 1983; Wynne-Thomas and Arnold 1984), were illustrative of an increasing Australian assertiveness and consciousness of a distinctive, if only embryonic, national identity. By the middle of the present century Australia was established as one of the major sporting nations of the world. The dramatic success of the country in the Melbourne Olympics of 1956, where it won more medals in relation to its population than any other country, confirmed, in the eyes of Australians at least, that it was the world's greatest sporting nation. Indeed in 1960 Australia was holder of the Davis Cup (tennis), the Canada Cup (professional golf), the Eisenhower Cup (amateur golf) and the Ashes (cricket). Although Australia's claims to global sporting pre-eminence are harder to sustain today, the country is still one of a small number of countries that combines breadth of sporting involvement with consistency of elite-level success. In attempting to explain Australian success, an information paper prepared by the Australian government referred to the benefits of 'A fine climate, plenty of room, plenty of time, an inbred love of sports and the wish to excel at them, the lack of competing interest, [and] the worship of the physical . . . ' (Department of the Interior: Australian News and Information Bureau 1962). Undoubtedly, the social status that accrues from sporting success and, with a few well-known exceptions, the relative absence of international celebrities in the arts are significant (Caldwell 1976: 142). Pearson and O'Hara (1977) point to the favourable topography and latitude, the bush tradition and the transplanted English sporting tradition (see also Daly 1972). Others have pointed to Australia's 'comparatively classless society and its absence of internal race problems, . . . (its) high standard of living, and . . . no underprivileged segment of the community' as key factors (Gordon 1976: 98). While the 'ignoring of' internal race problems is a more accurate observation than the 'absence of' them, the general homogeneity of the settler community was, for a considerable period, distinctive.

Explanations of high levels of participation framed in terms of climate and environment, and assumptions about the classlessness of Australian sport are, as Lawrence and Rowe point out, rarely supported by evidence (1986). However, they form part of a persistent perception of the role and significance of sport in Australian society. The tendency to mythologise the role of sport in Australian society has meant that there has been rather less critical investigation of the phenomenon than one would hope for and expect, even when survey data suggests that fewer than one in five Australians regularly and frequently participates in organised or informal sport (Arnold 1989; Souter 1989). In particular, it is important to place the development of sport in twentieth-century Australia within the context of the politics of race, gender and commercialism, all of which are important elements in the fabric of domestic sport.

In terms of race, little account has been taken of the systematic marginalisation of the Aborigines. Stratton (1986) notes that the tentative involvement of Aborigines in boxing and cricket in the mid-nineteenth-century period did not provide an opportunity for social mobility. Unlike the experience of black Americans, sport did not provide even that modest escape route from poverty. Stratton suggests that whereas in the United States the black American was portrayed as 'a noble savage' . . . ' primitive, powerful and to be feared', the Australian Aborigine was characterised as 'primitive, degenerate and to be despised' (1986: 92). By the 1870s Aboriginal participation in imported sports was negligible. The Victorian association of sports participation with civilised values and the nascent sense of Australian nationalism by definition demanded the exclusion of Aboriginals. As sport became ever more closely associated with national identity in the twentieth century, it has become increasingly difficult to incorporate Aborigines within the accompanying symbolism. As Stratton observes: 'By the 1970s even the national boomerang throwing champion was white' (1986: 94). The marginalisation of the Aborigine people in sport, as in general Australian society, has persisted up to the present. In 1982 the Queensland government, fearing Aboriginal protests at the forthcoming Commonwealth Games, passed an Act that provided the police with wide-ranging emergency powers relating to the removal of potential troublemakers. The recent competition to host the 2000 Olympic Games provided an opportunity for Aborigine protest groups to draw attention to their peripheral role in Australian sport and society.

'In Australia, sport is constituted as a site of maleness' (Stratton 1986: 104). The development of opportunities for women to participate in sport have been slower to emerge than in many other developed countries. This has been because of two factors in particular. First, the dominance of English Victorian patriarchal values, which provided only very restricted and controlled sporting opportunities for women such as the suburban garden sport of tennis, and second, the prominence of an exaggerated version of social Darwinism, which stressed the need to demonstrate 'manliness'. As in many other countries the pattern of stereotypical assessments of women's inability to participate fully in sport, especially at the elite levels, are also evident in Australian schools, media, sports clubs and governing bodies. What is possibly more pronounced is the use of sport to 'ritually support an aura of male competence and superiority in publicly acclaimed skills, and a male monopoly of aggression and violence' (Bryson 1983: 413, quoted in Lawrence and Rowe 1986).

In common with developments in the United States and the UK the links between sport and commercial interests have progressively strengthened. The involvement of corporations in sponsoring individual athletes, specific events or complete competitions has steadily increased, paralleling the growth of television ownership in the post-war period. Equally significantly, governing bodies were adopting a business approach to the management and development of their sports. The selling of franchises by leagues and the operation of clubs as commercial enterprises are now well-established features of the national sports scene (Stewart 1986). Of greatest significance is the interpenetration of television interests with sport. The dependence of television on sports programmes to fill its schedules had led inevitably to attempts by the purchaser to control more closely the source of supply and to shape the product to meet its own requirements. For example, in 1977 Kerry Packer moved from sponsoring sports events for his Channel Nine television company to organising international cricket tournaments in direct competition with the domestic and international governing bodies. The brief, but bitter, dispute was resolved clearly to Kerry Packer's advantage. Packer got everything he wanted: exclusive broadcasting rights for ten years, an increase in one-day matches, day/evening matches, coloured clothing and a say in which teams toured Australia. What is especially noteworthy is that the impact of the dispute was felt beyond the shores of Australia and affected other major cricketing nations. The more recent involvement of Australian media in Rugby League is in many ways more dramatic as Rupert Murdoch and Packer conduct chequebook battles to establish a broadcasting monopoly over elite-level competition.

Policy process

As the previous section demonstrated, sport has a high cultural profile in Australia and contains a number of particularly powerful interests, especially within business. The purpose of this section is to provide a summary of the main features of the policy-making process within which sport has to operate.

Given the influence of the British political and administrative system on the origins and early development of Australian political structures and processes, it is not surprising that many observers use similar analytical frameworks when discussing the national policy process. However, there is a degree of disagreement over the most appropriate conceptualisation of contemporary processes. Few would endorse wholeheartedly Emy's (1978) conventional pluralist model of Australian politics with its emphasis on the significance of competitive party politics and the underlying assumption of state neutrality. Laffin, in criticising Emy, suggests that, as in Britain, Australian policy-making is best seen as taking place within a series of relatively discrete policy communities comprising 'senior public servants, experts and professionals in the field and representatives of "respectable" interest groups . . . enjoying close, informal consultative relations on a continuing basis with public servants' (Laffin 1989: 39). Yet within analyses of the policy process there is a variation in the emphasis given to government, particularly with regard to its capacity to structure relationships within policy communities and also regarding the nature of the relationship with key interest groups in each policy field. There are a number of analyses that describe the policy process in corporatist terms, stressing the existence of strong cohesive interest groups capable of acting authoritatively on behalf of their members and also emphasising the capacity of government to co-opt and organise interests (Schmitter 1979; Panitch 1979b; Stewart 1984; Gerritsen 1986). This is in contrast to those who describe, especially in the pre-Bob Hawke years, a more open competitive relationship between interests and a more fluid relationship between interests and government (West 1984).

Schmitter defines corporatism as:

> a system of interest representation in which the constituent units are organised into a limited number of single, compulsory, non-competitive, hierarchically ordered and functionally differentiated categories, recognised or licensed (if not created) by the state and granted a deliberate representational monopoly within their respective categories in exchange for observing certain controls on their selection of leaders, and articulation of demands and supports.
>
> (Schmitter 1979: 13)

Within the terms of this definition it is indeed possible to examine a number of policy sectors in Australia and identify corporatist features. In economic policy, for example, the employee unions are organised into a series of 'peak' associations at both state and federal government levels. At national level the Australian Council of Trade Unions (ACTU) can claim to represent 90 per cent of trade unionists. Producer interests have until comparatively recently been highly fragmented, but from 1977 the formation of the Confederation of Australian Industry (CAI) seemed to announce the arrival of a national partner with the potential to participate in corporatist politics. For a number of observers Australia experienced a period of corporatist policy-making in the economic sphere during the late 1970s and early 1980s (West 1984). However, as Matthews (1983) makes clear, there is a wide gap between corporatism as an ideal type and Australian experience. In particular, Matthews (1989) draws attention to the extent to which the attempts to establish corporatist structures were undermined by, for example, their lack of authoritative status and the presence of welfare and consumer interests. Further, Ravenhill (1989) draws attention to the diversity of business interests over crucial issues such as trade tariffs, attitudes towards trade unions, and foreign investments (see also Glezer 1982).

In his conclusion Matthews (1989) stresses the capacity of political systems to contain a range of policy-making styles and processes and that it is possible for corporatist and more fluid, pluralist arrangements to co-exist. However, what is most striking about the Australian policy-making process is the extent to which attempts to develop national policy are affected by the strength of the interests of the component states. The fragmentation of the political system and the considerable powers vested at state level are probably the overriding factors preventing the persistence of corporatist structures. As Ravenhill suggests the fragmentation within the business community is 'further complicated by Australia's federal system as most business associations are organised on a federal basis' (1989: 230).

The federal nature of the constitution is of major importance in understanding the policy process in all areas, but especially in social, welfare and economic policy. It was the problems in developing economic policy, 'where key areas of the economy remain balkanized' (Wiltshire 1992: 165), that provided the impetus for recent attempts to remodel the pattern of federalism in the early 1990s. The reliance on institutional arrangements that effectively bypass state and federal parliaments has created a form of executive federalism that involves federal ministers and federal and state civil servants in labyrinthine decision-making processes. The blurring of responsibilities between levels of government has led Wiltshire to comment that 'The federal system with its lack of policy harmonization, absence of uniformity, fragmentation, overlap, and duplication has been seen as one of the key impediments to the microeconomic reform necessary to achieve macroeconomic efficiency' (1992: 168). Stewart goes further and argues that:

> one of the reasons for Australia's current difficulties is that the pattern of relationships between interests and government is neither corporatist nor pluralist but fragmented. Fragmentation means that Australia has neither

the advantages conferred by well-organised interests on the one hand, nor those offered by a diversity of competing interests on the other.

(Stewart 1991: 361)

The fundamental problem arising from fragmentation is that bargaining and negotiation is difficult to organise, interests become entrenched and conflict is often displaced to the courts. At worst the result may be paralysis, where national policy programmes are frequently extremely difficult to implement.

Given the serious difficulty in achieving agreement at national level in key policy areas such as the economy, it is hardly surprising that where the requirement for co-ordination is less acute there is a greater tendency to tolerate variety in many policy areas at state level and to accept a substantial degree of overlap between federal- and state-level policy initiatives. Thus, interests need to be active within states and at federal level, but may develop policy commitments at state level that militate against a national community of interest and effective lobbying at federal level. As regards the policy process for sport and recreation, there are few signs that an effective policy community exists and that policy development suffers from a similar degree of fragmentation to that found in other policy areas. For sport, the primary consequence of fragmentation is to enable the Commonwealth government to take a powerful policy lead on selected issues, but a secondary consequence is the absence of effective checks from among sports organisations on ministerial actions. For example, the resignation of Ros Kelly as Minister for Sport in 1994 was prompted by a critical report from the Auditor General alleging that the distribution of facility grants through the Community, Cultural, Recreation and Sports Facilities Program was motivated less by identified need than by a desire to 'buy' votes in marginal constituencies.

CANADA

The structure of government

Canada has much in common with Australia in terms of its imperial origins, its size and sparsity of population, and its relative youth as an independent country. It also shares with Australia a federal structure of government. Canada has a population of 25m. people within a territory of just under 10m. sq km. Politically it comprises ten provinces, of which only six have populations over 1m., and two northern territories.

The Canadian political system is the product of the British North America Act 1867 which established a structure based on parliamentary sovereignty and federalism (see Landes 1983). Although the 1867 Act has been revised on a number of occasions and additional legislation has altered the character of the constitution, it remains the foundation of the current system and the attempt to reconcile the inherent tensions between parliamentary sovereignty and provincial rights. The provisions of the Act created a balance in favour of the federal government. In particular, the architects of the constitution allocated the bulk of significant responsibilities to the federal government including the regulation of trade and commerce, defence, the system of taxation and control over public debt and the banking system. In contrast, the provinces were granted responsibility for 'all matters of a merely local or private nature in the province' (Section 92.16), which in practice included the administration of justice and prisons, and municipal institutions. Other sections of the constitution enabled provinces to develop their role in welfare provision later in the twentieth century. The relationship between the federal and provincial governments is best illustrated by their respective powers of taxation. The federal government is the superior taxing authority, able to generate income from any system of taxation. In contrast the powers of the provinces are limited to direct taxation for provincial purposes only. Over the years the financial weakness of the provinces has led them to trade control over policy for federal grant.

The primary intention of the devisors of the constitution was to delineate discrete spheres of responsibility for the two levels of government. Where concurrent powers were given, as was the case with agriculture and immigration, superior power rested with the federal government. In addition, a residual powers clause was included in the constitution which enabled the federal government to adopt extensive powers should it perceive an emergency to exist. Finally, the federal government was given the right to review provincial legislation prior to implementation. Subsequent legislation, such as the War Measures Act 1914 and the Bill of Rights 1960, added to and amended the constitution but did little to alter the basic distribution of power. However, the constitution has been subject to fierce debates over its interpretation and application and while Canada has experienced periods of intense centralisation, for example during the Second World War, it has also seen the pendulum swing towards extensive decentralisation, as was the case in the 1960s and 1980s. Part of the explanation for the trend towards decentralisation lay in the expansion of previously minor state responsibilities such as education, part in changes in judicial sentiment which affected interpretations of the constitution, and part in the changing policies of political parties on the issue of provincial autonomy.

It is within this ambiguous constitutional context that Canadian government operates. At the federal level the basic model for the organisation of the central bureaucracy was that of nineteenth-century Britain. The Cabinet system provides a strong link between the bureaucracy and the legislature, with ministers having to defend their actions and those of their civil servants before Parliament. As in most other countries, a functional division of responsibility at federal level predominates, with a few territorially based departments, such as Indian Affairs and Northern Development. Canada also uses public enterprises (nationally owned industries) for the delivery of some public utility services, such as electricity and water, and for the management of politically sensitive services, such as the national airline. Although more concerned with policy formulation than service delivery, the use of commissions of inquiry, task forces and advisory councils is an important and distinctive feature of Canadian administration. Advisory councils, which tend to have more long-lasting functions, not only fulfil a number of administrative roles such as grant distribution, but also provide an institutionalised link between the government and a very broad range of interest groups. As will be discussed below, this link is a distinctive feature of the policy process.

There is no specific mention of local government in the constitution and, as in Australia, local government is the creature of the provinces. The pattern of local government is not uniform across Canada but does possess a number of common features (Norton 1994; Kingdom 1993; Tindal and Tindal 1984; Andrew 1983). Generally, provinces contain a number of single-tier most-purpose authorities for their larger urban areas, with the rest of the population receiving their services through a two-tier system of municipal and country/regional authorities. Overlying this pattern are a series of single-function special agencies, such as school boards, planning boards and health units. In the larger metropolitan areas, such as Toronto and Montreal, special two-tier arrangements have been established with the upper tier enjoying the greater authority. Many provinces contain unorganised areas with no munic-ipal institutions. Party politics at local government level is slight by comparison with the UK. While turnout at local elections is respectable, local government is not normally seen as an important element in the democratic system. With one or two notable exceptions the public priorities for local government are low tax and efficient service delivery as opposed to the provi-sion of a platform for ideological debate and party politics.

Finance for local services comes from three main sources: provincial and federal government grant (*c.* 50 per cent); local property tax (*c.* 33 per cent); income from utilities, investments and sale of goods and services (*c.* 17 per cent). Provincial grants tend to be linked to specific services or projects such as police, water and sewerage, and parks and recreation. Although the federal government has no direct constitutional link with local government, it provides an increasing proportion of total expenditure usually because of the inability of local and even provincial authorities to meet the cost of major services. Local property taxes suffer the usual disadvantage of being electorally unpopular and therefore difficult to raise in line with service cost increases. Of the total income of local authorities, some 40 per cent is spent by special school boards on education, with environment consuming 7.5 per cent and recreation and culture 6 per cent. Recreation services are generally the responsibility of the municipal and regional authorities although in some provinces park boards have been established.

Sport in Canada

The dominant theme in the development of sport in Canada over the past hundred years or so has been identity, although race and commercialism provide important subsidiary motifs. The early phase of Canadian sports history, up to the last quarter of the nineteenth century, was characterised by a commitment to British patterns of recreation adapted to Canadian conditions and the incorporation of a number of native Indian games.

Within the emerging private school system, sport seems to have been accorded the same privileged position as in the English public (fee paying) school system (Cosentino and Howell 1970). But, as Roberts (1973) points out, while the 'character forming' sports of the English public schools were present they soon had to compete (and give way) to emerging Canadian sports such as lacrosse. Yet, even though the range of sports was different, the context was similar (Brown 1984). The prominence of the ideals encapsulated in the notion of 'muscular Christianity' was such that 'the importance of this set of ideas to Canadian sport and physical education cannot be over-emphasised' (Metcalfe 1974: 69). However, as education became more widely available, the Christian motivation for an emphasis on sport was combined with an expansion of physical education derived, in part, from interpretations of Darwinism.

By the latter part of the nineteenth century the relationship between the settlers and the native Canadians was already firmly established. Like white settlers in Australia, Canadian colonists sought to expropriate the property and marginalise the influence of the native people. In terms of sport the native people suffered the expropriation of their cultural heritage and subsequent marginalisation in organised sport as it emerged in the early twentieth century. Cosentino (1975), in his history of the development of professional sport, notes how sports such as lacrosse and snowshoe racing were adopted by white settlers and redefined as EuroCanadian products, which excluded participation by native Canadians. In a similar vein, Salter (1977) demonstrates the extent to which the native Canadians were permitted to continue their participation in lacrosse only as long as their novelty value at the box-office was maintained and only until white participants became equally proficient (see also Paraschak 1989 and Kidd 1983). Native Canadian athletes, such as Michael Thomas and Tom Longboat were also prominent in distance and marathon running during the early part of the current century but their presence faded in later years leaving few role models for subsequent generations (Ballem 1983; Kidd 1981).

Establishing a sporting culture distinct from native Canadians was relatively easy for the white settlers: more problematic was redefining their relationship with the imperial power. Metcalfe comments that 'Although Canada became a semi-independent political identity in 1867, it is doubtful whether a particularly Canadian way of life or culture existed during the nineteenth century' (1974: 63). Just as Canada acquired its financial investment and people from abroad, it also imported its attitudes and values from Britain, the United States and France. Indeed Gruneau and Whitson suggest that the priority in the late nineteenth century was with institution building rather than cultural manipulation (1993: 41–2). However, the period from the 1880s to the Second World War was marked by emergence of national governing bodies to organise sport, a steady distancing in cultural terms from the British shadow and a consolidation of commercialism. The founding of the national governing bodies for lacrosse (1867) and baseball (1876) both pre-date the establishment of similar bodies for British sports. The Dominion Football (soccer) Association was formed in 1878 and the Canadian Rugby Football Association was formed four years later. As Brown comments:

> while the moral theory of games was unquestionably British in its associ-
> ation, there is no doubt that in actual form, sport was illustrative of an
> emerging sense of Canadianism. Ice hockey, lacrosse and Canadian foot-
> ball were games which extolled the individuality of a people in search of
> their own identity.
>
> (Brown 1984: 132)

The end of the First World War prompted a period of intense reflection on the nature of Canadian identity and the relationship with Britain. As MacGregor observes, the war had 'undoubtedly heightened the affection for Great Britain, but it had an even more marked effect in developing a strong national consciousness within the Dominions themselves' (MacGregor 1965: 29). During the 1920s Canada gradually asserted its collective personality on the international stage by, for example, delaying its support for British policy towards the Turks in 1921 and by sending diplomatic representatives to Paris and Washington. This process was also apparent in the development of sport, where Canada maintained strong links with British sport mainly through support for the Commonwealth Games (Canada hosted the first British Empire Games in 1930). However, over the period from the end of the First World War, the influence of British sport waned to be replaced by increasing involvement in US-owned and dominated leagues for ice hockey and football, and later basketball and baseball.

From early in the current century, Anglo-Canadians have expressed a deep concern at the potential for cultural degradation from the US. In much of the literature that examines the relationship between Canada and its southern neighbour, commercialisation and cultural dilution are combined. More than any other major sport in Canada it is ice hockey that illustrates graphically the factors and pressures that shaped sport in the present century. Ice hockey emerged as the major ice, stick and ball game in the 1880s. Based on rules adapted from field hockey, it displaced alter-native sports such as shinny, rickets and hurley. The establishment of a governing body to formalise play in 1886 was followed by a rapid increase in the formation of clubs, largely committed to amateurism and motivated in many cases by a moral utilitarianism. However, by 1910 or so, moral entrepreneurialism had given way to economic entrepreneurialism with pro-fessional ice hockey teams well established throughout Canada. This development was some twenty years after a similar accommodation between baseball and commercialism. From the early days of commercialism, the future of Canadian ice hockey was closely intertwined with developments in the United States. Kidd and Macfarlane (1972) provide an account of the gradual undermining, by American business interests, of an autonomous Canadian sports structure for ice hockey and its progressive absorption into a US-dominated professional league. Within fifteen years of the formation of the National Hockey League (NHL) in 1917, Canadian teams found them-selves in a US-dominated organisation. Although there seems to have been little initial disquiet at the change in NHL control, by the middle of the century an increasing number of observers of the game were asserting that ice hockey represented an essential aspect of Canadian identity which was being debased through US domination of the NHL.

The commercial success of professional ice hockey helped to shape Canadian attitudes to other, predominantly amateur, sports which were increasingly seen as being second-rate. The poor performance of Canada's national ice hockey teams in the Olympic Games and World Championships of the 1960s confirmed this perception, but also made the country more receptive to Trudeau's proposal to commit federal resources to help improve international sporting success. From the late 1960s to the present day, the Canadian government has provided substantial financial and organisational support for sport, especially Olympic sports, and thereby complemented the increased commercialisation of sport over the past thirty years.

Policy process

In his analysis of the evolution of the policy process in Canada, Pross (1986) describes the transition from a period in the early part of the century domi-nated by the executive where interest groups were weak, through a period from the mid-1930s to the early 1960s where interest groups were more prominent but in a 'tutelary' relationship with the bureaucracy, to the current position where policy fields are the focus for the activities of an increasing number of active and more independent interest groups. The tute-lary relationship of the 1950s and 1960s was based on bureaucratic control of access which encouraged, or more accurately required, a high degree of discretion on the part of the interest group and an acceptance that the price paid for access was limited and muted public criticism. The 1960s was marked by a rapid expansion of the role of the federal state, particularly in areas such as education, urban deprivation, health and welfare. New issues also emerged, including those relating to the environment, and to consumer, gender and cultural rights. The increasing burden on the federal government was managed by distributing policy responsibility between a series of agen-cies. Paralleling the growth of government was a similar expansion in the number of interest groups actively involved in lobbying: the Directory of Canadian Associations of 1992 lists more than 20,000 associations and the 1991 Spicer Citizens Forum received the views of 13,000 groups. However, what is distinctive is the extent to which the growth in the number of groups was encouraged by the government. In a number of policy areas where organised interests were lacking, the government took steps to stimulate their formation through the establishment of consultative fora, the creation of regulatory frameworks that require group formation (Pross 1986: 65), and as Faulkner noted 'the decision to permit the public funding of interest groups' (1982: 248).

Despite the centralising tendency that is usually found in systems based on parliamentary sovereignty and Cabinet government, the trend towards an ever greater diffusion of power continued in the 1960s and 1970s. While this trend created an increased number of access points for organised interests it has also resulted in an increase in the number of 'clearance points' for policies where power of veto or delay might be exercised beyond those inherent in federal systems (Weaver and Rockman 1993). The stimulation of interest groups' formation by government agencies was seen by Pross (1986) as a deliberate attempt to establish policy communities, which, rather than being characterised by dependency relationships are better described as mutually beneficial relationships between agency and interests. Interest groups have now been accepted as an integral part of the policy process where they perform a number of functions including legitimating the role of 'their' agency. Parliament, through the establishment of a wide number of committees that hear evidence from interest groups, provides publicity and legitimation to groups and by implication to the activities of the relevant agency. The essential characteristics of Canadian policy communities are that they demonstrate commitment to a set of shared values, possess an implicit organisational and authority structure and display established patterns of behaviour. For Pross:

> A policy community is that part of a political system that – by virtue of its functional responsibilities, its vested interests, and its specialised knowledge – acquires a dominant voice in determining government decisions in a specific field of public activity, and is generally permitted by society at large and the public authorities in particular to determine public policy in that field. It is populated by government agencies, pressure groups, media people, and individuals, including academics, who have an interest in a particular field and attempt to influence it.
>
> (Pross 1986: 98)

Pross distinguishes between the sub-government of a policy community which comprises the government agency and approved interest groups and the 'attentive public', which is a much looser group of individuals and organisations whose participation in policy discussions is sporadic and less effective. Using rather different terminology, but making a similar distinction,

Coleman and Skogstad (1990) identify the policy network as a broad equivalent to the sub-government. The operation of policy communities is such that
they will decide between alternative policies, arrange implementation and
effectively 'dominate decision-making in fields where they have competence'
(Pross 1986: 131). A further characteristic of policy communities in Canada,
according to Pross, is that in marked contrast to the policy process operating
within Australian federalism the role of provincial governments is viewed as
frequently marginal in many key social and welfare policy areas. However, as
in Australia it is acknowledged that the specific character of individual policy
communities will vary.

The characterisation of the policy process as relatively open, where interest
groups count for as much if not more than political parties and where they
operate largely in a co-operative relationship with government is common but
not universally accepted. For example, there are those (Presthus 1973; Mcleod
1978; Atkinson and Coleman 1989) who have emphasised the corporatist
tendencies within the development of the Canadian policy process. During
the economic crisis of the early 1970s attempts were indeed made by the
Trudeau government to involve both business and unions in tripartite discussions aimed at achieving agreement on prices and incomes. However, as
Panitch (1979a) points out, the unions were at best lukewarm towards the
proposal and ultimately hostile. Experiments in the economic sphere with
tripartism need to be seen within a context where the state relies traditionally
upon high unemployment and selective welfare expenditure to moderate
working-class union militancy (Panitch 1977). In non-economic policy areas
corporatist experiments were rare, with relations between the state and
interest groups generally closer to a pluralistic-policy community model.

Pross concludes that, while there is a tendency towards state structuring of
relations with interest groups and a preference in parts of the state bureaucracy for corporatism, a tendency is not a trend. 'Both in terms of practice
and of ideology Canada has followed a path that is far from corporatism'
(Pross 1986: 225). The favoured image of the policy process is one where the
agency-interest group relationship lies at the heart of the policy community.
Although the government adopts a promotional attitude to interest groups
the power of the policy community is moderated by the central role of the
Cabinet and the legitimating role of Parliament. From the viewpoint of
government agencies, a coterie of broadly supportive interest groups provides
a set of valuable allies in the task of stimulating support for policies. However,
the development of policy communities is hampered by the tensions that arise
from federalism and the many occasions when provincial interests conflict
with those of the federal government, including, for example, the recent
examples of conflict over oil exploration (Doern and Toner 1985) and also
over environmental policy (Skogstad and Kopas 1992). In addition, Canada
faces the particular problems arising from Quebec. The simmering separatist
movement compounds the policy tensions between Quebec and the federal
government, based on cultural differences. Consequently, the effectiveness of

policy communities is, on occasion, moderated by the political priority given to the maintenance of the good relations between the provinces and the federal government. Simeon (1972), for example, suggests that, in the early 1970s at least, in a range of policy areas the sectional interests of groups was regularly sacrificed in favour of inter-governmental objectives. However, Knopff *et al.* (1994) urge caution against exaggerating the impact of the federal system and stress the tendency of interests to organise at the national level due to an acknowledgement of the power of the federal government.

THE REPUBLIC OF IRELAND

The structure of government

The Republic of Ireland[1] is a small country on the edge of Europe, with a population of just over 3.5m., approximately one-third of whom live in the capital city, Dublin. Ireland is culturally homogeneous with the over-whelming majority subscribing to the same religion (Roman Catholic) and speaking the same language (English). Despite recent rapid urbanisation, the country possesses one of the most rural populations of the European Union with 35–40 per cent still living in rural areas; a figure that rises sharply as one moves from east to west (Chubb 1992).

Given the revolutionary origins of the Irish state, the political system has remained remarkably stable. The main political cleavage is still derived from attitudes adopted in the early 1920s to the Treaty with Britain. Sinn Fein, the pre-independence nationalist party split into pro- and anti-Treaty factions which, following the short but bitter civil war, formed the basis of the two major parties in the Republic today, namely Fine Gael (pro-Treaty) and Fianna Fail (anti-Treaty). Images of class-based politics do not readily fit the Irish party system (Mair 1987). The Labour Party is small and has not benefited significantly from increasing urbanisation largely because of the success of Fianna Fail in maintaining its support across class and region, and between rural and urban areas. The enduring appeal of Fianna Fail has given the Republic a high degree of stability in government.

The stability of Irish politics was enhanced by the high degree of conti-nuity in administrative structures and practices between the colonial and post-colonial periods. The British colonial administration was based on the pattern in Whitehall and was adopted without substantial amendment by the Irish government in 1921. There was an initial emphasis on a simplifica-tion of the administrative system by locating the responsibilities of government either in one of the functionally defined central ministries or with local government. However, between the 1920s and the middle of the century a large number of semi-independent state-sponsored bodies were established often to manage public utilities or were associated with agricul-ture policy. To a very large extent this is a similar pattern of development to that found in the UK up until the 1970s, when Ireland adopted a centralised form of economic development policy which required a higher degree of administrative centralisation. According to Chubb (1992: 220), 'from 1970, the propensity to centralise was without doubt the major feature of Irish public administration'. However, Chubb also makes clear that the pace of change has been slow and has encountered considerable resistance both from within the civil service and from the private sector.

Currently Ireland possesses an administrative system where responsibility for public services is divided between a series of functionally organised central ministries, local government and a less clearly defined cluster of semi-independent, but government-funded bodies. Following the establishment of the Irish Free State in 1922, a central administration focused on eleven main departments was introduced. Although the intervening seventy-five years has seen the introduction of new departments and the reorganisation of others, the pattern has remained substantially unchanged. In the early 1990s there were over ninety state-sponsored bodies, the majority of which fall into one of three broad categories. First, there are those that operate along largely commercial lines and are responsible for public utilities, such as the Electricity Supply Board. The second category contains those bodies involved in promotional activities and includes the Irish Tourist Board. The third category is more amorphous and includes bodies that are responsible for regulating or administering a particular service, such as the Medical Registration Council.

The third element in the pattern of national administration is local government. As with the pattern of central government, the Irish Free State inherited a British model of local government which in many respects is still in place today. A period of post-independence rationalisation produced a system where county councils were the key unit of local government although some of the larger urban areas were granted county borough status. Within the counties a number of districts have borough status and some towns have local services provided through urban district councils. The range of services provided by local authorities are similar to those found in many other European countries and include public/social housing, highways, water supply and sewerage, planning, and recreation and amenity.

Among the distinctive features of the Irish system of local government are the low proportion of total public expenditure at its disposal (15 per cent in the late 1980s), the existence of a single local government service (for staff appointments) controlled by the centre, the adoption of the 'city manager' as the focus for service delivery and the weakness of the local tax base and consequent dependence on central grant. According to Barrington, the shapers of the Irish state had 'a clear vision – unperturbed by thoughts of democracy – of a streamlined, efficient, workaday system of local government operating basically as a dispersed agency of central government' (1991: 157).

Reform, and revitalisation, of the local government system has been discussed on a number of occasions without any significant progress. The most recent review was undertaken in 1990 following the announcement by the government of 'its commitment to a major reorganisation of the local government system' designed to 'strengthen local democracy in Ireland and to devolve additional functions to local authorities' (Barrington Committee 1991: iii).

Sport in Ireland

The history of the development of sport in Ireland is intimately tied in to the history of the independence movement and resistance to British rule. Before Ireland won independence from Britain, a distinctive sporting tradition had been established, supported by an elaborate organisational infrastructure. The Gaelic Athletic Association (GAA) had played a central role in stimulating cultural and political resistance to Britain and consequently provided the Irish state with a supportive network of sports clubs throughout the country. The effectiveness of the GAA partly explains the absence of direct state intervention in sport until comparatively recently.

The GAA is significant in any discussion of the administration and politics of sport in Ireland, not simply because of its network of clubs, but also because it has a cultural resonance and political weight that has shaped government policy towards non-GAA sports and sport policy in general. In order to appreciate the contemporary significance of the GAA it is necessary to understand the context in which it emerged in the nineteenth century and the part it played in the independence movement.

The GAA was founded in 1884 as part of a wider campaign of cultural resistance to British rule. The Association aimed to rescue and promote traditional Irish sports, such as hurling and Gaelic football, provide an Irish organisational framework for a range of sports, including track and field, and prevent the spread of 'alien' English sports such as soccer, rugby and cricket. That the GAA should emerge at this time is not surprising, for Ireland was not immune to the nationalist ferment which had hold of much of Europe. Yet, there were also specific factors that prompted the formation of the GAA in the mid-1880s. In 1874 the Irish Football Union had been formed to organise rugby and six years later the Irish Football Association was founded to fulfil a similar role for the growing number of soccer clubs. The concern among a number of prominent Irish nationalists was that the establishment of a series of governing bodies modelled on the English pattern would further undermine Irish identity. Michael Cusack, a founding member of the GAA, referred to rugby as 'a denationalising plague' while an article in the *United Irishman* described English games as a 'demoralising and prostrating tide' (both quoted in Mandle 1977: 420).

As significant as the network of sports clubs established by the GAA was the close relationship between the Association and nationalist politics, particularly those of the Irish Republican Brotherhood, a forerunner of Sinn Fein and the IRA. Following independence the GAA confined itself to organising hurling and football, leaving other sports, especially athletics, to the newly formed National Athletics and Cycling Association (NACA) (Mandle 1977). The government encouraged the GAA and the NACA to organise the sporting life of the country, with extremely modest and infrequent finance and without significant interference. As Hussey notes, the Irish 'avidity for all things sporting has not translated itself into financial support from government, which until 1992 managed to escape without really major provision being made' (1995: 446).

The explanation for the lack of government involvement in sport lies partly in the financial conservatism of both the major political parties, partly in the sophistication and geographical coverage of the GAA organisation, but primarily in the lack of need for government intervention. As already made clear, governments rarely provide support for sport unless it can serve some ulterior purpose, particularly associated with nation-building or international prestige. The central position of the GAA in Irish political and cultural life left little for the Irish state to do.

Although the level of support for the GAA still remains high, there are some signs that its dominance is being challenged by soccer and, to a lesser extent, rugby union. While part of the explanation of the increasing popularity of soccer lies in ubiquity of soccer on television, it is the considerable success of the Irish soccer teams in the 1988 European Championships and especially the 1990 and 1994 World Cup finals that has contributed most to the growing popularity of the sport. However, there is also a deeper cultural change within Ireland that may make Gaelic sports less attractive. For much of its early history the domestic politics of the Irish Republic had been dominated by its relationship with Britain – a relationship which was close and generally amicable, but also stultifying. A key development for the Republic was the decision (following the British lead) to apply for membership of the then Common Market. The persistence of the conflict in Northern Ireland ensures that Ireland's most significant foreign policy relationship will continue to be with the UK (Keatinge and Laffan 1992). However, the period since 1973 has not only produced sustained economic growth but has, more importantly, taken Ireland on to a European stage. The role of Ireland in the European Union, its membership of the European Monetary System and its support for the Maastricht agreement have all contributed to the foreign policy goal of taking Ireland out of Britain's shadow and making its presence felt on a broader stage. Soccer can be seen as both an element in that process of engagement with the world and symbolic of Ireland's confidence. As Holmes succinctly observes when assessing the significance of Irish soccer success, 'the isolation inherent in Gaelic games contrasts with the international outlook of football' (1994: 91). A complementary view was expressed, somewhat more tangentially, earlier in 1979 in a Foreign Affairs Department publication when it was noted that 'Quite often in the past the vigour displayed in pursuing these [nationalist] principles has clouded the vast contribution made by the [GAA] association to the sporting life of the Irish people' (Carroll 1979: 9).

It is not just soccer that marks Ireland's growing sporting cosmopolitanism. During the 1980s Barry McGuigan's winning of the world featherweight boxing championship and Stephen Roche's victory in the 1987 Tour de France generated immense interest both from the public and from political figures, including the Taoiseach (Prime Minister), Charles Haughey, who travelled to Paris to meet Roche as he crossed the finishing line (Hussey 1995: 445). Possibly the most significant international success was achieved at the 1992 Olympic Games where Michael Curruth won a gold medal in boxing. His victory prompted a series of rancorous exchanges between the Irish Olympic Council and the government over the absence of world-class training facilities for the Irish Olympic team; a complaint compounded by the fact that the triple gold-medal winner, Michelle Smith, trained for the 1996 Games in the Netherlands because of the absence of adequate Olympic facilities in Ireland.

This increasing engagement with the international community has been partly responsible for the recent pressure on the government to take a more active role in providing facilities and other resources for Ireland's sporting programme. As the following chapters will demonstrate, there exists an administrative infrastructure for sport policy at central government, local authority and agency levels but the government's utilisation of it has been slight. However, in the past ten years or so there has undoubtedly been an intensification of pressure on the government to participate more effectively in sport policy, particularly regarding the improvement of existing facilities for elite athletes.

Policy process

Such is the seductiveness of alliteration that one is tempted to summarise the Irish policy process as typified by centralism, corporatism, and Catholicism. Unfortunately, while being substantially accurate as a generalisation, it fails to capture the diversity in process between policy areas and also the direction of change in policy style.

In their review of Irish politics Collins and McCann emphasise that one of the distinctive features of the Irish policy process is the significance of decisions made outside the Republic. '[A]s a small country with a heavy dependence on international trade and with many large multi-national companies having Irish plants, decisions made in Chicago, New York, London, Tokyo and elsewhere can have immediate impact in Ireland' (1993: 59). The nature of the industrial base, the openness of the Irish economy, and its membership of the European Union all combine to enhance the significance of external constraints on domestic policy-making relative to those found in many other European countries. Acknowledgement of the significance of the external environment does not, however, result in an emasculated domestic policy process.

The extent of centralisation in the Irish political system has already been noted in relation to the limited powers of local government. Yet, even at the centre there is a comparatively small inner core of policy-makers who 'belong to the higher levels of the government bureaucracy, economic pressure groups, major companies and senior politicians' (Collins and McCann 1993: 61) and number fewer than 500. For Collins and McCann the policy process in Ireland is dominated by civil servants, and especially those in the Department of Finance and the Department of the Taoiseach. The senior civil servant is 'particularly powerful . . . (and) operates at the core of the highly centralised, secretive, self-protective, pervasive and unrivalled administrative machine' (1993: 48). Not surprisingly, even where opportunities are created for the introduction of new ideas to policy debates, for example, through special Commissions or the semi-official organisations such as the National Economic and Social Council, the contributions are heavily mediated by party and bureaucratic politics.

Chubb (1992) comes to broadly similar conclusions, but emphasises more heavily the variety of policy-making patterns found in different policy areas (see also O'Halpin 1992). Corporatism is most evident with regard to economic policy where 'this is a mode of policy-making that has now to be considered as a characteristic, if not yet a permanent, feature of Irish politics' (Chubb 1992: 158). Other policy areas tend to be rather more open with the determination of health policy, for example, involving significant non-state groups including the medical professions, the church and the voluntary sector (Carswell 1994). Environmental policy is also formed outside the corporatist framework where it is possible to identify the effect of successful pressure-group tactics in a number of recent policy changes, including the Environmental Action Programme adopted in 1990 (Baker 1994). However, whether the particular policy style tends towards corporatism or a more open form of sectorised interaction between government and interest groups, a comparatively small political and bureaucratic elite plays a determining role.

Providing an ideological context for the current pattern of policy-making is first, a largely unchallenged assumption of the coterminous nature of the interests of business and those of the state, and second, the position of the Catholic Church and Catholicism. The relationship between government and business is, to a very large extent, taken for granted; it is assumed that policies that enable businesses to prosper are largely consistent with governmental interests. This picture of government–business relations is similar to that outlined by Lindblom (1977) in his examination of the relationship between capitalism and pluralism, where he suggests that the privileged position of business in the policy process must be recognised in any analysis. In Ireland there is ample confirmation of this argument with the priority of business enshrined in the constitution which confirms that 'the state shall favour and, where necessary, supplement private initiative in industry and commerce' (quoted in Chubb 1992: 249). As Chubb makes clear, the establishment of state-sponsored bodies took place within the context of the weakness of the Irish private sector and 'owed little to socialist theory' (ibid.).

In a country where over 90 per cent of the population is Roman Catholic, 95 per cent of all schools are under Church control, and in the early 1980s over 80 per cent of adults went to church at least once a week it is hardly surprising that religion has a significant impact on public policy. The influence of the Church is rarely overt as Catholicism is so deeply embedded in the national culture. But the Church will exert its influence explicitly if it feels that core Catholic values are under threat. Thus, in the mid-1980s when referenda on divorce and abortion were held, the clergy 'made it abundantly clear to politicians and people where their Catholic duty lay' (Chubb 1992: 31). That the necessity for such explicit intervention is rare is an indication of the extent to which the interests of the Church are tacitly incorporated into everyday political discourse. Whyte (1980) draws attention to the 'taken for granted' nature of the relationship between the Church, government and policy: like business the church also has a privileged position in Irish politics. Consequently, the liberalisation of social policy in areas of censorship, divorce and contraception is slow; although the fact that movement is taking place is a sign of a change, and weakening, in the Church–state relationship.

UNITED KINGDOM

The structure of government

The United Kingdom comprises England, Wales, Scotland and Northern Ireland with all four countries returning elected representatives to the House of Commons. Key features of the UK political system are an established two-party structure – a simple majority electoral system and a weak second chamber, the combination of which produces a pattern of government characterised by a strong executive centred on the Prime Minister and Cabinet.

At central government level, responsibility for particular policy areas is determined largely on a simple functional basis augmented by a number of territorial ministries for Northern Ireland, Scotland, and Wales. Responsibility for sport is primarily located in the Department of National Heritage (DNH), although there is a broad range of ministries with an interest in sport policy, including the Home Office (control of gambling), the Department for Education and Employment (sport in the school curriculum) and the Department of the Environment (control over local authority spending and land use planning).

Although central government ministries take a key role in shaping national policy, they have few executive responsibilities. A trend that developed in the 1970s to devolve responsibility for service delivery to semi-independent agencies was given additional impetus during Margaret Thatcher's period as Prime Minister. In many policy areas, including sport, the arts and tourism, important roles are fulfilled by agencies such as the Sports Councils, the Arts Council and a range of Tourist Boards. Devolution of responsibility for policy implementation to agencies is complemented by a similar pattern of devolution to units of local government (local authorities). Unlike most federal systems of government, the powers, finances and responsibilities of local authorities in the UK are determined by Parliament. Consequently, although local government is a major provider of opportunities for sport and recreation, the scope for variation and discretion has become increasingly limited over the past twenty years.

Governments have generally been reluctant to acknowledge sport as an appropriate responsibility of the state and when acknowledged, there has been uncertainty about status and location within the machinery of government. From 1974 to 1991 responsibility for sport was located within the Department of the Environment (DoE). In many ways this was a logical choice as the DoE also had responsibility for local government, which was the main provider of public sport and recreation facilities. In addition, the DoE was responsible for land-use planning policy, water and countryside issues, and environmental matters. Yet, this location isolated sport from a number of important related policy areas, particularly school sport (in the then Department of Education and Science) and tourism (Department of Trade and Industry). In 1991, as the issue of sport in schools rose on the political agenda, the new Prime Minister, John Major, transferred responsibility for sport to the Department of Education and Science (later retitled the Department for Education and Employment). However, this arrangement was short-lived as the function was soon transferred again, in 1992, to its present home in the Department of National Heritage (DNH). The DNH was, in part, an attempt to group together a series of functionally related responsibilities. In practice the development of the hoped-for synergy in policy between tourism, the arts and sport has, so far, failed to emerge as each section of the DNH tends to work independently.

The DNH has responsibility for the Sports Councils, which have a major executive role in sport policy. The Sports Councils were reorganised in 1997 when the British Sports Council was replaced by two Councils, one for England and the other for the UK. There are now five Sports Councils in the UK, one each for Scotland, England, Wales and Northern Ireland and the UK Sports Council. Traditionally, the Councils have adopted a very broad range of responsibilities under the slogan 'Sport For All'. They aimed to support sports involvement from the elite level to the foundation/introductory level across a very wide range of sports. More recently the government has sought to narrow the focus of sport policy, giving priority to a more limited range of sports and concentrating on youth/school sport and elite development. The Councils work very closely with the local authorities, governing bodies and clubs in their region and as such provide an extremely important focus for sport development. At local government level, the distribution of responsibilities for sport and recreation is as complex as at the centre. The structure of local government and the responsibilities of the different units in the UK varies. Throughout the UK there is a mix of single and two-tier authorities. In the two-tier authorities sport is a major responsibility for the lower-tier body, though the upper tier will also have some sports-/leisure-related functions, such as country parks.

In order to provide a complete picture of the involvement of government in sport in the UK, it is necessary to comment briefly on the growing significance of the European Union (EU) (Houlihan 1994). The various changes in the title of the organisation (from Common Market to European Community and now EU) indicate clearly the gradual widening of its range of interests. Currently there are a number of policy areas where the EU is already having or could have a significant impact on domestic sport policy. At one level the EU has recognised and exploited the value of sport in contributing to the development of a sense of 'European citizenship' which, for many member states, is part of the progress towards the 'ever closer union' referred to in the Treaty of Rome. EU funds have been used to sponsor EU-wide sports events such as the EU Swimming Club Championships in 1987. More significant than these attempts at building a sense of supra-national identity is the treatment of sport by the EU as primarily an industry that needs to conform to EU regulations regarding, for example, the free movement of labour. This is a particular problem for soccer, where the European federation (UEFA) has resisted, without success, attempts by the EU to overrule the limit on the number of foreign players that can be fielded in international club competitions. Discussions between the EU and the UEFA have resulted in a temporary acceptance by the UEFA of the current position although it is clear that the UEFA intends to seek ways in which it can reassert its control over the composition of club teams.

Sport in the United Kingdom

As in many European countries Britain possessed a 'remarkable range of popular games and contests' (Holt 1989: 13) in the pre-industrial period. A variety of forms of hunting and animal baiting, together with a range of village-based team games blended with the seasonal activity in the agricultural industry. Yet, from the outset, the expansion of sport and recreational activities was paralleled by growing government involvement, frequently stimulated by a concern with the potential for disorder that sport was seen as providing. As Brailsford notes: 'There were numerous medieval and Tudor statutes defining the opportunities for recreation and their proper use' (1991: 33). By the seventeenth century 'holidays, gambling, and the effects of recreation on trade were all live issues' (ibid.: 31) with sport 'a regular theme of political dispute' being intimately intertwined with the major issue of the day – the conflict between Parliament and the monarch (ibid.: 32). Thus, the many bills passed by Parliament to regulate recreation and sports on the

Sabbath which the king vetoed were usually indirect ways of raising the key issue of monarchical power. During the Commonwealth the Parliamentarians instigated rigorous controls over all forms of sport and recreation on the Sabbath, but as Brailsford (1991) points out, instituted alternative holidays for recreation and had to contend with extensive evasion of the law.

The link between morality and recreation remained a constant thread in the development of sport. A second constant theme was the relationship between sport, privilege and class. In hunting, for example, the law was used to protect the sporting interests of the powerful through the Game Laws (Thomas 1983). The Law of 1671 limited hunting to the rich and imposed severe penalties on poorer people who poached game, even on their own land. Later Game Laws increased the severity of penalties and made the right to hunt more restrictive. The history of the Game Laws is a reflection of the social divisions of the time and the fact that the laws were produced by a Parliament dominated by the land-owning aristocracy and gentry and enforced by a magistracy composed of people from the same social classes. Indeed, it was not until the early part of the nineteenth century that the most repressive clauses of the Game Laws were modified or repealed. During the nineteenth and twentieth centuries the law has continued to reflect the power of particular sporting and social interests and the weakness of others. For example, the 1835 Cruelty to Animals Act outlawed bull- and bear-baiting but did not interfere with hunting and although repeated campaigns have attempted to outlaw fox-hunting, they have, so far, proved notably unsuccessful.

The association between class and sport was at its strongest during the Victorian period and is best reflected in the distinction between amateurs and professionals. The growing desire for social exclusivity in sport was achieved partly through the promotion of expensive sports, including hunting, game-fishing and shooting, as suitable for the elite and also partly through the exercise of control over the governing bodies of organised sports. The British system of public schools and the Universities of Oxford and Cambridge played a central role in articulating and refining the culture of athleticism and also in developing the organisational framework to manage its development. The formation of the Football Association in 1863 followed by that of the Rugby Football Union in 1871 were both inspired by ex-public schoolboys.

The debate over amateurism dogged UK sport well into the twentieth century. While only a few sports, and often only for a limited time, used amateur rules as a means of excluding manual workers, the use of amateur rules to exclude those who made a living from the sport itself persisted. Athletics (Lovesey 1979) and rowing (Holt 1989) fought long and hard to resist any dilution of the amateur rule while rugby split into two codes – union and league – over the issue. Where amateurs and professionals were allowed to participate in the same team or event, social distinctions were rigidly enforced. As Holt notes, in cricket where mixed teams were common, clear social rules were applied:

> There was a rough division of labour whereby the amateurs mainly batted and the professionals mainly bowled. . . . Bowling was thought to be too much like hard work; and, besides it was undignified for a gentleman's bowling to be struck nonchalantly round the ground by a social inferior.
>
> (Holt 1989: 107)

If the nineteenth-century sport was characterised by a preoccupation with social demarcation, it was also characterised by a concern with social unrest and the contribution that sport might make to its prevention (Bailey 1979). The 'muscular Christian' movement was based on the belief that sport instilled, among the social elite, a set of values essential to a vigorous and successful society, including self-control, fairness, determination and solidarity. The middle-class advocates of muscular Christianity operating through organisations such as the YMCA, the Boys' Brigade and the Church Lads' Brigade saw sport as a key instrument for the maintenance of social order among the urban working class. The perception of sport as a means of social control contributed greatly to the spread of organised sport in the late nineteenth and early twentieth centuries. By the start of the present century organised team sports were well established and very much part of the social fabric of the whole UK.

The twentieth century has been marked by a steady growth in commercialised sport, the grudging participation of Britain in international sport, and the increasing involvement of government in the administration and organisation of sport. A number of sports, most notably soccer, but also boxing and rugby league, adopted a commercial basis for organisation early in their histories. In more recent years, tennis, golf and athletics have all become more firmly committed to commercialism whether this has taken the form of sponsorship or an acceptance of professional players or more frequently both. The advent of television has had the most profound effect on the character and organisation of sport in the UK. Few sports have been able to resist the financial rewards available from television.

Policy process

Any description of domestic policy-making is an exercise in capturing the essential features of a dynamic process. At best such attempts will identify the central and most stable elements of the policy process and give some assessment of the areas of greater fluidity and the dynamics of change. Nowhere is the production of a satisfactory overview of the policy process more difficult than in Britain. The difficulties arise, first, from the persistence of long-established attempts to summarise and interpret an important, but unwritten, part of the UK constitution, second, from the blurring of the dividing lines between normative theorising and description and third, from the significance of the period when Margaret Thatcher was Prime Minister.

The traditional nineteenth-century model of the constitution stresses the centrality of Parliament in the policy process and the strength of representative democracy. While few, if any, would defend this view of the constitution as providing an accurate description of the actual policy process, the model is significant because, as Greenaway *et al.* argue, it provides 'the dominant language of political discourse' (1992: 50). At best it is a normative aspiration and at worst it acts as a rhetorical smoke screen. More recent summaries of the policy process stress the significance of organised interests and the variability between policy areas. Debates continue regarding the significance of political parties and the capacity of the Cabinet to determine policy. During the late 1960s and early 1970s the view gathered ground that what typified policy-making in Britain was fragmentation of policy and the strength of sectoral, and particularly departmental, interests. The Cabinet lacked a strategic capacity and while the Prime Minister could be influential, his/her influence was limited to a narrow range of admittedly key areas such as the economy and foreign policy. As the 1970s progressed, analyses of policy-making gave increasing prominence to the notion of a policy community as an apt characterisation of the way policy was made. As with earlier descriptions, the emphasis was placed on fragmentation and variation between policy fields. According to Richardson and Jordan 'problems are handled similarly irrespective of what government is in power' (1979: 43). The explanation for the similarity of response, and the implicit marginality of party and government, is due to the structuring of the policy process in such a way that sub-systems exist which exhibit strong boundaries between policy areas but less distinct and more permeable boundaries between departments and relevant interest groups within individual policy areas.

> It is the relationship involved in committees, the policy community of departments and groups, the practices of co-option and the consensual style, that better account for policy outcomes than do examinations of party stances, of manifestos or of parliamentary influence.
>
> (Richardson and Jordan 1979: 73)

The image of the UK policy process as discrete, segmented, focused on government departments, allowing minimal public involvement, with a central role for professions, and a high degree of cohesion founded on shared perceptions of problems and solutions has proved to be resilient. However, the conceptualisation, which tended to become part of the conventional wisdom during the 1980s, was seriously challenged by the Thatcher governments from 1979 which proclaimed the return to ideological (conviction) politics. This style of politics, which led to confrontations with the miners, teachers, fire fighters and civil servants in the 1980s, also led to the introduction of a sweeping privatisation programme and a significant increase in central control of local government. Yet when Jordan and

Richardson re-examined UK policy-making in 1987 they confirmed their original conclusions, but did admit that the style of the Thatcher governments was a break with the past. However, they stressed that the confrontational style on issues often gave way to a more conventional bargaining process. The development of education and social welfare policy during the 1980s would appear to confirm this conclusion. However, more importantly, the Thatcher period also highlights first, the cyclical nature of the influence of many interest groups and second, the broad resilience of many interest groups. It is undoubtedly true that up to the mid-1980s public sector interests were marginalised, but in the later years of the decade teachers, welfare workers and doctors all began to regain some of their lost ground.

Nevertheless, the 1980s witnessed the disruption of 'normal politics' in a number of key areas. The retreat from the politics of accommodation and bargaining was reflected not only in the willingness of the government to 'take on' what they saw as vested interests such as miners and public sector unions, but was also reflected in the way in which a number of policies were produced. The most notable example was the development of a new tax to be levied at local government level, the community charge. The community charge was introduced in April 1989 in Scotland and a year later in England and Wales with its withdrawal announced in April 1992. For Butler *et al.* the policy, which contributed much to a series of by-election defeats for the Conservatives and to the downfall of Margaret Thatcher, was the product of 'elective dictatorship'. Butler *et al.* conclude that:

> responsibility for initiating and pushing through the policy can be attributed narrowly. . . . The poll tax [community charge] was elevated from 'bold idea' to 'government policy', in the space of barely three months, because of the enthusiastic backing of the Prime Minister and key colleagues.
>
> (Butler *et al.* 1994: 287 and 289)

What is clear from the history of the community charge is that attempts by government, or parts of the government, to determine policy can be successful, but they are extremely difficult to sustain without an infrastructure of support from the civil service and affected interests. The increasing complexity of the policy process and especially the growing significance of the European Union and other international considerations make it less likely that government-inspired radical policy change can be sustained even over the medium term. Indeed Rhodes (1985) notes that policy communities will be less effective where 'grand' issues are concerned and are most effective where ordinary or routine issues are involved. The distinctive feature of the Thatcher governments was to translate many problems into 'grand' issues. However, as Jordan notes, 'there is a tendency for grand issues to be transformed in the process of resolution into sub-questions that are amenable to policy community bargaining' (1990: 333).

While this discussion confirms the utility of the policy community description, it also emphasises the need to develop a greater awareness of the variability and dynamism of communities. As Sharpe points out, 'communities vary in strength, influence and composition since some public services, for various reasons, are better suited to attracting a policy community than others' (1985: 84). As regards the question of the source of dynamism in a policy community there is a clear need to refine and develop the resource dependence theory that underpins much of the recent literature. Nevertheless the UK policy process broadly conforms to the imagery of the policy community and, from the point of view of sport, draws attention to the need to assess the importance of organised interest groups, a clear focus for contact and lobbying within the machinery of government and the development of common values and policy perceptions.

THE UNITED STATES

The structure of government

The most significant features of the American political system are the separation of powers and federalism. The framers of the Constitution were guided by a fear of a powerful executive and consequently devised a pattern of government which divided power horizontally between the executive, legislative and judiciary and also vertically between federal and state government. The Constitution has evolved substantially from its eighteenth-century origins and the initial separation of functions has broken down largely due to the steady expansion in the responsibilities of government. In the late twentieth century the branches and levels of government are not so clearly isolated and often become involved in the same range of policy areas. Peters refers to the evolution of an administrative federalism which operates within a complex pattern of intergovernmental relations 'of overlapping authority and interdependence of relationships [which] is more functionally specific and lacks the central co-ordination that occurs among levels of government' (1986: 18).

At the federal level the President holds executive authority subject to four-yearly elections. The President, plus his senior departmental staff, whose appointment is subject to confirmation by the Senate, and a number of personal advisers, constitute the heart of the country's executive branch. Legislative authority lies with the Congress. The legislature comprises two chambers, the House of Representatives and the Senate. Although Representatives are elected every two years, compared with the six-year term of office for Senators, they exert greater control over public expenditure. The Supreme Court, as guardian of the Constitution, completes the framework of federal government.

Despite the deep-seated suspicion of a concentration of political power in the hands of the executive, it is undoubtedly the case that the office of

President has changed substantially over the past two hundred years through a gradual accretion of influence and power within the political system. The inability of the other branches of government to act decisively in a crisis such as wartime and the steady growth in the prominence of foreign policy are two of the factors that have transformed the modern presidency. That transformation is reflected clearly in the scale of the federal bureaucracy. Although the number of departments has increased only from seven in the 1930s to thirteen in the mid-1980s as new functions, such as Housing and Urban Development, Education and Energy have been acknowledged, it is the rise in the number of employees that has been most spectacular, rising from approximately 400,000 to almost 3m. over the same period. Yet, while the growth in the bureaucracy provides the president with considerable influence over policy Maidment and McGrew comment that 'all modern presidents, regardless of party and their location on the ideological spectrum, have seen the civil service, their nominal subordinate, as a political enemy, and in some cases their principal opponent' (1991: 76). Rather than seeing the federal bureaucracy as their ally, presidents have been daunted by the problems of exercising control and have harboured the suspicion that departments are all too easily captured by external interests. One consequence of the uneasy relationship between the President and the bureaucracy has been the development of the Executive Office to provide the President with advice, information and analysis about the federal departmental functions. The current Executive Office employs about 5,000 people and many of its units have exerted a greater influence over policy than the departments. For example, the National Security Council and its principal officer, the National Security Advisor, have frequently pushed the State Department and even the Department of Defense to the periphery of the foreign policy process. Unlike the leaders of most other countries the President does not have a strong political-party powerbase to support him and support his attempts to control the executive. Although America has a long-established two-party system, party discipline is extremely weak due in part to the overriding emphasis given by Representatives and Senators to the views and interests of their constituents, or at least the key interests within their constituency.

State political structures generally mirror those found at the federal level. The state Governor is the focus for executive action, but frequently has less discretion over the appointment of his departmental heads than the President as, in many states, these posts are filled by election. With the exception of Nebraska all states are bi-cameral and operate within a similar balance of power to that found at federal level. The status and boundaries of states in American government are protected by the Constitution. Further, the tenth amendment specified that all powers not delegated to the federal government are reserved for the states. One of the areas where states enjoy autonomy relates to the structure of local government. The Constitution makes no reference to local government and consequently the structure of local government and the powers that units of local government possess are derived wholly from state-level decisions. While the federal government has formal links with states, it has none with local government. However, care needs to be taken not to underestimate the influence of the federal government at state and local government levels. The rhetoric of states' rights belies the extent to which they have become dependent on federal resources. Washington's willingness and capacity to make grant aid dependent on policy compliance has facilitated forceful interventions in education policy (for example, equal access for disabled students), environmental policy (for example, drinking-water standards), and health planning.

Given the extent of state autonomy with regard to local administrative structures, it is surprising to find that there is a reasonable degree of commonality of patterns of local government between states. Most states provide a mechanism through which larger communities (*c.* 20,000 plus) can obtain municipal (city) status. Most commonly, municipal status is achieved following a request from a community, confirmed through a referendum. Outside the cities the states will normally establish a pattern of county government where county authorities act largely as agents of the state government. In some states, particularly in the New England region, townships are established which fulfil many of the functions of municipal authorities but which do not have city status. In addition to counties and municipalities there exist an increasing number of special districts, many with independently elected boards, established to fulfil a specific function. The most common special districts are school boards, which administer primary (junior) and secondary (high) schools. A distinctive feature of many special districts is their power to levy tax. In 1987 there were 83,186 units of local government: 3,042 counties, 19,200 municipalities, 16,691 townships, 14,721 school districts and 29,532 other special districts (Wolman and Goldsmith 1992). As Wolman and Goldsmith note, 'The American "system" of local government is thus characterized by a proliferation of local governments and fragmentation' (1992: 65).

While it is a comparatively simple task to describe the structure of local government as each unit is independent and not part of a hierarchy of authorities as in many parts of the UK, it is far more difficult to link clusters of responsibilities with particular types of authority. Not only is there considerable variety in the powers of, for example, municipal authorities between states, but even within states cities may be able to select the charter they adopt. Generalisation about function is therefore difficult. However, most city authorities are responsible for highway maintenance, land-use planning (zoning), parks and recreation, and police and fire services. In addition, some cities will provide public utilities such as water and sewerage.

The distinctive political structure outlined above is supported by an equally distinctive political culture. The racial heterogeneity, religious diversity, absence of both a feudal past and contemporary class-based political parties, and the considerable sustained wealth provide a context that differs markedly from that found in any other advanced industrial country. Yet, there are a number of features which are not dissimilar to those found in western European countries, including a commitment to liberal democracy, a gradual extension of the franchise, and an economic system founded on an acceptance of capitalism and private property. However, as Maidment and McGrew (1991) make clear, it might be comparatively easy to describe the main features of the political culture but it is far more difficult to determine ownership and advantage. While there are many who would argue that the parameters of the contemporary political culture are the product of an unconstrained expression of individual social and political preferences, there is a more persuasive argument that suggests the capitalist democracy found in the US is an ideology which supports and protects sectional interest at the expense of general welfare. Katznelson and Kesselman (1979: 29, quoted in Maidment and McGrew 1991) argue that 'so powerful is the dominant ideology in this country that existing economic and political arrangements frequently appear not merely as the best possible arrangements but as the only possible ones'.

Sport in America

The overriding themes in the history of sport in America are class, social integration and commercialism. Although in the late colonial period and the early phase of independence the tension between the differing views of sport derived from Calvinism and other Protestant religions on the one hand and Catholicism on the other helped to shape the early development of sport, they soon faded in the face of stronger social forces. In the colonial period different attitudes towards leisure existed in different regions. In the southern states leisure was clearly used as a status symbol for a landed class intent on emulating the English aristocracy. Hunting, horse-racing and cricket served to demonstrate wealth and distance the social elite, Veblen's (1925) leisure class, from those who had to work for a living and those, the slaves, who were forced to work to live (Carson 1965). Sport in the New England region developed in marked contrast to the south. The strong puritan influence prevented not only the development of a strong association between economic success and extensive leisure, but also an association between leisure and excess. As Gorn and Goldstein note, 'New Englanders were much less likely than Virginians to assume that humans worked in order to play; rather, play renewed men for work' (1993: 37).

The pre-independence tensions were evident throughout the remainder of the eighteenth century although interest in sport continued to expand. During the nineteenth century the successive waves of immigration resulted in the importation of a wide variety of sporting cultures including the gymnastic movement of the Germans, and the rural games of the Scots and Irish. In addition to the introduction of specific sports, the immigrant groups reinforced the practice of establishing sports clubs. By the end of the century the United States had an elaborate infrastructure of voluntary and semi-commercial clubs catering for the various permutations of class, religion and ethnic origin. The desire to use sport as a means of preserving cultural identity created a tension with the countervailing pressure for the assimilation and Americanisation of the new arrivals. The latter purpose was increasingly well served by the establishment of national governing bodies for sports in the last quarter of the century. The United States Lawn Tennis Association was formed in 1881, followed by the Amateur Athletic Union in 1888, the United States Golf Association in 1894 and the National Collegiate Athletic Association early in the twentieth century in 1905. The emergence of commercial bodies to organise leagues and control professional sport represented a second wave of organisation of sport. The baseball National League was formed in 1876, that for ice hockey (the National Hockey League) in 1917, followed by football (the National Football League) in 1922 and basketball (the National Basketball Association) comparatively recently in 1946.

By the early part of the present century the organisational infrastructure of American sport had been firmly established. Provision of opportunities to participate in sport was primarily through commercial or voluntary bodies and clubs; professional sport was tightly controlled by a series of commercial interests; and federal government involvement was marginal. The development of sport in general as an integral part of American culture and the association of particular sports with American citizenship was given substantial impetus by the First World War. 'Never before had the rhetoric of Americanization and socialization taken on such urgency, even stridency' is how Gorn and Goldstein (1993: 177–8) describe the enthusiastic involvement of sports organisations in proselytising the virtues of sport to the five million Americans in uniform.

The pattern of participation and provision that followed the end of the war was typified first, by the continued rapid growth of mass spectator sports controlled by the commercial sector. The pattern was also typified by extensive public involvement either through the school and college system or through the provision established by local government, particularly by city authorities. However, what was also typical of the period between the end of the First World War and the early 1970s was the dominance of white male interests in sport. Although there were some examples of women's sport in the nineteenth century, it remained limited and subject to general social opprobrium. The early twentieth century saw the emergence of a small number of female sports stars, while the development of women's sport in general was helped by the social upheaval of the two world wars. As will be seen below, the most significant breakthrough came in the 1970s with the passing of the 1972 Educational Amendments Act which forced schools and colleges to direct a fairer proportion of expenditure on sport towards women. While the Act led to a significant increase in women's participation in sport, involvement by women in coaching and administration has, by contrast, declined (Sage 1990).

For black Americans the path towards greater equality of access to sports opportunities has been similarly tortuous and equivocal. Up until the early post-war period segregation was the norm in the major sports. In baseball, for example, it was not until 1947 that Jackie Robinson broke into the Brooklyn Dodgers first team (Tygiel 1983). In more recent years access to participation has undoubtedly improved. In the late 1950s barely one professional football player in six was black; by the mid-1980s the figure was one in two. Similarly, over the same period in basketball, the proportion of black players had increased from one in six to four out of five. However, the number of black Americans in administration and coaching significantly lags behind these figures.

The commercialisation of sport in America is reflected not only in the scale of professional sport, but also in the spread of commercial attitudes and values within college sport. Professional athletes and teams have always been a prominent feature of American sport, but in the past forty years professional sport has moved from prominence to dominance. This process has been made possible by the growth of television coverage of sport and the powerful symbiotic relationship that exists between the two. The number of (male) professional teams in football, basketball and baseball has grown steadily from the 1950s, paralleling the increasing emphasis given to sport by broadcasters. The three major networks broadcast about 1,600 hours of sport each year; there are now a number of sports-only 24-hour channels; and over half of the twenty-five programmes with the highest ratings are broadcasts of sports events (Eitzen and Sage 1986). Income from television fees is now a major part of the overall income of professional clubs. Over 60 per cent of the income of the National Football League (NFL) is from television; the sale of broadcast rights by the major league baseball teams generated $15m. for each team; and in 1989 CBS signed a seven-year contract with the National Collegiate Athletic Association (NCAA) totalling $1bn for Division 1 men's basketball (Sage 1990).

The size of the NCAA contract indicates that commercialisation is not simply limited to professional sport; college sport is equally big business with even high school sport beginning to attract interest from cable stations. The combination of a strong amateur ethos and marketability has resulted in the transformation of the governing body of college sport, the NCAA, into a thorough-going commercial concern. In many ways the college sports system is an excellent example of successful capitalism. The scholarship system ensures that costs are kept low and that athletes are tied to their college while the NCAA monopoly ensures that the media pay a maximum price for broadcasting rights. The poor academic performance of students on sports scholarships is merely one further illustration of the systematic exploitation of sporting talent in the guise of providing access to education for those on low incomes (Sperber 1990).

Policy process

Among the factors that shape the American policy process are the extent of administrative and political fragmentation and decentralisation, the degree of complexity of the political system and a deep-seated public scepticism regarding government involvement in many policy areas. Fragmentation has a positive side in that it provides a wider range of entry points to the political system (Kelman 1987), but fragmentation obviously also increases the number of clearance points for policy and, in a system where the opportunity for authoritative intervention in the policy process is low, there is an inherent tendency towards incrementalism (Peters 1986: 21). While the apparent incapacity of government to act on many policy issues, particularly in the fields of health and social policy, is frustrating for many, the level of disappointment is lessened by the high level of scepticism towards the actions of government.

Metaphors of the policy process abound and within a political system as complex as the American one, it is not surprising that there is considerable disagreement about the nature and dynamics of that process (Jordan 1990). Whether the process is best described as a series of sub-governments (Ripley and Franklin 1976), 'iron triangles' (Peters 1986), sub-systems (Truman 1951) or policy communities (Kingdon 1984), there is considerable agreement that the American policy process operates within a highly sectorised context such that 'each functional policy area tends to be governed as if it existed apart from the remainder of government' (Peters 1986: 22). At the heart of Peters' conceptualisation is an 'iron triangle' comprising the interest group, the relevant congressional committee or sub-committee and the responsible administrative agency, who are locked into an interdependent relationship. For Peters, 'much of the domestic policy of the United States can be explained by the existence of these functionally specific policy sub-systems and by the absence of effective central co-ordination' creating a feudal structure where central authority is bypassed and undermined by aggressive policy sub-systems (Peters 1986: 24).

Although the metaphor of the 'iron triangle' encapsulates the key linkages in many policy sub-systems, it does not capture the variation between policy areas nor the dynamics of the relationships. Kingdon, for example, prefers to talk of policy communities that are composed of governmental and non-governmental specialists in a given policy area. Kingdon is at pains to stress the degree of variety between policy communities especially in terms of the degree of fragmentation. The health community, for example, despite having a diverse membership, was relatively close-knit and, through regular contact, 'exchanged information, developed more common ways of looking at problems, and cultivated their informal contacts in the health network' (Kingdon 1984: 124). By contrast, the transportation community was much more fragmented with communities of specialists for particular modes of transport but with 'very few people . . . concerned with issues that involve two or more of these modes' (ibid.: 124). For Kingdon a key feature of the more tightly integrated community was the extent to which it generated a common perception of problems and solutions. Thus, as in the more general social science use of the term 'community', key attributes are structured interaction and common values and attitudes.

The prominence of the bureaucracy in many of the descriptions of the policy process requires comment and is best explained in terms of the discretion given to it by Congress. Although Gilmour and Halley argue that Congress increasingly involves itself in policy and programme implementation in a way both 'detailed and sustained' (1994: 366), others (Kelman 1987) argue that very often Congress legislates in a broad-brush fashion leaving the details to be determined by the departments or agencies. For example, the Environmental Protection Agency has made a number of interpretations of legislation, which have subsequently had the force of law. The decision to delegate may be made for a variety of reasons, including the highly technical nature of the subject of legislation and the desire to avoid difficult political choices. The second reason for the centrality of the bureaucracy is that 'government agencies are often an important source of the information about policy problems that other participants in the policy process use' (ibid.: 89).

One important, but not unexpected, feature of analyses of the environment of domestic policy-making in America is the extent to which external factors are down-played or, more commonly, ignored. Kingdon (1984), for example, when exploring the process of agenda setting refers to crisis, the gradual accumulation of research, the vagaries of public opinion, and luck as possible initiating factors; all of which are internal to the political system. Kelman (1987) refers to a similar list of sources, emphasising the role of advocates or policy entrepreneurs who possess the skills and knowledge of the political labyrinth. In marked contrast to the Irish Republic, for example, the United States policy process operates in an environment that is far less vulnerable to events beyond national boundaries. However, it is equally clear that the United States policy system is not immune to international developments. There are many examples of policy diffusion (Japanese developments in manufacturing processes; central European sports training methods; soccer), of policy reinforcement (Thatcherite economic policy; state support for elite sport) and also of policy constraint (loss of value of the dollar; European athletics Grand Prix circuit; IOC drug abuse policy), all of which have their source beyond the boundaries of the domestic political system.

CONCLUSION

The five countries examined above have a number of important characteristics in common, most notably a mature (or in the case of Ireland a rapidly maturing) capitalist economy, a liberal democratic political system, a broadly common cultural background and a high level of public interest and participation in organised sport. These countries also face a number of similar problems in the area of sport, including the place of sport in schools, the balance between fostering elite success and mass participation, the proper role of the state in sports regulation and development and the control of drug abuse. But, what should be clear is that the countries also possess significant differences derived from differing administrative arrangements, political and socio-economic pressures and contemporary cultural patterns. What should also be clear is that a number of common themes were evident in the foregoing discussion which are likely to shape and contextualise policy responses.

Of particular importance is the steady increase in the involvement of government in sport whether as a provider, exploiter or regulator. For some countries with a welfare state tradition, such as the UK, Canada and Australia, the expansion of the government's role has not been problematic but for the United States the growth of government involvement has been more sharply contested but no less significant. A second theme is the intensity of association between sport and identity politics. In a number of countries a key motive for government involvement has been to acknowledge or exploit the symbolism of sport and its significance for the maintenance of notions of national heritage and the external projection of national imagery. A third theme concerns the increasing strength and organisation of sports interests. While commercial interests have generally been effectively organised for some time, it is only more recently that athletes, non-commercial sports and specific user groups such as women and people with disabilities have begun to lobby more effectively. In part, this expansion in the number of organised interests is the result of rising public expectations regarding access to sports opportunities, but it is partly a consequence of increasing government administrative involvement and especially the creation of specialist administrative agencies and departments to manage and oversee sport policy. Finally, at a time when government involvement in sport has been increasing, so, too, has the need for greater international co-ordination in terms of policy consideration and implementation. On the one hand, the four-yearly cycle of many major international sports events such as the Olympic Games, the soccer World Cup and athletics world championships provides a rigid framework for countries aiming at elite success. On the other hand, there are a number of issues such as sponsorship, eligibility of athletes and anti-doping which can only be addressed satisfactorily at an international level.

3 Patterns of government involvement in sport

WHY DO GOVERNMENTS BECOME INVOLVED IN SPORT?

Until the late 1950s or early 1960s, sport was of only marginal interest to most governments. Prior to this, government intervention in sport was generally a reaction to specific problems such as poor standards of health in urban areas, military requirements or outbreaks of disorder and rarely the consequence of the recognition of sport (and recreation) as a distinct policy area. Yet, despite the absence of an explicit and sustained recognition of sport as a distinct focus of government interest there are, in a number of countries, clear thematic continuities between the early and more recent phases of government involvement.

Governments have frequently intervened to control the sports and pastimes of the community. In England, as mentioned in Chapter 2, intervention was designed to preserve privileged access to particular sports, such as hunting, through the Game Laws. Similar laws existed in France where, up until the revolution of 1789, hunting, with the exception of rabbits, was reserved for the nobility (Holt 1981: 18). Later, in Britain in 1835, the Cruelty to Animals Act again reflected the exercise of power to preserve class privilege, outlawing bull- and bear-baiting, which were both town 'sports', but leaving fox hunting or stag hunting unrestricted.

The history of the campaign over access to the countryside reflects a similar tension between the political power of landowners and the growing demand for opportunities to use the countryside for sporting and recreational purposes from an increasingly urbanised population (Donnelly, 1986). While the passage of the National Parks and Access to the Countryside Act 1949 marked a defeat for the landowners, the issue persists today with frequent disputes between the Ramblers Association and landowners over access to footpaths and bridle paths (Shoard 1987; Ramblers Association 1984). The contrast with France is interesting. Unlike in Britain, where the structure of land ownership led to the development of large estates, the French revolution confirmed the rights of the peasant to land and engendered a degree of confidence in their security of tenure so that land was rarely fenced and access was not an issue (Holt 1981: 21).

In seventeenth-century America a number of attempts to outlaw gambling, horse-racing, cockfighting and other sports were made by colonial governments whose Protestant sensibilities were offended. In Philadelphia, for example, the Quaker-dominated town council outlawed blood sports and gambling as well as the theatre. As the influence of Protestant groups weakened, many prohibitions were repealed. However, the early nineteenth century saw the rise in influence of the lobby against cruel sports and by 1866 blood sports were outlawed in twenty states (Gorn and Goldstein 1993: 37).

A second theme in the development of sport policy is a sporadic concern with the health benefits of recreation and sport. In Victorian Britain there had been a number of items of legislation concerned with public health which laid the basis for the development of sporting and recreational opportunities. For example, the Baths and Wash-houses Act 1846 gave powers to local authorities to build facilities to improve the standards of personal hygiene of the urban poor. A number of local authorities took advantage of this legislation to build facilities for swimming and in 1936 the Public Health Act gave explicit recognition to the recreational role of public baths by enabling local authorities to build baths exclusively designed for swimming. The development of open spaces for recreation and sport follows a similar pattern. Initially the laying out of urban parks under the terms of the 1875 Public Health Act was in part a response to the enclosure of common land and in part an attempt to ameliorate the appalling living conditions in Britain's major industrial towns and cities and as such had no explicit concern to meet sporting needs. Later, the parks became the basis for the provision of soccer, cricket and rugby pitches, bowling greens and tennis courts. The pattern of development of urban recreation facilities in Britain can also be found in many other countries, including America (Cranz 1982) and Australia (Cuneen 1980), and reflects the dominance of the Victorian concern with rational recreation.

In Canada, the 1961 Fitness and Amateur Sport Act was also partly the product of an increasing concern among physical educators and health professionals, with the health consequences of an increasingly sedentary lifestyle. The Act, which represented the first major intervention in the policy area by the federal government, was supported by $5m. per annum and the centrality of health concerns was emphasised by locating administrative responsibility for sport with the Minister for National Health and Welfare.

The third theme relates to the attempt by government to use sport as a means of social integration. In Britain during the latter half of the nineteenth century there was considerable concern among the English middle class about the potential for social instability within the urban working class (Bailey 1979; Holt 1989). The endeavours of the 'muscular Christianity' movement to instil discipline in the urban poor were reinforced by legislation (the Education Acts of 1870 and 1902), which emphasised the value of physical training and military drill. Later, the 1918 Education Act allowed

local authorities to provide a range of sports facilities for 'social and physical training' revealing, as McIntosh noted, the 'utilitarian attitude' of the
government to sport (1987: 100). In the early post-war years there was a
series of reports that drew attention to the problem of 'too much leisure',
particularly for the increasingly affluent urban male working class. Both the
Crowther Report (1959) and the Albermarle Report (1960) associated the
issue of juvenile delinquency with the absence of opportunities for physical
recreation in the immediate post-school years. This theme was echoed by the
Wolfenden Committee on Sport (1960), which suggested that there was an
association between the shortage of sports facilities and the rise in
delinquency. The association between sport policy and social integration
continued through the 1980s and 1990s. A recent example occurred in 1981
when, following a series of urban riots, the British Sports Council launched
the 'Action Sport' project which was designed to put sports leaders into local
communities with the aim of fostering the integration of disaffected social
groups.

Other countries have used sport in similar ways. During the Vichy
government of wartime France, sport, particularly gymnastics, was promoted
as a means of 'social discipline and a means of regenerating French youth'
(Holt 1981: 58). More recently in the 1980s the French government turned to
sport and other forms of leisure as a way of confronting 'the serious risk of
social problems as a result of social tensions in the suburbs of some cities'
(Poujol 1993: 23). This latter concern finds many echoes in Australia where
Boag (1989), in tracing the shifts in the rationale for government intervention
in recreation, notes that historically, the development of community integration has been a central goal of public provision.

In nineteenth-century America and Australia the 'muscular Christian'
movement followed similar lines of development to Britain with, in
America, baseball in particular being seen as preferable to the main urban
male sports, especially prize-fighting (Lewis 1966; Swanson 1968). The
development, and underlying philosophy, of the Young Men's Christian
Association best reflected the Christian concern to provide an alternative to
commercial entertainment, which emphasised physical sports, intellectual
activities, and Christian fellowship. According to Gorn and Goldstein the
emerging nineteenth-century sports ideology was underpinned by the
assumption that 'sports could be a socially stabilising force that would help
Americanize foreigners, pacify angry workers, clear the streets of
delinquents, and stem the tide of radicalism' (1993: 104). During the 1920s
the American Legion sponsored junior baseball leagues as a means of
combating radicalism and ensuring that 'all citizens stayed "100 per cent
American"' (Gorn and Goldstein 1993: 182). More recently, in the period
from the 1930s to the 1960s, creating greater equality of access to parks and
outdoor recreational facilities for black Americans, especially young black
males, was seen as an important step towards reducing racial tension (Cranz
1982: 231). A very similar pattern of sports development took place in

Australia, with the churches and private schools providing the momentum for the 'muscular Christian' movement, with 'many clerics regarding the cricket field as a suitable moral classroom' (Cashman 1995: 57).

In Canada the problems of social integration focused mainly on the division between the anglophone and francophone communities and the periodic pressure from Quebec for greater autonomy and later for independence. The preoccupation with national unity is evident in all major policy statements from the late 1960s. As Helmes noted following an analysis of a series of policy documents throughout the period, '"nationalism" was a dominant ideological component of the "Sports policy" – direct references to "unity", "national goals" and "Canadianism" made up a large percentage of the coded entries' (1981: 214). However, there was also a concern, particularly in the interwar depression, to use sport as a way of avoiding the potentially destabilising effects of male youth unemployment on society (Schrodt 1984). Similar concerns with nation-building can be found in a review of Irish (Sugden and Bairner 1993; Holmes 1994) and Australian (Mandle 1976) sport policy. For both these countries sport was (and still is) an important source of national symbolism.

A fourth policy theme concerns the use of sport as a means of improving the military preparedness of the state. As early as the 1860s Australian state governments were providing facilities for rifle clubs with the justification that they would provide the core of local militias in times of crisis (Lawson 1973: 210). Eighty years later in 1941 the federal government passed a National Fitness Act motivated in large part by defence needs. A little earlier in Britain the government sought to improve the quality of potential conscripts for the anticipated war with Germany and passed legislation in 1937. Under the terms of the Physical Training and Recreation Act the government voted to provide funding of £2m. to support the work of the National Fitness Council and the objective of making the youth of the nation 'fit for service'. The American decision to enter the First World War provided an opportunity for the statement of government support and financing of sport as a means of ensuring that young men would be fit enough for military service. Similarly, the development of urban parks was often justified by the contribution that they made to public health and 'via physical exercise to improv(ing) soldiering and keep(ing) up morale' (Cranz 1982: 212). Canada's 1943 National Physical Fitness Act was also introduced owing, in part at least, to the high rejection rate of military recruits.

A fifth theme in state sport policy is the increasing concern with the relationship between sport and international prestige. Governments are acutely aware of the potential of sport to reflect, enhance and undermine the prestige of the country. In Britain the growing success of East Germany (GDR) and the Soviet Union in the 1960s and a perception of national sporting decline prompted an increase in government funding and was an important stimulus for the establishment of the Advisory Sports Council in 1965.

Also in the early 1960s the Canadian government was prompted to act to support elite athletes. The Fitness and Amateur Sport Act of 1961 had the twin aims of improving the level of fitness of the general population and meeting the government's 'concern about national prestige and the success of elite athletes' (Franks and Macintosh 1984; Macintosh and Hawes 1994; see also Helmes 1981). Initially the policy objectives were supported by the provision of financial support for provincial government initiatives and those of governing bodies of sport. Later, in 1970, financial support was supplemented by the provision of administrative support with the creation of a national sports administration centre and a series of task forces aimed at particular sports or events. A similar strategy was adopted in France in 1984 with the government's decision to restructure the administration of sport and give responsibility for elite development to the Ministry of Youth and Sport.

An associated use of sport is as a diplomatic resource. Peppard and Riordan (1993; see also Hulme 1990) illustrate with reference to the United States and the former Soviet Union the long history of government use and manipulation of sport for diplomatic ends. Both countries used sport as a cipher for their ideological rivalry, as a way of attempting to entice countries into their respective camps and as a way of cementing links with their allies. Macintosh points to role adopted by Canada in shaping Commonwealth policy towards South Africa over apartheid and the use of sports development aid to poorer countries as a way of achieving its leadership on policy (Macintosh 1991: 271; see also Macintosh and Hawes 1994). Australia, too, was not averse to using sport for diplomatic purposes. For example, Prime Minister Menzies encouraged the Australian Cricket Board of Control to undertake a cricket tour of the West Indies in the mid-1950s in order to enhance his standing in the Commonwealth (Cashman 1995).

The definition of sport as an element in economic development and particularly the regeneration of declining urban areas is, in Britain at least, one of the more recent motives for governmental support for sport. The accumulation of evidence of the value added by sport to the national economy and to local economies has reinforced the long-held view that sports facilities are an important aspect of the marketability of an area for inward investment (Houlihan 1996). Cranz points to a similar perception in the USA where urban parks and recreation facilities were 'advocated as a way to revitalize neighbourhoods economically and stimulate the surrounding business district' (1982: 208). In the United States 'civic boosterism' through sports facility development is well established and documented (see, for example, Baade and Dye 1988; Johnson 1985; Reiss 1989) and is also evident in Japan (McCormack 1991). Macintosh noted a similar trend in Canada where both the federal and provincial governments were providing major subsidies for prestigious stadium developments on the grounds that the policy 'provides jobs and incentives for profits for the private sector as well as stimulating the local economy by bringing tourists and spectators to the community' (1991: 271).

This brief survey is designed to indicate the range of motives for government intervention in sport and also to suggest that, while each country has its distinctive pattern, there is considerable commonality of motive. The survey also makes clear that governments view sport almost exclusively in instrumental terms, as a convenient and malleable means towards some other policy objective. The exceptions to this conclusion are scarce. It cannot be denied that sport has benefited greatly from increased government interest, but government patronage, like business patronage, comes at a price. One of the few countervailing pressures on the tendency of governments to exploit sport is that, especially from the 1960s, government support for sport has proved to be attractive to voters. The increased salience of sport to the electorate has limited the extent of government manipulation, or at least the more blatant examples.

The pattern of government responsibility for sport

If the motives for government support and involvement in sport are becoming increasingly uniform, the same cannot be said of the administrative arrangements adopted by governments where a considerable variety persists (Sports Council 1990). Within industrial countries, including Australia, New Zealand and those in North America and the European Union, five overlapping types can be identified. First, there are those countries where a central government department fulfils a major role in the execution of sport policy. France and Greece both have strong ministries responsible for sport. In France, the Ministry for Youth and Sport has specific responsibility for competitive sport although most of the actual service delivery is delegated to state-approved Sports Federations. In Greece the pattern is similar although the sport function is administered within the Ministry of Culture, which has a much broader remit. Of the countries covered by this study, Ireland fits most comfortably into this first category. Although Ireland has a National Sports Council (NSC also known as COSPÓIR), it is closely integrated into the Sports Section of the Department of Education which provides the secretariat.

The second category includes those countries where the administration of public policy is more fragmented, with the impetus for policy development lying partly outside the centre at sub-national government level. The most obvious countries to locate in this category include those with federal systems such as Canada and Australia, and would also include Belgium. In Canada, the US and Australia, the provincial/state governments enjoy considerable autonomy in the area of sport and recreation although they are strongly influenced by central policy objectives, particularly when they are supported by generous revenue-sharing initiatives. In Belgium the existence of parallel administrative structures for the French- and Flemish-speaking communities provides a stronger check on the capacity of the central government to direct policy effectively.

The third category contains those countries where significant authority for sport is delegated to a quango (quasi-autonomous national governmental organisation) or similar semi-independent agency. In Spain, for example, sport is delegated to the largely autonomous Higher Sports Council (HSC) which is ultimately accountable to the Ministry of Culture. The HSC's main functions are to advise government on policy and distribute government finance for sport. New Zealand adopted a similar pattern of administration comparatively recently when in 1987 the Hillary Commission for Recreation and Sport was established (Jobling 1991). The Commission replaced both the Ministry and the Council of Recreation and Sport ostensibly to 'remove the duplication represented by the Ministry and the Council, to avoid complex bureaucratic processes, (and) to give sports people more influence over matters relevant to them' (Hillary Commission for Recreation and Sport 1987: 2). The UK is also included in this category because of the prominent role of the various Sport Councils, as is Australia because of the central role of the Sports Commission, especially since 1987 when the original Commission took responsibility for the Australian Institute of Sport which has responsibility for elite development.

The fourth category contains those countries where responsibility for sport is shared between a non-governmental organisation (NGO) and government as found in Germany and The Netherlands. In both these countries the NGOs have considerable sources of finance independent of government, usually from the subscriptions generated by an extensive and successful network of large sports clubs or through commercial sponsorship. However, government provides substantial additional finance to support the sports development activities of the NGO. There are also examples of countries, such as Sweden and Norway, where the NGOs have the primary responsibility for sport and operate with a substantial degree of independence from government. In some cases, the role of government is limited to facilitating access to finance, usually through the creation of a national lottery.

The final category contains those countries where government involvement is minimal. Of the countries covered in this study the US fits most clearly into this category although Italy has developed a similar pattern. In Italy the National Olympic Committee (CONI) is independent of the government and is responsible for co-ordinating sport, in conjunction with the major sports federations, at both the elite and mass participation levels. In the US the two key organisations with responsibility for sport are the US Olympic Committee (USOC) and the National Collegiate Athletic Association (NCAA). The former is responsible for co-ordinating elite athletes in Olympic sports while the NCAA controls the college-level competition, which is the main source of top-class sportsmen and sportswomen.

Explaining the variation in the patterns of administration is difficult but a number of significant factors can be identified, such as: wealth; tradition of voluntary organisation; political, geographic and demographic characteristics; and salience of sport to the government and major political parties. In general, those countries where sport is politically salient tend to create specialist quangos; those that are geographically compact or have small populations tend to rely on centralised authority; and those where the level of disposable income is high tend to rely on NGOs. As with all generalisations there are important exceptions such as the absence of a state agency for sport in Italy, and the comparatively high level of central control over sport in France and Canada. As a result it is important to explore the particular mix of factors that have produced the distinctive pattern of policy-making and administration for sport.

THE DEVELOPMENT AND PATTERN OF CENTRAL GOVERNMENT INVOLVEMENT

Australia

While there was some government support for sport in the nineteenth century, it was indirect and informal. In the early part of the century sport was encouraged largely as a form of social control; as a distraction for a predominantly male population especially around garrison towns (Cumes 1979; Hamilton-Smith and Robertson 1977). Towards the end of the century when urbanisation was further advanced, local politicians were important in determining the distribution of land for sporting use and frequently deciding between competing demands on particular venues. The emergence of sport as a focus for local party-political interest was not the result of a recognition of the social value of sport by party leaders, but rather due to the clientelistic nature of Australian politics where politicians had 'long cultivated sports clubs and acted as boosters for them, and in turn clubs have welcomed the active involvement of their local representatives' (Cashman 1995: 114). The spatial segregation of ethnic groups in urban areas and the strong links between political parties and particular ethnic communities reinforced clientelism with probably the best example being the close relationship between the Irish community, the Australian Labor Party, the Catholic Church and rugby league.

Despite the close association between sports provision and party politics at the local level there was generally little federal government involvement in sport before 1945. Apart from occasional diplomatic involvement (Harte 1993), regulation of gambling and horse-racing, and the attempt to improve the quality of military recruits through the passage of the National Fitness Act during the Second World War, the federal government was content to leave sport in the hands of voluntary bodies. Indeed, the federal contribution was limited to the award of modest grants to some voluntary sports organisations (Baka 1982), small contributions towards the cost of participation in Olympic Games and the British Empire Games and a larger contribution towards the hosting of the 1938 Empire Games. The federal contribution to the £2m. infrastructure costs for the Melbourne Olympics in 1956 was a major break with the past, but did not herald a continuing federal involvement. The acknowledgement that sport was significant and a long-term issue for the federal government was not given until the early 1970s. The catalyst was the election of a Labor government after twenty-three years of rule by the Liberal Party. The Labor Party had a long history of involvement in the local politics of sport and was, by inclination, a more interventionist party than the Liberal Party, which generally favoured limited government and low public expenditure. The specific policy concern of the Labor Party was the need for leisure provision, especially for young people, in a highly urbanised and affluent society (see Jaques and Pavia 1976a).

The shift in the salience of sport to the federal government in the early 1970s was dramatic. Following the 1972 election victory, the government of Gough Whitlam not only greatly increased the commitment of public resources to sport and recreation, but also established a Department for Tourism and Recreation (see Tables 3.1 and 3.2). The new Department was given a number of well-funded programmes to manage, which reflected the government's primary commitment to fostering mass participation and secondary concern with elite development. The new programme included the Capital Assistance Program, designed to boost the availability of local sports facilities, the Sports Assistance Program, aimed mainly at supporting governing bodies, and Fitness Australia, aimed at increasing the participation of Australians in active recreation. The primacy of mass participation over elite development was asserted in the comments of the then Minister for Tourism and Recreation who stated that:

> we have no intention of imitating some countries which regard success in sport as some sort of proof of the superiority of their way of life, ideology and race. Our task lies clearly elsewhere, in meeting more basic needs, in catering for masses, not just a small elite.
>
> (quoted in Semotiuk 1986: 162)

However, policy implementation did not echo the rhetoric of the Minister.

The new government initiated a number of reviews, of coaching and recreation, for example, to plan policy development. The intensity of federal activity had the effect of stimulating parallel developments at State level, where a number introduced similar changes to their machinery of government. However, the rapidity of implementation took many governing bodies by surprise as they 'were ill-prepared to handle the increased physical and financial involvement in central government' (Hartung, quoted in Baka 1982: 29). A degree of confusion was also to be found in the Department of Tourism and Recreation itself, which was encountering increasing difficulty in integrating its broad range of administrative responsibilities (Hamilton-Smith and Robertson 1977).

The momentum developed by the Labor victory was not to last as, in 1975, the Labor Party lost power to a Liberal-led coalition that was far less enthusiastic about sport and far less clear about its policy objectives

(Hamilton-Smith and Robertson 1977). The Department of Tourism and Recreation was abolished, sport was accorded much lower status and administrative responsibility was moved three times in eight years. A more severe downgrading of sport was avoided due to four factors: first, a well-organised sports lobby focused on the newly formed Confederation of Australian Sport, determined not to see the gains of recent years slide away; second, a recognition that sport and recreation expenditure was electorally popular; third, the support of Bob Ellicott, minister responsible for sport from 1978 to 1980; and fourth, the dire performance of Australian athletes in the 1976 Montreal Olympics. As Cashman notes, 'The Montreal Games represented a nadir in the Australian Olympic movement and helped to transform federal and State government attitude towards the promotion of sport' (Cashman 1995: 120). However, what was most notable during this period was not the reduction in priority accorded to sport but rather the reversal, or more accurately, the abandonment, of a balance between elite development and provision for mass participation (McKay 1986). The budget for facility development, for example, was reduced much more significantly than support for the Sports Assistance Program, although the latter survived only after intense lobbying by national sports organisations (NSOs). The shift in government sports policy priorities is also reflected in the establishment of the Australian Institute of Sport (AIS) in 1981 and in the provision of substantial grants for the 1982 Brisbane Commonwealth Games.

The establishment of the AIS was seen by the government as a crucial policy innovation designed to enhance Australian prospects in international competition. Located at the National Sports Centre in Canberra, the AIS provided top-class coaching, world-class facilities and scientific support. Initially the Institute catered for about 150 athletes in eight sports: weight-lifting, netball, swimming, track and field, soccer, gymnastics, basketball and tennis. Within eight years the Institute had expanded greatly providing support for over 300 resident athletes in seventeen sports and over 2,000 athletes involved on a part-time basis in over thirty sports. As more sports were added, the functions of the Institute were steadily decentralised with hockey relocated to Perth in 1984, diving and squash to Brisbane in 1985 and cycling (in 1987) and cricket (1988) to Adelaide.

The election of a Labor government in 1983 marked a return to the earlier commitment to sport. But while funding doubled to $50m., 'the election promise of seventy-five community leisure centres . . . was quietly dropped' (Vamplew *et al.* 1994: 161). The incoming government re-established a senior department, Sport, Recreation and Tourism, which was provided with a wide-ranging policy document, 'The Australian Labor Party Sport and Recreation Policy', to guide its activities. The renewed commitment to sport and recreation was reinforced by the 1983 House of Representatives report, 'The Way We P(l)ay', which while adding to the momentum of policy also, *inter alia*, drew attention to the contribution of the Department of Aboriginal Affairs and the National Aboriginal Sports

Foundation (NASF) to sports provision, but was critical of the lack of clarity of objectives and spending plans. Despite links between the Aboriginal Development Commission, the NASF and the AIS, Aboriginal sporting activity remained outside the broad policy debates of the 1980s and 1990s. Part of the explanation lies in a general lack of concern with Aboriginal interests within recent governments, whose attitude towards Aboriginal participation in sport is reflected in the immensely patronising objective of the NASF which was 'to encourage Aborigines to become more a part of the General Community and to perhaps achieve a satisfactory relationship with other people' (National Aboriginal Sports Foundation 1980: 5).

The first major administrative change introduced by the Labor government was the establishment of the Australian Sports Commission (ASC) in 1985. While the Department would continue to fund major sports events and the building of major facilities, the ASC would assume primary responsibility for managing a series of programmes associated with sports development and particularly elite development. Four years later the basis of the ASC relationship with government was altered to give it a greater degree of independence. The ASC currently operates under the Australian Sports Commission Act 1989 and, like other quangos, is funded by the federal government but managed by a board appointed by the relevant minister. The Commission's mission is to 'enrich the lives of all Australians through sport' and reflects the twin objectives associated with increased participation and improved elite performance. Current policy is dominated by the forthcoming Sydney Olympics in 2000, which is seen as a major opportunity to market sports participation to the Australian public, although as will be shown below, the award of the 2000 Games has also had the effect of distorting the activities and priorities of the Commission.

Balancing the twin priorities of the mass participation and elite success has proved problematic for governmental sports bodies in Canada, Ireland, and the UK: Australia is no exception. Bearing in mind that much of the provision relating to mass participation will, quite legitimately, be the responsibility of state and local government, it is noticeable that the proportion of ASC resources devoted to the promotion of participation is low and reducing. Only 11.3 per cent of the 1995–6 budget was spent on 'Sports Development' (down from 14.4 per cent in the 1993–4) and this covered funding for Aussie Sport. One significant impact of the ASC has been to modernise, but also marginalise, NSOs. NSOs have been modernised in so far as they have been required to develop strategic plans and contribute more systematically to the promotion of their respective sports and the development and refinement of their elite athletes. However, as in other countries NSOs are now so heavily financially dependent on the government and so tightly locked into the state infrastructure of sport centred on the ASC and the AIS, that it is difficult for them to justifiably claim independent control over the development of their sports. Yet, it is important to note that the changed relationship between the NSOs and government is as much the product of NSO lobbying as a recognition by government of the value of elite sport. The Confederation of Australian Sport lobbied very effectively throughout the mid- and late 1970s for government intervention to fund and co-ordinate elite sport (Nauright 1996; Daley 1990). Currently, with federal largesse flowing so freely, NSOs have little cause for complaint, but should government priorities change, few NSOs have the capacity to survive independently.

The early 1980s also marked the emergence of a period of broad cross-party agreement on the rationale for federal government involvement in sport. Of particular importance was the perception of sport as a unifying force best reflected in the decisions to fund the AIS (and its later decentralisation) and the initiation of the Australia Games. Of equal importance was the growing recognition of the value of sport as a tool of diplomacy and as a vehicle for the promotion of Australia abroad, reflected in the government's direction of public finance towards the development of elite sport rather than mass participation. Finally, and more recently, the government has acknowledged the considerable benefit to tourism of the hosting of major sports events. Research conducted by the Centre for Applied and Business Research into the economic impact of the hosting of the America's Cup in 1987 highlighted the potential benefits to tourism of major sports events. The Centre estimated that the event resulted in expenditure of $464m. and generated the equivalent of 9,500 full-time jobs. In the Department of Sport, Recreation and Tourism's annual report for 1986–7 it was noted that despite the failure of Brisbane's bid to host the 1992 Olympic Games, 'it did focus world-wide attention on Australia, its tourism potential, its excellent sporting facilities and its professional sports administration' (1987: 49). 'Sydney 2000' is expected, according to the Australian Tourist Commission, to attract an additional 2.1m. visitors between 1994 and 2000, due to the city's raised profile, and contribute further to an aspect of the economy which already in 1993 accounted for 11 per cent of Australia's exports. The diplomatic and economic motives for federal government involvement have dominated policy development in recent years to such an extent that McKay observed that sport has been 'denuded of its expressive, experiential and humanistic components . . . (and) has now become work, a utilitarian, instrumental, rational way of assisting economic growth while also stimulating national pride' (1986: 125).

As regards participation, the cornerstone of ASC activity is the much-imitated Aussie Sport set of programmes. 'Ready Set Go!', one of the key programmes that promotes modified versions of adult sport, is now firmly established in most of the nation's schools with, for example, 539 out of 800 schools in Western Australia involved. A second programme, 'Sport Search', is a sport software talent identification package for upper primary and secondary pupils, which helps children identify the sports they are best suited to both physically and physiologically. Although launched only in November 1993, over 25 per cent of secondary school pupils have access to the package. Elements of Aussie Sport notwithstanding, it is fair to say that the fostering of participation has been downgraded by government and left to states to pursue should they feel inclined. Unlike the production of sports stars, 'increased participation was a policy goal aspired to rather than actively sought' (Vamplew *et al.* 1994: 162). While the Aussie Sport programmes have been highly successful, it is debatable whether they are primarily concerned with increasing participation or with the provision of a secure foundation for continued elite success.

As in many other countries the federal government has found it difficult to identify an appropriate administrative location for sport and recreation. The current distribution of responsibility for sport and recreation is shown in Table 3.1. But as can be seen from Table 3.2, the sports function has been located within a number of central departments.

The decision by the International Olympic Committee (IOC) to award the 2000 Games to Sydney has had a profound impact on sport policy. Table 3.3 shows the pattern of distribution of ASC funds between various programmes and also shows the allocation of the Olympic Athletes Programme funding. Although it is difficult to disaggregate funding, approximately 45 per cent of the ASC budget is currently directed to Olympic sports, which account for only 25 per cent of sports participation. Of the top twenty most favourably funded sports in 1995–6, all but one are Olympic sports; the exception being netball, which is to be a 1998 Commonwealth Games sport. Despite the skewed pattern of distribution, the ASC funds a broad range of sports. In 1995–6 allocations varied between sums of over $A3m. to athletics, rowing, cycling and swimming down to a few thousand dollars to bobsled, tug-of-war and wave-skiing. Over the past four years there has also been a high degree of stability in funding, measured by the comparative rarity of a sport having its funding removed and of new sports receiving ASC funds. Less stable has been the year-on-year funding. As one would expect, percentage shifts in funding are more noticeable among the sports receiving smaller allocations but even among the heavily funded Olympic sports funding changes can be quite severe. For example, between 1994–5 and 1995–6 yachting had its allocation reduced by $A0.25m. (22 per cent) while the allocation to wrestling jumped by 65 per cent to $A521,000 following its identification by the ASC as a 'soft' target for Olympic medals.

The policy impact of Sydney 2000 is illustrated not just in the distribution of ASC funding, but also in the relative immunity of sport from public expenditure cuts which have severely affected other branches of government since the election of the budget-cutting Liberal coalition government of John Howard. It is as though normal politics in the area of sport has been suspended until after the Games have been held. The government's preoccupation with the Games is illustrated by the policy rhetoric of the current Minister who, when asked soon after his appointment to identify the major challenges that face his department gave clear priority to success in the Games and pointed out that for 1996–7 only the funding allocation for the

Table 3.1 The pattern of responsibility for sport and recreation in Australia

Federal government departments and agencies	Environment (sport, territories and local government)	Social security (including housing)	Health and family services	Defence	Foreign affairs and trade	Immigration and multicultural affairs	Industry, science and tourism	Employment, education and training
Main responsibilities	Elite sport and mass participation National parks and wildlife Urban playgrounds	Some funding of youth clubs and other community facilities	Health and fitness promotion	Use and management of services' sports facilities	Foreign travel by Australian teams Olympic visiting teams Sport Development Aid via AIS and ASDA	Support for minority sporting and cultural activities Some aspects of Aboriginal sport	2000 Olympic marketing	Youth affairs/service Sport and PE in schools Promotion of community use of school facilities
Examples of national government agencies and organisations	Australian Sports Commission Sport and recreation Minister's Council Parks and Wildlife Service ASDA		National Drug Strategy Committee				Australian Tourist Commission	
Examples of national non-governmental organisations	Confederation of Australian Sport							Australian Society of Sports Administrators Australian Schools Sports Council

Table 3.2   Australian federal government expenditure on sport and recreation, 1972–96

Year	Agency/department	Expenditure ($Am.)
1972–3	Department of Tourism and Recreation	1.2
1973–4	Department of Tourism and Recreation	3.8
1974–5	Department of Tourism and Recreation	8.1
1975–6	Environment, Housing and Community Development	11.4
1976–7	Environment, Housing and Community Development	7.6
1977–8	Environment, Housing and Community Development	5.6
1978–9	Home Affairs	5.8
1979–80	Home Affairs	6.8
1980–1	Home Affairs and Environment	9.0
1981–2	Home Affairs and Environment	13.1
1982–3	Home Affairs and Environment	14.5
1983–4	Sport, Recreation and Tourism	22.5
1984–5	Sport, Recreation and Tourism (inc. $0.8m. ASC)	41.2
1985–6	Sport, Recreation and Tourism (inc. $8.7m. ASC)	32.1
1986–7	Sport, Recreation and Tourism (inc. $9.1m. ASC)	31.9
1987–8	Arts, Sport, the Environment, Tourism and Territories (inc. $15.9m. ASC)	32.8
1988–9	Arts, Sport, the Environment, Tourism and Territories (inc. $10.6m. ASC)	30.4
1989–90	Arts, Sport, the Environment, Tourism and Territories (inc. $42.5m. ASC and AIS)	44.9
1990–1	Arts, Sport, the Environment, Tourism and Territories (inc. $54.6m. ASC and AIS)	57.1
1991–2	Environment, Sport and Territories (inc. $59.6m. ASC and AIS)	82.9
1992–3	Environment, Sport and Territories (inc. $60.8m. ASC and AIS)	86.0
1993–4	Environment, Sport and Territories (inc. $63.4m. ASC and AIS)	137.9[1]
1994–5	Environment, Sport and Territories (inc. $64.9m. ASC and AIS)	159.0[2]
1995–6	Environment, Sport and Territories (inc. $66.0m. ASC and AIS)	139.9[2]

Notes: 1 Includes a grant of $50m. to fund the preparations for the 2000 Sydney Olympic Games.

2 Includes additional funding from an Olympic Athlete Program supported by the federal government with $A135m. over six years.

Source: Departmental annual reports 1986–96.

Table 3.3   Australian Sports Commission: program allocation, 1995–6 ($A'000s)

Program	Allocation	Olympic athlete program	Total allocation	Percentage of grand total
AIS residential sports	12,153	1,109	13,262	14.7
AIS other elite	8,839	6,817	15,656	17.4
Sports management	20,437	10,178	30,615	33.9[1]
Sports development and participation	10,196	0	10,196	11.3[2]
Australian Coaching Council	922	0	922	1.0
Sports sciences	3,773	1,690	5,463	6.1
National Sports Research Centre	813	500	1,313	1.5
Other	12,758	0	12,758	14.1

Notes: 1 Includes funding of $A26.8m. for National Sports Organisations.

2 Includes funding of $A4.8m. for Aussie Sports.

Source: Sport Report, Spring 1995, vol. 15.3.

Olympics was guaranteed (Moore 1994: 8). Although the ASC budget has been cut by $A2m. for 1996–7, the scale of the cut is very modest by comparison with that imposed on other public services. It is undoubtedly the case that if Sydney had been unsuccessful in its bid to host the 2000 Games, deeper cuts would have been made. There is also speculation that the ASC might have been abolished, as many similar bodies have been, had it not been for the forthcoming Olympics. However, the impact of 'Sydney 2000' has not been limited to matters of funding and agency survival. Of equal interest has been the (re)discovery that Aborigines are interested in sport yet are still largely excluded from elite-level competition. The 1996–7 budget consequently included $A4m. (up from $A80,000 four years ago) for a new indigenous Sports Program within the ASC aimed at 'building bridges' with white sports organisations and conveniently timed to attempt to defuse Aboriginal protest in the lead-up to the Games.

The character of government intervention in the lead-up to the 2000 Games is further evidence of its domination of sports policy development. In general, the government, operating through the ASC, has effectively by-passed the NSOs in a number of crucial areas of sports administration and development: the top 200 athletes were directly funded by government in 1994–5; talent identification programmes are organised by co-ordinators appointed by each state; ASC funding is closely tied to elite achievement; and overall co-ordination of elite development is the responsibility of the National Elite Sports Council (established in 1993), which is dominated by the AIS, the ASC and the state institutes of sport. Most worrying is the air of unreality that pervades many Australian sports organisations about the consequences of even a modest withdrawal of public funding, let alone the scale of reductions that are likely after 2000. Some NSOs are aware that substantial grant reductions are likely but dependence is so deeply ingrained that few are planning effectively for the future.

Canada

Until the early 1940s, federal government involvement in sport had been *ad hoc* and limited. Apart from relatively small grants to support the participation of a Canadian team in the Olympic Games, federal involvement was confined to cost-sharing arrangements, from the 1930s, with a number of provinces designed to support sport and recreation projects whose primary aim was the creation of employment (Baka 1976). Despite some debate and lobbying within Parliament for greater federal aid following a poor performance in the 1936 Olympics, it was not until 1943 that the federal government intervened directly in sport policy (West 1973). Following the announcement that 33 per cent of military recruits had been rejected as unfit, Parliament passed the 1943 National Physical Fitness Act, which established a National Council on Physical Fitness, composed largely of provincial representatives, to advise the government on implementation. For the next eleven years the Council oversaw the cost-sharing programme and effectively lobbied for increased federal funds. However, in 1954 the federal government unilaterally withdrew from the programme because of continuing wrangling with the provinces over money, and for the remainder of the decade avoided further involvement in the policy area (Broom 1986).

The Fitness and Amateur Sport Act 1961 not only marks the re-engagement of the federal government with sport, but constitutes 'the cornerstone of the huge fitness and amateur sport edifice that has grown up in Canada' (Dubin Report 1990: 7). The Act was prompted by a dual concern: first, with the low levels of physical fitness among Canadians; and second, with the relatively poor performance of Canadian athletes in international competition in ice hockey and the summer Olympic events. Despite the earlier disillusionment with cost-sharing, the federal government adopted the same policy tool as before. As Macintosh notes, 'In the first few years following the passage of this bill, the federal government appeared content to play a passive role in the promotion of fitness and amateur sport' (1991: 270). Considerable care was taken not to undermine the autonomy of the sports governing bodies and federal involvement was indirect, as it operated through an agency, the National Fitness and Amateur Sports Advisory Council, which made recommendations to the government on the distribution of grants to sports governing bodies and other sports organisations. The decision to establish the Council was due to a range of factors, including the need to achieve a compromise between the wishes of many sports governing bodies for an independent agency and the suspicion of the government of such bodies. In addition, the government was aware of the value of having a semi-independent body to protect it from direct criticism. As Franks and Macintosh note, 'In establishing a national advisory council, the federal government created a buffer group which would protect it from criticism and, at the same time, would provide advice from various regions and from different program biases' (1984: 203). Third, where issues concerned joint federal/provincial programmes, the prevailing management fashion was for the establishment of advisory committees linked to departments. Finally, the government was also aware of the absence of appropriate expertise within the ranks of the permanent civil service (Macintosh *et al.* 1987). To the disappointment of many in sport, the Advisory Council was provided with only weak powers and was 'not given any executive powers, program funds, or an independent secretariat' (ibid.: 31). However, by the end of the decade, a number of significant changes had taken place: first, the Fitness and Amateur Sport Directorate (FASD) developed greater expertise in the sport policy area; second, pressure from governing bodies for federal financial support had also increased; third, the assertiveness of the Advisory Council had grown; and finally, growing calls, particularly from politicians, for action to improve the performance of Canadian athletes and the ice hockey team. Most importantly, in the late 1960s the Liberal Party adopted sport as one element in its strategy to disarm the increasingly powerful forces seeking to separate Quebec from the federation.

The growing salience of sport to the government was reflected in the White Paper, *A Proposed Sport Policy for Canadians* (Canada 1970). Under Prime Minister Pierre Trudeau the federal government pursued a more interventionist policy, particularly with regard to elite sport and the activities of the country's NSOs. As part of this policy, the government established a National Sports and Recreation Centre in the capital, Ottawa, which was intended to house the major governing bodies and provide them with effective administrative support. In addition, a new division, 'Sport Canada', was created within the Fitness and Amateur Sport Directorate (FASD) to take responsibility for elite sport, and a separate division, 'Recreation Canada', was also established to pursue policies aimed at stimulating mass participation. However, the latter never received the same degree of political support or resources as Sport Canada, due in large part to continued disputes over the appropriate spheres of influence of federal and provincial governments. Recreation Canada was consequently disbanded in 1980 with the federal government content to leave the development of recreation to the provinces. Indeed, the provinces were so insistent that recreation and mass sport were their prerogative that in 1978 a joint statement from federal and provincial ministers responsible for sport, recreation and fitness was issued, making it clear that provincial governments had primary responsibility for recreation and that the federal government was expected to withdraw gradually from the policy area, which it finally did as part of one of the recent rounds of discussions over the Quebec. The Beaudoin–Dobbie Committee recommended that the federal and provincial governments should 'negotiate constitutionally protected recreation agreements to better define the roles of each government' in which the federal government would recognise the exclusive jurisdiction of the provinces (Mirecki 1992: 8). Before its abolition in 1980, Recreation Canada was divided and a new organisation was established, 'Fitness Canada', to reflect the government's increasing concern with health. However, the relative priority of elite success over the general fitness of the population was reflected in the financing of the two units with the budget of Fitness Canada increasing from $6.6m. to $7.6m. between 1980–1 and 1986–7, and that of Sport Canada increasing from $26.4m. to $50.6m. over the same period (Harvey 1988: 326).

The growing significance of elite sport was also reflected in the steady rise in the status of the Fitness and Amateur Sport Directorate which, in 1973, was upgraded to 'Branch' status with its own assistant deputy minister. By 1976 the political salience of sport had increased to the extent that sport gained a minister of state with Cabinet rank. During this period the National Advisory Council faded into the background and exerted a declining influence on policy and by the end of the 1970s was virtually dormant. By contrast, during the 1970s the federal government established or strengthened a number of semi-independent agencies which, although nominally responsible to an independent board, were heavily, if not totally, reliant on federal funds. Among the most significant were: the National Sport and Recreation Centre, which provided office accommodation and administrative support for governing bodies of sport; Hockey Canada, which had responsibility for the operation of the national team; the Coaching Association of Canada; and the Canada Games Council. Such was the significance of the federal government in sport policy that the Dubin Inquiry referred to the 'dominant role' the government plays 'at the level of high performance athletics' (Dubin Report 1990: 27). The elaboration of federal administrative structures for elite sport gave considerable momentum to policy development only undermined by the inability to agree on an appropriate location for the Fitness and Amateur Sport Branch (FASB). In 1979 it was moved from health and welfare to the secretary of state's department, then moved to Labor Canada for a short period before returning to the Secretary of State's department, only to be moved back to where it started from, Health and Welfare, in 1982.

The growth in federal grant aid to governing bodies during the 1970s and 1980s was considerable and achieved the desired 'seduction of amateur sport' (Carlson 1992: 30) with an increasing proportion tied to specific objectives and projects (Kidd 1981). The federal government also provided grant aid direct to elite athletes through Sport Canada (Athlete Assistance Program (AAP)) and, by so doing, was effectively marginalising the National Advisory Council and with it an independent voice for sport in the policy process. As Franks and Macintosh observe, the culmination of the federal policy initiatives in the 1960s and 1970s was that 'the relative autonomy from government which sport had enjoyed for 100 years in Canada was lost' (1984: 206).

The administrative centralisation of sport was reinforced by the 1981 White Paper, *Challenge to the Nation: Fitness and Amateur Sport in the '80s.* The White Paper also accelerated the emphasis on elite sport and the government's intention to 'ensure that the momentum generated by the 1976 Olympics and the 1978 Commonwealth Games is carried into the 1980s and taken to new heights' (Canada 1981: 5). As a result, financial support was directed to those governing bodies that 'demonstrated a commitment to, and a consistent record of, excellence' (ibid.: 6). This policy direction was given a further boost with the choice of Calgary by the International Olympic Committee (IOC) for the 1988 Winter Olympic Games. Calgary's selection brought not only renewed federal largesse, but also federal consultants from Sport Canada who would liaise with governing bodies in the preparation of sports development plans focused on maximising medal success in the Games. The elaboration of a policy infrastructure for sport at federal level stimulated parallel administrative developments at provincial level. But as Macintosh notes:

> In the rush to get on the high-performance bandwagon provincial govern-
> ments abandoned their previously strongly held position as champions of
> mass sport . . . and commenced to compete with the federal government
> for the attention and glamour associated with international sports events.
>
> (Macintosh 1991: 271)

This was particularly true of Quebec, which recognised the value of elite sports success for its own separatist agenda (Broom 1986).

At the heart of the administrative arrangements in the mid-1980s lay Sport Canada, a directorate of FASB. The main functions of Sport Canada were to provide policy direction and financial support for the establishment and maintenance of a Canadian sports system, develop and promote elite sport, and, somewhat as an afterthought, promote mass participation: 'the Fitness and Amateur Sport Program endeavours to attain the highest possible level of success by Canadians in competitive sport . . . thereby . . . enhancing national pride' (Canada 1985: 7–12). Sport Canada, while adopting a rhetoric of respect for the autonomy of sports governing bodies, has been consistently and consciously assertive and interventionist. Fifty-six per cent of the income of the sixty-five or so recognised governing bodies (NSOs) comes from Sport Canada and, in the words of the Dubin Report, 'federal funding props up the entire sports system' (Dubin Report 1990: 27). The 1992 Task Force Report (usually referred to as the Best Report after its chairman) referred to the 'excessive day-to-day control . . . over sports organisations [and the] failure to adapt to more mature and effective sports organisations' (Best Report 1992: 192). Sport Canada plays a significant role in staff appointments made to governing bodies and influences their strategic development through the Quadrennial Planning Process (QPP) which, to the critics of the process, 'is more beneficial to Sport Canada than to sport organisations' (ibid.: 195).

Legislative and regulatory intervention has been important, but it is the steady extension of federal funding for sport that has been the primary source of government leverage in the policy area. Table 3.4 provides a breakdown of total federal expenditure on sport and fitness between 1961 and 1991. Excluding funding for the 1976 Montreal Olympics and the 1988 Calgary Olympic Games federal expenditure reached almost Can$1bn.

Table 3.4   Canadian federal expenditure on selected aspects of sport and fitness, 1961–91

Expenditure category	Total (Can$'000s)
A Subsidies to sports organisations and sportspersons	
National sports organisations	295,905
Athlete Assistance Program	42,332
'Best Ever' Winter (Olympics)	42,285
'Best Ever' Summer (Olympics)	59,400
Coaching Association	32,885
Canadian Sport and Fitness Administration Centre	59,953
Doping control	3,790
Other	51,692
Sub-total	588,242
B Subsidy to sports events	
1994 Commonwealth Games	11,000
Canada Winter Games	29,915
Canada Summer Games	31,156
Arctic Winter Games	2,364
1996 Toronto Olympic bid	2,407
Other	36,521
Sub-total	113,363
Total sport subsidy	701,605
C Subsidy to fitness projects	
National organisations/recreation	84,825
'ParticipACTION'	15,186
Other	12,768
Total fitness	112,779
D Fitness and amateur sport	
Directorate/Branch (running costs)	135,837
Total A,B,C and D	950,221
E Hosting the Olympic Games	
1976 Olympic Games (Montreal)	537,000
1988 Olympic Games (Calgary)	224,848

From the period 1961 to 1966 there was a steady rise in federal funding following the introduction of the Fitness and Amateur Sport Act. However, during the period from 1971 to 1984–5 the level of subsidy increased almost six-fold and increased by a further 50 per cent up to 1990–1 before declining sharply by the mid-1990s as Table 3.5 shows.

Over the same period the operating costs of the FASD/B have increased from approximately Can$0.3m. in the mid-1960s to just under Can$5m. by the mid-1970s and almost Can$11m. by the late 1980s. Over the thirty-five years of involvement in sport, the federal government has constructed a sports infrastructure that, to its defenders, is comprehensive, interventionist and highly supportive, but to its detractors is narrowly focused, elitist, manipulative and a threat to the autonomy of sport.

The political context within which the 1990 Dubin Report and the 1992 Best Report were published was one that was apparently highly supportive of the key conclusions that federal intervention was smothering voluntary NSOs and that the emphasis on elite sport was distorting, or even corrupting, the objectives of sports participation. However, while both reports led to important changes in the administration of Canadian sport, neither led to a shift away from the government's central concern with elite international achievement. The Dubin Report had significant implications for anti-doping policy but its trenchant criticism of the manipulation of elite sport by the government, and its highlighting of what one commentator referred to as the 'moral bankruptcy . . . of federal involvement' (Storey 1990: 7), was quickly forgotten. Similarly the underlying critique of the direction of federal sport policy found in the Best Report was ignored in favour of acceptance of its more palatable recommendations about the management of the relationship between the government and the NSOs.

The developments in sport policy since 1992 need to be placed within the broader context of recent Canadian politics: the collapse of the

Table 3.5   Canadian federal expenditure on amateur sport, 1961 to 1996–7

Year	Expenditure (Can$'000s)
1961	100
1966	4,700
1971	8,200
1976	23,300
1984–5	47,600
1986–7	86,000
1990–1	72,000
1996–7	48,800 (est.)

Source :   Minister of State, Fitness and Amateur Sport (1992) and Federal Budget Estimates, various years.

Charlottetown Constitutional Accord, aimed at defusing the resurgence of Quebec separatism; the weakness of the economy; and the election of the cost-cutting government of Prime Minister Chrétien have forced sport down the public policy agenda. One of the first actions of the new government was to restructure radically the machinery of government. In 1994 the number of ministries was drastically reduced and Sport Canada was downgraded and incorporated within the new Department of Canadian Heritage. The mission of Canadian Heritage is to 'strengthen and celebrate Canada' and within it the mission statement of Sport Canada is to 'strengthen the unique contribution that sport makes to Canadian society, identity and culture' (Sport Canada 1996: 2). While officials within Sport Canada feel that the location of sport within Canadian Heritage is appropriate, they are also aware that the unit has lost much of its previous autonomy and now has to conform to broad departmental goals and also compete for the attention of the Minister.

The 1993 election and the restructuring of federal departments (see Table 3.6) marked a number of important shifts in federal policy. First, the restructuring marked the final separation of sport from fitness. The transfer of Fitness Canada to the Department of Health, where it is a very minor unit, completed the gradual redefinition of policy goals away from a narrow focus on the contribution of sport-related physical activity to fitness to a more holistic definition, termed Active Living, which was defined as 'a state of total well-being of the individual – physical, mental, emotional, spiritual and social' (Fitness Canada 1991: 3). The second shift in federal policy concerned the refinement of the objectives of Sport Canada. In November 1994 the Minister announced a revised set of objectives for Sport Canada which largely ignored the thrust of the Best Report and its argument for a broader and less elitist approach to sport, and confirmed the priority of elite success by making it clear that federal funding would be used primarily to support high-performance athletes. To help realise these objectives, the government introduced a new funding framework for NSOs, the Sports Funding and Accountability Framework (SFAF). As the Best Report made clear, not only was the federal government spreading its funding too thinly, but the vehicle for fund distribution, the Quadrennial Planning process, had also been a major irritant in the relationship between the NSOs and the government. The Framework was therefore designed to concentrate funding on a more select group of sports and move away from the previous relationship of detailed oversight to one that gave the NSOs greater autonomy over the use of funds, or a shift from 'accounting to accountability' as one Sports Canada official termed the change.

The SFAF was introduced in pilot form in 1995 as a means of determining which NSOs were eligible for federal funding. The second stage of the process was to assess the eligible NSOs according to a set of funding criteria heavily weighted towards elite success. Although the government's 1994 policy statement did dilute its emphasis on elite athletes with some

Table 3.6 The pattern of responsibility for sport and recreation in Canada

Federal government department	Department of Canadian Heritage	Department of Health	Environment Canada	Department of National Defense	Human Resources Development Canada
Main sports responsibilities	Elite sport; doping control; ethics in sport; national centres policy; national parks; maritime parks; historic trails	Health and fitness promotion	Conservation	Provision of sporting opportunities for members of the armed forces	Grant towards provision of playgrounds Funding for CPRA (Canadian Parks and Recreation Authority)
Federal sub-unit	Sport Canada Parks Canada	Fitness Canada			
National-level semi-independent agencies	National Sports and Recreation Centre Coaching Association of Canada Hockey Canada Canada and Arctic Games Council Canadian Commonwealth Games Federation Canadian Centre for Drug-free Sport	Active Living Canada ParticipACTION Canadian Fitness and Lifestyle Research Institute			
National independent sports/leisure organisations	Canadian Olympic Association National sports organisations Canadian Parks and Recreation Association	Canadian Association for Health, Physical Education, Recreation and Dance YM/WCA Canadian Intramural Recreation Association Boys/Girls Clubs Canadian Council on Children and Youth	Canadian Nature Federation Canadian Wildlife Federation		
Provincial/municipal responsibilities	Mass participation Contribution to elite development for the Canadian Games Hosting and funding sports events Provision of facilities			Education School Boards Curriculum and sports facilities in schools	Urban playgrounds Play schemes Youth service

social goals including increased access for women, athletes with disabilities and Aboriginal athletes, there is little reflection of broader objectives in the funding formula.

A third recent policy development is the move towards giving athletes a greater voice in policy-making. According to a recent discussion paper the preferred definition of an athlete-centred sport is one where athletes are seen less as adjuncts to the mission of an NSO and more as key stake-holders to whom the NSO is accountable. To this end the NSOs have been encouraged, partly through the SFAF process, to ensure that athletes are represented on their Boards and on main committees and that they should be directly involved in developing policy, particularly regarding codes of conduct, selection and discipline (Canadian Heritage 1994). To help strengthen the voice of athletes, a new organisation, Athletes Canada, has been established with government funding and part of its role is to lobby the more recalcitrant NSOs.

Given that these major shifts in policy are so recent, it is difficult to assess their impact on the Canadian sports infrastructure. However, a number of tentative conclusions can be drawn. The most obvious is that many NSOs are having to search for alternative sources of funding to make good the shortfall in federal funding (a decline of Can$0.8m. over the past two years for Athletics Canada, for example). The Best Report (1992) illustrated not only the extent to which NSOs had become dependent on government, but also, and more significantly, their attitude to federal funding. The report pointed out that on average in 1989, 70 per cent of NSO income was from federal funds, with some receiving 95 per cent. More significantly, the report devoted barely ten of its 300 pages to finance and undertook no discussion of alternative sources of finance and did not challenge the central assumption of continuing federal funding. The sharp reduction in federal funding in 1994–5 has therefore come as a shock to most NSOs which have little experience of fund raising on a scale necessary to fill the gap. However, there are a number of Sport Canada initiatives under way including the 'Business Plan for Sport' designed to enhance the financial self-sufficiency of sport, in part through greater corporate funding. Despite this and similar initiatives, a number of NSOs have had to reduce drastically their activities. In the past eighteen months, more than twenty NSOs have moved out of the Ottawa administration centre to cut costs.

A more serious consequence of recent policy shifts is the policy vacuum that has been created. On the one hand, there is much public and party political sympathy for the sentiments that underpinned the Dubin Inquiry report and the Best Report. Yet, the exhortations to put elite success in perspective have been contradicted by the 1994 funding decisions taken by minister Michel Dupuy. There is some indication that the current minister, Sheila Copps, is sympathetic to a less elitist sport development policy, but this has yet to be reflected in funding criteria. However, what is painfully apparent is the inability of the NSOs and the Canadian Olympic

Association to take the initiative in shaping sport policy. They seem to be locked into a culture of dependence that prevents a proactive policy role. The weakness of the NSOs is amply illustrated by the fate of the Canadian Sports Council, established (with Sport Canada funding) to provide a collective voice for the NSOs and other sports organisations. Although the Council recruited successfully during a recent period of lobbying, the organisation faded once federal funding was scaled down as few sports bodies thought it was worth supporting out of their own funds.

Ireland

There are four sources of current government policy: first, the long-standing relationship between the Irish state and the Gaelic Athletic Association; second, the development of PE and sport in schools; third, the consequences of Ireland's increasing involvement in international sport; and fourth, the significance of sports tourism to the Irish economy.

As regards the first source, it was made clear in Chapter 2 that the pace and extent of government involvement in sport is intimately bound up with the activities of the Gaelic Athletic Association (GAA). The relatively recent and limited involvement of the government in sport and recreation is substantially the result of the cultural dominance of Gaelic sports and the comprehensive provision at local and regional levels of facilities by the GAA and local government. Just as the GAA played a key role in organising opposition to British rule, it played an equally central role in stabilising Ireland in the aftermath of the short, but bitter, civil war that followed partition. As Sugden and Bairner note, 'Operating in hundreds of parishes throughout the country the GAA served as neutral territory within which a common sense of national identity could be rebuilt' (1993: 33). The fledgeling government of the Irish Free State consequently relied heavily on the GAA and forged a close relationship that has persisted to the present day.

The centrality of the GAA to rural community life also influenced the character and development of both sport in schools and especially extra-curricular sport. However, the significance of the GAA in the development of school sport is in marked contrast to the marginal contribution of the Irish state until comparatively recently. Although physical education was strong at primary school level under colonial administration at the turn of the century, there was a sharp decline following independence. Part of the explanation for the decline lay in the directive to teach physical education through the Irish language, which 'was largely responsible for the almost total elimination of PE from Irish primary schools at that time' (Carroll 1979: 89).

In 1938 the government published a *Report on Physical Education* which argued strongly for the restoration of the subject within schools and emphasised the role of government in funding sports facilities. Among the report's main recommendations were the establishment of a specialist teaching college for PE, the requirement for compulsory PE in all schools and the provision of improved facilities, including swimming pools, in schools. However, the impact of the Report was undermined by the start of the Second World War and it was not until 1965 that the ideas were resurrected.

The third source of current government policy is in part the result of the general rise in the international significance of sport from the 1960s and also the increasing engagement of Ireland with the international community, particularly its involvement with the Council of Europe and later membership of the then Common Market. This shift towards a more outward-looking policy led to a greater concern to achieve prestige through the production of elite athletes in the major international, particularly Olympic, sports. By the early 1990s the Minister's introductions to the annual reports of the National Sports Council were emphasising the success of elite athletes and saying very little about progress in providing opportunities for mass participation. The impression of a greater priority being placed on elite success is reinforced by an analysis of the distribution of revenue funding. In 1992 just over IR£1m. was spent on elite programmes compared with fractionally under IR£1m. on 'Sport for All' programmes. In 1993 the figure for elite sport had barely changed at just under IR£1m. compared with a decline to just under IR£400,000 for the promotion of 'Sport for All'. Needless to say, caution must be exercised in attempting to draw firm conclusions from these figures as other elements of the overall budget such as those for local programmes and aid to governing bodies are difficult to disaggregate, but the overall impression is of a shift in emphasis to the promotion of elite success.

The final source of current sport policy is the growing recognition of the economic significance of sport. Tourism has always made an important contribution to the Irish economy, particularly as a source of foreign exchange, and sports-related tourism has for many years been an integral part of marketing strategy of the tourist board. Consequently, sports facility development has frequently been distorted by the need to give priority to tourist demands rather than domestic sports needs.

To sum up, the Irish government has, only from the late 1970s, begun to refine its policy on sport and, more importantly, establish an administrative capacity backed by the commitment of significant public funds for policy implementation. But while much of the increase in the prominence of sport within public policy has been stimulated by government, it has not been possible to establish neat administrative arrangements. As is the case in many other countries, the diffuse nature of the sport and recreation policy area has produced a fragmented administrative structure.

Although there are few central departments that do not have some interest in sport policy there is a clear clustering of responsibilities, including the location of the Sports Section, within the Department of Education (see Table 3.7). In contrast to specialist sports units in other countries, which often attract and retain civil servants that have a particular interest in sport, the staff within the Sports Section see themselves as career civil servants

Table 3.7 The pattern of responsibility for sport and recreation in Ireland

Central government ministry	Department of Education	Department of the Environment	Department of Justice	Department of Tourism and Trade	Department of Marine	Department of Agriculture, Food and Forestry	Department of Health	Department of Foreign Affairs	Office of Public Works	Ministry of Culture and Language
Main responsibilities related to sport and recreation	COSPÓIR Anti-doping policy Sport and PE in schools Grants to governing bodies and athletes	Funding of amenity provision by local government	Control of gaming and lotteries Control of firearms	Funding to support the hosting of international sports events	Aquatic leisure and recreation Licensing of angling	Outdoor recreation Rural land use	Health promotion	Cultural/exchange agreements Council of Europe	National Parks and Wildlife Canals Shannon navigation including The Burran	Protection and promotion of Gaelic culture, including sport
National governmental specialist units and semi-autonomous agencies	COSPÓIR	National Co-ordinating Committee for Mountain and Cave Rescue		Bord Fáilte (Irish Tourist Board)		Forestry and Wildlife service	Health promotion unit	Advisory Committee on Cultural Relations		National Heritage Council
Major national non-governmental sports and sports-related organisations	OCI GAA and other governing bodies of sport PEAI and other teachers' organisations	ILAM			National Coarse Fishing Federation					
Local-level public sector units of administration and government	Schools, colleges and universities Sports advisory committees, e.g. City of Dublin SAC	County and district councils								

working in the Education Department first and members of the Sports Section second. As a result there are few of the tensions that exist in other countries between a sports and an education policy culture. In Ireland the Education policy framework is one that Sports Section staff are happy to operate within, but it is essentially a highly conservative and traditional culture which finds the more entrepreneurial and populist aspects of sport policy difficult to accommodate. However, as is the case in the UK, the most significant tension arises over the role of sport in schools and its relationship to physical education (see Chapter 7) .

The policy framework within which the Sports Section operates includes an emphasis on participation as a means of promoting good health and enhancing the quality of life. In addition, sport is seen as possessing the potential to develop social skills, leadership and to 'act as an antidote to anti-social behaviour and vandalism' (Department of Education 1993:2). A considerable emphasis is placed on the contribution of sport to the economy in the form of job creation resulting from sports tourism. Finally, as already mentioned, the current policy framework draws attention to the capacity of 'Meritorious performances by Irish sports persons in the international arena to increase the country's prestige and image among the community of nations' (Department of Education 1993: 2). Given the broad range of interests of the Sports Section, the co-ordination of policy development and implementation is a primary concern with the main problems centring on the co-ordination of the activities of the Sports Section of the Department of Education and the Bord Failté (Irish Tourist Board) on the one hand and the Department of the Environment on the other.

Although sport is increasingly being recognised as a significant policy area in its own right, it is still strongly influenced by the priorities of the tourism policy community. For many years tourism development has been a central component of the government's economic strategy. Recent sports projects initiated by the Bord Failté include the development of a series of long-distance walking routes and the establishment of outdoor education centres. Both schemes require the approval of the Department of Education, which contains the Sports Section, but approval tends to be routine. There are also some joint-funded schemes, particularly relating to golf, aimed at expanding the golfing holiday market, which one officer described as 'essentially a Bord Failté initiative'. There is also some joint funding designed to bring major sports events to Ireland, such as the 1995 Eubank–Collins boxing bout. However, Bord Failté also funds some sports events without reference to the Sports Section including a series of golf competitions (IR£600,000 in 1995), such as the Irish Open, and also makes a major contribution to the cost of operating the Jordan Formula One racing team. Co-ordination, such as it is, is through a series of irregular meetings between officers of the Sports Section and representatives of Bord Failté, although the meetings function largely for the exchange of information and the presentation by Bord Failté of its forthcoming programme.

The relationship between the Sports Section and the Department of the Environment is also managed through a series of irregular meetings. There is little attempt to use these meetings to stimulate the preparation of sports/recreation plans at local level or to consider broader strategic issues as the meetings tend to focus on discussions over specific capital projects rather than over broader strategic questions.

Not only is effective co-ordination between the various branches of government a concern, but there is also a need to link the government's efforts with the extensive and longer-established voluntary sector. The primary link between the public and voluntary sectors is through COSPÓIR, the National Sports Council (NSC), established in 1978 in the wake of the development of the Sport for All policy by the Council of Europe. In the early years of its life the main terms of reference of COSPÓIR were:

a   to act as adviser to the Minister of State at the Department of Education in relation to the implementation of the government's policy on Sport for All, and
b   to promote initiatives and innovative measures in regard to:
   i the development of sport and physical recreation and leisure pursuits, and
   ii the raising of standards of performance in competitive sport.

From 1978 to 1988 COSPÓIR operated within these terms of reference and was established on a three-year renewable basis. In 1988 the government failed to reappoint the NSC mainly because of a growing uncertainty regarding its proper role in the policy process, but also because there was a concern that the body had expanded its remit (and membership) rather too liberally. The dismissive treatment of COSPÓIR by the government prompted little comment from the sports governing bodies or the Physical Education Association of Ireland, which had developed an increasing antipathy to the Council due to the latter's unrepresentativeness. Finally, bearing in mind the clientelistic nature of Irish politics and the importance of capital funding decisions within the Sports Section budget, the Minister wished to be able to make allocations unencumbered by a Council which he felt obliged to consult.

When COSPÓIR was re-established in 1992 its membership had been reduced from over forty to twenty-three and its remit was simplified and was 'to advise the Minister of State on all aspects of sport and recreation'. Like the earlier NSC, the current body has no executive powers. However, it is organised into a number of sub-committees, two of which correspond to the main policy priorities of the Sports Section – namely the Sport for All Committee and the Outstanding Sports Persons Committee. The former committee provides advice on the distribution of approximately IR£400,000 annually to a range of specialist bodies, particularly the Irish Mini-sport Movement, Special Olympics Ireland and the National Community Games, which organise major mass participation events. In addition, the Committee funds a broad range of individual projects including the Dublin Marathon and the 'Sport For All Day' in primary schools. The Outstanding Sports Persons Committee provides advice on the distribution of over IR£120,000 each year (in amounts ranging from IR£1,000 to IR£7,500) to elite athletes to cover the costs associated with training and competition preparation. The NSC provides the government with expert advice and also access to a wide range of voluntary bodies whose co-operation is essential if policy implementation is to be successful. In return, the various organisations represented bask in the illusion of influence.

The gradual extension of the policy ambitions of the Sports Section has been paralleled by a steady growth in its funding. In 1970 the total amount of grant aid distributed to sports organisations amounted to just over IR£100,000 but as Table 3.8 shows, by 1979 it had risen to IR£620,000. Funding continued to increase steadily during the 1980s, and received a major injection of funding with the introduction of the national lottery (Lotto) in 1986. The lottery was designed to provide additional funding for youth, sport/recreation, arts and culture and the Irish language and from 1988, the first full year when lottery funding was available, the total distributed to sport and recreation has averaged almost IR£10m. per year. However, this sum represents only 14 per cent of the total available for distribution and in 1992 the proportion allocated to sport dropped below 10 per cent. With some ten departments, including the Department of Defence, now receiving lottery funding, the allocation to sport is likely to remain under severe pressure.

The influence of the NSC on sport policy is at best modest. Although the agenda of the NSC is open, it is rare for members of the Council to raise

Table 3.8 Government funding for the Sports Section, 1970–94 (IR£)

Year	Total grant	Revenue	Capital
1970	100,000	n.a.	n.a.
1979	620,000	n.a.	n.a.
1986	3,113,000	1,604,000	1,509,000
1987	2,741,000	1,706,000	1,035,000
1988	8,410,000	5,370,000	3,040,000
1989	9,482,000	6,124,000	3,358,000
1990	9,121,000	5,599,000	3,522,000
1991	12,348,000	5,587,000	6,761,000
1992	9,884,000	5,649,000	4,235,000
1993	11,352,000	5,999,000	5,353,000
1994	17,104,000	6,775,000	10,329,000

Source: Department of Education Annual Report: Sport in Ireland, various years.

issues; consequently the Council is reactive rather than proactive on policy. For example, the introduction of the fund to provide grant aid for Olympic athletes was the initiative of the Minister. However, nominations for grants are made by a sub-committee of the Council and it is rare for the Minister to alter its suggestions.

There is currently some debate about the future role of the NSC. The existing remit of the Council is sufficiently vague to allow wide interpretation but so far there has been little attempt to sharpen the focus of its activities. This is partly due to the infrequency of meetings and partly due to the parallel funding given by the Sports Section to the Institute of Leisure and Amenity Management (ILAM) which fulfils a number of the technical functions, such as project appraisal, that one might expect the NSC to undertake. One sports administrator described the NSC as 'peripheral to sports policy development' and contrasted the inactivity of the current Council with the achievements of its predecessor which, between 1978 and 1985, was instrumental in introducing a series of innovative policy initiatives including the national lottery to fund sport, the establishment of the National Coaching and Training Centre and the establishment of a National Sports Centre (still under discussion). However, it should be borne in mind that successive governments have promised comprehensive policy statements on sport but have, so far, failed to deliver.

United Kingdom

The development of government involvement in sport has for much of its history been haphazard. Generally, governments have been reluctant to intervene in matters of sport and leisure, and such interventions as there have been have tended to be reactive rather than the outcome of a strategic overview. Travis's reference to the nineteenth-century practice regarding sport and leisure policy of 'identifying *separate* or *specific areas* of failure' the solutions to which 'should *not* be seen as a normative planning and management process in a welfare context', but rather as 'a scatter of items of isolated legislation' (1979: 1 and 2) could also be applied to most twentieth-century sport policy development. With some notable exceptions, recent governments have been prompted to intervene owing to particular crises such as outbreaks of soccer hooliganism in the mid-1980s. However, the evolution of the role of government has produced a number of recurring themes stretching from the early nineteenth century to the present day. The first is a strong element of paternalism towards the 'lower classes'. Nineteenth-century philanthropy, which was so important in influencing the shape of education and housing policy, was also significant in affecting the character of policy towards sport (Holt 1989). The second theme is the concern to defend privilege as evident in the conflicts over access to the countryside and hunting (Shoard 1987; Ramblers Association 1984; Donnelly 1986; Thomas 1983). The third theme is the belief that too much (undisciplined) sport and leisure for the poor was a danger to social stability. For much of the last half of the nineteenth century there had been growing concern among the middle class about the potential for social instability arising from the swelling ranks of the urban working class (Bailey 1979; Birley 1995). The fostering of 'rational recreation' was complemented by an attempt to prohibit the more undisciplined sports of the street and waste ground and was seen by many as an important element in maintaining social stability.

The piecemeal and reactive approach to sport and recreation continued until the early 1960s, by which time both the Labour and Conservative Parties had accepted that sport was a legitimate governmental responsibility. For Hargreaves the acceptance by government of a more central role in sport policy was due, in part, to a continuing concern with the potential for urban disorder led by young people, but was also due to 'the realisation . . . that state aided sport could help to improve Britain's international sporting performance' (1985: 221) and that this may have diplomatic benefits. The policy themes of the 1960s of social order, desire for international success and the increasing demand for wider sport and recreation opportunities need to be set within the broad political consensus surrounding the maturation of the welfare state, the ideological pre-eminence of social democracy and an expanding economy, described by Coalter as recreational welfare (Coalter 1990). This economic and political context for sport policy was supportive of notions of service planning, public participation and equality of opportunity, all of which were important in affecting the shape of policy development following the establishment of the Advisory Sports Council in 1965. Not only did the Council introduce a strong element of planning and co-ordination into the provision of sport facilities, it also provided a focus for the campaign to expand participation in sport.

The publication, in 1975, of the White Paper, *Sport and Recreation*, confirmed the place of sport and recreation services as a legitimate element of the welfare state and also reiterated a conventional rationale for intervention, namely a concern with social order, international prestige, and individual wellbeing (Department of the Environment 1975). While for much of the 1970s these three priorities were broadly complementary they also provide the dimensions of the conflicts running through the government's policy. In the years that followed the tensions between elite and mass provision, Sport for All and targeted groups, participation in sports and general fitness, organised sport (through clubs and governing bodies) and casual play, school sport and post-school provision, new sports and traditional sports reflected the unresolved conflicts in a policy that was both too broad and too vague.

In the late 1970s and early 1980s, the British Sports Council was the vehicle for a policy shift that downgraded the 'British Sport for All' campaign and gave greater prominence to 'concentrating resources instead on the symptoms, as opposed to causes, of social unrest in the inner cities, and to promoting the elite sector . . . ' (Hargreaves 1985: 223). The stimulus of the 1981 urban riots resulted in a number of initiatives (though many would argue that they were palliatives) involving sport, for example, the extension of the Urban Programme to cover the provision of sporting and recreational opportunities and the development by the British Sports Council of the 'Action Sport' programme (Coalter 1984: 26). The mid-1980s was dominated by the government's attempts to eliminate spectator violence from soccer matches. Although the initial policy response which involved a club membership scheme was ill thought out and quickly dropped, other policy initiatives, the banning of alcohol at grounds, closed-circuit television to survey the terraces and the grant of new powers to police and magistrate, seemed more effective. However, the government's response was, as so often in the past, short term and narrowly focused.

Sport was also affected by other policies introduced in the mid-1980s which, although not directed specifically at sport and recreation, have had a significant impact on provision of opportunities for mass participation. Central objectives of the Conservative governments of the 1980s were: on the one hand, to reduce the scope of government, and especially local government, and on the other, to introduce a market approach to the provision of public services. Implementation of these policies within sport and recreation services took the form of the introduction of Compulsory Competitive Tendering (CCT) which not only gave private contractors the opportunity to run publicly owned leisure facilities, but which also forced existing public sector management to adopt strategies and practices of the market sector. While there is some evidence that 'privatisation' is forcing sports and leisure facility managers to be more innovative, there is also evidence that the policy has resulted in a reduction in sports development activity and a preference for activities that generate a more rapid return on investment (Sports Council 1993).

While the emphasis on a market-oriented service remains, there has been an undoubted change in the government's approach to sport, especially since 1991. In general, this change was a consequence of the election of John Major as leader of the Conservative Party and Prime Minister, but it is also indicative of a longer-term trend towards a greater centralisation of control over sport policy. Since the early 1990s the main changes have been the raising of the status of sport within government through the creation of the DNH, the replacement of the British Sports Council with a UK Sports Council and an English Sports Council, and the abolition of the regional councils for sport and recreation. These structural changes have been complemented by the introduction or expansion of new sources of finance which have had a major impact on facility provision. Of particular note are the Football Trust which, through the use of money derived from a levy on the football pools, has helped soccer clubs to meet the requirements of the Taylor Report to improve the design and facilities at stadiums and make the larger stadiums seating only; and the National Lottery, which is likely to bring approximately £200m. of additional funding into sport each year.

Finally, the government issued a comprehensive policy statement, *Sport: Raising the Game* (Department of National Heritage 1995), in 1995 which has provided a strong context for policy development over the medium term.

Sport: Raising the Game provides a clear indication of government priorities. In particular it adds momentum to the withdrawal of central government and the Sports Council from the provision of opportunities for mass participation on the assumption that a substantial facility infrastructure is securely in place and that local authorities are a more suitable provider or co-ordinator of this aspect of provision. The policy document therefore concentrates on the development of elite sportsmen and women and suggests, *inter alia*, that an elite training centre be established along the lines of the Australian Institute of Sport, that higher education institutions should become more involved in the fostering of elite athletes and that grants to governing bodies will be conditional upon explicit support for government objectives. The third policy theme reflects the government's concern to promote and protect heritage sports partly by requiring schools to ensure that traditional competitive team sports are part of the curriculum.

Given the range and diversity of objectives that sport policy was seen as fulfilling over the past thirty years, it is no surprise that there has been considerable uncertainty over the appropriate status and location of sport within the central administration. The uncertainty arose from a number of sources: first, the reluctance by both the major political parties to bring sport and recreation policy into the mainstream of parliamentary debate; second, the lack of an obvious parent department for such a broad policy area; and third, the lack of civil service expertise in the area. As there was already an emerging management fashion within government for the establishment of 'arm's length' administrative units it was no surprise that the government decided to establish an Advisory Sports Council in 1965 and later, in 1972, a series of executive Sports Councils, for Britain, Wales and Scotland, under Royal Charter (the Sports Council for Northern Ireland was established in 1974). As with all quangos, the British Sports Council was linked to a central government department and a minister. Initially, the British Sports Council was responsible to a junior minister in the Department of Education and Science (DES) because of the links with school sport and the Department's existing responsibility for distributing grant aid under the terms of the 1937 Physical Training and Recreation Act. However, the responsibility was soon transferred to the Ministry of Housing and Local Government (MHLG) which was a more appropriate location given the priority of developing rapidly a network of sport facilities which required close liaison with local authorities. The British Sports Council remained within the orbit of the MHLG, and its successor the DoE, until December 1990, when it was transferred back to the DES due largely to the salience to the government of school sport. In 1992, after a brief and generally unhappy period in the DES, sport moved to its current ministry, the DNH.

The creation of the DNH took place at a time when there was a growing awareness of the links between tourism and sport, a sharper concern with the place of sport in the configuration of English identity, and the increasing commercialisation of sport. In addition, the new ministry reflected the personal commitment to sport by Prime Minister Major and was also an attempt to resolve the continuing problem of leadership and co-ordination in a traditionally fragmented policy area. The DNH brought together a range of loosely related functions including arts, museums and libraries (formerly with the DoE), film (Department of Trade and Industry), broadcasting (Home Office), sport (DES), and tourism (DoE). Table 3.9 shows the current distribution of responsibility for sport and recreation throughout the machinery of central government.

Two of the major problems facing the emerging sport policy area in the UK were first, the absence of a voice at Cabinet level and second, the fragmentation of responsibility for the service across a number of departments. The establishment of the DNH has gone some way to overcoming these weaknesses. Undoubtedly the status of sport within the government has risen, although whether this survives John Major's premiership remains to be seen. In the few years since its creation it has managed to keep a surprisingly low profile and, to date, is best known for the introduction of the National Lottery. It has also made little progress in establishing a departmental culture that is capable of integrating the common themes found in its various responsibilities. More worryingly, it has yet to provide the strong policy lead for other government departments, especially the powerful DoE and the Department for Education and Employment (DfEE) (see Table 3.9). A continuing problem regarding government involvement in sport is that school sport is firmly under the control of the DfEE and a cluster of entrenched interests within the education policy community and consequently is difficult to influence. Mass participation in sport is also firmly outside the remit of the DNH as it is the DoE that is responsible for funding and overseeing the activities of local government.

The upheaval at departmental level has been paralleled at agency level, with the British Sports Council being subject to considerable uncertainty over its future since the late 1980s. Since 1989 there have been seven major reviews of the Council, a number of which have led to proposals for reform, which were later abandoned. Since the establishment of the Sports Council as an executive agency in 1972, it has been the focus and driving force for government policy, although its position at the heart of British sport policy has been constantly challenged by the Central Council of Physical Recreation (CCPR) and to a lesser extent by the British Olympic Association. The CCPR is an umbrella organisation that represents a broad range of sports organisations, including the major governing bodies and specialist organisations for the disabled, armed forces and teachers, for example. The CCPR was instrumental in the creation of the Sports Councils, transferred many of its assets to the new organisations and was on

Table 3.9 The pattern of responsibility for sport and recreation in the UK

Central government ministry	Department of National Heritage	Department of the Environment	Department for Education and Employment	Ministry of Agriculture, Fisheries and Food	Home Office	Foreign Office	Ministry of Defence	Welsh, Scottish and Northern Irish Offices
Main responsibilities	Sports Council; anti-doping policy; after-school sport; sponsorship; international issues; National Lottery	Local government organisation, functions and finance; land use policy; countryside issues	Sport in the curriculum; community use of school sports facilities	Alternative uses (including leisure) for surplus farm land	Control of gambling; crowd safety at sports events; law and order at sports events	Foreign travel of sportsmen, sportswomen and supporters	Community use of sports facilities	Responsibility for sports policy in each area, although extent of responsibility varies
Examples of national government agencies	UK Sports Council; English Sports Council	The Countryside Commission; The Nature Conservancy Council	School Curriculum and Assessment Authority		The Gaming Board; The Horse Totalisator Board		Royal Air Force Sports Board	
Examples of national non-governmental organisations	Central Council for Physical Recreation; Foundation for Sport and the Arts; British Olympic Association; Sports Aid Foundation; sports governing bodies; The Football Trust; British Sports Association for the Disabled[1]	Inland Waterways Amenity Advisory Council; Society for the Promotion of Nature Reserves	Physical Education Association; English Schools Athletic Association	National Farmers Union; Country Landowners Association				Equivalent bodies for Education, Environment and National Heritage

Note: 1 Many of these bodies depend heavily, and some exclusively, on public funding, thus putting them in a more ambiguous category. It is possible to argue that it is more accurate to treat organisations that rely on public subsidy as part of the infrastructure of government than as part of the independent sector or 'civil society'.

the point of dissolving itself in 1972. However, its membership decided to continue the organisation and it remained closely tied to, and financially dependent upon, the British Sports Council. The existence of three national organisations not only led to a weaker and occasionally contradictory voice in domestic sport policy, but also led to confusion in attempts to project and protect UK sports interests within international sport (Houlihan 1991; Coghlan 1990). It is hoped that the new UK Sports Council will provide the much sought after unified voice for UK sport.

Funding for sport has been shaped by the uneasy accommodation between an established welfare state ethos and, more recently, the Conservative government's antipathy to both public expenditure and local government. Funding has also been affected by the tension between the ideological preference among many Conservative politicians to treat sport as an element of 'free time' and therefore minimise state intervention and the desire for international prestige. The outcome of this mix of motives is a position in the mid-1990s where sport is funded through a combination of direct public subsidy and state-supported, but essentially commercial, sponsorship schemes (Houlihan 1996).

Direct public subsidy for sport is organised either through the Sports Council or through the expenditure of local authorities. In the financial year 1994–5 the grants to the four Sports Councils totalled £67.18m., fractionally down on the total for 1993–4 of £67.26m. A substantial proportion of the income of the Councils (*c.* 50 per cent) is distributed in the form of grants to governing bodies of sport or to other national sports organisations (such as the British Deaf Sports Council, the National Council for School Sport, and the Young Men's Christian Association). Table 3.10 shows that British Sports Council expenditure has risen steadily over the past twenty-five years, but remains a modest total.

Table 3.10   Government grant to the British Sports Council between 1972–3 and 1996–7 (£m.)

Year	Grant	Year	Grant
1972–3	3.6	1986–7	37.35
1974–5	6.58	1988–9	38.41
1976–7	10.2	1990–1	42.6
1978–9	15.73	1992–3	47.6
1980–1	19.31	1994–5	49.8
1982–3	28.0	1996–7	47.4
1984–5	28.6		

Source: GB Sports Council, annual reports, various years.

The main function of Sports Councils' funding is 'pump-priming' and support for innovative projects. Although the finance that flows into sport through the Councils' grant aid is an important contribution to the development of sport, it is dwarfed by the volume of investment in sport allocated by local authorities. In the financial year 1992–3, local authorities spent £560m. on revenue support for sport and a further £130m. on capital projects. While these figures are substantial revenue expenditure has declined as a proportion of total local government revenue expenditure over the five years from 1989–90 and capital expenditure has fallen by 60 per cent over the same period.

Although public expenditure on sport is likely to remain under severe pressure, the government has supported the introduction of a range of new funding sources which rely on a mix of public and private support. In 1991 the government supported the establishment of the Foundation for Sport and the Arts (FSA), which distributes about £40m. each year for sports projects. The FSA's income is derived partly from a reduction in the tax imposed on gambling on the outcome of soccer matches (the football pools) and partly from a voluntary contribution from the Pools Promoters Association. A second source of grant aid for sport comes from the Football Trust. During the 1980s the Trust provided over £10m. to aid local authorities in improving the quality of pitches and providing changing facilities for amateur teams. The third scheme designed to provide financial support for sport is the National Lottery, which was introduced in November 1994. The lottery is expected to generate funds, largely for capital projects, for sport totalling between £100m. and £150m. in 1995, rising to £250m. in 1999.

In conclusion, sport in the UK in the mid-1990s has a more secure central government administrative framework, although serious problems of policy co-ordination remain unresolved, and is experiencing a boom in investment, much of which is the result of public policy decisions. However, the mid-years of the decade have also witnessed the emergence or continuation of a number of trends that are likely to reshape the character of the policy sector. First, there is the continued marginalisation of governing bodies through the establishment of the British Academy of Sport and the pressure on the Sports Councils to make elite development a higher priority. Second, there is the more determined intervention by government to shape the general development of sport, particularly by influencing the school curriculum, but also through directing the Sports Councils to narrow the range of sports they grant-aid and finally, by influencing the funding priorities of indirect public expenditure, such as that from the National Lottery and the FSA. With regard to the distribution of grant aid, the Sports Council announced in mid-1996 that it was intending to be more selective in the support that it provided for governing bodies. Targeted for 'enhanced' support are those governing bodies considered to be especially supportive of the key policy thrusts of the Council. Ten criteria, many similar to those in use in Canada as part of its Sports Funding and Accountability Framework, were used to evaluate sports with particular emphasis placed on their contribution to excellence and youth sport development. Eleven sports have been identified as contributing to objectives associated with excellence and young people and a further eleven deemed to be contributing significantly to one or other of the objectives. Included in the eleven core sports are the main Olympic sports plus the main traditional English team games of soccer, cricket and rugby.

The United States

As made clear in Chapter 2, the constitutional impediments to state intervention are reinforced by a deep-seated popular scepticism towards the efficacy of state action. Restraining federal expenditure and preventing federal expansion have often been the most rewarding electoral platform for aspiring candidates for Congress. It should therefore come as no surprise that federal government intervention in sport policy is rare, especially when compared with the other countries in this survey. The dominant perception of sport among the public and in Congress is that amateur sport is rarely, if ever, a proper focus for state action and that intervention directed at professional sport should be aimed at maximising entrepreneurial freedom. However, as will also become clear, state intervention, particularly through the courts, although rare, has done much to shape sport and recreation in the modern United States. In common with many other countries, state involvement with sport was sporadic and highly fragmented until the 1960s. As Wilson notes: 'Before 1950 Congress virtually ignored [sport]. In the next thirty years, however, nearly three hundred pieces of legislation dealing with professional sport alone were introduced in Congress' (1994: 24). Although few became law, it is important to bear in mind that the introduction of bills is as much part of the lobbying process as it is an element in the legislative process and as such does not contradict Clumpner's assessment that 'the American government adheres to a "less-government-the-better" rule when it comes to sport' (1984: 10).

Any cursory review of federal government involvement in sport reveals that, by comparison to the other countries in this survey, the form that involvement takes is through regulation and the provision of grant aid rather than through direct provision. Moreover, there is relatively little involvement of the federal government in attempting to promote and co-ordinate the strategic development of the policy area. As Kraus noted: 'the federal government has developed a multitude of programs related to recreation – more than 90 departments, bureaux, commissions, or councils and 300 different operations – without a systematic plan to determine priorities' (1990: 210). Apart from the generally low salience of sport and recreation to federal politicians, the emergence of federal involvement in the policy area was, as in many other countries, a by-product of other higher priority functions such as flood control, education and environmental control and management. Finally, despite the plethora of bills relating to sport that have been introduced in recent years, it has been the courts as much as the legislature that have helped to shape public policy for sport and recreation.

The emergence of a federal interest in sport and recreation was slow and piecemeal and followed in the wake of service development activity within the municipal, voluntary and commercial sectors. Although there had been some state involvement in the early part of the century, a turning point came with the economic depression of the 1930s. Of particular significance was the establishment of a number of federal job creation agencies, such as the Works Progress Administration (WPA) and the Civilian Conservation Corps, which focused on the provision of sport and recreation facilities. According to Shivers: 'By 1937, about 10 per cent of the entire WPA budget had been expended on the construction of more than 10,000 recreational structures, facilities or places' (1993: 86). Although these projects were aimed at responding to, and further stimulating, mass participation in sport and recreation, they provided part of the infrastructure for performance and elite sport. A further stimulus to the expansion of recreational facilities and opportunities came with the Second World War. Federal support came in the form of grant aid to voluntary bodies such as the American Red Cross and from the armed forces, which developed specialist sections to cater for the sport and recreation needs of service personnel. The wartime experience not only added to the range of available facilities but, more importantly, created, among service personnel, an expectation of good-quality sport and recreation opportunities. According to Butler, following the end of the war, 'A renaissance of the movement for living war memorials, initiated after World War I, took place and prompted the construction of memorials in the form of recreational buildings, playgrounds, parks and athletic fields, swimming pools, band shells, and forests' (1975: 83).

The momentum for the development of sport and recreational facilities lay clearly with the multiplicity of municipal authorities. The federal government, although occasionally significant, generally played a more peripheral and irregular role largely as a source of pump-priming funds. Examples of federal programmes included time-limited initiatives such as Mission 66, a ten-year plan introduced in the mid-1950s to develop recreational facilities in the national parks, and Bureaux initiatives such as that from the Bureau of Outdoor Recreation in 1958 to provide expert advice on service strategy to municipalities. Federal interest and support for sport and recreation initiatives tended to vary in relation to the seriousness of unrelated policy problems. For example, the injection of resources into local sport and recreational facilities in the 1930s was a by-product of a concern to ameliorate the worst effects of the economic depression. Some thirty years later during President Johnson's Great Society programmes and following a series of riots in inner-city areas there was a further, largely fortuitous, injection of programme aid to urban sport and recreation projects. As in many other countries the federal government perception of sport and recreation was instrumental: sport was a means to other non-sport ends such as job creation or social control. However, it should also be noted that the late 1960s also saw the passage of some important legislation which had a lasting impact on service development, such as the Federal Water Project Recreation Act 1965, the Wild and Scenic Rivers Act 1968 and the National Trails System Act 1968.

While the mid- to late 1960s marked a growth in interest in sport and recreation within Congress and the executive, there were few signs of the lasting shift in status and political salience of sport that took place in many other countries. Following in the wake of the Great Society initiative substantial amounts of federal money were channelled into inner-city recreational and sports projects, including approximately $650m. through the Urban Park and Recreational Recovery Program. Shivers, reviewing the decade of the 1970s, argues that 'it can be asserted that the entire recreational service movement, but particularly the public sector, has made tremendous strides' (1993: 110). However, Shivers also notes the failure of the federal government to sustain its commitment to the policy area. He notes that the flagship agency, the Heritage Conservation and Recreational Service (HCRS), which was established in 1978 to replace the Bureau of Outdoor Recreation within the Department of the Interior, was abolished in 1981. The closure of the HCRS was followed during the Reagan years with a substantial reduction in the flow of federal funds to local sport and recreation projects, such as the Comprehensive Employment and Training Program, which made a major contribution to many municipal parks systems. The period of retrenchment in federal expenditure inaugurated by Reagan's election continued into the late 1990s despite the election of a Democrat President in 1992.

In summing up, the development of federal involvement in the provision of opportunities for mass participation in sport and recreation a number of characteristics are clear: first, an infrequent, but often unintended involvement in the policy area; second, a lack of strategic commitment; third, a highly fragmented administrative pattern; and finally, a preference for short-term pump-priming intervention over long-term administrative commitment. Set alongside this profile of involvement in mass provision there is a history of significant and often dramatic intervention in elite and college sport. Both the courts and Congress have intervened to regulate professional sport, to provide a more effective administrative framework for elite sport, and thereby achieve foreign policy objectives as well as domestic objectives such as securing equality of access to sport.

Intervention to ensure fair competition among sports businesses and to regulate their employment practices is one of the most consistent motives for federal intervention. The application of anti-trust (anti-monopoly) legislation has been particularly controversial. The courts and Congress have been exercised by two issues in particular: first, the attempts to form national elite leagues; and second, the selling of broadcasting rights to sports events. At the heart of much of the debate on these two issues is a general uncertainty in the minds of justices, legislators and the public over the status of sport and a specific reluctance to treat sport as merely a business where the pursuit of profit is the overriding motive. In 1922 the Supreme Court decided that baseball was not a trade and was consequently granted exemption from anti-trust legislation, thus allowing the two major leagues to organise elite baseball so as to exclude rival leagues and control entry of new clubs. Such a view became increasingly difficult to sustain across a range of sports as both leagues and clubs became the source of substantial profits in the second half of the century. During the post-war period, basketball and football both attempted to manipulate the market in order to protect their investment. As television revenues began to become more significant, leagues sought monopolistic positions in order to restrict entry and thereby ensure that broadcasting revenues were kept high and were divided among a small group of clubs. Consequently, the period from 1960 to the mid-1980s saw a number of bitter disputes argued out before Congress or the courts concerning attempts by rival leagues to merge, as with football in the mid-1960s and basketball in 1976. What made the disputes both long-running and highly politicised was the ambiguous perception of sports organisations. As Wilson observes, following the court decision that the NFL was guilty of monopolistic practices but only awarding damages of $1:

> The decision in this case neatly captures the anomalous status of all sport leagues without grant of baseball's immunity. They appear so vulnerable to the charge of monopoly but judges and juries have great difficulty thinking of them as a 'predacious conspiracy'.
>
> (Wilson 1994: 133)

But as Wilson makes clear, some professional leagues and clubs conducted their affairs in a manner that could *only* be described as both predatory and conspiratorial. Possibly the clearest illustration of the true character of the major sports organisations is the behaviour of the National Collegiate Athletic Association (NCAA) in its relations with individual colleges. The source of disagreement between the colleges and the NCAA was the division of television revenues which, during the 1970s, led to a prolonged and rancorous series of court cases between the elite colleges (which wanted to negotiate separately with the television companies) and the NCAA, which wanted to maintain the existing cartel. Once again the attitude of the judiciary was more one of pained surprise that sport, and especially college sport, could behave in such a mercenary way.

The other major issue that led to federal intervention concerned a growing perception of inefficiency and disorganisation within elite sports administration, a perception fuelled by the increasing frustration among politicians at the virtual domination of summer and winter Olympic competition by communist states. The nub of the problem was to be found in the vested interests of the NCAA and its concern to maintain its control of college sport, the American Athletic Union (AAU), concerned to control amateur sport, and the USOC, with its concern with Olympic success. As Chalip (no date) makes clear, from the mid-1950s and throughout the 1960s there was growing awareness of the foreign policy significance of international sports competitions against the Soviet Union and its allies and mounting disquiet among politicians at the administrative inadequacies of the country's major sports organisations. From early in the 1960s there had been considerable discussion in both houses of Congress of the issues surrounding international sport and its private government. There had also been a number of attempts to encourage greater co-operation between the NCAA, the AAU and the USOC but to no avail. Matters came to a head following the 1972 Olympic Games where American athletes were perceived to be handicapped by a series of shortcomings within the USOC administration. The outcome was a rare but emphatic legislative intervention by Congress to produce the 1978 Amateur Sports Act, which forced American sport to restructure. In brief, the Act provided a central role for the USOC, fatally weakened the AAU and laid the foundation for a working relationship between the USOC and the NCAA (see Chapter 5 for a fuller discussion).

The second Congressional intervention to impact significantly on sport was a consequence of legislation designed to ensure equality of access by women to educational facilities. The Education Amendment Act 1972 (Title IX), a product of the tide of civil rights activism in the late 1960s, required that bias based on sex should be eliminated from any education programme or activity receiving federal financial assistance. Thus defined, the Act covered nearly all institutions of higher education and therefore all elite college sports activities. In the period following the passage of the Act, the NCAA led a powerful rearguard action to limit the impact of the Act by lobbying for an extremely narrow interpretation which would leave the privileged position of male college sport largely intact. The courts, especially during the Reagan administration, interpreted the Act in a highly conservative way. Of particular significance was the Supreme Court's ruling in the case of *Grove City College* v *Bell*, which successfully undermined the campaign by civil rights groups for a liberal interpretation of the Act. However, the liberal coalition in Congress regrouped and overrode the Presidential veto and passed the Civil Rights Restoration Act in 1988. Although sport was not a major theme of the conflict over the Act, it was a beneficiary and the 1988 Act gave a new impetus to those seeking a broader interpretation of Title IX. The Americans with Disabilities Act 1990 had a similar, though less dramatic, impact on provision of sport and recreational opportunities. Although a general piece of civil rights legislation, it imposed substantial obligations on educational establishments as well as local government facilities. Like the 1972 Act the full implications will take some time to work through into changes in provision but the impact on facility design and access has already been significant (McGovern 1996).

From this brief survey of the intervention of federal government in sport policy it should be clear that one is not going to find an elaborate pattern of federal departmental involvement. Yet, despite the rhetoric of 'small government' and the often expressed desire to avoid involvement in the sport and recreation policy area, it is surprising the range of federal departments that have an interest in sports-related services. It is clearly the case that for many departments their interest is at best tangential and inadvertent, but it cannot be denied that a substantial proportion of sporting and recreational activities are affected indirectly, if not directly, by state policies. However, what is clearly missing from the federal administrative machinery is any one department with a clear brief in relation to sport. The Department of the Interior probably has the greatest involvement, but the Department would reject any notion that one of its core responsibilities was for the development or management of sporting and recreational activities: still less would it feel any responsibility for co-ordinating the activities of other departments.

Yet as Table 3.11 makes clear, the range of departments and agencies with a sport and recreation interest gives the federal government, however unwelcome it might be, a significant responsibility for the development of the policy area. The Forest Service, for example, owns about 190m. acres, the Bureau of Land Management some 270m. acres, the Park Service 80m. acres and the Fish and Wildlife Service 90m. acres (*Economist*, 4 November 1995). In terms of finance, the land owned by these four agencies generates over $1,250m. in revenue, mainly in the form of fees from oil, gas and coal extraction, of which almost half is returned to the Treasury. Much of the remainder is used by the various services to manage the land for a variety of uses including recreational and sporting uses. Just as the prevailing disdain for federal administrative entanglement in sport and recreation is belied by the extensive actual involvement, much the same can be said regarding the scale of federal financial support for the policy area. Although the revenue expenditure of the four land-owning bodies is considerable, it is difficult to disentangle budgets to arrive at a fair estimate of the scale of total federal investment in the sector. Part of the problem lies in the preference within Congress to fund on a project basis rather than to give departments a global budget which they then allocate in discussion with their political head. However, some indication of the scale of federal expenditure can be gained from noting that the budget for the National Parks Service alone amounted to just under $1,500m. in the mid-1990s.

CONCLUSION

Perhaps the most striking feature of the way in which governments have become involved in sport is the assumption that they can achieve such a wide variety of purposes. The intervention by governments in the late 1930s and early 1940s to use sport as part of the solution to the problem of unfitness among recruits and conscripts is the easiest to understand. The problem

Table 3.11 The pattern of responsibility for sport and recreation in the United States

Federal government departments and agencies	President's Council on Physical Fitness and Sport	Department of Agriculture (Forest Service)	Department of Justice (Federal Trade Commission)	Department of Labor	Department of Commerce	Department of Transportation	Department of Health and Human Services (Vocational Rehabilitation Administration, Public Health Service; and Rehabilitation Services Administration)	Department of the Interior (Bureau of Outdoor Recreation, Public Roads, Indian Affairs, Land Management, Reclamation, National Parks Service; Fish and Wildlife Service)	Department of Defense (US Corps of Army Engineers; Morale, Welfare and Recreation Departments)	Department of Education (Office of Education, Children's Bureau)	Department of Housing and Urban Affairs
Main responsibilities and programmes	High-profile publicity events	Provides advice to state agriculture departments on recreational use of land	Approval of mergers and acquisitions involving professional sports clubs	Providing grants to fund sport and recreation projects in inner-city areas	Application of laws on monopolies to sport	Provision of access to the countryside	Grants to the NPRA for leadership training		The US Corps of Engineers manages rivers, other waterways and reservoirs which are heavily used for recreational purposes; Morale, Welfare, Recreation Program	Physical education and recreation for mentally handicapped; provision of outdoor recreation centres	Provision of grant for development of sport and recreational facilities as part of urban renewal projects
Examples of non-governmental organisations[1]		4-H[2]	Police Athletic League					National Recreation and Parks Association		Catholic Youth Organisation; Boys/Girls Clubs of America;Boy/Girl Scouts of the USA; National Therapeutic Recreation Association	YM/WCA
State/municipal-level departments		Department of Agriculture (functions similar to federal level)	Police (youth recreation programmes)					Parks and Recreation Departments (land management and development, and planning of recreational use); City or County Parks and Recreation Departments		Department of Education (sport in the curriculum; PE needs of special groups); universities; School Boards (provision of sports facilities often in co-operation with City Parks and Recreation Department)	Public Housing Departments (often incorporate recreation provision into new developments)

Notes:
1 The activities of non-governmental organisations are frequently wide-ranging and bring them into contact with a number of federal and state departments. In the table they have been located close to one of their major governmental partners.

2 4-H is a voluntary organisation which, among its range of activities, provides recreational opportunities for rural communities, although in recent years it has shifted its focus to urban areas.

was clearly defined and specific and the identification of sport as a solution was a logical selection from a limited range that also included dietary changes and better child health care. Following the end of the Second World War, governmental interest in the use of sport in the promotion of health and fitness waned, reappearing on the agendas of governments only sporadically, and much less urgently, until the mid-1980s. Over the past ten to fifteen years health and fitness has re-emerged as a political issue, partly as a result of the accumulation of medical evidence of the consequences of an increasingly sedentary lifestyle, but partly due to the willingness of the electorate to support leisure expenditure. There is a high degree of uniformity regarding the salience of the issue of fitness and health to politicians today. All the countries in this survey have policy targets related to general health that have been easily adapted to support public investment in sports facilities.

A second policy area where sport has been fairly uniformly adopted as a policy tool is in relation to economic development. The United States and, to a lesser extent, Canada have a long history of investment of public money in municipal sports facilities either as a means of alleviating unemployment and stimulating the local economy (especially in the 1930s) or more frequently as a way of producing a civic status symbol. Up until the 1970s most of the investment in sports facilities was funded by states/provinces with little central/federal involvement. More recently, the level of involvement of central governments has increased partly in recognition of the economic impact of being able to host major international sports events and partly because the cost of sports infrastructure has grown dramatically. The net effect of the recognition of the economic benefits of hosting major events such as the Olympic Games, the soccer World Cup and Euro '96 is that the scope for local or state initiative has greatly declined. The IOC and the major federations expect (and receive) clear statements of support from central governments. Even the major cities and states in the United States are unable to host major international sports events without the explicit support and funding from the federal government. The claims of Los Angeles and Atlanta to have organised 'private enterprise' Olympic Games reflect a highly selective method of accounting and one that, in the case of Atlanta in 1996, ignored the $350m. contribution to infrastructure from the public sector, of which just under $100m. was contributed by the federal government.

In addition to using sports investment as an element in economic policy, governments have also been uniform in the use of sport as a means of achieving greater social integration. Australia, the United States and Canada have all used sport as a means of assimilating recent immigrants, whereas the UK, Canada and Ireland have attempted to use sport as a way of healing sectarian, cultural and political rifts. In addition, UK governments and to a lesser extent the others in this survey have all attempted to use sport as an instrument of social control, especially in urban areas. Finally, governments in all five countries have intervened to foster elite development to help establish and project a favourable international image.

The trend over the past thirty years has clearly been for central governments to become more closely involved in sport and to seek to exploit sports
in pursuit of a broad range of domestic and international policy objectives.
However, governments have found it far less easy to establish a stable set of
administrative arrangements for sport within the machinery of government.
There have been two key problems: first, establishing a viable relationship
with the sports governing bodies, and second, the identification of a suitable
departmental location for sport. As regards the former problem, only the
Irish government has not found great difficulty in establishing a stable relationship with domestic governing bodies. But even in Ireland's case this
accommodation was achieved by the development of an extremely close
relationship with the GAA at the expense of any significant contact with the
governing bodies of other sports. It is only in the past ten years that the Irish
government has begun to develop links with the governing bodies for soccer,
rugby and the Olympic sports. For the other countries the increase in
interest in sport by central government has resulted in the steady undermining of the autonomy of sports organisations.

More problematic is the second issue of finding an administrative home
for sport in central government. Leaving aside the United States which,
apart from the occasional Presidential commission or committee, has not
sought to establish an administrative capacity for sport within the
Washington bureaucracy, and Ireland, where the function is still fairly novel,
Australia, Canada and the UK have tended to move the function fairly regularly. On the one hand, the frequency of transfer of the sports function
reflects the recent identification of sport as a focus for government interest
and also the fact that sport and recreation impinges on a number of other
major policy areas, including education, tourism and land use planning.
However, the relatively frequent relocation of the sport (and recreation)
function may, on the other hand, reflect not government indecision, but
rather the steady evolution of the perception of the contribution that sport
can make to the solution of the problems facing government. In the UK
sport has moved from the environment ministry to education and most
recently to heritage; in Australia the progression has been from tourism to
environment and community development, back to tourism, before currently
residing with environment; the sport function in Canada has also moved
between ministries concerned with health, labour and, more recently,
heritage. Although the patterns vary, they all reflect the progressive redefinition of the function of sport over the past twenty years with the early
concerns of facility development and health giving way to a more recent
emphasis on heritage and tourism promotion. Thus, rather than reflecting
the difficulty of integrating sport within the machinery of government, the
regular transfer of responsibility reflects the rapid evolution of the perception of the policy area by governments.

Unfortunately the main consequence of the willingness of governments
to exploit the malleability of sport as a policy instrument is the steady

erosion of governing body autonomy. Despite being the recipients of substantial public funds, the price paid by NSOs has been high and has seriously undermined their capacity to act independently within a putative sport policy community. From the analysis of the development of central government sport policy there is little evidence to suggest that it would sponsor the emergence of a policy community, except to ensure tighter control over policy implementation. There is certainly little evidence so far to suggest that sports organisations have been able to force the formation of a policy community due to government resource dependence.

4   Sub-national government

The term sub-national government is used to refer to elected units of government rather than administrative agencies or units of central departments found at local, regional, provincial or state levels. The pattern of sub-national government found in the five countries covered in this survey varies considerably. Australia, Canada and the United States have federal structures that reserve significant powers to the state level. In all three countries the federal government–state/province relationship is an issue of continuing salience within the political system and the past twenty years or so have seen considerable ebb and flow in the power relationship between the centre and periphery. By contrast, Ireland and the United Kingdom are both highly centralised political systems where the powers of units of sub-national government are tightly circumscribed and, furthermore, where there is little grassroots demand for a more decentralised pattern of government.

Attempts to provide a convincing theoretical context for the comparison of systems of local government has proved elusive (see Dunleavy and O'Leary (1987) for a review of the literature). There was a flurry of theorising in the 1970s and early 1980s which has since lost momentum. Some of the most interesting ideas came from the neo-Marxists such as Castells (1976) and O'Connor (1973). Castells (1976) argued that local government would be the locus of a crisis of capitalism resulting from the attempt to reconcile the demands of the working class, expressed through urban social movements, for increased social expenditure with the long-term need of capital to maintain the rate of profit by transferring production costs, such as health, education and housing, to the (local) state. The pressure on the rate of profit would in turn reduce the sums available for the provision of social consumption at the local level, thus creating the ingredients for political conflict. As Henry (1993) points out, the consequences for sport and recreation services would be significant as one would expect them to be among the services most vulnerable to cuts in public expenditure. However, sport and recreation services are not simply aspects of collective consumption (goods and services provided centrally by the state but consumed individually), they are also social expenses which, along with the police and fire service, are necessary costs of the maintenance of social order.

Although this analysis was severely criticised largely for the tautological nature of its explanation of policy, it was useful in raising more forcefully the question of the particular role of local government in advanced capitalist economies. A rather different attempt to theorise the division of function between central/federal and sub-national government came from the proponents of the dual-state thesis. Saunders (1982, 1984, 1986), focusing on Europe, suggested that it was possible to differentiate the roles of central and local government along two primary dimensions, namely: a concern at central government level with production and at local government level with consumption; closed corporatist modes of decision making at central level, but more pluralist modes of decision making at local level. Thus, while the centre asserted tight control over production issues, it left the local level as an arena for pluralist competition for the diminishing resources available for welfare services. The dual-state thesis came in for much criticism, particularly from those (for example, Wolman and Goldsmith 1992) who argued that in a range of capitalist states the local level was closely involved in production issues as well as consumption politics, but more significantly from those (Peterson 1981) who had already demonstrated the inability of American cities to engage in extensive redistributive welfare politics owing to the mobility of business and population and their willingness to move out of high-tax local authorities.

While these attempts to theorise the relationship between central and local government have not fulfilled their promise, they have sensitised scholars to the potential for distinctive roles for different levels of government and also reinforced the pluralist and competitive nature of the relationship between tiers. One possible way forward is to take greater account of the differential power of central (and in general, federal) government and the way in which it uses its power to dominate certain policy areas and distance itself from others. In general, one might hypothesise that central/federal governments will seek to retain tight control over production issues, much as Saunders argued, and that while local government will also seek to influence production issues (particularly business location), its capacity to exercise influence is constrained by its limited access to political and financial resources. This differential capacity is also evident when redistributive and collective consumption issues are considered. The attractiveness to central/federal governments of exporting their expenditure problems to local government is overwhelming. The origin of budget cuts for education, health and welfare may lie with the centre, but if the responsibility for delivery rests with a lower tier, then there is the possibility of avoiding some of the electoral fallout. The capacity of the centre to export its problems is matched by the weakness of lower tiers to resist the assumption of responsibility. Thus, there may well be a strong division of labour between tiers of government, not for reasons inherent in the logic of capitalist development, but for reasons of pragmatic organisational politics.

Bearing these comments in mind, a review of the most common motives for local or municipal government involvement in sport and recreation shows a concern with mass participation, social control and economic development. The objectives of this chapter are: to examine whether there is a common set of policy priorities among the various units of sub-national government; to identify the main contours of the policy process at sub-national level; to explore the relationship between the centre and the periphery; and to provide an outline of the administrative and financial context of the sub-national policy process.

AUSTRALIA

The paradox between the elite achievement and the cultivation of the myth of a sporting nation on the one hand and the low levels of participation in sport among the general population on the other is at its clearest in Australian local government and in the debates over the land use priorities. Although matters have improved greatly it is comparatively recently that Mercer wrote of the 'low priority that has traditionally been accorded recreation land-use planning' at local government level and that 'recreation is assigned to land for which no other use can be envisaged, and the standard of site design is appallingly low' (1977: 16). Where land was set aside in major cities such as Sydney and Melbourne for recreational use, it has been continually vulnerable to redesignation for other uses, including commerce and highways, with the result that in the early 1970s parts of Sydney had only 2–2.5 acres of open space per 1,000 population. One of the clearest examples of the problems faced in attempting to preserve open space is in Adelaide where the parklands that originally surrounded the city have gradually been encroached upon (alienated) by a mix of commercial and governmental interests (Daley 1987). Land has been redesignated for use by the railway service, the university, schools, the police and the prison service. Unsurprisingly the steady alienation of the parklands by non-recreational uses generated considerable public opposition but interestingly, what stimulated as much opposition was the development of both indoor recreational facilities, such as the aquatic centre, and the fencing of land allocated for sporting uses and the introduction of floodlighting. As Daley wryly observes, sport was the 'sacred cow trespassing on the Adelaide Parklands' (1987: 153).

Part of the explanation for this situation lies in the weakness of local government, but part also lies in the fragmentation of responsibility for parks and recreation at the state level. As is the case in many countries, parks and recreation services is a peripheral interest of many departments, but a core interest of few if any. To make matters worse, not only is responsibility fragmented within particular levels of government, it is also divided between levels. For example, the Port Phillip Authority ostensibly manages the Port Phillip Bay area, one of the most important parklands in Victoria. In reality the management of the area is subject to the competing priorities of twelve state government departments, fifteen municipalities, two regional planning authorities and over twenty locally elected committees of management. This pattern is typical in the recreation policy area. Chapman and Wood (1984: 40), using a typology designed by Harris (1979), identify recreation and cultural services as one of the services that is delivered concurrently by all three levels of government.

Although many local authorities are becoming more assertive and valued as democratic institutions, they are still a minority. Historically local authorities have played only a marginal and strictly circumscribed role in the development of local services and the urban social fabric. While the nineteenth-century origins of local government were cloaked in the rhetoric of their democratic educative function, many local authorities were in fact fostered by state governments, who were seeking ways of shifting some services to a local property-related tax base. As a result, even when local authorities had strong local support, state governments saw them as their creations and consequently exercised close supervision. Indeed, states retain the power to dismiss councils and replace them with a commissioner. Although rarely exercised, the dismissal of district councils in central Melbourne in 1981 and Sydney in 1987 had the effect of further weakening the self-confidence of local government politicians and administrators. The dominant role of state departments is complemented by a self-imposed limitation on function within local authorities. For many years authorities defined their responsibilities in terms of the primary source of taxation, namely a concern with the provision of property-related services, such as street cleaning, highway maintenance and refuse collection.

The functional modesty of local government is reinforced by the nature of local politics which is 'highly parochial and particularistic' (Painter 1989: 171). Councillors tend to seek local solutions to local problems and rarely demonstrate a willingness to scan the broader environment for information or examples of good practice. Second, there is a lower level of political party involvement, particularly outside the major cities, than would be found in the UK or Ireland. Third, because many councils are small and are formally responsible for all decisions, there is a tendency to dwell on detail rather than develop a concern with strategic questions.

The general 'conservatism and timidity' (Jones 1993: 3) of local authorities has led many to ignore the opportunities to expand their responsibilities presented in the 1970s to include a broader range of community welfare services including sport and recreation. However, the trend, slow though it is, is towards an expansion of local services stimulated, in part, by the increasing prominence of federal grants. Initiated by the Whitlam government of the early 1970s, federal grants have grown steadily in importance over the past twenty-five years increasing from $A56m. in 1974–5 to $A900m. in the mid-1980s and to over $A1,100m. by the early 1990s. The expansion of federal grants has created a direct link between local and federal government and, despite a determined rearguard action by state administrations, has both weakened state influence and enhanced the self-esteem of local government (Chapman and Wood 1984: 15). However, old habits die hard and as Painter notes, 'most councils have used these grants more to balance their budgets than to undertake new initiatives' (1989: 169).

Nevertheless a number of federal grants were specifically directed towards recreation services and did much to stimulate investment in facilities during the mid- to late 1970s. However, momentum diminished in the early 1980s as the federal government turned its attention to the financing of sport rather than recreation, leaving local authorities to fund the development of recreational services. Federally funded programmes which did much to stimulate recreation such as 'Life. Be in it' and the Community Assistance for Leisure Facilities Program were scaled down substantially in the late 1970s and later terminated. However, the decline in federal assistance for local authority recreation may be put in perspective by acknowledging that federal expenditure on sport and recreation in the 1970s and 1980s was always dwarfed by state and local government expenditure. In 1970–1 federal, state and local government expenditure was \$A4m., \$A18m. and \$A175m., respectively; in 1980–1, \$A9m., \$A55m. and \$A280m.; and in 1990–1 estimated to be \$A80m., \$A300m. and \$A900m.

As Table 4.1 shows, spending on recreation and culture has grown steadily over the past twenty-three years and while it is difficult to isolate the proportion of the recreation and culture budget that is spent on sport and physical recreation, there is clear evidence that, in common with Britain, the 1970s and 1980s was a period of rapid development in the quantity and quality of sports facilities at the municipal level. Currently the sport, recreation and culture budget is the second-largest budget in most authorities and has consequently generated considerable political commitment at local level.

Table 4.1   Pattern of local government expenditure for selected services between 1973–4 and 1995–6 (percentage)

Service	1973–4	1975–6	1978–9	1981–2	1984–5	1990–1	1995–6
Highways	41	45	41	36	36	35	36
General	18	21	24	23	17	18	19
Recreation and culture	12	17	17	18	20	19	21
Sanitation and environmental protection	5	6	6	8	7	7	8
Education, health and welfare	5	5	6	6	7	7	7
Housing and community development	n.a.	2	3	4	3	4	5

Source: Adapted from Painter 1989 and Commonwealth budgets.

The strength and limits of political commitment to sport and recreation is easily illustrated in the Australian Capital Territory (ACT) where, unlike other urban areas, the state and local government functions are combined because of the status of the area as the federal capital and its compact area and small population. Although the ACT Bureau of Sport, Recreation and Racing accounts for only just over 1 per cent of the total ACT budget, the sporting infrastructure is extensive and includes more than 300 hectares of open space, four swimming pools and 120 sports grounds, and also supports the highest participation rate in the country.

Sport and recreation is not a politically controversial service within the ACT and benefits from a high level of cross-party support. However, while the service is clearly valued for its intrinsic qualities it is also viewed instrumentally, especially in terms of its capacity to stimulate tourism and provide the high quality of life thought necessary to retain a mobile middle class and counter the attractions of other major cities, particularly Sydney. There is also an appreciation among the electorate that the sport and recreation budget helps protect property values.

Despite the strength of electoral and political support for the service, there has been a steady reduction in the direct provision of services and an increasing acceptance of a facilitating or enabling role. Only thirty head-quarters staff are employed to manage the $A20m. budget. The ACT provides a strategic lead which it supports through the management of its own facilities and through the distribution of grants to voluntary organisations, particularly the 'peak bodies' of sport. Sports 'peak bodies' (state-level branches of NSOs) provide a three-year strategic plan and take responsibility for the allocation of ACT grant to specific projects and clubs and the subsequent evaluation of implementation.

It is not only in the involvement of peak bodies that the Bureau is developing partnerships. There is a parallel trend regarding the management of new facilities. For many years it had been common for the Bureau to provide capital for the development of tennis clubs and to transfer the lease to the clubs which then took responsibility for maintenance and general management. Increasingly, similar arrangements are being entered into, covering softball, netball and soccer. Partnerships are not just confined to the voluntary sector. The Bureau recently grant-aided a partnership with a voluntary body and a commercial basketball club in developing a major indoor sports centre.

Community use of school facilities is also an important, if somewhat problematic, part of the Bureau's overall facility strategy. State schools generally control their indoor facilities but depend on the Bureau to provide outdoor facilities. Consequently, there is an incentive on both sides to make community agreements work. However, there are a number of problems in maximising community access: first, state schools are obliged to pay union rates for janitorial (care-taking) services and as a result have to charge relatively high fees for public access; and second, the trend towards devolved control of schools to management boards (school governors) involves the

ACT in a series of bilateral negotiations. The position is less problematic in the private schools, which account for about 33 per cent of all ACT schools, with Catholic schools being the most significant group. Private schools are more aware of the need to generate revenue, can rely on voluntary janitorial services and are increasingly conscious of the marketing opportunity that community use presents.

The range of problems and policies found in Sydney is similar to that found in ACT despite the latter's unique status. In New South Wales (NSW) the state government, through its Department of Sport, Recreation and Racing, has a modest involvement in provision for sport and recreation, but one which is none the less greater than that found in most other state governments. The NSW Department is responsible for managing a series of twelve outdoor recreation centres designed particularly for use by schools during term time with more general access during the school vacation periods, although priority is given to various disadvantaged groups. Apart from a limited contribution to service delivery through the centres, the bulk of the state's involvement with sport and recreation is through a series of grant-aid programmes, including the provision of capital assistance to clubs and local councils, but only averaging less than $A9,000. The state also runs its own sports academy, aimed at developing youth talent, and from 1995 a NSW Institute of Sport aimed at fostering elite success. The state is also heavily involved in promoting the Aussie Sport programme in conjunction with the state Department of Education and the ASC.

The fact that most of the state programmes require the co-operation of clubs or more commonly local government for their effective implementation is an acknowledgement of the primary role of local authorities in the direct provision of services to the public. Sydney City is typical of local authorities in the major cities in that it is small (only 6–7 sq km) and has relatively little open space. As in ACT, sport and recreation, while not being a politically controversial service is one which has a high level of political and electoral support: a perception heightened by the forthcoming Olympics. In general, the work of the Department of Leisure, Information and Community Services is seen as a 'good news' department by politicians, who are also aware of the high level of community commitment to the authority's sports centres and limited amount of open space. In general, the City's sports facilities are seen as fulfilling a strong welfare function and also helping to maintain the vitality and viability of the city centre as a residential area in keeping with the City's slogan, 'The Living City'. In common with the ACT the City is slowly embracing a wider range of partnerships with the voluntary and commercial sectors with a form of CCT being introduced very similar to that existing in the UK. Also paralleling developments in the ACT, the City is experiencing a slow increase in sports facilities owing to a greater willingness of schools to open their facilities to the public. However, the primary motive for many schools is income generation rather than social welfare and consequently, they are just as likely to hire their facilities for an indoor market as for sports use. Where policy development is distinctive is in relation to the spillover effect of Sydney 2000, where there is a clear skewing of policy, especially as reflected in facility development, towards the needs of elite athletes rather than the casual participant. For example, there has been a tendency to approve the building of 50-metre rather than 25-metre pools and to build full-size basketball courts rather than a half-court when in both cases the smaller facility would be a more cost-effective investment for recreational use.

The picture in North Sydney is broadly similar to that in the City authority. Like the City, North Sydney is a small authority (10 sq km) but with a highly mobile and predominantly middle-class population of 52,000. Despite pressure on the council finances, the Parks and Recreation Department has seen its share of the overall budget slowly increase in recent years due to a number of factors, including the attempt by the council to improve the quality of life, preserve property values (for an unusually mobile population where 55 per cent moved address in a five-year period) and enhance the marketing of the area to inward investment. Where the authority differs from its neighbour is in its limited use of privatisation of the management of its sports facilities. Part of the explanation lies in the shortage of facilities and the necessity for most facilities to be multi-use, thereby making it difficult to transfer responsibility for management to one club. However, community management of community centres is well established as a cost-cutting exercise and the authority has negotiated a number of partnerships with commercial providers, which involve mixing public access with commercial club use.

In both Sydney and North Sydney the most striking feature of service provision is the general weakness of strategic planning for sport and recreational services, prompting the government to require local authorities to produce management plans for all open spaces (including playgrounds, playing fields and specialist resource-based facilities) under the 1993 Local Government Act, which identifies objectives in relation to access, use and maintenance and specifies action needed to enable the plan to be fulfilled.

North Sydney is as keen as Sydney City to maximise public access to school facilities but has had very little success owing to the willingness of schools to pay lip service only to the objective of community use. Consequently there is very little effective community access in an authority where there is a general shortage of both facility-based and resource-based sport and recreation opportunities. North Sydney also shares its neighbour's interest in privatisation and partnership schemes but has so far made only limited progress.

As in most other countries, the bulk of service provision for sport and recreation rests with local government with, in the case of Australia, a limited degree of support from the state-level government and little involvement beyond occasional funding programmes from the federal level. Australian experience is also similar to that in both the UK and Canada in so far as its local authorities are making slow but steady progress towards a pattern of service delivery that involves the local authority placing more emphasis on an enabling rather than a providing role. Australia is clearly moving along a policy trajectory determined by UK experience of the early 1980s with recognisable imitations of compulsory competitive tendering and partnership arrangements with both the voluntary and commercial sectors. A final point of similarity with the UK is the problems in establishing an effective pattern of community use of school facilities.

CANADA

With a few exceptions, Canada has, like the UK, a mix of unitary and two-tier local authorities but, unlike the UK and closer to the USA pattern, Canada also delivers some services (education and planning, for example) through specialist boards which are independent of the municipal council and are either appointed or more commonly elected independently of the council. A further similarity with the United States is a lack of a direct constitutional link between the federal government and local authorities, which is more than redressed by the degree of financial dependence of many local authorities on federal grant. In general, and in common with Ireland, 'local government has a particularly low status' (Norton 1994: 434). According to Tindal and Tindal 'municipal government in Canada has never really had an opportunity to develop as an extension of the community' (1995: 5), due first to the attempts of early reformers to exclude politics from local government; second to a response to urbanisation that frequently involved the shifting of responsibility for services outward to specialist boards and upwards to the province; and third to a series of reforms that (as in Britain) focused on structure and tended to define local government in terms of the services provided rather than the communities served. One significant feature of the Canadian system of local government is the low level of involvement of national political parties. Of the major parties 'only the NDP (New Democratic Party) has made a concerted effort to run candidates in municipal elections, and then only with limited success (Tindal and Tindal 1995: 274).

Historically, local government has rarely been the product of local demand for democracy. Indeed, the introduction of frameworks of local government has frequently been viewed with suspicion and, for example, as an element of colonial oppression (Quebec) or as an excuse for the province to shift some of the tax burden to a local property tax (the Atlantic and western provinces). Attempts to stimulate local democracy, such as through the creation of a single-tier authority for the metropolitan area of Winnipeg, have had a variable impact, leading Kingdom to conclude that recent structural changes in local government 'have not generally been favourable to local democracy and, even where they have, the popular response has not been enthusiastic' (1993: 167). A further factor that undermines local government is the continuous close supervision of local activities by the provinces, which have separate ministries to oversee local government matters. Finally, D.J.H. Higgins (1986) reports that frequently local governments are keen to transfer expensive services, particularly education, to the province as this reduces pressure on local property taxes. Not surprisingly, local authorities have been equally reluctant to accept new responsibilities for the same reason (Norton 1994: 443).

In the post-war period Canadian local government has experienced a series of efforts at structural reform, driven partly by a general dissatisfaction with existing arrangements (voiced by the provincial government or by the local community) and by the specific pressures arising from rapid urbanisation. In Toronto, for example, a metropolitan authority was created in 1953 in a bid to cope with the rapid growth in population. The metropolitan authority was superimposed on the existing thirteen municipalities with major services, including water supply, sewage disposal, major roads and some elements of the parks and recreation function, such as major open spaces, being transferred to the upper tier. Over the intervening years the number of municipalities has dropped, from thirteen to six, and there has been some adjustment to the distribution of services with the lower-level authorities consolidating their central role in the provision of sport and leisure services.

The Toronto experience provided a template for reform efforts elsewhere in Ontario, which led to the adoption of a form of regional government based around existing county authorities (the upper tier having responsibility for a similar range of services to those found in Metropolitan Toronto). Currently two-thirds of Ontario's population live within the boundaries of the twelve two-tier metropolitan authorities. However, the existing structure is far from secure. One persistent problem is the difficulty of matching boundaries to population movement.

Outside Ontario the pattern of local government is more varied, although most major urban areas have adopted a version of the Toronto model. One of the major exceptions is found in Manitoba where the two-tier structure for Winnipeg was replaced in 1972 with the Winnipeg Unicity. This single-tier experiment has not been viewed universally as a success due in part to the secession of one of the middle-class neighbourhoods and the reluctance or inability of councillors to move beyond a parochial perspective on issues and adopt a city-wide view of service needs and location. Quebec, which has three metropolitan authorities at Montreal, Hull and the city of Quebec, is also an exception, although more in terms of the motives for their creation than in terms of structure or functions. The Montreal Urban Community (MUC) was created in 1970 primarily as a solution to a funding crisis associated with a strike by police officers. The creation of the MUC allowed for the reorganisation of the police force and a settlement of their dispute by increasing tax levels in suburban areas. Similarly, the regional government formed in the Hull area was motivated by a fear of loss of influence to the adjoining metropolitan area of Ottawa–Carleton over the river in Ontario.

The financial context of local government is one where in recent years local authorities received an increasing proportion of their income from the provincial level, much of it in the form of conditional grants which have the effect of further undermining the scope for local decision making and the vitality of local political processes. An exception to this pattern, and possibly an indication of future trends, is found in Alberta, which recently elected a radical right-wing government. Under the revised funding arrangements most conditional grants to local government have been replaced by unconditional grants. However, the overall size of the grant transfer to local government has been drastically reduced from Can$169m. in 1994–5 to Can$88m. in 1996–7 (Tindal and Tindal 1995: 217). The parks service, which was protected through the allocation of a conditional provincial grant, now has to compete each year with a range of other services, all of which are competing for a rapidly shrinking pool of funding. The implications for recreational services of a squeeze on local government leisure spending is evident from the fact that whereas, in 1991–2, only 0.7 per cent (Can$1,168m.) of federal expenditure and 1 per cent (Can$1,810m.) of provincial expenditure was concerned with recreation and culture, the figure for local government was 6 per cent (Can$3,985m.) (Howard 1992).

Starting from a pattern of internal organisation that largely mirrored that developed in nineteenth-century Britain, Canada has steadily moved towards a pattern of administration more frequently found in the United States and Ireland. Up until the 1970s most units of local government had a series of functionally specialist departments overseen by a specialist standing committee of councillors, the major difference from Britain being that the size of the council is usually much smaller, rarely more than fifteen members. From the mid-1970s reforms were made, designed to overcome the problems associated with a perceived lack of political leadership and long-term planning, service fragmentation and the poor quality of co-ordination between municipalities and functional boards. The response to these problems was generally two-fold and concerned the appointment of a more powerful chief administrative/executive officer and the establishment of some form of executive committee of the council.

As with structural reform the preoccupation of those concerned with the internal organisation of the council focused on improving the quality of service delivery rather than the enhancement of local democracy. The past thirty years has witnessed a steady increase in the number of 'council managers', closely modelled on the American city manager, and in the number of municipalities that have appointed panels of two or three commissioners to manage public services. Parallel developments have taken place among elected members, where there has been a steady trend towards the creation of small executive committees.

Because of the history of political and administrative passivity at local level, it has been argued that the main source of policy innovation lies with the provincial or federal governments (Frisken 1988), although as Tindal and Tindal point out, the Canadian examples pale by comparison with the intervention in the affairs of local government by the Thatcher government in the UK (1995: 272). By the mid-1970s most provinces had specialist departments concerned with leisure. To these bodies must be added the sixty-four federal departments or agencies that had some involvement in leisure services (Burton and Kyllo, 1974, quoted in Kraus 1990). Provincial governments have provided and continue to provide a wide range of grants to local authorities including funds for new facilities, supporting Provincial Games, grants to sports federations and granting permission for lotteries (Redmond 1985), although as previously mentioned the grants are less likely to be earmarked for parks and recreation services.

There are four main features of the pattern of local government in Canada that affect the context within which the parks and recreation service operates. The first feature is the conceptual priority of service over representation. With a few exceptions, in the larger urban areas local representatives, the electorate and the provincial government all give greater weight to the efficient and economic delivery of services than the effective representation of interests. The second feature is the administrative fragmentation of responsibility for parks and recreation, as reflected in the overlap of responsibility between the local levels and the province and the relative autonomy of boards. A third, and closely related, feature is the problem of strategy development due, in part, to the absence of organised political parties and the parochial nature of municipal politics. The final feature is the heavy dependence of local authorities on the province for finance and legitimacy.

The administration of the parks and recreation service in the city of Toronto provides confirmation of many of these features, but also provides a number of variations. Within the city of Toronto the parks and recreation function is located in a broad-based department of community services, which includes the fire service, public housing and the management of the municipality's property. The distinctive, if not unique, feature of Toronto's parks and recreation service is the fact that access to the service is free. For a city with a population of 0.63m. the range and number of facilities is impressive and includes 780 hectares of parkland, 22 ice rinks, 107 tennis courts and 32 community recreation centres.

Although Metropolitan Toronto has an involvement in the service, it is limited to a responsibility for major areas of parkland and thus raises few issues of co-ordination. Within the City the administration of the service is through one of only four broad-based departments and thus reduces further the problems of fragmentation. In addition, the City and the two school boards have a long-established tradition of shared use of facilities. In terms of funding, the service was responsible, in 1995–6, for just over 10 per cent of the City budget (Can$54m.), a figure that has grown slightly in percentage terms in recent years despite a steady reduction in the overall

City budget. The success of the service in maintaining its budget share reflects the political salience of parks and recreation to the council, which sees recreational services as a central aspect of a policy designed to avoid the problems of urban decay experienced in the United States, and also reflects the unusual strength of neighbourhood activism. Within the City there seems to be a consensus among politicians and the electorate that the parks and recreation service has an important part to play in maintaining the viability of the downtown area as a place to live and work.

The neighbourhood focus of the City is acknowledged by the extent of decentralisation of administration and management authority. The importance of neighbourhood offices is partly a reflection of the strength of locally based interest groups, but is also partly a consequence of the lack of a strategic capacity (through party organisation) among the elected representatives. As a result, conflicts over the use of facilities and the allocation of time for particular sports is resolved locally as are issues regarding facility development. While this has the possible advantage of responsiveness to majority preferences, it does make it difficult for recreation centres to schedule time for minority sports, new sports and for meeting the needs of women and ethnic minority groups. In summary, while the range of facilities is impressive, it is often difficult to provide specialist facilities for minority interests which could be met only if planned on a city-wide basis.

Although the city has a substantial commitment to direct service provision, there is also a well-established tradition of partnerships with voluntary groups, and particularly provincial sports organisations, according to which the city will, for example, provide a facility with the provincial sports organisation or club providing coaching and having responsibility for officiating and league organisation. Probably the most important partnership that the city has is with the two school boards (one state and one Catholic). Under the agreement, which has existed for over twenty years, most community recreation centres are integral parts of school campuses with the school having priority or exclusive use during school hours and with community use at other times. In addition, the city has similar arrangements with neighbourhood groups, professional sports clubs (such as basketball and ice hockey) and, increasingly, private developers.

Despite what appears to be an enviable position for leisure services in the city, there are increasing signs of strain due primarily to the financial pressures affecting the entire local government system in Canada. For example, the renegotiation of community use agreements with schools is having to cope with increasing friction over the apportionment of maintenance and running costs. The city is also seeking partnerships which involve a more limited financial commitment, for example, with the more affluent clubs concerned with racquet sports or with semi-commercial organisations. Most significantly, the city is considering the long-term viability of its commitment to free access to facilities. Finally, there is growing pressure from the provincial and federal levels to emphasise those aspects of the service that contribute most clearly to welfare goals, particularly where the young, ethnic minorities and the unemployed are concerned.

It is not surprising that Ottawa shares many of the policy concerns of Toronto and has undergone very similar administrative reorganisations. Like Toronto, the city of Ottawa's internal structure was recently, in 1995, reorganised into four broad-based departments with parks and recreation forming part of a Community Services Department which also includes the fire service and cultural services. The city is the most significant provider of leisure services, but there is some overlap with a number of other agencies and levels of government including Parks Canada and Agriculture Canada, both of which control major parklands in the city. Other important organisations include: the National Capital Commission which has a broad planning responsibility for Ottawa; and the Regional Municipality of Ottawa–Carleton, which has a broad land-use planning function and a specific involvement in parks and recreation services because of its ownership of major facilities, such as the Marlborough Forest.

Ottawa is also similar to Toronto in having a highly decentralised pattern of service administration based at the neighbourhood level. Thus the city's 325 parks and 138 built facilities are all covered by a series of neighbourhood plans. The emphasis on the neighbourhood is a reflection of the strength of local activism and also the clientelistic nature of local representation where councillors are much more dependent on the goodwill and support of their electorate owing to the weakness of local political parties. One important consequence of the strength of community interest groups is that they are valuable in defending local leisure services against expenditure cuts but also hamper the development of a more rational service strategy. Over recent years Ottawa's budget has been cut from Can$350m. to Can$250m. largely through the transfer of responsibility for police to the region but also because of budget cuts of over Can$20m. The city also faced a budget cut of Can$ 7–12m. for 1996–7. During a round of public consultation it was made apparent through a survey that parks and recreation, with a budget of Can$18m., was not a key service and was ranked twelfth behind services such as public protection and highways. A particular problem for the Community Services department is that the bulk of its budget is accounted for by the fire service which is largely immune from cuts. However, when the department proposed to cut seven wading pools as part of its contribution to the required savings, the strength of local lobbying forced the abandonment of the plan and its replacement with an agreement to close all pools for one day each week. Similarly, when there was a proposal to rationalise the provision of community centres in the Glebe area by closing two centres in need of extensive and expensive refurbishment and building a new centre adjoining an existing sports complex, local opposition forced councillors to abandon their plan and opt for the more expensive policy of refurbishment.

In the 1995–6 budget round the parks and recreation service managed to protect its budget at least to the extent that it suffered cuts no more severe than other major services. If the ability to protect its budget is a reflection of the positive side of community politics, the weakness of strategic service planning and the development of corporate priorities in the city is one of the costs.

As regards co-operation with the city's five school boards, there are well-established shared-use agreements, according to which schools get free access to municipal facilities during school time and, in return, school facilities are available for community use outside school hours. Although most school boards have gradually transferred their 'after school' service to the municipality with the effect of making the relationship less evenly balanced than intended, the city still perceives the policy of shared use as cost effective.

Like Toronto the city of Ottawa has had to face increasing pressure on its budget in the past five years and has been forced to explore ways of maintaining service levels at reduced cost. Although, by comparison with the UK the moves towards privatisation are tentative, they are receiving ever greater consideration (see, for example, Panther 1995; Tindal 1995). To date, the management role in one major new facility, St. Laurent, was put out to tender with the contract being won by the in-house management team. Cost recovery has also been the guiding principle behind the city's attempt to entice an elite AAA baseball team to the area. The city agreed with private companies that if they would meet the cost of the franchise, the city would fund the stadium. The city was able to build a new stadium at no cost to the taxpayer by selling executive boxes, individual seats and advertising space. Other examples of privatisation include the provision of facilities, which are then run by community organisations, and the conscious decision not to provide for some sports, such as squash, on the assumption that the private sector will satisfy the demand. Privatisation, or partnership as the city prefers to refer to the policy, has yet to be extended to many existing facilities and there is a clear wariness among the public sector unions that the most serious consequences of competition with private providers may be felt by their members.

The current strategy within the Department of Community Services is to give greater emphasis to its enabling role or as the department prefers 'a business-like approach [designed to] orchestrate the most cost-effective and efficient provision' (City of Ottawa 1996: 3). In addition, the department has adopted a three-fold categorisation of basic, enhanced and specialised services. Basic services are those that 'benefit all citizens generally', such as open spaces and parkland, and where cost recovery is not a high priority; enhanced services are those where the 'direct participants receive the most of the benefit', such as sports pitches, and consequently cost recovery will be a high priority; finally specialised services are those that 'benefit the participant almost exclusively', such as sports arenas and specialist sports facilities, and where revenue generation is a high priority (City of Ottawa 1996: 10 and 11).

Until very recently it would have been true to say that by comparison with other systems of local government, that found in Canada was characterised by a lower level of local policy innovation and policy momentum. As Redmond noted, the 'implementation of Federal and Provincial policy in the domain of sport has been a major factor in the increasing role of municipal governments' (1985: 317). Local service delivery has normally been accompanied by a high level of provincial, and increasingly, federal oversight (Tindal and Tindal 1984).

Part of the explanation for the general policy passivity of Canadian municipalities lay in the tradition of limited government: even today many local authorities are reluctant to adopt a broader remit for service provision and innovation. The tradition of establishing school and park boards as a means of minimising the intrusion of politics has also had the effect of increasing service fragmentation and making policy co-ordination more difficult to achieve. In addition, it must also be accepted that the generally slow pace of municipal reform, which was itself the product of provincial reluctance to allow the establishment of local authorities which might challenge its power, has encouraged a drift of service responsibility from the local to the provincial level. Finally, the inflexibility of a property-based tax has also limited local initiative.

However, over the past ten to fifteen years there have been developments in Canadian national and provincial politics which have had a significant impact on local government. First, the withdrawal of federal funding from the area of fitness (and recreation) has had a major impact on local provision. Throughout the 1970s and 1980s federal pump-priming funding of municipal projects was a crucial stimulus to policy innovation. However, there was growing concern among the provinces that federal funding was creating an expectation that the provincial government would continue funding once federal interest ceased. Provincial government therefore lobbied Fitness Canada to reduce the extent of its direct funding of municipal programmes. The withdrawal of Fitness Canada from municipal programmes was more abrupt than the provinces and the municipalities had expected and was prompted less by a wish to respond to provincial concerns than by a refocusing of objectives away from a concern with physiological fitness and towards a more holistic conception of 'good health and fitness'. Second, the financial implications of the policy change at federal level was compounded by the election of a number of radical conservative political leaders, most notably in Alberta but also, more recently, in Ontario, committed among other things to a drastic reduction in the scale of the provincial bureaucracy and policy involvement. Among specific changes was the introduction of block rather than specific grants which, in many municipalities, forced parks and recreation to compete with other services.

For many municipalities the consequence of a more hostile financial environment has been the need to explore a wider variety of forms of privatisation including the contracting-out of facility management, public–private sector partnerships, the greater use of volunteers or even the closure of older, less economic facilities (see Vail and Roth 1994; Davis-Jameson 1990; Gair 1994;

and Milton 1994 for examples of recent service innovation). Yet as was seen in Toronto, the adoption of rational decision-making methods with regard to facility planning are frequently thwarted by effective lobbying by sectional interest groups (see Smyth 1992; Crompton and Lamb 1980). Furthermore, costs in the parks and recreation service have tended to rise much faster than inflation and Canadian local authorities have a poor record of cost recovery. In a study of local government in Western Canada between 1980 and 1989, service costs rose 113 per cent, almost twice the inflation rate of 64 per cent with cost recovery declining very slightly from 38 per cent to 37 per cent (Harper and Johnson 1992).

A third development, and a further consequence of Canada's belated engagement with Thatcherite and Reaganite economics, was the drive to return power to the citizen (Robertson and Barlow 1995). In Alberta this objective was realised in a number of ways, including the introduction of 'school-based management' which is designed to undermine the role of school boards. Such a development, should it spread to other provinces, would threaten the stability of many of the shared-use agreements between school boards and municipalities.

Finally, despite the moves in some provinces to promote municipal amalgamation in the pursuit of economies of scale (O'Brien 1993; Tindal 1996) or provincial–local government administrative 'disentanglement' (Sancton 1992) the combination of the growth of defensive neighbourhood activism aimed at protecting local facilities in the face of radical right economics designed to force down municipal budgets, and the possible spread of school-based management will undoubtedly undermine the capacity of local government to plan parks and recreation services strategically.

IRELAND

Centralisation, the distinctive feature of Irish local government, is the product of a number of factors including the sparsity of population, the 'extraordinary degree of Irish clientelism' (Barrington 1991: 167; see also Komito 1984), a history of inefficiency, the disruption caused by the anti-colonial conflict, the civil war that followed independence and, in Barrington's words, 'a lethal mixture of cynicism and neglect' (1991: 156; see also Roche 1982). The changes that have taken place in the structure and functions of local government since independence have generally intensified centralisation, for example, through the removal of significant powers of local taxation in 1977 with the abolition of domestic rates (Knox and Haslem 1994). Where there have been moves to strengthen the capacity of local government, it has tended to be at the expense of local democratic participation, for example, through the introduction of city and county managers, who normally report their decisions to the council with little expectation that they will be overturned (Collins and McCann 1993: 99; see also Collins 1987). The widespread appointment of city and county managers has both strengthened the centre and furthered weakened local democracy. Although there have been a number of attempts to protect the policy-making role of the council in relation to the manager, they have generally failed to stop a steady expansion of the manager's role to encompass policy-making. However, it should be noted that the expansion of the manager's role has been largely uncontentious for 'though there may be a semblance of conflict when councillors at meetings may wish to be seen as championing the interests of those who elected them as against the tyranny of the bureaucracy . . . real conflict is rare' (Dooney and O'Toole 1992: 140). Of particular importance is the role of the manager as a major link between the centre and the locality for the dissemination of national policies (McManus 1993).

In addition, the role of the TD (Teachtá Dala – member of parliament) tends to limit and undermine the role of the local councillor. TDs (a substantial number of whom are also councillors) tend to be closely involved in local matters, such as planning decisions and project development, which frequently leaves the councillor with only the most trivial of issues to handle. The local focus of the TD also has the effect of encouraging interest groups to focus their activities on the centre either directly or via the local TD. Where interests groups do operate at local level they tend to bypass councillors and communicate directly with the city or county manager. But interest group activity at local level is slight and particularly so for cultural and sporting interest groups (Collins and McCann 1993: 104 and 105). The vogue for regionalism and the tendency to introduce *ad hoc* regional bodies, often as a way of compensating for the weaknesses of local government, has the effect of further undermining the vitality of local democracy and strengthening the hold of the centre. The 'indifference to the place of local democracy in the modern [Irish] nation state' (Barrington 1991: 155) provides a general explanatory context for both the current position and the absence of any substantial ground swell of electoral discontent at the current position. There is little opposition to an agency model of central–local government relations and a highly marginal role for local democracy. Finally, the financial position of local government reinforces the drift to centralisation. While Ireland ranks beside Sweden and Denmark as a country where public expenditure accounts for a high proportion of GDP, it is near the bottom of rankings based on the proportion of GDP spent by local government. In the late 1980s when public expenditure accounted for almost 50 per cent of GDP, the percentage of total public expenditure accounted for by local government was only 15 per cent.

Not surprisingly, Irish local government has a much narrower range of functions than that found in most other European countries. By comparison with Italy, France and Switzerland, where thirty-one services are provided by local government, and Britain, where the figure is twenty-seven, the total for Ireland is only ten. In general, Irish local government is confined to dealing with environmental matters and some limited cultural services, including sport and recreation.

In 1994 IR£1,123m. was spent on local government services with some IR£116m. being spent on recreation and amenity services, which included swimming pools, libraries, parks, open spaces and recreation centres. Of total local government expenditure, by far the largest proportion was spent by county councils (IR£740m.) followed by city boroughs (IR£296m.) and urban districts (IR£87m.). The main source of income came in the form of central government grants which totalled IR£424m., with IR£393m. raised through the sale of goods and services and the remaining element, IR£305m., raised locally through commercial rates.

Table 4.2 shows that the volume of recreation and amenity expenditure has remained fairly steady over the past decade, while Table 4.3 shows that it has grown steadily as a proportion of total local government expenditure.

Part of the explanation for the relative success of recreation and amenity service advocates in defending their budget lies in the gradual expansion in the scope of the policy area. From an initial limited concern with the provision of modest leisure facilities for the local community, the service is now seen as part of the tourist industry and investment in leisure facilities is increasingly judged by its capacity to attract tourist expenditure as well as its capacity to meet local leisure needs. A closely related element in the overall explanation is the receptiveness of the European Union to tourism-related

Table 4.2 Expenditure patterns for recreation and amenity services, 1985–94 (IR£m.)

Year	Pools	Libraries	Parks, open spaces and other recreation centres	Other recreation	Administration and misc.	Total
1985	6.3	25.3	23.1	10.3	13.5	78.5
1986	9.8	24.2	32.6	16.0	20.8	103.4
1987	6.5	27.4	30.3	17.5	25.0	106.7
1988	6.6	26.0	30.8	16.3	30.3	110.0
1989	6.4	24.1	30.1	17.0	7.9	85.5
1990	6.9	25.3	34.7	18.1	7.3	92.3
1991	7.3	27.8	38.8	19.7	6.9	100.5
1992	8.0	28.0	38.4	19.1	7.6	101.1
1993	7.4	29.2	44.7	14.9	9.4	105.6
1994	7.4	31.0	50.2	16.7	10.8	116.1

Source: Department of the Environment, local authority estimates, various years (Stationery Office, Dublin).

infrastructure bids and the priority for EU funding that Ireland has held over the past fifteen years (O'Toole 1995). The EU has recently provided 75 per cent funding for a number of major weather-independent water-based schemes such as Waterworld at the seaside resort of Bundoran.

Although funding looks relatively buoyant, there are some serious problems, particularly concerning the mismatch between the demand for central government support for schemes and the sum available to the Department of Education. In 1994–5, for example, the Department of Education had IR£6m. available to fund IR£60m. project bids under the Recreational Facilities Scheme and the Major Facilities Programme. Swimming poses particular problems as there were recently 30 bids for grant aid totalling IR£30m. competing for an allocation of IR£1.3m. in 1993–4 and IR£2m. in 1994–5 (Holohan 1995: 3).

Within local authorities the organisational location of sport and recreation services is strongly influenced by the grouping, since 1976, of services into eight programme areas. Sport and recreation are located within the 'Recreation and amenity' programme head which covers parks, swimming pools, libraries, museums, art galleries and national monuments. While not all authorities use the programme groupings as a template for departmental organisation, it is the most common basis for the allocation of function.

One of the distinctive features of the organisation of service delivery at local authority level is the frequency with which specific recreation facilities are managed by bodies outside the local authority such as sports clubs,

Table 4.3 Proportion of total local authority expenditure allocated to recreation and amenity services, 1982–94

Year	%
1982	6.17
1983	6.34
1984	5.61
1985	5.48
1986	6.77
1987	6.31
1988	8.47
1989	8.32
1990	8.41
1991	8.62
1992	8.5
1993	9.67
1994	10.08

Source: Department of the Environment, local authority estimates, various years (Stationery Office, Dublin).

voluntary management committees or private companies operating under licence from the county manager. Dublin, for example, has a wide range of sporting and recreational facilities including eight swimming pools, 261 playing pitches, 190 tennis courts, five golf courses, and five leisure/sports centres of which three are managed by the community.

Outside Dublin the use of non-local authority management is even more common. In South Tipperary county two of the three swimming pools are managed by an independent management committee (Ahearn 1995). For example, the pool at Clonmel, built in the early 1970s, closed in 1989 owing largely to underinvestment in maintenance, which was partly the result of dissatisfaction with the operation of the facility. The pool reopened in 1991 following a major refurbishment, but while the county retained ownership of the facility, a management committee was established comprising leisure-services senior officers, elected members and community representatives. The management of the pool is left in the hands of the manager and the committee with the county retaining responsibility for maintenance. A similar arrangement exists at the pool at Carrick-on-Suir. For all three swimming pools the county strategy is to set commercial targets for the manager and to use the management committee more as a buffer between the management and the council and the public sector unions rather than as a mechanism for controlling or overseeing the decisions of the facility manager. Marren, commenting on the decision by Dublin County Council to establish a Board of Management to run the new Loughlinstown Leisure Centre, refers to the fact that the management of other leisure facilities by the county had 'all become a source of concern – over staffing, restrictive practices, declining numbers using facilities, poor marketing (and) high costs of maintenance' (1995). In part, this is a reflection of the desire to bypass public sector unions, but it is also a reflection of a long-established practice whereby local authorities were able to choose whether to undertake a project themselves or whether to contribute to its completion by others. For example, under the terms of the 1955 Local Government Act, authorities could develop swimming pools themselves or support their development, possibly by a local swimming club (Roche 1982: 268–9).

Given the general weakness of local government, it is not surprising that sport and recreation provision and planning at local level is poor. Perhaps the major problem is the number of factors that conspire to prevent the development of a strategic service planning capacity within recreation and amenity departments. First, there is the dependence of the local authority on a DoE grant to fund new facilities. The party political nature of the decision-making process, which gives a prominent role to the TD, marginalises the role of local authority service professionals. To an extent, professional judgement is incorporated into the decision-making process through the use of the Institute of Leisure and Amenity Management (ILAM) as an independent source of advice on the appropriateness and viability of individual schemes. However, while it true to say that a scheme is highly unlikely to be supported if it does not receive ILAM approval, the willingness of politicians to refer projects to ILAM is only partly a desire for an element of rationality in their deliberations. Frequently politicians will use ILAM reports to deflect criticism from themselves when projects are rejected. A final difficulty with the current decision-making processes is that while some much-needed schemes fail to acquire political support, others receive a grant but remain half completed because of the inability of the local community to make available the matching funding.

Second, the capacity to plan strategically is undermined by the concern to bypass the strong public sector unions. The designation of sports and recreation facilities as community resources and the consequent transfer of management to a committee or board results in a distinct loss of capacity on the part of the county to move much beyond the use of financial objectives as tools of strategic planning. Third, strategic service planning is further weakened by the dominance of the tourism policy paradigm which distorts attempts to respond to local community need or the needs of particular sports for specialist facilities. Fourth, while it is true that the total amount of public funding available for sport and recreation provision has increased in recent years, doubts have been voiced about the appropriateness of its distribution. Investment in facilities tends to be incremental and *ad hoc* rather than strategic, to the extent that it would be extremely difficult for either the government or most individual local authorities to demonstrate that their investment programme is giving value for money (Stanton 1995).

The review of local government completed in 1991 offers little prospect of any significant change in the status and scope of local government. The legislation that followed made some changes to boundaries (Local Government (Dublin) Act 1993), and also restated the powers and functions of local authorities (1991 and 1994 Local Government Acts). However, the changes have done little to alter the fundamental relationship between central and local government. The creation of regional authorities, which offered the possibility of a reduction in central authority have been a disappointment. It appears that 'regions' have been established primarily to provide a framework more supportive of EU funding bids. In addition, the Minister made it clear in the Dáil that the Regional Authorities would not be local authorities 'in the normal sense'. Knox and Haslem (1994: 69) observe that the situation in the Republic is mirrored by the state of flux in the relationship found in Northern Ireland and is not peculiar to the south. The distrust of local democracy by the centre and the lack of enthusiasm for it among the electorate make it unlikely that there will be any significant change in the role of local authorities in recreation and leisure services in the foreseeable future. Indeed, the 1991 report of the Advisory Committee paid scant attention to recreation, tending to subsume it under heritage or tourism (Government of Ireland 1991: 23). The recent comment of one county manager that 'it is abundantly clear that there is a crucial need for a strengthened local government to continue to provide relevant essential public services into the next century' (Bradley 1995: 5) echoes similar comments that long pre-date the recent round of reform and suggest that reform has simply streamlined centralism rather than weakened it.

UNITED KINGDOM

For most of this century, up until the mid-1970s, local government in the UK was complex, but stable. In 1974 the government introduced sweeping changes to a system which had become dated because of urbanisation, population growth and a steady expansion in the range of services delivered by local authorities. The period since 1974 has been characterised by continual tinkering with the structure, the powers of local authorities and the method of funding. Currently, England has a mix of unitary and two-tier authorities. Unitary authorities deliver all local government services and generally are found in the major cities and larger towns. The rest of the country has a two-tier system of counties with a number of districts within them. Wales, Scotland and Northern Ireland have a pattern of unitary authorities (see Table 4.4). Local government in the UK is responsible for a broadly similar range of services with the exception of Northern Ireland, where the range is significantly more restricted .

The continuing sectarian division is the primary reason for the different pattern of functions in Northern Ireland. While local government in Britain has substantial responsibility for major services such as public sector housing and education in Northern Ireland, these functions are the

Table 4.4   The distribution of responsibilities for sport and recreation in the United Kingdom

Service	Unitary Councils	County Councils	England District Councils	Wales, Scotland and Northern Ireland District Councils
Outdoor sport	*		*	*
Indoor sports facilities	*		*	*
Informal outdoor urban recreation	*		*	*
Countryside recreation	*	*		*

Note: The table indicates the primary provider of the various services and does not indicate exclusive provision.

responsibility of central government (the Northern Ireland Office) due, primarily, to the misuse of public housing allocation powers as a means of manipulating the composition of the electorate and maintaining sectarian privilege. Sport, along with tourism, are among the small number of significant services left to the province's local authorities to administer.

As in many other countries, sport and recreation emerged as a discrete local government service in the late 1960s and early 1970s. Its emergence was stimulated partly by the creation of new public agencies such as the Countryside Commission in 1968 and the British Sports Council in 1972, which encouraged the development of new types of facilities such as sports and leisure centres, and country parks, and which coincided with a rapid growth in both free time and disposable income (Veal and Travis 1979). The development of the service was also stimulated by the discussion of structural reform of local government and particularly the appropriate internal organisation of the new authorities. There was a consensus that not only should there be a small number of departments, but also that one of the departments should provide a specific focus on recreation and leisure. Although responsibility for leisure services remained fragmented in some authorities, the restructuring did result in the creation of a larger number of specialist leisure services departments, a trend that peaked in the late 1980s but has since slightly reversed.

Financially, local government in the UK, as in the US and Ireland, has been under sustained pressure in recent years. From a position in the late 1970s when local government had relatively buoyant expenditure levels and considerable financial autonomy, particularly over the level of the local property tax (domestic and commercial rates), local authorities now operate in a financial environment where their expenditure is tightly controlled by central government and where allocative discretion is more limited. Given a steadily worsening environment for local government, it is surprising that leisure services which, with the exception of Northern Ireland, are not statutory have been able to maintain their relative share of total local expenditure. In 1979 expenditure on leisure services accounted for 4.8 per cent of total local government expenditure; the figure peaked in 1984 at 5.0 per cent before dropping back to 4.8 per cent in 1993. However, leisure services have not been immune from cuts in public expenditure. Although both capital and revenue expenditure grew steadily in absolute terms during the 1970s, they levelled off in the late 1980s and since the early 1990s have declined, only marginally with regard to revenue but sharply (from £300m. in 1989–90 to £130m. in 1992–3) in the case of capital.

The sharp decline in capital expenditure in recent years should not detract from the enormous growth in facility provision that took place between 1960 and the late 1980s. For example, 84 per cent of current swimming pool area was provided between 1960 and 1989. There has been an equally dramatic growth in the provision of sports halls, with their number increasing from under 300 in 1970 to 700 in 1981 and 1500 in 1991. As these figures show, the growth in the significance of local authority involvement has been recent, rapid and accomplished without the benefit of a statutory foundation on which to base bids for central government funding.

Explaining the relative stability of spending on leisure and recreational services by local authorities is difficult, but is partly explained by the diversity and evolution of policy objectives. While part of the stability of local expenditure can be explained by the strength of popular demand for a widening of provision, part of the explanation lies in the increasingly common perception of leisure services, by both central and local government, as an element in economic development. During the 1980s, as the government's regional policy has been wound down, local authorities have become more concerned to market their area to investors, and recreational and cultural facilities are seen as important in attracting investment. Also, for many areas, tourism has been identified as a potential growth industry and this has resulted in local expenditure on the sport and leisure infrastructure as well as on the promotion of special leisure events such as sports and arts festivals.

As indicated earlier, Northern Ireland (also referred to as Ulster) is an exception to many generalisations about the pattern of responsibility for sport at local level and the nature of local policy processes in the UK. But what makes Northern Ireland especially interesting is the explicit use, by both the Labour and Conservative parties, of sport and recreation as a tool of social engineering. Displaying a disturbingly high level of historical naiveté, mainland political parties perceived sport and leisure as 'an area of personal opinion, freedom and choice, and as such a "de politicised" arena, properly outside the realm of adversarial politics' (Coalter *et al.* 1986: 127). Forgetting the significance of sport and the GAA in fostering Irish nationalism the central government attempted to use sport and recreation as an instrument to build bridges across the sectarian divide in cities such as Derry and Belfast by designating the service as one of the few to remain at local level (Sugden and Bairner 1986 and 1993; Holmes 1994; Bairner 1994).

The Local Government (Northern Ireland) Act 1972, which reorganised local government in the province, was the outcome of a compromise between the desire for management efficiency and service effectiveness on the one hand and the reality of sectarian politics on the other. The new district councils were responsible for the delivery of a narrow range of comparatively minor services such as refuse collection and disposal, burial grounds and crematoria, tourist amenities and recreation. Within this range, recreation was a relatively important and, it must be added, in contrast to England and Wales, a mandatory service. Starting in the early 1970s from a poorer base of provision than the rest of the UK, Northern Ireland benefited from substantial investment in the following twenty years. Relying heavily on the advice of the Northern Ireland Sports Council, local authorities developed a wide range of good-quality facilities (Knox 1987). The methods used to determine need and location were a mixture of spatial analysis combined with the notion of a hierarchy of provision throughout the province. This rational approach to location and type was supported by the Northern Ireland Office, which perceived the investment as a key means of reducing the level of intercommunal tension.

Despite the level of central government commitment, it soon became clear that leisure services were no more immune from sectarian politics than housing or education had been. The location of new facilities in particular was used by the various religious/political factions as a means of seeking sectarian advantage. Location was determined less by rational planning than by the political need to be seen to be even-handed in investment in Catholic and Protestant areas (Knox 1986 and 1987). While leisure investment has had little effect on sectarian politics, it has left both Derry and Belfast with an enviable range and quality of facilities. However, the peculiarities of Northern Ireland politics make it difficult to determine the impact that the statutory nature of sport and recreation services in the province has had on overall levels of investment.

Within the UK generally, the most significant policy change in the past ten years, even acknowledging the growing financial problems, is the introduction of privatisation, in the form of compulsory competitive tendering (CCT). As part of a policy to reduce the size of the public sector and to introduce 'market discipline' to those elements that remained, the government introduced CCT in 1988 for a range of government services (Clarke 1994). The essence of CCT within the leisure services policy area was that while the local authority would retain ownership of the facility, its management would be subject to a process of competitive tendering with contract periods running for four to five years. CCT was introduced for leisure services in 1992 with government expecting a reduction in management costs of 20 per cent (Audit Commission 1989: 17). While most local authorities successfully prepared an in-house tender in the face of competition from private companies, a major consequence of CCT has been to worsen the pay and conditions of public employees as in-house management teams sought to reduce costs in order to compete with private sector companies (Henry 1993).

As might be expected there was considerable apprehension about (and opposition to) the introduction of CCT and although it is early in the life of the policy, it is possible to draw some tentative conclusions about its impact on provision. On the positive side CCT has reinforced pressure from the Sports Council for local authorities to prepare strategic plans for sport and recreation. Unfortunately, not only is the pace of plan preparation slow, but there is evidence to suggest that even when they are available the extent to which plans are used as a basis for constructing the tender specification is limited. Although the client (the local authority) may use the plan to set explicit targets regarding particular priority groups and sports development activity, it is often the case that these are substantially ignored by the contractor, even when the contract is won in-house. Indeed, recent research suggests that CCT has had the effect of marginalising sports development activity. 'In many cases sports development objectives are becoming irrelevant to what local authority facilities are actually delivering' (Sports Council 1993). Part of the problem lies in the failure of the client to match the tender specification to the strategic plan and also the failure to monitor progress towards the objectives set in the tender specification. The collection of reliable management information by the contractor is often poor and the capacity of the client to analyse data is often inadequate.

There is a clear tension within many privatised sports facilities between the financial objectives and those relating to elements of the service, such as sports development, which generate little revenue. The overriding concern of management is to meet income targets even if this means giving priority in bookings to established sports, such as five-a-side soccer, in preference to the creation of opportunities to develop new sports and activities.

Although the initial assessments of the impact of CCT are negative, there are one or two more positive views. In the early days of the policy the Regional Councils for Sport and Recreation hoped that local authorities would think more creatively about how they could achieve their policy objectives. The most promising examples to date include a number of schemes which involve closer links between voluntary clubs and local authority sports facilities. In one authority the local badminton club has agreed to provide coaching for the public (casual user) in return for lower hire charges for courts; in another the swimming club has agreed to provide coaching at the sports centre in return for cheaper hire rates for club activities. It is this latter example which is developing fastest as clubs offer coaching expertise to the public in exchange for reduced user fees.

Despite these promising examples of innovative co-operation between the public and the voluntary sectors, the key question remains whether CCT will undermine the rapid progress in increasing participation that took place in the 1980s. On the basis of the information available so far, it would seem that the quantity of participation may continue to expand but that the quality of the participants' experience, especially when assessed in terms of choice, may deteriorate.

Apart from the introduction of CCT, the other major policy innovation in recent years has been the attempt to develop greater shared use of facilities owned or controlled by different branches of the public sector. The policy of community use covers a broad range of facilities, mainly those controlled by schools, but has also been applied to those controlled by private companies, government departments, colleges and universities. The prime target for this policy has been the extensive sports facilities attached to schools, which generally are open only during term time and school hours and where use is restricted to pupils. Ideally under community use, once the pupils have gone home the facility would be available for use by members of the local community. Walsall is an example of a successful community-use scheme where a network of schools is the basis for a hierarchy of provision ranging from simple facilities available at local primary schools, through more sophisticated and specialist facilities at secondary schools, to specially built centres of excellence (*Sport and Leisure* 1985; Nixon 1985). The additional revenue and maintenance costs are subject to a separate agreement between the education and leisure services departments.

The expansion of community use offers a cost-effective means of creating greater recreational opportunities but the potential is slow to be exploited. In large part, the problem stems from the unwillingness of many schools to co-operate often because of disagreements over management arrangements or because of a suspicion that the school will be left to meet the costs of the replacement of equipment. Finally, with an increasing number of schools opting to move from local authority control to a more autonomous, grant-aided relationship with central government, there is an increasing tendency for schools to see that sports facilities are their own assets rather than those of the community.

In conclusion, local government sport and recreation departments face a policy environment that is more uncertain than in previous years. Of particular concern is the decline in capital expenditure. More serious than the obvious effects of the reduction in the development of new facilities is the difficulty of financing the refurbishment of existing facilities. The pattern of construction which peaked in the mid-1970s has resulted in many facilities, especially swimming pools, requiring major refurbishment during the late 1990s. Estimates suggested that some £63m. will be required to be spent each year from 1995 to 2000 to cover the cost of refurbishment (Sports Council 1995). In addition, there remain many areas of underprovision particularly in the inner cities, but also in a number of rural areas. Equally worrying is the exclusion of local government from any role in the current central government policy statement – 'Raising the Game' published in 1995. While the policy document discusses at length the role of the Sports Councils, commercial sector, voluntary sector, schools, colleges and universities, it makes only passing reference to local government.

More generally, local government's key role in fostering the widening of mass participation is under threat partly as a result of financial pressures but mainly due to the introduction of CCT, which has had the effect of homogenising provision and reducing the incentive to take risks with innovative policies designed to attract underparticipating groups such as certain ethnic minorities and age groups.

However, all is not gloom for local government. The guidelines for distribution of the proceeds of the National Lottery give a priority to proposals aimed at mass participation in under-resourced areas and changes to the application procedure have recently been introduced to make it easier for schemes in poorer areas to be supported by relaxing the requirements to raise matching funding. In addition, despite the lack of enthusiasm among many schools for community-use schemes, there is strong government support for a more intensive use of educational facilities by the community. It remains to be seen whether the statements of support will be turned into

policies to require or at least encourage, greater co-operation in the implementation of the policy. Finally, one consequence of the increasing financial
pressure on local authorities has been a greater willingness to develop joint
projects with local voluntary clubs, many of which successfully combine the
coaching expertise of the club with the facilities of the local authority. In
brief, the quality and quantity of provision at local government level is a
significant achievement but the challenge for the future is to protect the
gains made in the face of privatisation, expenditure cuts and a central
government which is antipathetic to local government.

THE UNITED STATES

In the overview of the structure of American government given in Chapter
2, local government was summarised as being characterised by fragmentation and a proliferation of administrative units. In addition, there is only a
limited pattern to the distribution of function, although parks and recreation services (the most common title for departments responsible for sport,
leisure and recreation provision) tended to be located with city and county
authorities. Finally, while the lack of a formal constitutional link between
the federal government and local government was noted, the ability of the
former to exert influence over the latter through grant-aid arrangements was
acknowledged.

Most sport and recreational services are located at the city or county level,
but there are some state-level services, usually those associated with the
management of major natural resources, such as bays, forests, lakes and parks,
which are seen as regional facilities and are also normally beyond city boundaries. It has been estimated that states are responsible for almost 14m. acres of
parkland, with 675m. person visits per year and an expenditure of $800m.
(Kraus 1990: 223). Some states have used their involvement in regional facilities as an opportunity to establish agencies designed to co-ordinate state and
local recreational provision, but in general the level of co-ordination between
lower-tier units and the state is slight. Where states do establish an administrative sub-structure for parks and recreation, it is often with the intention of
stimulating tourism or other forms of economic exploitation of the resources
rather than to achieve improved service co-ordination.

In general, the role of state agencies is marginal compared with the
involvement of municipal and county authorities. Both these units are the
creation of the state, which will also grant and determine their powers. As in
all industrialised countries the process of urbanisation has resulted in city
boundaries rapidly becoming outdated. In some cases states have responded
to this development by enforcing mergers between city and county units
with the former effectively incorporating the latter: in other cases the state
will establish a special district to exercise responsibility for particular
services including parks and recreation. However, in many instances the
state simply leaves the municipal and county authorities to work together as

best they can. The preference for special districts creates particular problems of service co-ordination. As Hjelte and Shivers noted in the late 1970s, 'So intent are these governmental entities in carrying out their narrow tasks that they fail to observe the effects that their total disregard of other functions promotes' (1978: 31).

It is at the city level that the core facilities and opportunities for sport and recreation are found. Although municipalities derive their powers from the state, they are generally sufficiently broad to allow a generous interpretation of service provision. Where state legislatures have been restrictive, it has frequently been the case that state courts have supported city governments in their attempts to develop recreational provision with liberal interpretations of existing legislation. For most cities the power to provide a recreational service is derived from the city charter, which will normally identify the responsible department, create a board or commission (appointed by the elected members of the city or common council) to exercise oversight of the work of the superintendent/director and the department, advise on policy and define the scope of the service.

The use of commissions (lay expert appointments made by the council to oversee a service) as the organisational form for the administration of recreational services is still to be found, but it is increasingly common to find recreational services organised under the auspices of a city manager or mayor and council. Under the city-manager structure the council will employ a city manager to act as the 'chief executive' on its behalf taking responsibility for the efficient and effective management of the city's services and its various departments. The mayor and council operate in a similar fashion to the city manager except that the 'chief executive' role is taken by the elected mayor.

Up until the 1960s it was still common for municipalities to have separate parks and recreation (P&R) departments but combined departments are now the norm. Although the P&R department is the primary provider, other municipal departments have some involvement in the service. For example, police departments often run youth sports leagues, youth boards operate outreach programmes for teenage gangs, and public housing departments may operate recreation centres. Outside the municipality one of the most significant providers of recreational opportunities is the school system. Throughout the twentieth century school codes have been broadened by legislation or liberal court rulings to enable school districts to make school facilities available for community sports use. The extensive use of school facilities for recreation is partly the consequence of the long tradition in America which places the school at the centre of community life, and partly an acknowledgement that municipal recreation departments have rarely been able to cope with the rising demand for recreational opportunities. The most common form of school involvement in the recreation service is through the provision of a summer recreational programme, either under the direct supervision of school staff or with external staff. There is also an increasing number of examples of year-round recreation programmes frequently funded partly by tax income and partly by charitable foundations.

However, it must be noted that enabling legislation does not create an obligation on the part of the school board and while community use of school facilities is extensive, it is still highly variable between states. Where community use has been established, it is often very difficult to achieve a high level of co-operation between schools and the municipality. In many areas the school service is the responsibility of a separate political and administrative entity, the school board/district. Not only is there a problem arising from the ambiguity over the role of school districts in providing sport and recreational facilities, but there is the more common problem of tension between city and school districts which inhibits co-operation. As Hjelte and Shivers noted, municipal and school services are 'difficult to co-ordinate and probably impossible to consolidate' (1978: 35).

Despite the serious problems of co-ordination that the relationship between schools and municipal recreation departments poses, the school fulfils an important role in meeting urban recreational demand. In rural areas the potential significance of the school service is even greater. Given the sparsity of population in many rural areas in America and the frequent inaccessibility of city facilities, the provision of recreational opportunities poses a major problem. In many rural areas recreational needs are met through a combination of voluntary provision often involving the YM/WCA and organisations, such as the Farmer's Union and the National Grange (which have a specific interest in protecting farming communities), school boards and county local government.

Unlike city government, county authorities are more the creatures of the state and are best seen as administrative sub-divisions of states rather than an assertion of the demand for popular control of services, which prompts the petition for city status. Counties consequently have far less scope for extending their range of responsibilities although there has been an increase in the willingness of states to grant some discretionary powers. Where counties are involved in recreational service provision, it is often in connection with the management of resource-based, as opposed to built, facilities. Wilderness parks, beaches and landscaped parks, which tend to have a regional function, are the most common facilities managed by the counties.

To the outsider probably the most striking feature of the American parks and recreation service is the range and quantity of publicly provided facilities. In some of the country's largest cities over 10 per cent of total land is parkland: Phoenix, 29,460 acres of parkland equivalent to 11.9 per cent of total land; Baltimore, 6,480 acres, 12.3 per cent; San Francisco, 3,300 acres, 11.1 per cent; and New York, 26,140 acres, 13.5 per cent. Taking New York as an example, of the 26,140 acres that the city is responsible for, most, just under 80 per cent, is open parkland.[1] In addition the city provides: 838 playgrounds, of which 226 are jointly managed with the Board of Education; 2,009 basketball courts; 1,885 handball courts; 760 baseball fields; 627

tennis courts; 13 golf courses; 6 skating rinks; 46 swimming pools and 33 mini pools; 183 recreational buildings; 12 miles of running paths; and 5 zoos. Funding for the P&R service in New York has been drastically affected by a succession of economic crises which, while more severe in New York, have been a general feature of most city administrations since the late 1970s. Following a steady rise in expenditure (measured in constant dollars) to just under $190m. in 1978, operating expenditure declined sharply to $148m. in 1984, recovered to $188m. in 1988, only to embark on another period of sharp decline to a budget of $109m. in 1992. Parks and recreation services fared badly during the mid- to late 1980s. The dramatic reduction or termination of many federal funding programmes severely affected local provision. Of particular importance was the termination of Community Development Block Grants and the CETA (Comprehensive Employment and Training Programme) which caused the near 'collapse of many park systems as personnel cuts had to be made' (Shivers 1993: 113).

More significantly, and in sharp contrast to major cities in the UK, the P&R budget for New York has been relatively more vulnerable to budget cuts than other services. As Brecher *et al.* (1993) demonstrate, P&R spending as a proportion of the total city budget has steadily declined from an average of 1.5 per cent between 1945 and 1955 to 0.6 per cent in 1979, and following a slight rise during the 1980s dropped again to 0.6 per cent in the early 1990s. They conclude that: 'Experience . . . suggests that the DPR [the Department of Parks and Recreation] will continue to suffer reductions substantially in excess of citywide averages' (1993: 324). The most obvious consequence of the cuts in budgets has been a significant decline in the quality of the service as measured across a range of performance indicators with, for example, a fall of 52 per cent in participation in structured recreational activities. One further consequence of the decline in tax income has been to encourage the pursuit of alternative sources of resources. In recent years the granting of concessions, whereby private companies will manage publicly owned facilities has rapidly grown. Currently, all the city's golf courses and five of its ice rinks are operated through concessions. Although the city loses the direct fee income, it receives an annual fee from the concessionaire and has no maintenance obligations. A further service innovation, though one which has been opposed by the unions (Kraus 1990), has been the development of voluntary organisations, often underwritten by corporate resources such as the Central Park Conservancy established in 1980, which has provided over $16m. for capital projects and also many thousands of hours of voluntary labour.

In general, there has been little attempt to generate systematically additional income either through corporate philanthropy or from increases in user fees. Part of the explanation lies in the difficulty of introducing policy change in a political system which is, at times, gridlocked by competing vested political, union and corporate interests. But part of the explanation also lies in the relative lack of salience of parks and recreation issues over many years within the Democrat-dominated political administration. This lack of administrative and funding innovation is not typical of American cities.

The fiscal problems facing New York and other cities such as Oakland are common, but Crompton and McGregor caution against a too ready assumption of underfunding. Indeed in contradiction to the New York experience, they argue that:

> In the broad context of the United States as a whole, park and recreation interests have been relatively successful in fending off disproportionate cuts in their budgets in difficult times, but have been less successful in securing proportionate increases in budgets when economic conditions improve.

> (Crompton and McGregor 1994: 29)

The authors also note that in parallel with the pressure on budgets that the 'range of services, intensity of use and number of facilities have all increased' (ibid.: 36). Colorado Springs is among those cities which, while not immune from the problems arising from fiscal pressures, has managed to protect the profile of its parks and recreation service with considerable success. In 1994–5 the service received 8.5 per cent of the total city budget ($11.8m.), a figure which has remained steady for the past ten years. The city also benefits by $3.5m. from the state lottery which is used for land acquisition, development and maintenance. Although politically conservative with strong anti-tax sentiments, the P&R budget has been protected due in large part to effective lobbying by local interest groups (such as the Springs Area Beautiful Association and the Council of Neighbourhood Organisations), which have managed to exclude the service from successive rounds of finance cuts. Second, the city has buoyant inward corporate investment and sees public expenditure on the maintenance of the quality of the general environment as of key importance. Third, the city has a highly mobile middle class (the average period of residence is under six years) which views investment in P&R as an important contribution to the maintenance of property values. Finally, P&R staff argue that a peculiarity of Colorado Springs is that virtually all sports activities take place in municipal parks, which fosters a very positive image of the facilities with the electorate.

However, even in a city which, by comparison with New York, has such a different experience of service development and priority, there are many policy similarities; most clearly in relation to privatisation. As in New York there is extensive use of commercial concessions as a means of generating income, but the most striking recent development has been the extent to which the revenue side of service provision has been transferred to voluntary sector partners. For example, voluntary organisations now organise youth soccer with the city only providing the pitches. Similarly, the city's ice rink is rented to a local club which also provides a coaching service to the general public. The city has also attempted to establish community use of the local Air Force Academy's huge sports resources but success has been variable because of dependence upon the attitude of the incumbent Commandant.[2] However, community use arrangements with the University of Colorado and Colorado College have been more successful.

Other important partnerships include those with the school districts. In the mid-1970s the city took the decision to reduce its investment in separate P&R facilities and to channel its funding towards the provision of community schools which agreed to include P&R facilities. Success has been variable but generally good. Of the twelve school districts in the city only one has refused to co-operate. Although financial pressures have led to an increase in disputes over cost-sharing arrangements, the development of partnerships has not lost momentum and is seen by the city as a major element in its strategy to maintain and extend sport and recreation opportunities.

Colorado Springs' commitment to co-operation with schools is mirrored in Oakland, where partnership with schools dates from the establishment of the city and is seen as a fundamental element in P&R provision. Similarly, in San Francisco there is extensive co-operation between the School Board of Supervisors and the Board of P&R over the use of school and city facilities. It is also increasingly common for new schools to be planned jointly.

In terms of the future development of P&R policy in the United States, a number of trends are clear. First, that for most cities P&R budgets will continue to be squeezed with the result that an increasing number of cities will see their funding as fulfilling a pump-priming function. There are a number of examples of innovative funding arrangements where the key facilitating role is played by either the municipal government or the state. One such example is the White River State Park in Indianapolis, a combined theme park, zoo and sports centre, which was provided through a mix of city, state and commercial funds.

The second development is a broadening in the rationale for public involvement in P&R from welfare (social control) motives to viewing P&R as investment in the marketing of the city to mobile corporations and tourists (as in Indianapolis, see National Recreation and Parks Association 1988), and as a means by which house owners can protect their personal capital. In Oakland the traditional defence of the P&R service based on its contribution to crime reduction is being supplemented by arguments that stress the potential to attract tourist dollars and aid urban regeneration. In many cities, such as Colorado Springs, house owners perceive parkland and good-quality sports facilities as helping to maintain property values, while for the wider community there is increasing recognition that leisure spending is a major source of income and profit. Anderson *et al.* (1986), for example, in a study of the economic impact of state parks in North Dakota estimated that visitors spent $71m. in the state by comparison with the $2.8m. cost of park maintenance. Third, there is evidence of a shift in departmental organisation which is resulting in the loss of separate P&R departments and their incorporation within multi-disciplinary departments. While this rationalisation might produce budget savings, there is the clear risk of a dilution of service objectives and expertise.

Finally, the most significant trend in the funding of P&R is the move towards a greater reliance on user fees, concessions and other forms of income generation (Kraus 1990). During the 1980s, user fees were the fastest growing method of financing leisure services (Pagano 1990). It is also increasingly the case that the effective preservation of city P&R budgets is the result of specific state or city bond ballots. San Francisco provides a useful, though not necessarily typical, example. The tax revolt of the 1970s resulted in a 33 per cent cut in the service budget and prompted a search for alternative sources of funding (see Howard and Crompton 1980, for a discussion of the impact of the tax revolt on parks and recreation services). Whereas income of only $1.5m. was produced in 1968, this figure had increased to $20m. by the early 1990s. Of that total, 25 per cent comes from charges for the use of car parks built under city parks; a further 25 per cent comes from municipally owned and managed golf courses; 5 per cent from the rent of the Candlestick Park stadium to the Giants and Forty-niners; and the remaining 45 per cent from various fees, charges (to enter the botanical gardens, for example) and concessions (for refreshment stands in the city parks). Although the contribution of self-generated income in San Francisco has been significant, the national pattern is more complex. In general, while the growth in self-generated income has been relatively substantial, it has 'not replaced tax supported revenues, but rather has been able only to supplement them to a relatively small degree' (Crompton and McGregor 1994: 25; see also Brademas and Readnour 1989).

Although the Californian tax revolt resulted in a growing reluctance to support ballots on bond issues, bonds have been successful in providing San Francisco with additional income for P&R (Goldberg 1991). A recent $73m. bond issue to cover infrastucture work within Golden Gate Park received the backing of 74 per cent of those who voted. Indeed, so highly valued is the P&R service in the city that not one ballot for additional expenditure has been lost. But even in San Francisco, 'the capital of progressivism' (DeLeon 1992), there has had to be the development of partnerships with the private and voluntary sectors to preserve levels of service. Volunteers are used to clean up Golden Gate Park; corporations are encouraged to sponsor tree-planting and the zoo is supported by the fund-raising activities of the Zoological Society.

CONCLUSION

From this brief review a number of common themes are apparent: first, the role of central (including federal) government in supporting facility development; second, the significance of a close relationship between the municipal parks and leisure authority and schools; third, the level of popular support for leisure sports and services; and finally, fiscal pressures.

In examining the provision of financial support for developing the sport and leisure infrastructure, a distinction has to be made between the provision of facilities for mass participation in sport and those that are designed specifically, though not always exclusively, for the use of professional sports teams. In the United States and Canada particularly there is a strong tradition of local investment in sports facilities, such as major sports stadiums, as a form of 'civic boosterism'. While federal governments might provide some form of tax and funding support for major projects designed to attract professional teams, these incentives tend to be limited. As regards the provision of facilities for mass participation, in all the countries surveyed the central government has played a key role. In Australia, Canada and the United States this was frequently through specific, and sometimes time-limited, funding programmes, often directly leisure related but also a by-product of programmes directed at other policy objectives such as job creation. However, what is also clear is that federal/central support is short lived, as few countries could claim that their governments have displayed a steady and continuing interest in the development and improvement of the facility base for mass participation in sport and recreation. The early rhetoric of commitment and partnership with local government soon evaporated with primary responsibility transferred, explicitly or by default, exclusively to the local (and occasionally state) level. From the perspective of federal/central administrations this is, in many respects, a logical development in the process of policy implementation whereby the federal/central level provides pump-priming funding to cover the capital costs of developing the physical infrastructure for sport and recreation and then passes the day-to-day management and maintenance over to the local authority, which should be closer to public needs. What tends to cause concern at the local level is the abandonment of a continuing commitment to support the, often substantial, refurbishment costs of facilities such as pools and sports halls. The behaviour of central governments can be explained by the general, and extremely convenient, assumption that routine maintenance, substantial refurbishment and eventual replacement are revenue costs or else costs which should be planned for through the provision of a sinking fund or some similar financial arrangement. Part of the explanation also lies in the weakness of commitment of central governments to provision of mass sport and leisure opportunities and the stronger attraction of a concentration on provision and support for elite success.

At local level a feature of the successful development of a broad range of community facilities was the extensive use of schools for community leisure. In Canada and the United States in particular community use is well established, while in Australia and the UK community-use arrangements are more uneven. In general, where these arrangements work well, they have been built into the expectations of school authorities from the establishment of schools. In all countries it has proved much more difficult to develop community-use arrangements once patterns of management have become established. What also seems to be important is the perception and commitment of the local community to sport and leisure services. In all countries sport and leisure services are seen as making a significant contribution to the quality of life and, generally, leisure services are salient to the local electorate, if not as a generalised service then certainly as a set of neighbourhood facilities. Yet, the motive for citizen commitment varies from the materialistic view of those who see leisure facilities and local open parkland as a support for local property values to those who see leisure facilities as an element of welfare provision. Whatever the precise motive for citizen support the impact of neighbourhood activism can be considerable, as the examples from Canada show.

Among local authorities there is also a range of motives for involvement in sport and leisure services. At one extreme there are those authorities, found most frequently in Ireland and north America, who view facility provision as an aspect of a broader economic strategy often focused on tourism or the attraction of inward investment. Other authorities, such as those in much of the UK and Australia and in parts of north America, view leisure services as an element of welfare provision. However, for all countries sport and leisure expenditure is now a significant element of the overall municipal budget, a development which reflects the level of past commitment and stimulates the development of a supportive lobby among citizens' groups, local politicians and administrators. The problems that this poses for local authorities during periods of fiscal stress have been amply illustrated. Pressure throughout much of the 1980s on leisure service budgets has not only stimulated local political activism in some countries, but more generally forced most leisure service departments to seek alternative sources of income through the privatisation of aspects of the service. Whether privatisation has been imposed, as in the UK, or has emerged gradually as a result of sustained budgetary pressure and the diffusion of the UK experience, it is now a feature of both the funding and the development of the service (with the notable, but possibly temporary, exception of Toronto). At present there are few assessments of the impact of the imposition of fees and charges, the sale of concessions and the introduction of CCT on the character of the service. But there are few signs that the implications are necessarily adverse either to the range of services provided or, more importantly, to the pattern of access. However, this optimistic view needs to be tempered by an acknowledgement that access to leisure facilities has generally been significantly skewed towards middle- and upper-income groups.

5 National sports organisations

There is temptation to juxtapose voluntary governing bodies (or NSOs) and commercial sports organisations, presenting the former as reflecting and sustaining a version of sport which stresses inclusion, participation, voluntarism and which is respectful of sporting traditions and the latter as promoting a sporting infrastructure which is exclusive, passive, specialist, innovative and fickle. To characterise the governing bodies as the guardians of the pure spirit of sport and the commercial sector as the vandals at the castle gates is to misjudge seriously both sets of organisations. It would be just as easy to paint a picture of governing bodies as socially elitist, exploitative of athletes, patriarchal, wilfully amateurish in administration and equally wilful in their reluctance to acknowledge the changing context of their respective sports. Within the commercial sector there are also those, albeit far fewer in number in the 1990s, who are more motivated by sentiment than profit and who have used their resources to sustain soccer and rugby league clubs, for example, when their cash would have been better kept under the mattress.

As the social, economic and political importance of sport has increased over the past forty years or so, the triangular relationship between government, the governing bodies (or voluntary sector) and the commercial sector has become more intense and more significant in shaping the development of sport. In most of the countries in this study, the US being a significant exception, it has for many years been possible to treat the role of these three bodies separately as they generally fulfilled related but largely discrete functions within the policy area. The governing bodies were responsible for establishing and enforcing the rules of sport, stimulating sport's development, selecting international teams, organising events and representing the interests of domestic sport in the relevant international federation. Government, from the mid-1960s, provided funds for facility development but generally kept its distance from more detailed policy issues. The commercial sector, television in particular, generally preferred to treat sport as a vehicle for self-promotion and advertising rather than as a source of direct profit. In the past ten years the relationship between the three has become more blurred, with government encroaching on governing-body functions; many governing bodies and individual clubs adopting commercial objectives; and the commercial sector seeking a greater degree of direct control over sports.

The focus of this chapter is primarily on governing bodies of sport and the aim is to examine their current role and influence within the policy process. However, any such analysis will require not only a study of the relationship with government, but also an assessment of the importance of commercial sport and its evolving relationship with government and the governing bodies. An emerging fourth actor in this pattern of relationships is the sportsmen and women either individually (plus their agents and managers) or collectively through unions or associations. While players' organisations have been influential in the major commercial sports in the US for some considerable time, their significance in the UK and Australia, for example, is relatively recent. A final element in the changing context of domestic governing bodies is the growth in importance of international sport and the consequential increase in significance of international federations.

AUSTRALIA

Australian NSOs retain a significant role in the shaping of domestic sport policy more out of sentiment than strategy and owing more to the indulgence of their rivals (government and commercial bodies) than to their own political power. For the government, the NSOs are an adjunct to their policy objectives for elite sport and are tolerated agents rather than partners. For the commercial sector the major governing bodies are either irrelevant and are bypassed or are co-operative partners in the business of sport.

In order to explain how this marginalisation occurred, it is necessary to trace briefly the evolution of Australian NSOs from their early days as imitators of British governing bodies. The first sports organisations developed at state level in the 1880s, but as in Britain the motivation for their establishment was often less a concern with the codification of rules and the development of the sport and more to do with the maintenance of social exclusivity under the guise of a concern to protect the amateur nature of a sport. Consequently, the emergent NSOs, coalescing around the issue of amateurism, were often complemented by usually looser organisations concerned to promote professional sports (Mason 1985). Thus, rowing, athletics and rugby were all divided along class and frequently religious lines, as Catholicism was viewed as an indicator of low status. Only cricket, among major sports, was an exception. Although the sport outgrew its pub-based roots by the middle of the nineteenth century, the new breed of cricket administrators were content to maintain the links with pubs and hotels and while amateurism was occasionally debated 'administrators were able to take a much more pragmatic stance in the amateur versus professional debate' (Cashman 1995: 66).

Once the rift between amateur and professional sport developed, it took far longer to heal than in the UK. Cashman explains the persistence of amateurism and the consequent distraction of governing bodies from more general sports development as due, first, to the association of professionalism with drinking and gambling and the bitter antipathy this provoked among Christian organisations, and second, to the status insecurity of the Australian middle class and the resultant need to reinforce their social position through the organised exclusion of working-class sportsmen.

Even where the nascent NSOs were overseeing a relatively united sport, as in the case of cricket, they were still in a precarious position being frequently short of funds and open to challenge from a variety of sources, most notably professional cricketers who were involved in many disputes with the Board in the early 1900s over the organisation and financial rewards of overseas tours (Wynne-Thomas and Arnold 1984; Harte 1993). As a result, where possible, sports administrators attempted to shelter under the patronage of state politicians which was used, for example, to secure privileged access to sports grounds. More importantly, as Cashman notes, 'Sports associations also looked to government for recognition [as this] . . . added to the authority of a governing body and offered the prospect of assistance' (1995: 116). However, in general, state and commonwealth governments showed little enthusiasm to get involved in sports administration and, apart from sporadic interventions to control gambling associated with professional sport, retained a marginal role until the second half of the twentieth century.

Probably the clearest and certainly the most dramatic illustration of the vulnerability of NSOs occurred in the 1970s and concerned the attempt by Kerry Packer to establish World Series Cricket (WSC). The conflict between Packer and the Australian Cricket Board (ACB) took place at a time when both government and the commercial sector had recognised the potential value of sport. Packer's intervention was prompted by his failure to secure, from the ACB, the broadcasting rights to domestic cricket for his own Channel 9 television company. His response was to challenge the authority, not only of the domestic governing body, but also of the international federation, the International Cricket Conference (ICC). He recruited enough first-class cricketers to organise an international cricket event to rival the Test Match series organised by the ICC. Packer's proposed WSC would, not surprisingly, be broadcast on his own Channel 9. By his actions Packer bypassed the ACB, realising that if he could overcome the ICC the opposition of the ACB would crumble. The response of the ICC was first, to ignore the threat, then ban players who had signed up with WSC and finally, to challenge Packer's proposal in the UK courts. None of these strategies worked; virtually an entire West Indies squad signed for WSC and the British legal challenge failed in the High Court. World Series Cricket went ahead and as Jack Bailey, at the time secretary to the ICC, commented, '[Packer] had introduced day/night cricket which did capture the Australian public and he had certainly hit the Australian Cricket Board where it hurt, chiefly in the pocket' (1989: 110). The ICC realised that a compromise was inevitable and suggested that the Australian Cricket Board negotiate a solution with Packer. The agreement that eventually emerged was more a capitulation than a compromise as Packer got everything he wanted; exclusive broadcasting rights to the domestic game for ten years; an increase in one-day matches; day/evening matches; coloured clothing; and a say in which teams toured Australia. Packer demonstrated that the love of money linked players to promoters more tightly than the love of the sport linked players to administrators.

By the 1980s other major sports, including Australian football and rugby league, had developed close links at the elite level with business, both as recipients of corporate sponsorship and as sources of profit themselves. Over a relatively short period the Victorian Football League as well as the clubs within it became significant corporations in their own right. New national competitions were introduced and the early 1980s witnessed the creation, death and franchise transfer of clubs from one city to another in a fashion more readily associated with North American professional sport than Australian.

Paralleling the growth of commercial patronage of sport was the steady expansion of governmental interest in the policy area. The growth in federal and state interest was not only reflected in the flow of public funds to sport, but also in the creation of additions to the sports administrative infrastructure. Of foremost importance was the creation in 1981 of the Australian Institute of Sport and the establishment of the avowedly interventionist Australian Sports Commission three years later. However, it was the election of the Labor Party in 1972 that marked the sea change in government attitude to the NSOs. As already noted in Chapter 3, the NSOs were unprepared for the injection of public funding and consequently leaned very heavily on government for administrative support and advice. One might argue that public investment produced more effective lobbyists as instanced by the successful campaign in 1977 to reinstate the Sports Assistance Programme, which provided financial support for NSOs, following its abandonment in 1976. However, it can also be argued that their vociferous opposition to the loss of grant aid was as much a reflection of the extent of their financial dependency as of their capacity to influence the direction of national sport policy.

By the early 1980s both major political parties, Labor and the Liberal–Country Party, had formulated policy positions on sport, which were broadly similar in nature, particularly regarding the support for voluntarism and the autonomy of NSOs. However, both parties also drew attention to the inadequacy of the administrative capacity of the NSOs. Although the policy solutions to this problem differed with Labor favouring a federal interventionist response and the Liberal–Country Party favouring various forms of privatisation, both were content to impose solutions on the NSOs.

The dominant position of the government operating through the ASC is easily illustrated by examining the financial position and policy development of the major NSOs. Australian Swimming Inc. (ASI) is one of the oldest NSOs in the country and also one of the most successful when judged in terms of membership and elite success. Membership of the ASI has steadily increased from 78,073 in 1987–8 to 94,581 in 1995–6 with the number of affiliated clubs increasing from 928 to 1,004 over the same period. In terms of elite success, Australia finished second to the United States in the Pan-Pacific Games of 1995, winning a total of thirty-five medals (thirteen gold) and in the Atlanta Olympics collected twelve medals (two gold, four silver and six bronze). This high level of success is paralleled by substantial dependence on the ASC for funding. As Table 5.1 shows, over the past three years ASC funding has steadily grown both in absolute terms and as a percentage of total income.

Table 5.1 shows the extent of dependence on ASC funding and the degree to which it sharply increased following the announcement of Sydney as the 2000 host. The level of support from state governments varies considerably, with New South Wales being one of the most supportive, inspired no doubt by the prospect of Sydney 2000, but is generally insignificant by comparison with support from the ASC to the national body. The ASI is aware that federal support is guaranteed only until 2000, but is clearly facing problems in locating alternative sources of funds. While the NSO has sponsorship arrangements with a number of companies, most deals involve the provision of goods and services rather than the transfer of money: Canon provide copiers, Qantas provide travel and Speedo supply swimwear. The signs are that following the 2000 Games corporate sponsorship will prove as difficult to sustain as will public funding.

The situation facing cycling is similar to swimming in some respects, especially the reliance on public funding, but distinctive in others. Australian cycling is reasonably successful, boasting three world champions and collecting five medals (one silver and four bronze) in the Atlanta Olympics. However, the Australian Cycling Federation (ACF) finds it difficult to market the sport to potential participants and, more importantly, to

Table 5.1 ASI funding by source between 1993–4 and 1995–6 ($Am.)

Year	ASC	Commercial sponsorship	Fees	Other	Total
1993–4	1.2 (45.4%)	0.78 (29.3%)	0.27 (10.2%)	0.41 (15.1%)	2.66
1994–5	1.9 (59%)	0.5 (15.5%)	0.27 (8.4%)	0.55 (17.1%)	3.22
1995–6	2.34 (59.1%)	0.6 (15.2%)	0.28 (7.1%)	0.74 (18.6%)	3.96

Source: ASI Annual Reports, various years.

sponsors because most of the Australian elite cyclists are competing outside Australia for most of the year. The shortage of top-class domestic competitions and the absence of elite cyclists has not prevented a steady rise in the ACF's membership from 5,285 in 1984 to 8,621 in 1990 and 10,623 in 1996. Despite the strong base of participation and elite success the ACF depends for almost 75 per cent of its income on the ASC, with a significant proportion of the remainder coming from the Commonwealth Games Federation and the Australian Olympic Committee. The dependence of the ACF on ASC funding has had an impact on Federation policy as exemplified by recent attempts to create a single head-coach position, which was stymied by the ASC. ASC policy of funding a limited number of AIS scholarships is also affecting the Federation's attempts to increase participation at the competitive levels. While the Federation is keen to take advantage of AIS scholarships, it is aware that the quality and intensity of training that scholarship holders receive generally results in a significant improvement in performance, which is dispiriting for those who just miss out on scholarships and frequently results in a decline in participation among the 'near-elite'-level cyclists.

The positions of swimming and cycling are broadly typical of the main Olympic sports, all of which are aware of the fragility of ASC financial support but which are also aware of the limited pool of potential sponsors, particularly in the post-Sydney Games years. Problems for the NSOs also arise from their changing relationship with their elite athletes. In general, the challenges to NSO authority come from individual athletes, but there is also in Australia a strong history of collective action by athletes. Both cycling and swimming have had recent experience of more assertive athletes, with cycling facing legal challenges over selection decisions and swimming facing court action over the use of an athlete's picture to promote the ASI sponsor.

Periodically throughout the history of modern sport in Australia, sportsmen (rarely sportswomen) have attempted to exert greater collective control over their working conditions, or over their share of the income, or indeed over both. As mentioned above, part of Kerry Packer's success in challenging the authority of the ACB was because of the readiness of elite players to abandon the governing body. However, the players' association formed by cricketers in the wake of the Packer challenge did not survive because of its unrepresentative membership which was lacking in non-WSC players and its failure to look beyond WSC and gain recognition from the ACB (Dabscheck 1991). Despite the failure of the Professional Cricketers Association of Australia, other players' unions have survived in rugby league, basketball and football and achieved a degree of modest success in protecting the interests of members in relation to proposals concerned with transfer, draft arrangements and employment during injury. While union successes until the early 1990s were unremarkable, there are signs that a more sophisticated approach to negotiating and a greater willingness to use the courts is beginning to raise their profile. The Rugby League Players

Union effectively used the courts to prevent the introduction of an internal draft in 1991 and in 1992 successfully used the courts again to force concessions from the league over payments associated with a pre-season 'sevens' tournament (Dabscheck 1994).

In conclusion, Australian NSOs have witnessed their support from the federal government expand rapidly over the past fifteen years and have accepted the funding and also the dependence that goes with it. The impact of the election of a budget-cutting government has been dulled by the forthcoming Olympic Games, and most NSOs expect public finance to be cut sharply after 2000. However, there are few NSOs that have an effective strategy to cope with the probable decline in public funding, with a number suggesting that it will be hard for a future government to announce that it is prepared to oversee a decline in Olympic success in 2004.

CANADA

As in most other industrial countries, the last quarter of the nineteenth century saw not only a rapid rise in sports participation, but also the equally rapid establishment of NSOs concerned to codify the rules and organise competition for new sports such as lacrosse and Canadian football and also for imported sports such as soccer, baseball and tennis. NSOs emerged in some sports, such as boxing, because of the need for amateur participants to distance themselves from the less reputable commercial version; in other sports, the Canadian form of rugby union, for example, NSOs were formed to preserve the social exclusiveness of the sport; and in further sports, basketball in particular, to foster the rapid expansion of the sport among the urban working class (Cox *et al.* 1985). During the early part of the century the capacity of NSOs to exercise authoritative regulation over their sports was hampered by the problems of communications in such a large and sparsely populated country and by the emerging pattern of club competition, which forged closer links between provinces and northern states in the US than with other Canadian provinces (Lappage 1985). This early period also saw frequent confrontation between clubs and athletes in the western provinces, on the one hand, and Ontario where most of the NSOs were located, on the other. As Lappage notes, rule changes initiated by Ontario-based NSOs were 'foist(ed) . . . upon Western Canada and the Maritimes', whereas changes initiated by the west 'were usually encountered with opposition from the more conservative Ontario' (1985: 273). Provincial distrust of Ontario and provincial links with the US are themes that recur in the history of Canadian NSOs.

By the 1920s major commercial sports, such as ice hockey, football, boxing and wrestling, were strongly influenced by the structure and pattern of sport in America. Even in amateur sport, such as rowing, sailing and marathon running, international contact with America was often more important than intranational competition. Apart from football, which for many years managed to retain a viable Canadian league, many other major sports have succumbed to US influence and dollars – such as hockey, where major Canadian teams aspired to join the American-controlled National Hockey League (NHL). The example of hockey illustrates the schizophrenic attitude of Canadians to its southern neighbour in sport. On the one hand, participation in the NHL offered an exciting series of national and international matches at which Canadians can display their talent at the country's national games: on the other hand, Canadians resent the American dominance of the NHL, illustrated by the League's repeated refusal by the League to admit further Canadian franchises, particularly in Quebec and Vancouver (Macintosh *et al.* 1987), and by the way in which the NHL frustrated attempts by the Canadian Amateur Hockey Association to develop an elite national team for Olympic and other international competitions (Redmond 1985). The ambiguous relationship between Canada and the US was repeated later in the 1970s in baseball when the two major US baseball leagues established Canadian franchises. Similarly, the US-based North American Soccer League established two soccer franchises in Canada, also in the late 1970s.

If Canadian NSOs have had to cope with the power of American commercial sports interests since the 1920s, their need to cope with federal government involvement in sport is much more recent. However, whereas American influence was largely confined to a limited number of commercial sports, federal intervention was much more sweeping. The Trudeau election in 1968 ushered in a period of intense analysis of Canadian sport and recreation sponsored by the newly formed Fitness and Amateur Sport Division of the government. It was also the start of a period that was to transform the organisation of Canadian sport and the role and influence of the NSOs.

Having previously largely ignored sport, any change to a more proactive policy altered significantly the relationship between government and the NSOs. In the early 1970s the shift in policy was modest, with the government content to exhort NSOs to adopt a greater concern with international achievement. In general in this period, government provided unconditional grants and left policy initiative in the hands of the NSOs. None the less, a number of changes were introduced that prepared the way for a much more interventionist stance by government. For example, the 1970 White Paper on sport described and, by implication, defined the role of NSOs and the 1969 *Report of the Task Force on Sport for Canadians* led to the positioning of the building blocks of a professionalised administration of sport with the establishment of a series of multi-sport bodies such as the Canadian Academy of Sports Medicine in 1969 and the Coaching Association of Canada in 1970 (Galasso 1972; Macintosh *et al.* 1987: 88ff). By the mid-1970s the federal government had moved from a passive and indirect involvement in sport to a more proactive role and the determined pursuit of political goals. Among the most significant measures adopted by the government were the offer to NSOs of funding for the appointment of full-time executive and technical staff and the establishment of a national sports administration centre in Ottawa to house key NSOs. However, the provision of funds for staff appointments was dependent on the agreement of NSOs to relocate to Ottawa. Other measures included the creation of Hockey Canada to review the 'national game', on which the NSO the Canadian Amateur Hockey Association had only minority representation; the establishment of a grant-aid programme designed to enable athletes to concentrate on their preparation for competition; and the formulation of a 'game plan' in preparation for the 1976 Olympic Games, scheduled for Montreal.[1]

In 1977, with the administrative and financial infrastructure in place, the government produced a discussion paper which put the development of elite sport at the heart of its policy programme (Ministry of State for Fitness and Amateur Sport 1977). The ensuing White Paper was not acted upon because of the temporary loss of power by the Liberals in 1979 and it was not until 1981 that the new Liberal Minister issued a slightly revised White Paper which, in addition to recommending the establishment of new training centres, extra funding for athletes, and a more energetic hosting policy, also 'made it clear that priority in funding was to be given to Olympic sports which demonstrated a commitment to, and a consistent record of, excellence' (Macintosh 1985: 385).

As Howell and Howell comment, 'Until the 1960s sport was in the hands of "pure" amateurs, volunteers working in the basements of their homes . . .' (1985: 413; see also Slack *et al.* 1994). By the mid-1980s the administration of Canadian sport, taken collectively, had been radically and irrevocably altered from amateur to professional administration, from a shoe-string budget derived from subscriptions and donations to a large publicly funded budget (Can$20m. by 1982–3), from a decentralised personalised structure to a highly centralised bureaucratic structure, and from a geographically dispersed organisation to one predominantly located in Ottawa. The great danger, but one largely ignored, was that: 'By removing the administration of sports from the kitchen table, the minister may also have excised it from the hearts of the many volunteer workers across the country' (Galasso 1972: 55). Although the scale and pace of change was dramatic, one needs to bear in mind the caveats offered by Kikulis *et al.* (1995) who point out that the response of NSOs was not uniformly compliant. A number of NSOs displayed a degree of ceremonial conformity (Meyer and Rowan 1977) and others exhibited a degree of inertia that resulted in selective conformity, particularly with regard to the centralisation of decision making in the hands of professional officers. However, none took action that jeopardised the flow of federal funding.

The rapid creation of elaborate sports bureaucracies within the Ottawa administration centre and the equally rapid expansion of the Fitness and Amateur Sport Branch resulted in a steep decline in the autonomy of NSOs during the 1980s. Federal dominance of NSOs was effected in a number of ways. First, there was the role of Sport Canada consultants in the selection of staff by the NSOs. The consultants were so closely involved that the Task Force observed that: 'In short, Sport Canada plays a significant employer role in personnel management of funded positions' (Ministry of State for Fitness and Amateur Sport 1992: 194). Second, the introduction in 1984 of the Quadrennial Planning Process (QPP) has been criticised not only for being too complex but also for being designed more for the benefit of Sport Canada than the NSOs. The QPP was introduced by Sport Canada as a condition of funding and as a means of encouraging strategic planning by the NSOs, but the process was resented because it was cumbersome, costly to produce, did not necessarily produce the promised additional funding and generally 'heightened the potential for conflict' (Slack *et al.* 1994: 318). In addition, according to Macintosh and Whitson (1990), the rational basis of the QPP was undermined by the self-interested behaviour of sports administration professionals who used the Process to defend their definition of policy problems and solutions against those of their volunteer board members and also against regional interests. Nevertheless, the QPP provided the government with considerable leverage with regard to the strategic objectives, organisational structure and internal management of the NSOs.

Third, the Athlete Assistance Program (APP) provides a central role for Sport Canada in determining the criteria for eligibility for what is referred to as 'carded' status. It also established a direct relationship between the athlete and the government as the monthly payments were sent direct to athletes, thus bypassing the NSO. Finally, Sport Canada introduced, in 1985, a complex Sport Recognition System to identify those sports which it would fund. The System was criticised for being arbitrary, favouring Olympic sports and overemphasising elite achievement at the expense of participation and sport development. 'In the comments received by the Task Force, it is apparent that no federal sport policy is more unacceptable and, in many cases, more offensive than the Sport Recognition System' (Ministry of State for Fitness and Amateur Sport 1992: 203).

The newly appointed professional officers were also faced with balancing the requirements of the largely voluntary managing committees and meeting the expectations of the government which was paying their salaries. Macintosh saw the almost total dependence on government funding as leading to an 'unprecedented level of federal government dominance of amateur sport policy' reflected in government intervention on issues relating to drug use, bilingualism in coaching, apartheid in South Africa and even athlete selection (1985: 391). Most significantly, the overbearing presence of government compounded the fragmented character of Canadian NSOs just at the time when an effective NSO lobby was essential. The attempts to strengthen the Sports Federation of Canada, an umbrella organisation of sports governing bodies, largely failed because of the reluctance of the NSOs to give up the little autonomy that they continued to possess, and also because of a growing mutual suspicion among NSOs fostered by the funding pattern of Sport Canada. NSO unity was also undermined by the strong rivalry between provincial sports organisations and their reluctance to cede too much authority to the NSO (Macintosh 1996). A further example of the dominance of federal policy over NSO interests was the comparative ease with which the Canadian Olympic Association was persuaded to join the US boycott of the Moscow Olympic Games in 1980 even though the Association had voted overwhelmingly to attend. The government wanted to create a successful elite but one that was also politically compliant.

The importance of federal policy to the NSOs is easily illustrated. Swimming is governed by Swimming/Natation Canada (SNC), a name adopted in 1987 as an acknowledgement of the government's commitment to bilingualism. SNC is one of Canada's major sports organisations with more than 50,000 competitive swimmers and 357 clubs in 1995. At international competitive level swimmers have won more Olympic, Commonwealth and Pan-American gold medals than any other Canadian sport. Yet, the income to the organisation is only just over Can$2m., of which approximately half comes from the federal government (see Table 5.2).

Table 5.2 demonstrates the degree of reliance on federal funding and also the weakness of commercial sponsorship. The table also illustrates the first effects of the government's policy to reduce the level of funding given to

Table 5.2 Swimming/Natation Canada: sources of revenue between 1987–8 and 1995–6 (Can$m. and percentage)

Source	1987–8	1988–9	1989–90	1990–1	1991–2	1992–3	1993–4	1994–5	1995–6
Sport Canada	1,247	1,152	1,265	1,268	1,233	1,221	1,104	1,131	962
	(50%)	(45%)	(58%)	(49%)	(46%)	(53%)	(50%)	(52%)	(42%)
Imperial Oil	440	345	0	50	33	0	35	4	35
Canadian Olympic Association	42	0	0	143	142	167	81	99	119
Fees	425	377	391	392	387	507	543	578	585
Sports marketing	151	349	342	547	700	262	304	236	320
Other	204	310	167	194	162	138	149	139	276
Total	2,509	2,533	2,165	2,594	2,657	2,295	2,216	2,187	2,297

Source: SNC Annual Reports, various years.

NSOs with the loss of Can$169,000 between 1994–5 and 1995–6. In terms of expenditure the largest amount is allocated to coaching, competitions, athlete travel and topping up the funding given to athletes from Sport Canada under the 'carding' system. A similar picture of dependence on federal funding is found in the accounts of Athletics Canada (AC). In 1995 AC received Can$1.8m. from Sport Canada, accounting for 67 per cent of its total income of Can$2.7m. This percentage figure remained steady throughout the 1990s, but in 1996 dropped dramatically to 52 per cent as Sport Canada cut its subsidy to Can$1.2m. Further cuts are anticipated in 1997. For both swimming and athletics the Canadian Olympic Association (COA) has played an important role in softening the blow of federal funding cuts by increasing its financial support for prominent Olympic sports. In 1996 Athletics Canada received an increase in funding from the COA of Can$90,000 from a 1995 figure of Can$94,700. Swimming/Natation Canada received a much more modest increase, possibly reflecting the relatively poor performance of swimmers in the Barcelona Olympic Games.

Like all the major NSOs, both Swimming /Natation Canada and Athletics Canada depend heavily on a strong provincial structure to provide a framework for coaching, athlete development and competition. Because of the size of the country and the cost of travel, provincial sports organisations are a key element in the NSO structure. However, provinces have not been immune from the change in attitude of government towards public sector finances and some provincial sports organisations (PSOs) have suffered severe cuts in funding. In athletics, for example, while provincial government funding to Athletics Manitoba has been maintained at the 1995 level, this is probably because the province is scheduled to host the Canada Games in 1997 and the Pan-American Games in 1999. These commitments notwithstanding, the provincial government is to undertake a review of sport funding during 1996. By contrast, the budget of Athletics Alberta has been cut by Can$25,000 plus the loss of previously free services and in Ontario the provincial government withheld funding for eight months in 1995 and the Ontario Track and Field Association is uncertain about the scale and release of funding for 1996–7.

For the major NSOs at least, both their organisational infrastructure and finances are strong although both are too dependent on the continuing interest and goodwill of federal and provincial governments. Despite the much harsher economic climate facing the NSOs it is unlikely that politicians will be prepared to see such a useful resource as international sport be weakened too greatly. In addition, some NSOs are having some success in attracting alternative sources of income with Athletics Canada increasing its sponsorship income 33 per cent to Can$205,000 between 1995 and 1996. However, the next few years will undoubtedly be difficult for all sports organisations and for those concerned with the minor and non-Olympic sports in particular.

The capacity of NSOs to weather the current funding crisis is dependent upon the extent to which they were able to build a firm foundation during the period of greater federal generosity. Certainly by the late 1980s Canada had established a sports system that was envied, if not always admired, in many other western countries. Success in the 1984 Olympic Games made challenges to the direction of federal policy difficult: new ambitious targets were set for the Seoul Olympics in 1988. Writing in 1987, Macintosh summed up the environment for national sports organisations in the following terms:

> At present, then, the federal government, through its control of funds to national sports associations, its indirect control of the two key national arm's-length sport agencies (the Coaching Association of Canada and the National Sport and Recreation Centre), and its grip on the sport bureaucrats who staff these arm's-length agencies and national sport associations in Ottawa, dominates sport policy making in Canada.
>
> (Macintosh *et al.* 1987: 183)

One can add to this summary that the federal government had established itself in a dominant position in the sport policy process, had also shaped that process to marginalise the NSO contribution, and had effectively excluded any public voice. Policy-making was now a closed activity. However, this period of self-confident federal dominance was about to be rudely shaken. The Ben Johnson scandal in 1988, when Johnson broke the world 100 metres record and won the Olympic gold medal at the Seoul Olympics only to be stripped of his medal due to drug use, was a traumatic time for Canadian sport and prompted a protracted period of introspection. The subsequent Commission of Inquiry, chaired by Charles Dubin, investigated almost every aspect of federal government sports policy.

Many of the recommendations of the Dubin Report had an air of unreality about them: exhorting government to develop an arm's-length relationship with the sports community with the statement that, 'I believe that Canada is unique among Western nations in having government control so closely the ordinary functions of the sport federations' (Dubin Report 1990: 530); encouraging a reorientation of policy to give priority to mass participation rather than elite success; and a downgrading of the value put on medal success. The government's response came in three phases and contained a number of decisions that affected its relationship with NSOs. Of particular importance was the acknowledgement by government that it was for the appropriate NSO to determine whether an athlete was eligible to compete. The government commissioned a number of specific studies of current aspects of sport including an examination of the national sport system. The report, *Amateur Sport: Future Challenges* (Porter and Cole 1990), recommended that the federal government should be less involved in the day-to-day affairs of the NSOs and that the latter be given greater discretion over the use of government grants. However, the report also confirmed that the major policy concern of the federal government was elite sport and also identified the federal government as playing a key role in the campaign against drug use. It remains to be seen how the level of involvement required to enforce an anti-doping policy can be reconciled with NSO autonomy.

While government was undergoing this rigorous bout of self-analysis, the NSOs were attempting to regroup and regain some of the ground lost over the previous fifteen years. Two Sports Forums were convened in an attempt to develop a collective position on the future of Canadian sport that would allow a more equitable partnership with government. If the aspirations of the NSOs can be summed up as a desire for greater autonomy from government and greater cohesion among sports organisations, then their recent behaviour suggests that the fulfilment of these aspirations may be difficult to achieve. As Semotiuk observed:

> The sports community's activity and response continues to be characterised by an element of mistrust and a lack of team spirit among its members. . . . National level coaches, national level high performance athletes, sports science representatives, the Canadian Olympic Association, and several national governing sports bodies have declined to participate in the Sports Forum conferences.
>
> (Semotiuk 1994: 372)

More recently, the government published the report of the Minister's Task Force on Federal Sports Policy (Ministry of State for Fitness and Amateur Sport 1992). The report was wide ranging and made over 100 recommendations and, apart from recommending that federal funding be more selective and target key sports, largely echoed earlier demands that athletes' interests be recognised and protected, that NSOs should have more autonomy and that federal policy should reflect a greater concern with participation. However, the report failed to address how a reoriented federal policy would be financed and what criteria should be used to prioritise the 100 or so recommendations. The report was long on rhetoric and short on pragmatism for, while it provided a powerful indictment of current policy, it gave the government too many opportunities to be selective in its response.

In conclusion, although the debates prompted by the Johnson scandal have forced the government to adopt a less aggressively promotional approach to sport, it has not altered the fundamental characteristics and underlying power dynamics of the relationship. While government has retreated on some fronts, such as athlete selection, it has acquired extensive new responsibilities in areas such as anti-doping and the identification of recipients for grant aid, which enable it to retain a central role in determining the direction of sport policy within the voluntary sector. Government may be less inclined to pursue so aggressively its authoritarian relationship with the NSOs, but while the NSOs remain so heavily financially dependent, the best they can hope for is a more benign attitude.

IRELAND

Any analysis of the policy significance of governing bodies of sport in Ireland is bound to have the dominant role of the Gaelic Athletic Association (GAA) at its heart. The extent to which the GAA is woven into the fabric of Irish society, religion and politics makes it difficult to talk of the organisation's role in policy-making, as this conceptualisation implies a degree of distance between itself and the institutions of the state. The complementarity between the geographic structure of the GAA and the parish structure of the Catholic church, and the significance of involvement in Gaelic sport in the advancement of political careers suggests an unconscious empathy between key power holders and the governing body. At one time in the mid-1970s the Taoiseach (Prime Minister), Jack Lynch, and the leader of the Catholic Church, Cardinal O'Fiaich, had both been prominent in the GAA, the former as a six-time winner of an All-Ireland finalist medal and the latter as a senior member of the Association.

Given the strong association between sport and nationalist politics, by the end of the nineteenth century it is not surprising that the emergence of a pattern of modern governing bodies to oversee the development of sport in Ireland was a politically charged process. Surprisingly, in the early years of the GAA, greater emphasis was given to the promotion of athletics and it was only by the late 1880s that stress was put on the revival of hurling and Gaelic football. However, even these early years were politically charged with rival anti- (or at least non-) nationalist athletic organisations, such as the unionist-controlled Irish Amateur Athletic Association formed in 1885, attempting to undermine the nascent GAA. But, as Mandle notes, the success of the GAA was derived from 'all the advantages accruing to an organisation avowedly nationalist, ostentatiously Irish, and, crucially, church-supported' (1977: 422). Governing body rivalry along political lines also affected other sports such as cycling in the early years of the present century where the unionist Irish Cyclists Association was in competition with the GAA-supported Gaelic Cyclists Association. The hostility of the GAA to the Irish Amateur Athletics Association (IAAA) and the general neglect of athletics by the nationalist body had the effect of stymieing attempts to develop a capacity to participate at international level and especially in the early Olympics.

The tension between competing governing bodies was paralleled by an equally acrimonious relationship between the GAA and the British government. Up to the establishment of the Free State there were many instances of petty harassment of the GAA by the government, including the attempt to impose an entertainment tax on Gaelic sports, interference with the provision of special trains for major sports events, periodic bans on GAA sports, the requirement of permits for sports events and police disruption of matches (de Búrca 1980). Matters reached their nadir in 1920 when police and soldiers raided a match at Croke Park, Dublin, leaving thirteen dead and over 100 injured. By 1922 the British had been forced out of most of Ireland and the GAA then had to build a relationship with a government which included a number of prominent GAA members. The transition was smooth, even with the divisions caused by the brief but fierce civil war, and as de Búrca notes, the GAA became part of the new establishment 'with ease' (1980: 157). The advent of independence ensured not only the privileged status of the GAA but also that other sports could begin to organise nationally without challenge from political rivals. By 1924 a new body (the National Athletic and Cycling Association) had been established and the Irish Handball Association had been formed to promote the Gaelic sport of handball.

The close relationship between the GAA and the government of the day did not inhibit the Association from lobbying forcefully for exemptions from both the entertainment tax and also income tax, a dual exemption not enjoyed by other governing bodies, nor by the GAA in Northern Ireland. However, what made, and makes, the GAA distinctive among governing bodies is not only its lobbying capacity, but its continuing expansion of activities beyond those purely concerned with sport. From the 1960s onwards the Association has expanded its involvement in a range of community and social services.

In terms of membership the Association has steadily, if occasionally fitfully, grown. Six years after its formation the Association had over 800 clubs affiliated, organised on a county basis and representing a membership of 40,000. By the turn of the century the GAA had established an administrative structure for sport throughout the whole of Ireland. More recently, in 1994, the Association had 280,000 players and 2,000 clubs, 80 per cent of which own their own pitches, with over 700 providing high-quality sporting and social facilities. The GAA is organised in a hierarchical fashion with a solid foundation at the parish level upon which is built a county and provincial structure. Not only does the GAA reach into every town and parish of the Republic, it also has a strong organisation in Northern Ireland, which adds the extra fuel of irredentism to the nationalist politics of the Association. A final demonstration of the intimate relationship between Gaelic sports and Irish political life is the fact that about 'one-third of those elected to the Dáil in recent years were actively involved in [Gaelic] sports' (Hussey 1995: 452).

Financially, while some receive a subsidy from national level or from their provincial council, most GAA clubs are self-sufficient. In 1994 some 38 per cent (IR£1.24m.) of total expenditure was devoted to ground improvements throughout the country. For the Association as a whole the bulk of its income is received from admissions (71 per cent) with a much smaller, but rapidly growing income from commercial activities such as sponsorship (12.8 per cent) and broadcasting rights (8.4 per cent). Finally, while it is rare for local government to provide grants to local clubs, the government has provided substantial and regular support to the GAA nationally. In the first years of the Republic the government allocated IR£10,000 to cover the cost of the Tailteann Games organised as part of the celebration of independence. More recently, the government provided a grant of IR£5m. as a contribution to the IR£40m. cost of the new stand at Croke Park.

The dominant position of the GAA in Irish sporting, cultural and political life provides the defining element of the context within which other governing bodies have to operate. Currently, Ireland has over fifty governing bodies for sports, ranging from the major team sports such as soccer and rugby union, the newer sports of triathlon and water-skiing, to the more idiosyncratic sports of baton-twirling and surfing. However, very few have the resources to support a full-time professional administration and an increasing number have relocated to the government-subsidised House of Sport in Dublin, which provides office accommodation and administrative support services. Almost all governing bodies receive financial support from the government either indirectly, through the House of Sport, or directly in the form of grant aid. In 1994 grant aid ranged from IR£104,000 to the GAA and IR£80,000 to the Irish Football Association to IR£2,600 to the Irish Amateur Fencing Association and IR£6,500 to the Irish Blind Sports Association. Most grant aid is given to help meet general administrative costs but some is earmarked for particular projects such as the employment of development officers or coaches, or else is allocated to meet the costs of attending international competitions, such as the Olympic Games. Table 5.3 shows the distribution of a variety of grants to the major team sports.

During 1994 Gaelic sport and hockey received exceptionally large grants for major stadium developments, which distorts the overall total. In general, the major sports receive a level of financial support that is broadly in line with their level of membership and activity, with the notable exception of rugby union. The Irish Rugby Football Union (IRFU) is an interesting contrast to the GAA. Like the GAA it is a thirty-two-county organisation and receives some funding from the Northern Ireland Sports Council largely for youth development projects. In contrast to the GAA, it has received very little finance from the Irish government, despite having over 15,000 adult participants and an active youth and schools development programme involving 15,000 youth and more than 20,000 school participants. There are four main reasons for the current low level of governmental financial support for rugby union: first, it is still perceived as an elitist sport confined to the ex-private school, Anglo-Irish middle class. Although the social basis of rugby is broadening slightly, its strongholds are still in the old garrison towns of Limerick, Cork, Dublin and Galway. The second reason for low level of grant is that the association of rugby with the breaching of sanctions towards South Africa during the anti-apartheid campaign still lingers in the mind of many politicians. Third, and very importantly, the IRFU has previously had very little reason to ask for financial support having an

Table 5.3   Department of Education (National Sports Council) grant aid 1994
(IR£'000s)

	Rugby Union (IRFU)	*Soccer (FAI)*	*GAA[1]*	*Field Hockey[2]*
Annual grant	0	98	104	42
Administrators and coaches	0	13	0	40
International competition	0	100	0	85
Development officers	0	0	21	0
Major facilities[3]	2 (100)	33 (650)	5,110 (6,140)	684 (1,240)
Recreational facilities[3]	30 (30)	86 (96)	128 (139)	0 (0)
Total	*32*	*330*	*5,363*	*851*

Notes: 1   Funding for football and hurling only.
2   Funding for the Irish Hockey Union and the Irish Ladies Hockey Union.
3   The number indicates the grant spent in 1994, while the number in brackets indicates the total grant.
Source: Annual Report, Sports Section, Department of Education 1994.

annual income from subscriptions sufficient to fund over IR£2m. of club development. The organisation also has reserves of over IR£15m. Finally, there seems to be little interest in the governing body for radically altering the social or geographic basis of participation. The priority is rather to consolidate and concentrate on maintaining the flow of young players into the adult game by supporting the network of schools that currently teach rugby and strengthening the youth development policy within existing clubs and to a lesser extent, universities. Part of this policy is a tacit agreement between the IRFM and the GAA not to attempt to poach schools from each other.

Although current relations with the government are cool and distant, there are two issues which may prompt the IRFU to seek closer links. The first issue is the long-term future of the Lansdown Road ground and the consideration being given at present to the development of a new stadium. The second issue is the recent and rapid professionalisation of the sport. Any attempt to keep Irish players with Irish clubs would radically reduce the proportion of income that the IRFU could retain and might make it less able to fund its development projects. Yet, the growth of a greater desire on the part of the IRFU to bring government within its policy orbit presupposes, at the very least, the emergence of a complementarity of interest between the two organisations. While the government is much more aware of the value, both domestically and diplomatically, of international sporting success, its policy is largely unformed. The central values within Irish sport policy are still primarily the product of a sensitivity towards British cultural dominance and an internationalism that has difficulty looking beyond the pattern of the Irish Diaspora. Recent popular and governmental enthusiasm for the soccer World Cup, the Olympic Games and even the rugby union Five Nations Cup is an indication of a tentative shift in the parameters of policy debate rather than being an indication of a change in policy itself. A redirection of governmental support towards the major international sports would involve a major redefinition of its policy towards the GAA. Such an explicit policy change is unlikely to be initiated by any of the Irish political parties at present. Rather, they will wait for public opinion and changes in the pattern of sports participation to push for greater investment in facilities for sports that rival the GAA. However, the GAA is acutely aware of its vulnerability to competition for talented sportsmen and sportswomen from other sports that benefit from intense media coverage and also from glamorous and high-quality international events and has demonstrated its capacity to protect its interests effectively on many previous occasions.

The overall effect of the current situation is that governing bodies have no effective collective voice in domestic sport policy. More significantly, the privileged position of the GAA inhibits debate on national sports development strategy. Consequently, governing bodies and individual clubs rely on clientelistic politics focused on the local TD, which devalues links with civil servants and undermines moves towards a more strategic and open approach to policy-making and helps to maintain a policy process that is fragmented and incremental.

UNITED KINGDOM

Among the defining features of British sport is the extensive network of governing bodies and their influence on the character of competitive sport up until the mid-1980s. Although this period has at times been turbulent, it was the epitome of tranquillity when compared with the past ten to fifteen years. There are currently well over one hundred governing bodies and while they follow a variety of organisational patterns they tend to have some or all of the following features in common: separate organisations for each of the four home countries of the UK; separate organisations for men and women; a pyramidal structure with individual clubs at the base supporting county/regional bodies and national organisations; volunteer officers supported by professional administrators, whose number varies considerably depending on the wealth of the body; and finally, substantial reliance on government grant aid via the Sports Councils.

In the early years the governing bodies concentrated on harmonisation and codification of the rules of their sport, the organisation of competition and, for many, the enforcement of eligibility rules designed to maintain amateurism and the social exclusiveness of many major sports such as rugby union, field hockey, athletics and cricket. The dramatic split in rugby that led to the development of a separate code and governing body for rugby league was one of the early signs of a tension between sport as a confirmation of wealth and privilege and sport as a career and source of livelihood. However, even when sports were organised to allow participants to earn a living from their involvement, the administrators, for many years, treated players in a highly exploitative manner. In soccer the attempts by the Football Association to resist the abandonment of the minimum wage and, more recently, to circumvent the European Union judgment on the free movement of players are the most dramatic examples of the feudal relationship between players and administrators/owners. Similarly, in the early years of organised cricket the distinction between 'gentlemen' (amateurs) and 'players' (professionals) was rigidly maintained with the latter being referred to by their surname alone, required to use separate dressing rooms and often having to take a different route to and from the pitch to the pavilion (Birley 1995: 18). Much of the history of UK governing bodies has centred on attempts to thwart the emergence of the professional player and, when that fails, to keep professionals in their place. For many governing bodies the antipathy towards professionalism was coupled with a willingness to make illegal payments to notionally amateur players.

The long history of snobbery, hypocrisy over professionalism and paternalism in management established traditions in major governing bodies of UK sport that have made them generally unable to cope with the pace of change in the past twenty years. To make matters worse, the prominence of these characteristics has distracted attention from the more positive qualities of the UK pattern of governing bodies, especially the high volume of club-level voluntary activity, estimated to be worth over £1.5bn per year (Sports Council 1996), and the occasional willingness to resist government pressure, as over the attempted boycott of the Moscow Olympic Games, and the concern with sports development.

In the past twenty years or so many British governing bodies have been through a period of prolonged and often traumatic change focused on responding to more forceful government involvement, aggressive intervention by commercial interests and challenges to the remaining vestiges of amateurism. The changes in the government of UK track and field provides a good illustration of the problems faced by the major sports and the pace of response required. The development of governing bodies for track and field was typical of the pattern found in many sports. Separate bodies were formed for each of the provinces and also for males and females with a British Amateur Athletic Board formed in 1932 to represent British (and UK) interests internationally and thereby thwarting the Scottish Amateur Athletic Association plan to affiliate independently to the International

Amateur Athletic Federation (IAAF) (Houlihan 1991). The problems of such a fragmented pattern of control and organisation were always apparent but became a source of concern in the 1980s when the existence of nineteen governing bodies began to cause serious problems for the funding and organisation of coaching, event organisation and sports development. In 1983 the Sports Council intervened at the behest of the Minister for Sport and undertook an inquiry into the funding of track and field and made it clear that unless there was considerable administrative reorganisation, the Council would review its financial support for the sport. As a result in 1988 the various bodies decided to form a new umbrella organisation, the British Athletics Federation (BAF).

The progress towards a greater degree of unity within track and field has been slow as there had been discussions about reforming the government of the sport on a number of occasions during the previous twenty years. The major stumbling block was the balance of power between the regions and the centre and the distribution of income and costs within the new body. At the heart of much of the in-fighting was the desire by some of the more prosperous regions to retain control over the television income generated by the sale of broadcasting rights for the more successful competitions. In addition, there was the vexed question of the allocation of responsibility and funding for coaching. Previously, coaching had been the responsibility of the British Amateur Athletic Board (BAAB), a burden which had nearly bankrupted the body on two occasions.

The establishment of the BAF took place at a time when other major changes were underway in the sport, the most important of which was the acceptance that amateurism was a damaging fiction. Yet, the acceptance of professionalism within track and field has not been as difficult as operating within a set of expectations from athletes and sponsors concerning the commercial capacity of the Federation. The demands from athletes for both enhanced governing body services and larger appearance fees have grown generally faster than the Federation's capacity to generate sponsorship income. In 1996 the Federation announced losses of £0.75m. in the previous two years and proposed to make cuts in administrative and coaching staff in an attempt to balance its books. This was despite the announcement of a £4m. sponsorship contract with Reebok and the likelihood of a new television contract. Significantly, and like many other governing bodies, the BAF is looking to the National Lottery to fill its funding shortfall. On the positive side the experience of track and field in the UK shows that a sport can successfully navigate the series of substantial financial and constitutional obstacles that have faced most modern sports. However, the experience of the BAF also highlights the perilous nature of the finances of some major sports. Despite the high international profile of track and field, it remains a sport run on an extremely fragile budget and where the failure of one sponsorship deal can threaten the stability of the sport and jeopardise its development plans. The resignation in 1997 of the BAF Chief Executive,

Peter Radford, suggests that the problems facing the Federation are far from being resolved.

The past few years have also proved traumatic for another of the UK's major sports. Both the rugby codes, but especially rugby union, have had to cope with profound change in recent years. Rugby union had for many years been one of the most vociferous upholders of the amateur tradition. Cracks began to appear in facade of amateurism during the 1980s when the income from broadcasting rights began to escalate. Allegations of illegal payments to players were rife and as Vernon Pugh, chair of the International Board commented, 'We had a situation which tended to make honest men dishonest' (quoted in the *Guardian,* 28 August 1996). The weaker level of commitment to amateurism in France and Australia (or their more pragmatic approach to sport in the 1990s) increased the pressure on the four home countries of Ireland, Wales, Scotland and England to accept the demise of amateurism. Despite some dogged resistance from within the English Rugby Football Union, the inevitable acceptance of payment to players came in August 1995 when the International Board, the sport's international federation, abandoned 120 years of amateurism and accepted professionalism.

The decision threw the national governing bodies into confusion. The Rugby Football Union (RFU) voted to impose a one-year moratorium on professionalism in order to create time to determine a number of key issues, including the nature of professional players' contracts, the balance of obligation between club and country, and the negotiation of broadcasting rights and the distribution of the subsequent income. The next fourteen months was a period of acrimonious dispute between clubs and the RFU and between the RFU and the other national governing bodies involved in the five nations championships. At the heart of the dispute between the clubs and the RFU was the distribution of income from broadcasting. The twenty-four major clubs formed the English Professional Rugby Union Clubs (EPRUC) to negotiate on their behalf with the RFU. Threatening not to release players for international matches and thereby jeopardising the lucrative £87.5m. deal with Sky television, there followed a protracted period of wrangling for control over the sport. The EPRUC has argued that it is more than capable of running the professional game and that the RFU should concentrate on the non-professional side of the game. On the other hand, the RFU argues that it controls the highly valuable international fixtures without which rugby union might well lose out to its rival, rugby league. At the time of writing a compromise seems to have been reached which gives the clubs a considerable share of the RFU's broadcasting income but which leaves the control of the sport in the hands of the governing body. Whether the compromise will hold remains to be seen.

The problems faced by the English RFU have been repeated, if in slightly different forms, in the other home nations. Each has struggled to establish a relationship with their elite clubs, although the lack of a large number of potentially wealthy clubs as in England has made the negotiations less fraught. In addition, the Scottish, Welsh and Irish clubs have had a common cause with their governing bodies in attempting to resist the RFU taking the lion's share of income generated by the Five Nations Championship. In April 1995 the RFU announced that it had negotiated a separate deal with Sky television for all England's international matches. Not surprisingly, the other home nations and France threatened to cancel their matches against England unless the deal was renegotiated. A final cause of conflict between clubs and the governing bodies was the attempt by the former to negotiate a television deal for a European club competition. However, Sky agreed to negotiate only with the governing bodies and not with organisations such as EPRUC.

The decision by Sky television to support the governing bodies is reminiscent of the problems that faced the Football Association when its elite clubs sought to achieve greater control over the commercial aspects of soccer. Here again the preference of Sky television to negotiate with the FA was a major source of leverage in the governing body's bargaining with the elite clubs, and reflects Sky's preference for dealing with a cartel rather than getting involved in a large number of bilateral negotiations. However, it is ironic that one of the main sources of support for governing bodies comes from commercial interests outside the sport rather from interests within the sport, such as the major clubs and the elite players.

The new environment that many governing bodies are having to operate within has highlighted the disadvantages of the multiplicity of organisations in the UK that claim to 'speak for sport'. The absence of an effective collective voice for British or UK sport is a persistent concern expressed by a number of governing bodies. In England and Wales the Central Council of Physical Recreation (CCPR) which, as indicated in Chapter 3, has the potential to act as a unifying force among the voluntary sector has dissipated its resources in an ultimately fruitless squabble with the British Sports Council. Seeking ways to sever the residual links between the Sports Council and the CCPR was one of the implicit factors influencing the recent restructuring of the Council. In addition, the antipathy of the CCPR to the Council also led other influential organisations in Britain, especially the British Olympic Association (BOA), to treat it with a degree of wariness. The BOA itself provides a potential alternative focus for collective lobbying by the voluntary sports sector, but it has deliberately maintained a peripheral role for a number of reasons: first, an extreme reluctance to become embroiled in the quarrel between the Council and the CCPR; second, the experience of 1980, when it was subject to intense pressure from the government over the American-inspired boycott of the 1980 Olympic Games, which left a deeply ingrained caution in its relations with government; and third, unlike its Italian counterpart, CONI, for example, a reluctance to expand its remit beyond its primary responsibility for Olympic sports.

It has also been suggested that the Sports Councils could and should fulfil the role of articulating the policy priorities of voluntary sport. Even if this had been a credible prospect in the 1970s, it has proved an even more remote possibility over the past fifteen years. The Conservative government entered office with a deep distrust of quangos such as the Sports Council. The government's distrust was based less on the lack of direct ministerial accountability and more on the fear that quangos are easily 'captured' by the interests they are involved with and become an internal lobby on their behalf. As a result, the Sports Council has taken particular care to distance itself from its client group. In 1996, the government reinforced its preference for 'clear blue water' between the Council and the voluntary sector by abolishing the Regional Councils for Sport and Recreation, which were serviced by the Sports Council's regional offices and provided a forum where voluntary, commercial and local authority interests could discuss policy developments with Council officers.

Recent indications of the policy priorities of the new English Sports Council suggest that it will continue to distance itself from the voluntary sector. It is clear that grant aid will be more selective and more closely tied to the current priorities of school sport and of elite success in Olympic and traditional team sports. In 1991–2, for example, the Sports Council grant-aided more than sixty sports, ranging from over £0.5m. for field hockey and sailing to £1,000 for kendo. A broad range of sports was supported, including the main Olympic sports, the major commercial team sports (though mainly for youth development), and a wide range of minority sports, some of which were on the fringe of a definition of sport such as rambling (£50,000), movement and dance (£162,000) and life saving (£50,000). In May 1996 the Sports Council announced that it was intending to be more selective in the sports it supported and identified twenty-two sports, that would receive 'enhanced' service from the Council. The sports selected were those that contributed most directly to the government's twin priorities of young people and the development of excellence. Among the ten criteria used to assess sports were the following: participation levels, potential for international success, achievement at 'excellence level', availability of facilities and governing body administrative, coaching and officiating infrastructure. Included in the twenty-two selected sports are all the traditional British team sports, such as rugby union and league, soccer, netball and cricket, one or two sports newer to Britain such as basketball and triathlon, and the major Olympic sports.

The progress towards a more formal and selective relationship between governing bodies and the Sports Council has been gradual but steady and follows closely in the footsteps of the Canadian and Australian governments. It remains to be seen whether the UK government, through the new Sports Councils, has the self-restraint, and whether the governing bodies have the political and organisational resolve to enable sport to work in partnership with government or whether governing bodies will be overwhelmed as in the Australian and Canadian cases.

THE UNITED STATES

Although different in scale, the development and modern pattern of United States national sports organisations is very similar to that found in the other countries in this study, with the exception of Ireland. The division between commercial and amateur sport in the late nineteenth and early twentieth centuries echoes similar developments elsewhere, as does the association between sport and social exclusivity, and the widespread practice of illegal payments to 'amateurs'. The treatment of sportsmen and women as commodities to be traded, exploited and discarded is also familiar. However, the United States differs from most other countries in the low level of contact between government and the NSOs and in the strong position of college organisations in the overall fabric of sport in the country. Among the broad range of NSOs, three categories are distinctive and require particular attention, namely, Olympic sports and the USOC, the NCAA and the structure of college sport, and finally, the major commercial team sports such as basketball, football, baseball and ice hockey.

Voluntary sports clubs spread in America partly as a focus for ethnic identity, as in Australia, and partly as a means of confirming and protecting social status, as in Britain. Thus, the establishment of Scottish Caledonian and German Turner athletics clubs reflected the first motive while the suburban country clubs of the north-eastern states best illustrate the status motive. This latter group, which emerged in the early part of the century, exerted a defining influence on the recently formed NSOs. As Sage notes: 'The Amateur Athletic Union (AAU) and the US Olympic movement were both primarily under the sponsorship of socially elite members of sports clubs' (1990: 97). For much of the twentieth century the charge of social elitism and amateur management levelled against the AAU by the professional staff of the NCAA provided one element of the context of interorganisational conflict over the right to control amateur sport. The other significant ingredient in the conflict was the tension between the international orientation of the American Olympic Committee and AAU (as the NSO recognised by the IAAF) on the one hand, and the NCAA with its primary concern with elite competition in a series of sports, particularly football, that had a domestic rather than an international focus, on the other. Much of the history of the development of the organisational infrastructure of American sport has been dominated by intense and destructive rivalry between key bodies with the effect of exasperating politicians and prompting their intervention, and also undermining the capacity of NSOs to lobby energetically and competently on behalf of American sport.

At the heart of the fragmentation in American amateur sport was the lengthy competition between the AAU and the NCAA for control of elite track and field sportsmen and sportswomen. At the start of the century, the AAU developed a strong link with the American Olympic Committee formed in 1896, primarily because of its existing control over track and field sports and ten other major sports, including swimming and gymnastics. The AAU organised the selection of American athletes for the 1904 Games held in St Louis and oversaw the administration of the Games. The problem the AAU faced arose from the absence in America of an extensive athletic club structure outside the universities. Consequently, the AAU was continually in competition with the growing college athletic circuit for the services of elite athletes. Unfortunately, the universities and colleges were unwilling to acknowledge the assertion by the AAU that students had a prior obligation to participate in AAU-sanctioned events. The rivalry between the AAU and the NCAA lasted until Congress made one of its rare legislative interventions in the administration of sport in 1978.

As the importance of the Olympic Games grew, so did the tension between the two bodies and particularly the desire on the part of the NCAA to challenge the status of the AAU as the Olympic 'franchise holder' (Wilson 1994: 358). Overall, the NCAA progressively weakened the link between the AAU and the Olympic movement, partly by encouraging the formation of rival 'governing bodies' and also by highlighting the poor organisational performance of the Union at athletic competitions. However, the NCAA did little to endear itself to the IOC, the IAAF and other major international federations by its suggestion that the legitimacy of the AAU was derived from foreign organisations and therefore suspect. In addition, the NCAA's support for college scholarships was seen by some in the Olympic movement as incompatible with the movement's commitment to amateurism. Later, when the Soviet Union returned to Olympic competition with its state-sponsored athletes, the force of the criticism directed towards the NCAA was greatly weakened, as was the value of the claim by the AAU to be the guardian of pure spirit of amateurism.

By the 1930s the AAU had agreed to allow the NCAA joint control over Olympic qualification for a number of sports including track and field, swimming and gymnastics (Wilson 1994). Although there was a lull in the dispute between the two bodies until the 1960s, the political context of sport had altered radically and thus made the renewal of conflict of sharper concern to the government. Of greatest significance was the abrupt rise and consolidation of communist athletic superiority in both the summer and winter Olympic Games and the first defeat of the United States by the Soviet Union in the annual track and field competition. Congressional interest in the organisation of amateur sport grew steadily from the late 1960s resulting in a series of bills and committee hearings, none of which had any significant impact. Matters reached a head at the 1972 Olympics in Munich where aspects of the disappointing American performance were deemed to be the result of inadequacies in AAU management. In 1975 a Presidential Commission on Olympic Sports was established. The report, published in 1977, provided a comprehensive critique of the deficiencies in the administration and planning of amateur sport with none of the major organisations involved escaping criticism. The Amateur Sports Act of 1978, which accepted many of the recommendations of the Commission, attempted to overcome the 'overorganisation and the demise of local–national control of amateur athletics' (Frey 1978: 361). In brief, the Act, deliberately tailored to fit into the Olympic framework, expanded the role of the US Olympic Committee by giving clear responsibility for co-ordinating the preparation of the teams for the Pan-American and Olympic Games and the right to grant recognition to NSOs for Olympic sports. With the latter power the Act significantly undermined the authority and role of the AAU and opened the door for the recognition of the range of single-sport governing bodies promoted by the NCAA. The final blow to the waning authority of the AAU came a few years later when the IOC agreed that athletes could receive payments, such as sponsorship money, but these would be held in a trust managed by the athletes' international federation. With the demise of amateurism, the AAU had no principle left to defend and with the international federations being given the responsibility for the trust it had no clear management function either.

Among Olympic sports the United States has an organisational structure superficially similar to that found in the other countries in this study, namely a series of single-sport governing bodies with representation on the Olympic Committee. However, the authority vested in the Olympic Committee by the Amateur Sports Act 1978 to establish governing bodies makes the latter more dependent on the Committee than is the case elsewhere. The dependence is the result not only of the legal authority of the USOC but also the precarious financial position of most governing bodies. Even USA Track and Field (USATF) received, in 1994, about 29 per cent ($2.7m.) of its income from the Olympic Committee. Out of a total of $9.2m. the major sources of USATF income, apart from the USOC grant, were sponsorship ($3.9m.), events ($1.2m.), television ($0.45m.) and membership ($0.5m.). In general, USATF has a good relationship with the USOC, helped by the scale of grant aid provided. However, there is a clear feeling within USATF that the Olympic Committee encroaches on issues, such as the organisation of coach education and development, that are properly the preserve of the governing body. Tension also arises because of the growing importance of sponsorship income and because Nike sponsors USATF while Champion sponsors the Olympic team, necessitating complex protocols designed to satisfy both corporations. Although there are a large number of clubs affiliated to USATF, the sport relies heavily on the NCAA to develop future elite athletes. There is little interclub competition owing to the cost of travel and the main function of local clubs is to provide coaching. However, this frequently means that young athletes will have a series of coaches during the formative part of their career; one each at junior school, local club, high school and college.

Other governing bodies have similar financial profiles and a similar dependence on the Olympic Committee. US Swimming, for example, owing to its large membership receives more than $5m. in subscriptions, but also receives $1.5m. grant from the USOC as well as many services in kind such as office space. In addition, US Swimming receives $2m. in sponsorship. By contrast, US Weightlifting with only 3,000 members relied on the USOC for over half its total income of $0.8m. in 1995.

The long and acrimonious battle for control of amateur sport sullied the reputation of all those involved and left a lasting impression among federal politicians that American sports organisations were small-minded, petty and barely competent. Although matters have improved substantially, the USOC and the NCAA are far from being in a position of having the confidence of government should either of them wish to lobby Washington.

Although the acceptance of payments to sportsmen and sportswomen seriously damaged the AAU, it also harmed the interests of the NCAA owing to the increasingly central role of domestic governing bodies, many of which had been sponsored by the NCAA as part of its battle with the AAU. Yet, the NCAA, because of its control over college sport and the relative weakness of non-college athletic clubs, retains a dominant position in the American NSO infrastructure. The Association was formed in 1905 as a result of the growing concern among politicians and academics at the extent of violence and injury evident in college sport.[2] In 1905 there had been eighteen deaths and 159 serious injuries in college football (Fleisher *et al.* 1992: 39). The Association helped to standardise rules and, in so doing, reduce the number of fatalities and serious injuries. As is common with many organisations, once the NCAA fulfilled its original brief it was reluctant to disband and began the process of extending its remit to include what Fleisher *et al.* refer to as the 'cartelizing of intercollegiate football' (1992: 35). Over the next fifty years the NCAA expanded from a body organising sport for a small number of elite universities to one that had, by 1961, a membership of almost 600 universities, and over 1,000 by the late 1980s. As early as the mid-1950s the NCAA cartel was well established and controlled entry of colleges and universities to the inter-university competition circuit, controlled the terms on which individual athletes might be recruited and compete, and also controlled the increasingly important negotiations over broadcasting rights. The most controversial aspect of the Association's activities was its tight control over student athletes. On the one hand, the NCAA set ground rules for the recruitment of athletes and, most importantly, set standard terms for scholarships which ensured not only that minimum conditions were met, but also that colleges could not compete for athletes by offering more generous scholarships. The latter control ensured that a free market in recruitment was prevented and consequently that the cost to the colleges of recruiting athletic talent was kept low. In addition, the NCAA imposed and rigorously enforced eligibility criteria which prevented athletes competing outside the NCAA circuit, thus precipitating the long-running conflict with the AAU referred to above.

With the expansion of television interest in college sport from the mid-1950s, the NCAA became the organising body for a multi-million dollar business. By the early 1980s television companies were already paying over $60m. for the broadcasting rights to college football and rapidly increasing sums for basketball. Attendances had also grown and stabilised around 35m. per season for football by the late 1970s. NCAA activity was not simply of interest to the physical education departments of colleges, it was also seen by most colleges as an essential element in their marketing effort and an important source of revenue. In contradiction to Sperber's (1990) suggestion that college sports is a drain on college finances, the analysis by Fleisher *et al.* (1992) suggests strongly that behind the public accounting deficit there is a genuine transfer of income from sport to central college funds. Although there was some weakening of the NCAA cartel in the early 1970s, with the establishment of the short-lived Association of Intercollegiate Athletics for Women, and in the mid-1980s when the Supreme Court allowed individual universities to negotiate directly with the television companies, the position of the NCAA in the late 1990s is still dominant in the college sector. Its determination to ensure that college athletes give due priority to college competition has brought it into conflict with the US Olympic Committee which, following the lead of the IOC and major international federations, has progressively liberalised athlete eligibility criteria. However, this tension over control of athletes is obviously less acute with regard to the non-Olympic sports such as football and, until recently, basketball, and consequently the NCAA has a better relationship with the commercial sports sector for which it acts as an athlete development department.

Apart from the Olympic sports governing bodies and the NCAA the third key element in the American sports infrastructure is the commercial sector and the major team sports of football, basketball, baseball and ice hockey. While many Americans cling to the fiction that sports businesses are qualitatively different from other commercial enterprises, there is little in the organisation and management of the National Football League (NFL) or the National Basketball Association (NBA) to suggest that they differ in any substantial way from Ford or McDonald's.[3] As Sage observes, 'The professional team sport industry is . . . one in which capitalist productive relations hold sway and in which power, dominance, and subordination are fundamental' (1990: 138).

The National Baseball League was founded in 1876 and was the earliest of the major team sports to organise non-college competition. Similar organisations followed with a second baseball league (the American League in 1900), the National Hockey League in 1917, the National Football League in 1922 and the National Basketball Association in 1946. From the earliest days of non-college competitive sport, there has been substantial commercial involvement initially through sponsorship of teams by local companies, and then through the trading of franchises. Recent estimates value the NFL, for example, at over $2.4bn (Reiss 1988, quoted in Sage 1990) However, rather than being the exclusive result of astute entrepreneurial skills, the economic success of football, and indeed the other major commercial sports, is also the product of an effective cartel and substantial public support in the form of tax breaks, stadium subsidies and anti-trust exemptions.

Nothing better illustrates the ambiguous attitude towards commercial sport than the application of anti-trust (anti-monopoly) laws. As with the NCAA, commercial sports attempt to function as cartels by restricting or controlling: the recruitment, employment and transfer of players; the entry of new teams; and the sale of outputs particularly broadcasting rights. The Sherman Anti-trust Act 1890 has been applied to sport with the prohibition of price-fixing, agreements not to compete and collective boycotts, but in general sport has been treated differently to other industries. Due to the unique nature of professional sports operations, such as the necessity of members of a league agreeing to abide by predetermined rules and regulations, the courts have found justification for violation of anti-trust laws' (Freedman 1987: 4). Of the four major team sports in America, only baseball has exemption from the Sherman Act 'upon the grounds that this professional sport was not engaged in interstate commerce or trade, and furthermore baseball was in essence not a commercial activity' (ibid.: 32). In large part, the decision of the Supreme Court in 1922 to exempt baseball was based as much upon sentiment as upon an interpretation of the Sherman Act. Sentiment has continued to give baseball a privileged position as the 1972 comments of the Southern District federal court of New York reflect: 'The game is on higher ground; it behoves everyone to keep it there' (quoted in Freedman 1987: 34).

The other major team sports have generally had to abide by the Sherman Act and, despite repeated attempts to argue that they should benefit from the same treatment as baseball, Congress has resisted any significant extension of exemptions although the 1966 agreement that the AFL could merge with the NHL was a major exception (see Wilson 1994: 131–7). However, the absence of anti-trust exemptions has not had a noticeable effect on the structure of team sports. As Roberts notes: 'Since World War II, one hockey, two basketball, and four football leagues have sprung up to compete against the NHL, NBA and NFL respectively, and not one has survived more than a few seasons' (1991: 139–40; see also Gorman and Calhoun 1994). There is within the American legal and political system a deep-rooted sympathy for major sports which results in a generally more favourable treatment than other businesses. Illustrations of sympathetic treatment include a favourable tax position that enables clubs to offset a proportion of player costs against tax liability. In addition, the NBA and the American Basketball Association were eventually allowed to merge in 1976 despite being refused permission on anti-trust grounds only six years earlier. All the major commercial sports also obtain considerable benefit from the subsidy provided by municipalities in the form of low-rent (often below cost) stadiums. Finally, as with the other sports leagues, the NBA sells national broadcasting rights on behalf of league members without challenge on anti-trust grounds.[4] In general, the owners of leagues and franchises have lobbied extremely effectively to preserve many elements of a sports cartel and those who sought to challenge their power, including players and would-be entrants to the sport, have received remarkably little encouragement or support from the courts or Congress. What makes the power of the owners greater is the absence of any countervailing pressure from international sports federations as only basketball and ice hockey have a significant international presence, at Olympic level for example, and both these sports have weak international governing bodies.

CONCLUSION

It is tempting to paint a picture of domestic governing bodies as institutions whose best days are behind them. For most sports the pioneering role of national governing bodies in harmonising rules, organising competitions and supporting clubs in their infancy is now long passed. In many sports clubs are well established and the international federations have taken over many of the key roles of domestic governing bodies. The increasing commercialisation of sport has not only increased the income of many sports at elite level, but has often driven a wedge between the elite clubs and their governing bodies and between elite sport and mass participation. In addition, the growth of government involvement in sport has also contributed to the marginalisation of governing bodies in areas of sports development. Finally, the extensive investment at local government level in facilities for sport has enabled much sport to be organised on a casual basis (racquet sports, for example) which makes the governing body largely redundant.

In a number of the major team sports, domestic governing bodies increasingly fulfil a legitimising role, making them part of the 'dignified constitution' of sport. They hold power only nominally as substantive control has passed into the hands of the major clubs, leagues, broadcasters and other commercial interests. The position of professional sport in Canada, the United States and Australia is the direction in which UK professional sports are moving. The recent realignment between the Football Association and the elite soccer clubs and the current realignment underway within rugby union are clear indications of a diminished role for governing bodies and a step closer to the United States model.

In the United States the weak and diminishing role of governing bodies is substantially the result of the intensity of commercialisation and the long-standing fragmentation and mutual suspicion between governing and organising bodies. United States sport has also not been able to exploit the interest of government in sport as a potential countervailing pressure. In preference to a long-term commitment to the sport policy area, the US federal government has tended to intervene infrequently but significantly in sport, thus increasing the level of uncertainty among governing bodies. Unfortunately in countries where governments have acknowledged sport as an aspect of public policy, governing bodies have frequently been overwhelmed by the weight of public resources and bureaucracy. At the heart of the vulnerability of governing bodies to commercial and governmental interference lies their inability to develop effective lobbying organisations. In the UK the acrimony between the CCPR and the British Sports Council and the consequent tendency of governing bodies to distance themselves from the CCPR undermined the CCPR's claim to be the 'voice of sport'. Attempts to form representative interest groups in Canada, Ireland and Australia have all been less than successful owing to a high degree of mutual distrust between governing bodies and a preference on the part of the government for bilateral links.

For some domestic governing bodies, such as those in Ireland, links with their international federation or with major events-organising bodies such as the IOC provide some leverage in relations with commercial and governmental interests. However, for most governing bodies strong links with international bodies provide few resources. In Canada the close and high-profile links between governing bodies and the IAAF and the IOC has done little to reduce the high level of control exerted by government. In general, domestic governing bodies run a significant risk of being marginalised as commerce, government, clubs and players all vie with one another to control an increasingly wide range of elite-level sports. The voice of governing bodies in policy debates on sport is getting progressively weaker and it is hard to see how they can maintain their control over elite sport in the coming years.

6 Doping and sport

Many articles and books that examine the incidence of drug abuse by athletes begin by stating that the use of drugs to enhance performance is not new. Research has demonstrated that ether, caffeine, brandy, cocaine and other substances were used throughout the history of competitive sport (Williams 1974; Hanley 1979; Donohoe and Johnson 1986; Woolley 1987; Asken 1988). However, a more appropriate emphasis is not the continuity in the use of drugs but rather, the persistence of the desire to cheat in competitive sport. Drug abuse needs to be seen in the same category as other methods of winning unfairly such as bribery, intimidation and collusion. Few issues in modern sport have generated so much passion and controversy as the prevalence of drug abuse in sport. It would be convenient to be able to trace the source of that passion to an acknowledgement that doping is directly at variance with the values of sport as reflected, for example, in the Olympic Charter. However, not only is it difficult to sustain the argument that sport possesses a set of agreed and immutable values, but it is equally difficult to identify a consensus within sport regarding the use of drugs (Hyland 1990). The attitudes of governing bodies, athletes and governments are frequently ambiguous.

Much of this ambiguity is reflected in the process of developing a policy towards doping and to an extent may be seen as a consequence of the relatively recent history of attempts to combat drug abuse by athletes.[1] Although modern policy can be traced back to the early 1960s, it was undoubtedly the discovery that Ben Johnson had used anabolic steroids in his dramatic victory in the 100 metres final at the Seoul Olympics in 1988 that transformed what might best be described as a largely private matter into a public concern.

The modern concern with drug use in sport emerged in the 1950s and 1960s. Among scientists, for example, there was a growing awareness of the properties of anabolic steroids as early as the 1930s and even though there were rumours that Soviet athletes were being given steroids in the mid-1950s, it was not until the late 1960s that research confirmed the value of steroids in increasing muscular strength (Banks 1992). Even in the 1960s much of the evidence regarding the use of steroids and other drugs was anecdotal.

Allegations about the extent of use abounded but corroborated evidence was in short supply. However, the small amount of reliable research that had been undertaken suggested that doping was not a marginal practice in sport (see, for example, Williams 1974; Ljungqvist 1975; Cooter 1980; Clements 1983; Donohoe and Johnson 1986).

As mentioned earlier, the issue of doping in sport reached the agenda in many countries through the disqualification of Ben Johnson, but the Johnson scandal was only one in a series of equally dramatic events, some involving positive tests and others the consequence of political change. Few countries were immune from the scandal of positive drug tests: the British Olympic bronze medallist, Kerrith Brown, also tested positive at the Seoul Games; Harry 'Butch' Reynolds of the United States tested positive for nandrolone in 1990; and in 1992 three German athletes, including Katrin Krabbe, were suspended for alleged doping sample manipulation. To compound the effect of these individual cases the ending of the Cold War brought fresh evidence of systematic state-administered drug abuse, particularly in former East Germany and in the former Soviet Union.

The early tentative steps towards developing a policy response to doping came in the 1960s from a range of domestic sports organisations and governments, including Norway, West Germany and the UK, and also from a range of international bodies. In 1962 the IOC passed a resolution against doping and, in 1967, the year of the televised death of the cyclist Tom Simpson in the Tour de France, established the IOC Medical Commission with a brief to devise a strategy to combat doping. Four years later the Medical Commission produced the first IOC list of banned substances (mainly stimulants and narcotic analgesics) and practices. The IOC list, which rapidly became the international standard, had anabolic steroids added in 1974 following the development of a reliable test to determine their presence in a urine sample. Caffeine and testosterone were included on the list in 1982 as were beta-blockers three years later along with the practice of blood doping. More recently, in 1987 diuretics were included on the list as was probenecid which inhibits the excretion of anabolic steroids in the urine. In general the IOC is reluctant to add a substance or practice to its list until a reliable method of detection has been developed. An exception to this policy was the inclusion of erythropoetin (EPO), which speeds up the body's production of red blood cells thus enabling athletes to absorb more oxygen. EPO was included on the IOC list in 1990 despite the absence of a reliable method of detection.

FIFA, the soccer international federation, introduced modest drug testing during the 1966 World Cup followed by similarly modest efforts by the IOC at the 1968 Winter Olympic Games in Grenoble and by the Commonwealth Games Federation at the 1970 Commonwealth Games. Among the international federations, the IAAF formed a Medical Committee in 1972 and began testing for anabolic steroids at the 1974 European Athletics Championships in Rome. By 1976 the Federation had developed an agenda for its anti-doping activities designed to improve the quality of its testing and to clarify its rules. However, it was not until the late 1970s that a systematic policy was implemented with, for example, the introduction of an eighteen-month minimum suspension rule, agreed standardised testing procedures and agreed criteria for the accreditation of laboratories undertaking the analysis of samples. Finally, in parallel to the activities of the federations, individual governments and the IOC, the Council of Europe was also active in attempting to stimulate action among its members. In 1963 it published a definition of doping. Later in 1979 the Council adopted a recommendation urging member states to develop domestic policies to combat drug abuse in sport and followed this, in 1984, with the publication of the European Anti-doping Charter, which outlined in detail a suggested policy response by governments.

Given the broad range of organisations with an interest in the issue and also bearing in mind the international pattern of sports competition and training, the development of anti-doping policy needs to seen within a domestic and, more importantly, within an international context. The framework for policy development is complicated by the interweaving of concerns regarding state sovereignty, the maintenance of a degree of autonomy by domestic governing bodies from their international federation (IF) and the tension between the Olympic movement and the major IFs (Houlihan 1994). It is within this complex organisational pattern, where each member gives the issue of anti-doping a priority in relation to its broader organisational goals, that policy has been, and continues to be, developed. The process of policy development has three distinct themes: first, the development of an agreed list of banned substances and practices; second, agreement on the testing procedure, which includes agreement on the technical conduct of the sample collection and its analysis, and also includes the administration of the testing regime, for example, agreeing who should be tested, how often and when; and finally, what penalties should be imposed for doping and also whether the penalty should be applied to the athlete alone or to his/her governing body as well. It is against this background of organisational complexity and suspicion that domestic sports organisations and governments in this study have sought to devise and implement an anti-doping policy.

AUSTRALIA

With only one or two dissenting voices (see, for example, Donald 1983), the majority of those involved in sport in Australia maintained for much of the 1980s that doping was an issue for other countries, especially those in the communist bloc. The steady success of Australian athletes was seen as the product of the Australian way of life and later, and more plausibly, the product of the professional support and training provided by the Australian Institute of Sport. However, the general complacency was rudely broken in the late 1980s when allegations of doping by a significant number of elite athletes began to be voiced more loudly and regularly. What gave the issue additional momentum was the suggestion that a number of staff at the Australian Institute of Sport were deeply implicated in doping. The Australian media were particularly important in forcing the issue on to the political agenda, with the broadcast of the 'Four Corners' programme in November 1987 having a major impact. The programme suggested that doping was widespread and especially so within the AIS. Additional impetus was provided by a number of Australian athletes who had tested positive and who offered the conventional defence that 'everyone' at the elite level was taking drugs. The response of the government was to appoint a Senate Committee of Inquiry, chaired by John Black, which, in its Interim Report, concluded that, on the one hand, 'there has been a problem with drug use in Australian sport and that this has extended to all levels, and included sportspeople of all ages' (Australia 1989: xix), but on the other, that the problem 'is by no means as serious, or as extensive, as sport drug abuse in many other countries' (ibid.).

The Interim Report provided a sharp insight into the complex motives surrounding anti-doping policy and the problems that inhibit effective implementation. Among the justifications given in the report for adopting a stringent anti-doping policy are the adverse consequences on health, the alienating effect of drug-induced achievements on public support and the undermining of Australia's attempts to host future Olympic Games. In terms of implementation the report illustrates the prisoners' dilemma that is evident in sport policy. The report acknowledged the adverse effects on national pride and the chances of hosting future Olympics if no action is taken, but also acknowledged that if a testing regime is introduced that is more stringent than that of other major sporting countries then 'Australian athletes will never be internationally competitive' (ibid.). The report therefore argues that 'there is no doubt that Australia's interests would be best served by the world-wide implementation of the kind of testing regime proposed in this report' (ibid.: xx). To this end it is suggested that the Australian Olympic Federation and its members on the IOC lobby hard for the development of similar international standards of testing.

As well as providing a snapshot of the then current state and direction of policy regarding doping, the Interim Report also makes clear that policy formation is not a linear process but a circular one, where initial problem definition is reviewed in the light of feedback on current policy and where the redefined problem sets in motion a new round of policy development. Thus, the linear ideal types of Downs or Hogwood and Gunn need to be modified to take account of the fitful pattern of policy development prompted by some issues. So, while it is attractive to see the formation of anti-doping policy as progression from agreement on definitions, through agreement on procedures, to determination of penalties, the situation in Australia makes clear that policy-making in each of these three areas is tightly interdependent.

As with most other countries, Australia followed the lead given by the

IOC and, to a lesser extent, that of the IAAF. While the major international bodies were grappling with the problems of defining doping, domestic governing bodies were faced with the problem of interpreting the IOC policy. For some governing bodies, for example, the Australian Weightlifting Federation, definitions of doping in the late 1980s were 'too general, confusing and open to various interpretation' (Australia 1989: 15–16). For example, while steroids were banned the AIS was involved in research into the benefits to throwers of the use of amino acids and inosene as agents to aid recovery from training, and the use of food supplements, vitamins and minerals as aids to performance. According to the Royal Brisbane Hospital Foundation, 'the Australian Institute of Sport is investigating safe, legal pharmacological ways to enhance endogenous growth hormone production and thus performance . . . ' (ibid.: 23).

Prior to the Senate investigation of drug use in sport, there was little co-ordination in the definitions of doping adopted by domestic governing bodies, considerable uncertainty over the interpretation of the prevailing IOC definition and clear attempts to probe the then limits of tolerance of the policy. Yet, the Senate investigation, like the Dubin Inquiry in Canada, proved to be a watershed in the evolution of Australian anti-doping policy. By the time the second report (Australia 1990) was published in May 1990, a broad consensus, based on the IOC list, had emerged regarding the substances and practices to be banned. Even the professional sports of Australian rules football, rugby league, soccer and basketball had accepted the IOC list as their framework for policy development. Currently there is little disagreement over the list of banned substances and practices with all major amateur and professional sports adhering to the IOC policy.

Up until the late 1980s the policy regarding who, when and how often to test, and indeed whether to test, was left largely to the discretion of individual governing bodies. The governing bodies for fourteen sports had testing policies and programmes in place and conducted tests usually at major competitions but also randomly. Two groups of athletes were subject to regular testing – those associated with the AIS and those who competed at the national championships. In general, the policy was haphazard and unenthusiastically implemented and covered fewer than 500 athletes, none of whom was involved in professional sports. According to Kemp, an athletics coach at the AIS:

> The testing program in Australia is basically regarded as a joke by the athletes. In the case of track and field the only tested meet is usually the national championships and they know when that is on, so athletes can easily organise their schedules to avoid the testing.
>
> (quoted in Australia 1989: 84)

For athletes holding an AIS scholarship the regime was slightly more rigorous as they were subject to random testing.

By the time of the publication of the Senate Committee's second report, there had been some improvement among the professional sports examined but most of the changes had been only recently agreed. Even so there was a considerable degree of variation concerning who was tested and how frequently tests were carried out. The Australian Soccer Federation adopted an anti-doping policy in 1989, but its representatives 'were vague about the number of tests that were envisaged' and up to the end of 1989 no tests had been carried out (Australia 1990: 103). Similarly, the Australian Basketball Federation adopted its anti-doping policy between the publication of the Senate Committee's Interim Report and the hearings for the Second Report. In common with soccer no tests had been carried out and the Federation was unsure how many tests would be conducted. An exception among professional sports was rugby league, which introduced drug testing in 1986 (well before many amateur Olympic sports), had carried out more than 300 tests in the following three years and in 1990 amended its policy to include out-of-season testing.

By the early 1990s there was a clear consensus among the proponents of an anti-doping policy that random out-of-competition testing was essential to combat steroid use. There was also a growing awareness within government and governing bodies of the difficulties associated with the implementation of an effective policy. For example, problems arise from the actual collection of the urine sample and laboratory handling of tests where a series of opportunities occur to interfere with or contaminate samples. A number of athletes commented in evidence to the Black Committee on the slackness of supervision of athletes when they were providing their urine sample. More significantly there was some doubt cast on the reliability of the Brisbane laboratory used to analyse samples. In January 1987 the laboratory, which had analysed samples from 1982, lost its accreditation from the IOC owing to its failure to identify correctly four out of eight test samples provided by the IOC. The laboratory continued conducting sample analysis for almost a further twelve months before the decision was taken by the governing bodies and the Australian Olympic Federation (AOF) to send samples abroad.

Irrespective of the particular problems of the Brisbane laboratory, there are a number of problems which all laboratories and governing bodies face in deciding how to respond to analyses. The problem has two aspects. The first is that laboratories differ in the detection thresholds that they are able to adopt. The more sophisticated drug users have been known to adapt their pattern of doping to remain just below the detectability threshold of the local laboratory. The second aspect of the problem concerns defining a positive test. This dilemma is especially acute with regard to the use of drugs that occur naturally in the body, but is also evident with regard to drugs such as caffeine. The problem may be illustrated with reference to testosterone which is present naturally in both males and females. Testosterone levels can vary considerably in any population but the ratio of testosterone to epitestosterone is more regular. As a result the IOC recommends for males a ratio of 6:1 outside which doping is deemed to have taken place. The problem is in determining a deviation from the norm that will indicate doping beyond doubt: the understandable practice is to err on the side of caution and ignore ratios that are significantly outside the norm but not extreme. A further problem is that some athletes may take an injection of epitestosterone prior to competition to produce a ratio closer to the norm.

An additional difficulty in demonstrating an effective doping policy in the late 1980s was the way in which laboratory results were dealt with by the governing bodies. In common with practice at IOC-accredited laboratories, drug samples are identified by number, not with the athlete's name. It is only the governing body that is able to identify the athlete concerned. The supervisor at the Brisbane laboratory told the Black Committee that during 1987 none of the samples that tested positive were acted upon. Each athlete's sample is divided between two bottles, A and B, and initially it is only the A sample that is tested. If a positive result is declared, the laboratory informs the relevant governing body which then decides whether to inform the athlete and request that the B sample be tested to check the original result. In 1987 no such requests were received from governing bodies, which, possibly from a desire to protect the image of their sport, individual athletes' medal chances or their government funding, quietly ignored the results or declared that they were technically faulty.

Among athletes and sports administrators there was also an acute awareness that not all countries could or would allow such testing. Coates, the President of the Australian Olympic Federation, pointed out that the American NCAA had been prevented by a Californian court from carrying out random tests at Stanford University because it breached rights to privacy (Australia 1989: 10). While this knowledge might have diluted the commitment of the Australian sports men and women, of much greater significance was the ambivalence of both the governing bodies, and particularly the government towards drug use and testing. It is quite apparent that a significant proportion of the Australian sports establishment was only weakly committed to prioritising drug-free sport over gold medals. The clearest indication of the variability of commitment to eliminating the abuse of drugs in sport comes from the comments made in the Senate Committee regarding weightlifting. Having singled out weightlifting and the role of the Australian Weightlifting Federation for particularly damning criticism in the Interim Report, the Committee, in its Second Report, concluded that 'the AWF has taken no effective action to prevent a recurrence of the activities outlined in the Interim Report' and recommended that the Australian Sports Commission should review its funding of the sport (Australia 1990: 156).

Evidence to the Black Committee makes it abundantly clear that athletes, coaches and other staff employed at the AIS were acutely aware of the need to justify the expenditure of taxpayers' money and one obvious way was through the production of gold medal winners. Not surprisingly, the Institute was at the centre of a series of allegations of collusion in the procurement and administration of drugs, particularly anabolic steroids. Some of the allegations were from athletes who had recently tested positive and who justified their behaviour with the familiar allegation that abuse is endemic. A more serious allegation was that anabolic steroids had been administered to two athletes 'for therapeutic reasons' by AIS staff without notification of either the IOC or the athletes' governing body. While there was criticism by the Black Committee of the secrecy surrounding the administration of steroids to the athletes, it was unlikely that they constituted a breach of IOC regulations because neither athlete competed during the period when they were taking the drugs. Despite the absence of firm evidence of collusion to aid drug abuse, the Committee found sufficient circumstantial evidence to draw a series of highly damaging conclusions about the running of the Institute.

The Committee found that the testing regime was flawed because 'there are major questions over the collection of urine samples, the selection of athletes for tests and the low frequency of testing' (Australia 1989: 494). The lack of firm commitment to anti-doping was reflected in the low number of tests: only 239 had been carried out and none had been positive. The standard of administration of testing was also low, with some athletes providing samples unchaperoned, and twenty athletes turning up to provide a urine sample between three and thirty days after the 48-hour deadline. 'Most surprising of all is that four athletes appeared to been tested before their names were drawn' (ibid.: 476). The Committee concluded that the Institute's testing programme:

> was a response to outside pressures to be seen to be 'drug-free', rather than from any real concern for the need to strictly apply IOC guidelines to ensure the integrity of Australian sport and the health of its athletes. . . . The Committee believes that in many ways the AIS drug testing program was worse than having no drug testing programme at all. It provided the protection of appearing to do something to prevent the use of drugs, but was conducted in such a manner that it may have been possible for athletes using drugs to claim that the program showed them to be drug free.
>
> (Australia 1989: 495)

Apart from the Institute the other main organisation with a responsibility for conducting drug tests was the AOF. In 1987 the AOF announced a revised testing regime which was introduced in January 1988. Unfortunately, the way it was introduced added to, rather than allayed, suspicions regarding the determination to eradicate drug abuse. It was announced in late June 1987 by the AOF that random testing would be introduced from January 1988. According to the Black Committee, not only did this degree of advance warning give drug users ample time to ensure that they were free of drugs by the time testing started, but more significantly it allowed any drug users to compete in the Olympic trials.

The most significant outcome of the Black Committee's report was the establishment of the Australian Sports Drug Agency (ASDA) in 1990 with the brief to 'reduce the harm associated with the use of drugs in sport in order to promote the well-being of the individual and enhance the value of sport to society' (ASDA 1991: 3). The ASDA, established by Act of Parliament, is managed by a Board nominated by the Minister who is responsible for the overall operation of the Agency. In 1996–7 the Agency had a budget of just over \$A3m., of which half was spent on testing and a further quarter was spent on educational activities.

The activities of the ASDA were reinforced by the requirement of the Australian Sports Commission (ASC) that any national sports organisation receiving government funds or using government-funded facilities had to have an acceptable anti-doping policy. The ASC agreed to provide additional support to the NSOs through the establishment of a Medical Advisory Panel to advise on the increasingly problematic question of when a positive result constitutes a doping infraction. The ASDA introduced a much more rigorous anti-doping programme, conducting 2,802 tests from a governing body-nominated pool of 2,220 athletes in 1993–4 covering forty-nine sports, with new sports, such as the triathlon, being added if considered that there is the potential for a doping problem. The testing programme is divided between 'public interest' tests and 'contract' tests. Within the former, emphasis is placed on testing athletes from the sports considered to be most 'at risk', including weightlifting, rowing, swimming and track and field. Fifty-six per cent of tests were during the out-of-competition period and 359 contract tests were conducted on behalf of a number of major professional sports, including basketball, soccer and rugby league. Contract tests are undertaken on behalf of professional sports with the threat by the government to withdraw access to publicly funded training and playing facilities often acting as the spur to professional governing bodies to comply with ASC policy (Buti and Fridman 1994).

Table 6.1 Summary of ASDA test results between 1992–3 and 1995–6

Year	In competition	Out of competition	Total tests	Actionable results	Prohibited or restricted substances	Inadvertent[1] drug use	Refusals
1992–3	1,386	1,491	2,877	54	10	22	22
1993–4	1,354	1,448	2,802	38	21	12	5
1994–5	1,414	1,694	3,108	34	24	1	9
1995–6	1,517	1,779	3,296	29	19	2	8

Note: 1   Most results in this category were for pseudoephedrine, a common ingredient in over-the-counter cold cures.
Source: ASDA Annual Reports, various years.

As Table 6.1 shows, there has been a steady rise in the total number of tests, with out-of-competition tests accounting for approximately 50 per cent each year. More significantly, the number of 'positives' has fallen as have the number of examples of inadvertent use and refusals to comply. The last two trends are indicative, according to ASDA, of the success of its education programme, while the general decline in the number of 'positives' might indicate the steady eradication of drug abuse, but might also indicate the use by drug-taking athletes of as yet undetectable substances such as EPO and human growth hormones.

Although the testing regime is much better co-ordinated and more respected than in previous years, there are still a number of areas of concern. For example, of the 38 problematic test results in 1993–4, 33 were due to positive results and 5 were due to failure to provide a sample. However, 'sporting organisations are responsible for investigating the circumstances surrounding positive test results and determining whether sanctions are appropriate' (ASDA 1994: 15). Twelve of the 33 positives were deemed to be 'due to the inadvertent use of banned substances and two were the result of legitimate therapeutic use of a banned substance' (ASDA 1994: 15). This compares with 22 out of 32 positive tests in the previous year and 22 out of 35 in 1991. To use inadvertency as a basis for inaction seems, on the face of it, curious and requires a more rigorous justification than is provided in the ASDA annual report.

A further issue concerns the preference for 'short-notice' testing (95 per cent of all tests) rather than unannounced testing as part of the out-of-competition anti-doping programme. Short-notice tests give an athlete 24 hours to attend a sampling station, thus allowing an opportunity to flush some of the more sophisticated steroids out of their system. These issues notwithstanding, ASDA has achieved a considerable improvement in the quality of Australia's anti-doping effort, most notably in achieving a greater degree of uniformity of policy and practice among governing bodies, but also in enhancing the credibility of and support for the anti-doping policy among athletes (Mugford 1993).

Until 1987 the penalties for doping were the responsibility of the individual governing bodies and were highly inconsistent and generally low. In the early 1980s the period of suspension could be as short as nine months (Donald 1983). In 1987, at the same time as the announcement of the new testing regime, the AOF agreed that any athlete found guilty of having taken drugs would be banned for life. However, while this was the strongly held view of Kevan Gosper, President of the AOF, it was equally strongly opposed by Ken Fitch, chair of both the AOF and Oceania medical commissions, who argued that Australia should adopt the emerging global penalties of a two- to four-year suspension (Gordon 1994: 369). The lack of agreement within the AOF was also to be found between the AOF and the government. During the 1988 Seoul Games the Australian pentathlon team lost its remaining member as a result of a positive tests (it lost one other member because of a positive test just prior to the start of the Games). The athlete's urine sample was found to contain excessive caffeine. Despite claiming that the positive was the result of numerous cups of coffee, he was consequently banned for two years by the pentathlon IF and although he was given a mandatory life ban by the AOF, it was reduced to two years in 1989. The handling of the incident and the penalty imposed by the AOF was subject to criticism by a Senate committee which accused the Federation of being excessively harsh (Gordon 1994: 382). Despite the intention of the AOF to adopt a tough stance on penalties, it was unable to sustain the policy in the face of internal criticism and, more importantly, the lack of international support. Interestingly, the 1992 Australian team took a lawyer with them to the Barcelona Games to act as advocate in discussions with the IOC should 'contestable' positives arise.

The reason for the difficulty in generating broad support for a life ban for doping was not necessarily a reflection of a lack of commitment to anti-doping policy, although this might have been the case for some of those involved in the implementation of the policy. A more important reason for the lack of support for a life ban was the belief that governing bodies might be less inclined to announce a positive where there is the slightest doubt because of the severity of the penalty, much in the same way that juries in murder trials are thought to be less inclined to convict when there is a mandatory death penalty. In other words, the severity of the proposed penalty, far from being an effective deterrent to athletes was seen as undermining the effective implementation of the policy.

Discussions during the early 1990s between domestic governing bodies and their international federations and also between sports organisations and the commonwealth government have led to a greater degree of harmonisation of penalties. Although there is still some variation between governing bodies, there is a general acceptance of the policy on sanctions included in the ASC doping policy, which states that there should be a minimum suspension of two years for a first infraction and a life ban for a second infraction. However, the policy does allow for a lower penalty if the substance may have been taken for therapeutic purposes or, more controversially, if the substance is taken when 'the athlete is "out of competition"' (Buti and Fridman 1994: 492). Increasingly, the ASDA is turning its attention to the maintenance of momentum in policy development at the international level and is especially concerned at a perceived decline in commitment from the IOC. Australia is party to a memorandum of understanding with the UK, Norway, New Zealand and Canada (France recently withdrew) aimed at a closer harmonisation of policy, and is also a signatory of the Council of Europe's Anti-doping Charter. It is also involved in discussions with the People's Republic of China, Malaysia, Singapore and the Philippines over anti-doping policy and best practice.

Overall, Australian anti-doping policy is far more rigorous than prior to the Senate Inquiry. The strong lead from the government, and especially the threat to withdraw funding, has achieved a high degree of consistency in policy implementation among NSOs. The ASDA has progressively tailored its testing strategy to meet the particular characteristics of individual sports. In addition, the government, through the Sport and Recreation Ministers' Council, is extending the anti-doping policy so as to establish a national policy framework that involves states and territories (Breiner 1995). The aim of the extension of the current policy is to encourage states and territories to introduce complementary legislation that will, *inter alia*, fund the testing of elite state athletes. It is anticipated that states will fund about 500 additional tests once the necessary legislation is in place, which is expected to be by 1997 (Richards 1994). The achievement of a testing regime that bears comparison with the more reputable national anti-doping policies, such as those in the Netherlands, Norway and Canada, has been a significant increase in governmental control and the consequent marginalisation of sports governing bodies (see Bryson 1989).

CANADA

It is impossible to deny the magnitude of the scandal produced by the revelation that Ben Johnson's record-breaking run at the 1988 Seoul Olympics was the result of drug abuse, but even so the reaction of the Canadian government seemed wildly out of proportion. A ninety-one day commission of inquiry, which involved over fifty lawyers, forty-eight admitted drug users and over 150 witnesses seemed more an exercise in public expiation, involving the 'mass crucifixion . . . of many of our own heroes' (Helmstaedt 1994: 16), than an inquiry and policy review. While much of the subsequent report (Dubin Report 1990) is routine in both its analysis and its recommendations, it does contain a number of interesting insights into the policy framework for drugs that had developed in Canada. Of particular interest is the degree to which the high level of activity in the development and promotion of international anti-doping policy contrasted with the neglect of domestic policy.

Before assessing the impact of the Dubin Report, it is necessary to examine the development of the domestic anti-doping policy which formed the context for Johnson's doping strategy. It is probably fair to say that Canada's anti-doping policy, in common with that in many other countries, was scandal-driven. Up until the early 1980s neither the government nor the governing bodies of sport had taken any serious steps to formulate a domestic policy or move much beyond a routine endorsement of the prevailing IOC policy. The IOC list of banned substances and practices was generally accepted but little attempt was made to institute a regime of testing outside major competitions. Even following the publication of the Sport Canada anti-doping policy in 1983, there was a routine acceptance of any revisions to the IOC list. Sport Canada did extend the IOC policy to make the *possession* of certain drugs, and not just the laboratory-confirmed positive test, an offence. However, few resources were allocated to the implementation of policy.

Although the first Canadian positive test occurred in 1975, the issue lay largely dormant until 1983 when two events combined to prompt political action on doping in sport. The first was the return, without competing, of a number of athletes from the Pan-American Games in Caracas, Venezuela, allegedly because they were deterred by a more rigorous testing programme than had been expected. Of those who remained, nineteen athletes tested positive, including two Canadians. The second event was the discovery of anabolic steroids in the luggage of a group of Canadian wrestlers on their return from a competition in eastern Europe. Minister Hervieux-Payette announced that federal funding of governing bodies would be contingent upon their development of a strategy to prevent athletes using drugs. These two events also spurred Sport Canada into formalising its opposition to drug abuse through the issuing of a policy statement, *Drug Use and Doping Control in Sport – A Sport Canada Policy*, and also in earmarking funds of Can$650,000 to support testing, an educational programme and research (Macintosh *et al.* 1987: 149).

The 1983 policy statement was extensive and relatively detailed. It placed the onus for the formulation of a detailed policy and its implementation on the NSOs. Among other requirements, governing bodies were asked to devise a plan for the 'regular testing of top Canadian athletes at major competitions and during training periods' (Sport Canada 1983: 1). The policy also committed the government to the punishment of athletes found guilty of doping offences by the withholding of any state financial assistance for one year in the first instance and for life for a second offence. In a revision of the policy in 1985 the penalty for the use of anabolic steroids was increased to a life ban for a first offence.

A leading role in the implementation of the anti-doping policy was taken by the Sports Medicine Council of Canada (SMCC), a federally funded agency. Between 1984 and 1989 over 3,500 tests were carried out, with the bulk of testing being directed at weightlifting, track and field, and cycling (see Table 6.2).

Between 1983 and late 1989, twenty-five Canadian athletes tested positive for breaches of doping regulations, of whom fifteen were weightlifters and seven track and field athletes. From the mid-1980s the penalties imposed were two years for the weightlifters, but between 18 months and two years for most of the track and field athletes.

Up until the early 1990s, responsibility for the implementation of the testing regime in Canada was divided between the SMCC and the governing bodies of sport. The main responsibility of the SMCC was to establish the details of the testing procedures and included the mechanics of sample collection, analysis, notification of results to the governing body and athlete, the conduct of appeals, and the organisation of arbitration arrangements. The responsibility for selecting who should be tested rested with the

Table 6.2 Drug tests conducted between 1984–5 and 1988–9

Sport	1984–5	1985–6	1986–7	1987–8	1988–9	Total
Canoe	18	23	92	23	28	184
Cycling	53	126	89	88	142	498
Judo	–	35	39	36	34	144
Swimming	–	112	71	63	43	289
Track and field	82	215	212	189	286	984
Weightlifting	21	53	121	181	219	595
Other	164	158	191	178	261	952
Total	*338*	*722*	*815*	*758*	*1013*	*3646*

Source: Sports Medicine Council of Canada, via the Canadian Doping Control Centre.

governing body as did the decision regarding the imposition of penalties. Up until 1989 the governing body submitted a plan to Sport Canada that determined how many athletes would be tested and at which events. The governing body was also responsible for nominating the particular athletes to be tested at each event. Despite the commitment to out-of-competition testing included in the 1983 Sport Canada policy statement, no such tests were carried out in the six years following the publication of the policy. Finally, it was also the responsibility of the governing bodies to co-ordinate testing at events although the SMCC provided the sampling equipment and notified the laboratory that a consignment of samples was to be delivered by the governing body.

Despite the apparent clarity of the 1983 policy statement and the commitment of the government, the administration of the testing procedure prior to the Dubin Inquiry was characterised by considerable ambiguity of accountability for key aspects of the process. In particular the intervention of Sport Canada in 1983, which led to the formulation of the anti-doping policy, was rhetorical rather than substantive, with the publication of the policy document being seen as a substitute for policy implementation. In addition, the central role allocated to the governing bodies and the scope for interpretation of their responsibilities was a crucial flaw in policy design and one that was compounded by the unwillingness of Sport Canada to engage in effective monitoring of policy implementation. One would have to agree with the conclusion of the Dubin Report that: 'I am satisfied that what impetus there was for the implementation of an effective anti-doping program which included out-of-competition testing came in large part from Sport Canada' (Dubin Report 1990: 225). The point that needs emphasis is that the level of impetus that did exist was extremely low.

The scale of drug abuse in the 1988 Olympic weightlifting team amply illustrates the weaknesses in the strategy to combat doping. During the Dubin hearings a number of elite-level weightlifters admitted that they had used steroids from the early 1980s. Jacques Demers, for example, admitted using steroids prior to the 1983 Pan-American Games. In late 1983 he was discovered at Montreal airport attempting to smuggle 22,000 doses of anabolic steroids into the country and in 1986 he failed a drug test, although he launched a successful appeal on a technicality (Dubin 1990: 145). At the heart of any discussion of doping in weightlifting is the role of the governing body. The Dubin Inquiry noted that two of the senior coaches 'were aware of the use of anabolic steroids . . . but they chose to ignore it' (p. 149). Further, the report notes that following the arrest of four members of the national squad for attempted smuggling, the failure of the Canadian Weightlifting Federation to conduct an inquiry was a clear indication that it 'did not take a serious view of such misconduct' (p. 150). The only action taken by the Federation was to suggest that the IOC should instigate a programme of random testing and arguing that the Federation's poverty prevented it from such an undertaking.

Yet, the actions of the Federation need to be seen in the context of the culture within international weightlifting and also the lack of commitment from Sport Canada. In the three Olympic Games of 1976, 1984 and 1988 over half the total of positive drug tests were from weightlifters, but rather than this providing the motivation to combat drug abuse, it perversely provided confirmation of the necessity of drug use if Canada were to continue to compete at the highest level. Although the Federation was aware of the prevailing culture within the sport, it did not ignore the issue or the damaging effect of the doping incidents on the image of the sport. In 1978, when no governing body was conducting testing, the Federation approached Sport Canada to request additional funding to conduct testing at national championships. The response of Sport Canada was to agree to the testing but to refuse to provide additional funds, thus forcing the Federation to subsidise testing at the expense of coaching or competition. Not surprisingly the Federation took no action. The lack of interest within Sport Canada in promoting testing was also evident from the continued financial support for individual lifters who had been convicted of the Montreal smuggling offence.

The positive tests on two lifters in 1984, five in 1985 and three in 1986 prompted Sport Canada to apply pressure to the Federation to develop a more effective anti-doping policy. The result was the introduction of an out-of-competition testing programme in 1987. Though rudimentary, the programme seems to have been an effective deterrent as no positives were detected during the year. Unfortunately, 1987 marked not only the introduction of out-of-competition testing, but also the decision by the Federation, on the advice of the national coach, Andrzej Kulesza, to send its elite athletes to Czechoslovakia for intensive training. The federation sent athletes to Czechoslovakia on three occasions in 1987 and 1988 in the run-up to the Seoul Olympics. The Dubin Report states that in the opinion of Pierre Roy, a Federation coach, the improvement in the performance of the athletes on their return was 'extraordinary' and that 'so great an improvement in such a short period of time would not have been possible without the use of anabolic steroids' (1990: 168). The subsequent positive tests on three of the seven-strong Olympic squad led to an internal inquiry into the role of the national coach which concluded that there was no evidence of wrongdoing on his part. He was subsequently confirmed in his post as national coach and given an extended contract.

Experience was very similar with regard to track and field athletes. Prior to 1982 there had been only two positive tests among track and field athletes, apparently confirming the view of the Canadian Track and Field Association (CTFA) that doping was only an issue in other countries. Although the Association declared against doping in 1976, no tests took place until the 1981 national games that in-competition tests were undertaken. The CTFA adopted a formal policy on in- and out-of-competition dope testing in 1982, but only 'where feasible'. As the Dubin Report noted, 'it took many years for the CTFA actually to implement a program of out-of-competition testing' (1990: 217).

The CTFA rather naively responded to enquiries from coaches about the likelihood of testing at particular competitions. By the mid-1980s rumours had begun to surface about doping at the high-performance centre at York University where Charlie Francis trained a group of athletes that included Ben Johnson. The CTFA President refused to arrange surprise dope tests for Charlie Francis' athletes on the grounds that the Association needed firm evidence rather than rumour in order to act. However, the Association did agree to introduce out-of-competition testing from October 1986, arguing that this was a sufficient response to the allegations. Unfortunately, out-of-competition testing did not commence for a further two years, until after the 1988 Olympics. Part of the explanation for the CTFA's inaction lies in the lack of the required investigative and quasi-judicial resources for tackling drug abuse. However, it must also be noted that until the Johnson scandal there was little indication that the Association was enthusiastic about developing the skills required to tackle doping. In addition to the simple cost of testing, the CTFA was also aware of the implications of testing for Canada's future as a host to major events, the likelihood of resistance from athletes and, of especial significance, the fear that the inevitable decline in performance would be punished by Sport Canada by a reduced grant. Unwillingness to address drug abuse was not confined to the NSOs. Within the Canadian Olympic movement there was a similar reluctance to confront the issue. When Richard Pound, IOC vice-president and most senior Canadian Olympic official, appeared before the Dubin Inquiry and was 'questioned why he did not ask Ben Johnson if he took steroids, following numerous rumours and allegations, he stated, "As a lawyer, I felt I was better off not knowing" ' (Moriarty *et al.* 1992: 25). The overall result of the inaction by sports organisations was that the opportunity to determine the direction and character of anti-doping policy was lost and the initiative passed to the government which had other interests beyond a concern with the future of competitive international sport.

The development of the CTFA's policy on testing parallels that of the Canadian Weightlifting Federation. Policy evolved slowly during the early 1980s, jolted occasionally by renewed scandal. The CTFA adopted the IAAF list of banned substances and practices and started to lobby Sport Canada for funding as early as 1983. Although some money was provided, it was slow in being allocated and rarely covered the number of tests requested by the Association. Neither body was keen to pursue a rigorous doping policy refinement and both were content for ambiguity to persist. Consequently, testing was minimal. The generally equivocal nature of the CTFA's commitment to anti-doping was reflected in the penalties applied for a positive result. Initially in 1985, the penalty was extremely mild being simply exclusion from the competition. Within a year the penalties had been raised, because of pressure from Sport Canada, to an eighteen, and later still a twenty-four month suspension. By 1986 Sport Canada began to press the CTFA to introduce more rigorous testing and in 1987 the Association published a much more detailed policy aimed at conducting out-of-competition tests among the top 250 athletes, but no tests were conducted until after the Seoul Olympics. Yet in 1988–9 under fifty out-of-competition tests were conducted by comparison with 200 in-competition tests. As the Dubin Report noted, '[t]he record of the CTFA on developing and implementing its anti-doping policy up to the Seoul Olympics is characterised by a tendency to philosophize, discuss, and delay' (1990: 225).

Following the Seoul Olympics and, more significantly, the publication of the Dubin Inquiry, anti-doping policy developed rapidly. The Canadian Olympic Association (COA), which had taken only a marginal part in the development of Canadian anti-doping policy up until 1988, now embarked on a flurry of activity. In addition to a series of resolutions exhorting others, such as the IOC, governing bodies and the international federations, to take action the COA resolved that unless the governing bodies for Canadian Olympic sports devised and implemented a programme of random out-of-competition testing approved by the Sport Medicine Council of Canada they would not receive COA funding or be allowed to participate in future Olympic Games. The exercise of the considerable power of the COA to withhold funding and to deny participation gave substantial momentum to the development of policy among the governing bodies. This highly effective action by the COA in 1989 underlines the Association's prior complacency and inaction.

As is clear from the foregoing discussion the Dubin Inquiry proved to be a watershed in terms of policy development and implementation. One of the central recommendations of the Dubin Report, and one endorsed by the

Best Report in 1992, was that the SMCC expand its role to become the 'central independent agency responsible for doping control' (Dublin Report 1990: 538). The SMCC had already begun to enhance its role during the Dubin Inquiry and had expanded a programme of unannounced out-of-competition testing funded by Sport Canada. The Dubin recommendation was in line with the advice of the IOC regarding the need for an 'arm's length' agency to undertake testing. The proposal met little opposition from the NSOs, which saw the transfer of responsibility for testing as a way of protecting their relationship with Sport Canada and avoiding a series of complex administrative problems associated with the implementation of anti-doping policy.

In late 1991 Sport Canada agreed that a new organisation was needed to manage the anti-doping policy and announced the establishment of the Canadian Centre for Drug-free Sport (CCDS). Established in 1992 the Centre is funded wholly by the government and is responsible to a Board of Directors which includes lawyers, doctors and two ex-Olympic athletes. In addition to managing the drug testing programme, the Centre aims to fulfil a central role in education about drugs at the domestic level and in shaping the development of anti-doping policy at the international level. For example, the Centre is currently heavily involved in an educational programme aimed at the young. During 1993–4 the Centre undertook a major survey of 11–18-year-olds on the issue of drug use for sports and body-image purposes. The research was used to shape the CCDS's educational campaign 'Spirit of Sport', which was directed at high-risk groups identified in the survey.

The main rationale for the CCDS is as an independent doping control agency. The Centre is responsible for all aspects of doping control, including sample collection, chain of custody, results management, protests, appeals and reinstatements. To date, the Centre has trained over 250 sampling officers and the impact of the Centre on the volume of doping control activity is amply reflected in Table 6.3.

The most obvious impact of the establishment of the Centre, apart from the increase in the number of tests, is the shift towards unannounced tests which, in 1995, accounted for three-quarters of the total. The slight decline

Table 6.3 Doping control activity, 1984–95

	1984	1985	1986	1987	1988	1989	1990	1991	1992	1993	1994	1995
Announced	292	542	625	667	630	1,313	917	1,125	1,042	845	616	419
Unannounced	0	0	0	83	120	229	583	958	1,292	1,440	1,584	1,326
Total	292	542	625	750	750	1,542	1,500	2,083	2,334	2,285	2,200	1,745

Source: CCDS Annual Reports, various years.

in testing from the peak in 1993 is accounted for partly by the cycle of major championships, especially the Olympics, and partly by the growing sensitivity of the testing regime. It is the view within the Centre that the targeting of tests is increasingly precise and therefore fewer tests are required. In addition, many NSOs requested more tests than were required as a way of 'educating' their athletes, and their coaches, about the new more rigorous doping policy. All the tests referred to in Table 6.3 are paid for out of public funds and are deemed to be 'public interest tests'. However, it is possible for governing bodies or organising bodies (such as the Commonwealth Games Federation) to purchase additional tests should they so wish.

In terms of the number and pattern of doping infractions, Table 6.4 shows that there has been a sharp decline from the peak years of 1992 and 1993. It also indicates the familiar pattern of problematic sports including body-building, football and weightlifting.

Of the eighteen doping infractions in 1995, the majority (ten) were for the use of anabolic agents, four were for the use of stimulants and the remainder were refusals. The impact of the CCDS has not been limited to an addition of funds to the testing programme and an increase in the number of tests. The Centre has also been active in refining almost all aspects of national anti-doping policy. Like most other countries the CCDS has endorsed the IOC list of proscribed substances and practices and, in common with the major international federations and indeed the IOC itself, the Centre is more

Table 6.4 Doping infractions, 1989–95

Sport	1989	1990	1991	1992	1993	1994	1995
Bodybuilding	0	3	2	34	27	16	8
Junior football	0	2	1	3	9	10	4
Weightlifting	5	2	3	1	2	2	0
CIAU: Football	0	3	2	2	3	1	0
Athletics	1	0	2	1	3	0	1
Bobsleigh	1	0	1	0	0	1	1
Powerlifting	0	0	0	0	2	1	1
Boxing	0	2	1	0	0	0	0
Wheelchair weightlifting	0	0	0	2	0	0	0
Other	1	1	1	1	1	1	3
Total	*8*	*13*	*13*	*44*	*47*	*32*	*18*

Source: CCDS, doping control: statistics and media releases (no date).

inclined to take account of the likely effect of a substance on performance rather than acting on the simple presence of a drug. For example, the Centre is more inclined to be sympathetic in its interpretation of results that indicate the presence of substances found in cold remedies, as the likely impact on performance would be slight.

In relation to testing procedures the most visible impact of the Centre has been to increase the number and proportion of unannounced tests. But the Centre has also made more systematic the criteria for determining the distribution of tests between sports and between athletes. The first stage is to receive from the NSOs a report which suggests the number of tests thought necessary and the pattern of competition and training during the year. Within the Centre a set of weighted criteria is used to apportion tests between sports. The criteria include the history of drug abuse in each sport, the potential advantage to be gained from anabolic steroids and the general relationship between the skills of particular sports (or positions in team sports, such as football) and the potential benefits of drugs. The Centre can also target-test individuals if it receives firm allegations of drug use. The selection of the actual athletes to be tested out of competition is the responsibility of a doping-control review panel which has a semi-independent relationship with the CCDS.

The Centre is currently reviewing a number of aspects of its sampling procedures. A recurring problem is the tardiness of the NSOs in informing the CCDS of the names of those athletes about to break through into national or elite squads. In addition, athletes are frequently poor at keeping their NSO informed of their location throughout the year with the result that the Centre is considering requiring athletes to phone in to their NSO every three days. A further issue relates to the difficulty of ensuring that sampling officers collect a sample from the correct athlete. Although there is little evidence that impersonation is a problem, the Centre is discussing the issue and collecting examples of methods used to ensure that the correct athlete has been tested, including the use of finger-printing or photographing athletes at the time of a test.

In the immediate aftermath of the Dubin Inquiry, one of the first actions of the government was to put pressure on NSOs to incorporate clear penalties into their rules and also a set of procedures should a positive result be declared. Although there was some resistance from NSOs, an agreement was eventually reached and published in the policy paper, *Canadian Policy on Penalties for Doping in Sport* (Canadian Centre for Drug-free Sport 1993), and subsequently endorsed by the government. In essence the policy required a four-year ban from competition for a first infraction and a life ban for a second infraction. Any athlete guilty of a doping infraction would also lose, for life, their entitlement to federal funding (Canadian Centre for Drug-free Sport 1994). Among a number of NSOs there was a feeling that the penalties were too lenient and they argued for a life ban for a first offence. As a result, the CCDS policy is seen as a minimum. However, in general, the level of disagreement among NSOs is small. A more substantial problem arises from the difficulty some domestic governing bodies have in reconciling their penalties with those of their international federation. The CCDS accepts that the vast majority of international federations have adopted a two-year ban for a first offence. As a result there is a continuing debate about the appropriateness of uniform penalties among such a broad range of sports. At the heart of the unease among many governing bodies is the difference in the length of time an athlete's elite career may last. In some sports such as shooting and riding an athlete may compete for twenty years at the top level whereas in gymnastics or sprint events the 'life expectancy' may be half that period. Thus a four-year ban will have a much greater impact on the sporting career of some athletes than others. Despite these problems the CCDS is reluctant to vary its policy on penalties at least until there is a clear lead from the IOC. However, it has undertaken an examination concerning the inadvertent use of drugs and is currently lobbying the IOC to instigate a policy review (Canadian Centre for Drug-free Sport 1995).

In general, it is the opinion of the officers of the CCDS and, indeed, that of many NSO officers that the current anti-doping regime in Canada is highly effective in identifying drug abusers and that there has been a significant reduction of the amount of doping within Canadian sport. As is the case with any attempt to control a prohibited activity, it is difficult to verify the effectiveness of the CCDS policy. The decline in the number of doping infractions may well be the result of an effective anti-doping policy, but may also reflect the increasing sophistication of drug users. It should also be noted that the implementation of an effective testing regime within professional sports such as ice hockey, baseball and football lags well behind the 'amateur' Olympic sports. However, the respect for the Canadian policy has been reflected in its endorsement by a number of international organisations such as the Council of Europe and the IAAF, which has decided to use the CCDS's doping control services throughout North and Central America, and also through the co-operation of New Zealand, Australia, the UK, Norway and France in exploring opportunities for harmonisation of policy.

Finally, the evolution of Canadian policy on doping in sport has marginalised the governing bodies of sport and placed the government at the centre of policy development and implementation. A generous interpretation of the actions of the governing bodies is that they neglected the issue of doping and underestimated the degree to which it would affect the perception of sport held by the government. A more realistic interpretation is that few governing bodies had either the inclination or the resources to make doping a priority and that this apathy was reinforced, up until the late 1980s, by a series of governments which demonstrated at best an ambiguous attitude towards doping and at worst a willingness to ignore the issue if it jeopardised the prospects for Olympic medals. The recent developments in Canadian policy have been significant but, as de Pencier observes, it:

remains to be seen if the independent testers and the lawyers who are replacing sports officials as the main actors in anti-doping matters will have any more success than their predecessors in eradicating the abuse of some drugs by some athletes and their entourages. Troubling is the fact that with lawyers comes the encouragement and the means for challenging doping control.

(de Pencier 1994: 299)

IRELAND

Ireland's experience of drug testing and of dealing with the consequences of positive tests is slight. To date, there have been only two incidents associated with drug abuse: the first concerned a positive test result from a professional cyclist and the second concerned the refusal by a track and field athlete to be tested. The latter mounted a successful legal challenge to his national governing body on the grounds that he had offered to be tested within days of the official request. Neither of these athletes had a high international profile nor were they involved in sports that attracted substantial media attention. Despite the lack of firm evidence of a doping problem in Ireland there is, among the major governing bodies, a growing awareness of a need to address the issue of doping policy. But this is not because they suspect that they have a hidden drug problem, indeed most governing bodies assert that an anti-doping policy has little relevance to them. The primary reason for the increasing interest among governing bodies is a concern that an anti-doping strategy is emerging due to the policy development of other governments and a range of international organisations. The main loci of policy-making still lies outside Ireland with the IOC, the international federations and with the Council of Europe. As a result, the domestic agenda for doping policy is being set by external organisations using their domestic members to raise the profile of the issue. For example, the activities of the Council of Europe have been particularly important in stimulating governmental awareness of the issue. Ireland's recently developed internationalism has involved it closely with the activities of the Council of Europe which has a strong involvement in a number of major sports issues such as doping, ethics, the promotion of 'sport for all' and soccer hooliganism.

Although the government signed the Council of Europe's anti-doping convention in 1992, action to implement the convention has been slow. The ostensible stumbling block is the lack of agreement regarding who should pay for testing. But a number of other problems exist which hinder the emergence of policy including the lack of a domestic accredited laboratory and a lack of urgency on the part of the governing bodies. As in other countries the impetus for policy development has come largely from government. Yet, the government is not the sole political actor with an interest in the issue of doping. The Olympic Council of Ireland (OCI) has also been lobbying both the government and the governing bodies of Olympic sports to take the issue of doping more seriously. Prompted in part by the policy of the IOC, the OCI undertook eight tests on Irish athletes in the three months prior to their departure for the Barcelona Games in 1992. The OCI has experience of IOC testing procedures at Olympic events and has organised a series of seminars on testing procedures for governing bodies aimed at encouraging them to develop the necessary commitment and organisational capacity to undertake testing. The OCI has also been lobbying government to underwrite the cost of testing by the governing bodies. The events at the Atlanta Games concerning the Irish athletes Michelle Smith and Marie MacMahon have provided a further stimulus to policy development. Smith's triple gold medal success was soured by repeated suggestions of drug abuse despite the lack of any firm evidence. While the Olympic Council of Ireland mounted a staunch defence of its star athlete, its case was weakened by the absence of a rigorous anti-doping policy in Ireland. However, the force of any criticism of the OCI was mitigated by the fact that Smith undertook most of her training outside the Republic in the Netherlands. More damaging was the case of MacMahon, who tested positive for phenylpropanolamine. The runner escaped a ban because the IOC accepted that she had taken the drug inadvertently as part of an influenza remedy and that she 'had not been properly advised about banned substances' (*Guardian*, 2 August 1996). This admission highlighted the limitations of the OCI's drug education and testing policy and has consequently added to the urgency for policy development.

That policy development is at an early stage is apparent from the current level of testing. In the 1993 Annual Report of the sports section of the Department of Education a commitment was made to 'implement a system of drug testing in 1994' (Department of Education 1994: 11). Progress has, however, been much slower and no mention was made of the policy in the 1994 report. In 1994 the National Sports Council carried out a survey to quantify the existing level of testing and to assess the willingness of NSOs to participate in what is referred to as a National Drug Testing Programme. Of the sixty-six NSOs contacted, replies were received from all but twelve, with forty-six agreeing to participate in a national programme and only one, the Irish Olympic Handball Association, indicating that it would not be prepared to participate at this time. In terms of current testing activity, nine NSOs indicated that they carried out testing at national championships; ten carried out tests at major international competitions held in Ireland; and fourteen carried out tests when hosting world championships. As indicated, all testing was conducted at competitions with no random out-of-competition testing programme.

The Irish Rugby Football Union (IRFU), for example, undertakes no testing during the domestic season and conducts testing only at international matches, selecting two players at random from each team. As is common with governing bodies only recently involved with testing, the IRFU has simply adopted the list of substances and practices banned by the IOC and also the conventional penalties of a two-year ban for a first offence and a life ban for a second positive result. Perhaps the most interesting feature of the IRFU's testing policy is the close relationship developed with the Northern Ireland Sports Council which organises the analysis of samples with the IRFU paying the laboratory fees. Part of the explanation lies in the nature of rugby union in Ireland where the national side is drawn from the Irish Republic and Northern Ireland. Participants in rugby union in Northern Ireland are subject to a much more rigorous programme of testing than their colleagues south of the border. Consequently, the pattern of testing in the North has established a set of benchmarks and expectations among players and administrators in the Republic. It is therefore difficult for the IRFU not to adopt a policy which broadly conforms to that so well established in the North (see Table 6.5).

The Gaelic Athletic Association is also in the process of determining its anti-doping policy and like the IRFU is in the position where it currently has no policy in place in the Republic yet finds that its members in Northern Ireland are subject to testing during the playing season. Even though the main GAA sports of football and hurling have few international matches, are not Olympic sports and are still overwhelmingly amateur, the Association has largely adopted the IOC list of proscribed substances and practices as its starting point for policy development. The only variation from the IOC list concerns the use of pain killers where the GAA is inclined to allow a wider range to be used. The Association is also likely to depart from the conventional pattern of penalties by imposing, for a first offence, a six-month ban for the use of anabolic steroids. Although the GAA has discussed its policy extensively and begun to shape the policy to meet the particular requirements of the Association's sports, it is reluctant to institute a testing programme due to uncertainty over the source of funding. Like most of the other NSOs, the GAA is lobbying the government to treat testing as a matter of public interest and therefore agree to underwrite the cost.

Within the government and among sports organisations there is undoubtedly growing interest in and commitment to anti-doping objectives but there remain a number of significant issues to be resolved. The first has already been mentioned and concerns who should pay for testing. In most other industrial countries the cost of testing, initially at least, is borne by the government. Governments tend to cover the cost of testing in the poorer sports and those sports where they consider that there is a public interest in ensuring drug-free sport. In the last two financial years the Irish government has earmarked between IR£20,000 and IR£25,000 for testing, which is roughly equivalent to the amount spent on testing in Northern Ireland. Unfortunately, because of the difficulty of resolving other issues, the money has not been spent.

The second issue concerns who will be responsible for managing and administering the testing programme. The government initially considered using the Olympic Council of Ireland as its agent but decided that the agency needed to be seen to be independent of any particular set of sports interests. It is likely that the responsibility for the programme will remain with the Ministry of Education, which has already accepted that it will arrange for the training of the sampling officers. The third issue concerns the selection of a laboratory to analyse the samples. Although Ireland has no IOC-accredited laboratory, there is a preference for using a domestic laboratory, such as that at Trinity College, Dublin. But there is a concern that the low volume of samples for testing will not be sufficient to justify the investment by the laboratory in the necessary staff training and equipment. The final issue relates to the necessity of ensuring that all governing bodies include a comprehensive anti-doping policy in their constitutions and specifically include rules which require athletes to agree to be tested. There have in recent years been a number of athletes who have legitimately refused to be tested on the grounds that an obligation to be tested was not part of the governing body's rules.

The final issue is to determine how the Irish policy will interlock with that already in existence in Northern Ireland. As mentioned earlier, the major stimulus to policy development is the recognition that policies developed by a number of external organisations are constructing an anti-doping policy in Ireland by default and without the Irish government and Irish governing bodies having the opportunity to shape domestic policy to suit the particular circumstances of the country and its particular mix of sports. At present, more Irish sportsmen and women are tested abroad than in Ireland and with a number being tested in Northern Ireland (see Table 6.5). It will therefore be extremely difficult for the Irish to develop a policy that does not simply mirror that found in the North.

Table 6.5 Tests carried out in Northern Ireland, 1992–6

Year	1992–3	1993–4	1994–5	1995–6
Total Northern Ireland	79	78	67	92
Ulster	33	52	46	46
GAA sports	4	0	0	0

Note: Northern Ireland contains six of the nine counties of the province of Ulster. The figure for Ulster in the table refers to those athletes tested whose NSO administrative unit was the Ulster province rather than Northern Ireland and would therefore have included some players from the Irish Republic when participating in sport in the North.

Source: Annual Reports of the British Sports Council's Doping Control Service.

UNITED KINGDOM

Anti-doping policy in the UK has been shaped by the parallel activity of the British Sports Council and the governing bodies of sport. As early as 1965 the British Sports Council formed a working party to examine the emerging issue of drug abuse. Prior to the involvement of the Sports Council, only one or two governing bodies had taken an active interest in the issue. The British Cycling Federation began discussing the development of anti-doping measures in the early 1960s and carried out tests at the 1965 Milk Race, but it was not until the mid-1970s that the major governing bodies, such as the British Amateur Athletics Board (BAAB) responsible for track and field events, began to introduce testing at major events.

Although in the mid-1960s some governing bodies were making tentative moves towards policy development, by the late 1970s the British Sports Council had adopted a central role in the development of policy which it was to maintain for the next twenty years. In 1978 the Council agreed to fund a research and testing programme at Chelsea College Drug Control and Teaching Centre and thereby established itself at the heart of the nascent policy network. During the 1980s the British Sports Council steadily increased its involvement in the development of anti-doping policy in part through the production and refinement of testing procedures and in part through the application of pressure on governing bodies to co-operate in policy implementation.

A key role for the British Sports Council was in achieving agreement on the list of substances and practices to be proscribed. Initially, during the late 1970s and early 1980s, the Sports Council encouraged governing bodies to adopt the IOC list and incorporate it into their regulations. The IOC list was generally accepted without significant objection in the UK. Objections tended to come from the professional and non-Olympic sports such as professional billiards and snooker which argued that beta-blockers, which help to reduce the heart rate, should not be added to their Association's list of banned substances because the sport did not feature in the Olympic Games and that participants played for longer periods than most other sportsmen and women. R.H. Nicholson, deputy director of the Institute of Medical Ethics and a life member of the National Rifle Association, also suggested that there was a case for not banning beta-blockers in full-bore target rifle competition because 'beta-blockers would make the sport fairer [because] it produces most enhancement in the less skilled marksman . . . [and would therefore make] the competition more equal' (1987: 35).

Despite these reservations, beta-blockers were banned by most governing bodies. A more sustained debate developed over the distinction between perfor-mance-enhancing and restorative drugs. In particular, there was a great deal of concern over the inclusion of easily available and commonly used preparations for colds and asthma. Many cold remedies contain mild narcotic analgesics such as codeine and many of the preparations for treating asthma contain ephedrine: both codeine and ephedrine are banned. Malcolm Bradbury of the BAAB's Medical Committee argued that the IOC policy needed to be more flexible to accommodate the therapeutic use of small quantities of some drugs. However, this was not a view that the IOC or the Sports Council shared in the early phase of policy development. The inflexibility of the IOC is based partly on the awareness that a large number of drugs fulfil more than one function. For example, frusemide which was the diuretic drug allegedly used by the British athlete Kerrith Brown, may be used to over-come pain by reducing swelling, but may also be used to flush other drugs out of the body.

By the late 1980s the vast majority of governing bodies, a number with the prodding of the Sports Council, had adopted either the IOC list of banned substances and practices or the variation on the IOC list produced by their international federation. What variation there was from the IOC list tended to be marginal. For example, in contrast to the IOC the IAAF permits the therapeutic use of codeine; the International Rugby Board prohibits the use of lignocaine, a local anaesthetic; and the International Federation of Professional Cycling bans a broader range of steroids. Whereas variation from the IOC list was unusual in the 1980s, it is now much more common reflecting both a more sophisticated approach to the development of policy and also a concern to tailor policy to reflect the char-acter of particular sports. An increasing number of sports are examining critically the IOC list often at the prompting of their athletes or as a result of the advice of their medical committees. For example, the International Tennis Federation does not ban the use of the small quantities of ephedrine or pseudoephedrine found in cold cures, claiming that the stimulant effect is so low as to be insignificant. The International Cycling Union, which removed the ban from beta-blockers in the late 1980s, does not prohibit the use of diuretics, arguing that neither substance is of any advantage in cycling. More generally, an increasing number of international federations are treating the use of social drugs like cannabis more seriously whereas the IOC continues to consider their use to be of minor importance.

The central role of the Sports Council in generating the current high level of policy consensus on banned substances and practices has been reinforced consistently at ministerial level. In the mid-1980s action by the then Minister for Sport, Colin Moynihan, was important in placing the issue of doping on the policy agendas of related policy communities. For example, Moynihan was able to encourage the Home Office to consider making the possession of anabolic steroids an offence under the Misuse of Drugs Act 1971 and to recognise doping in sport as part of the wider problem of social drug use. More importantly, the Minister was also able to support initiatives within the Council of Europe concerning control of drugs in sport.

As the issue has developed, the UK government, along with the major British governing bodies, has recognised the importance of ensuring that domestic policy development has progressed in parallel with the evolution of policy at the international level. In part this is an acknowledgement of the expansion of the international competition calendar for major sports and of the increasing practice of overseas training, which means that a rigorous domestic anti-doping policy can easily be avoided. However, it is also a reflection of the reluctance felt, even among the most committed anti-doping campaigners, to institute an anti-doping policy which is significantly more rigorous than that in force in most other countries.

As a result the British government and many UK governing bodies have sought to pursue national policy goals through international bodies. The British government, for example, has strongly supported the activities of the Council of Europe in encouraging national governments to treat doping in sport seriously and to develop a broadly consistent policy response (Houlihan 1994). To this end, the agreement on the European Charter on Doping in 1984 was a particularly significant landmark. The value of the Charter and the Council of Europe's interest in anti-doping was reinforced following the end of the Cold War when a large number of previously communist states, many of whom were either suspected or known to have officially sanctioned the use of drugs in international sport, applied for membership of the Council.

In parallel to the discussion of the issue in governmental bodies such the Council of Europe, the IOC and the IFs were also keen to develop an effective international response to the problem. The urgency within the IOC and IFs was primarily due to a recognition that were doping to be ignored, international sports events might lose their attraction to sponsors and the public. However, the international sports organisations were also concerned about losing the initiative on doping to governments and international governmental bodies, which might be intent on pursuing objectives other than the future success of international sport.

The initial dominance of the IOC list of banned substances and practices and the subsequent refinement and variation of it by the federations has led to a dialogue between the IFs, governments and the IOC about harmonisation of policy. In part it is a recognition by the Olympic movement that the IFs are much more knowledgeable about doping and also an acknowledgement that the IFs are not as deferential as they once were. To this end the IOC has established a sub-committee with representatives from a cross-section of federations and also from a small number of governments, including Britain through the Sports Council, primarily to discuss questions of harmonisation, but also in the process to attempt to assert its position of policy leadership.

The current position in the UK on the list of substances and practices to be banned is that while the IOC list is still seen as the benchmark, more NSOs, following the lead of their international federations, are adapting the list to suit the character of their particular sport. Likely future additions to the list include a test for human growth hormone (hGH), which has a similar effect to anabolic steroids, and rEPO, which simulates the benefits of high altitude training. A project funded by the European Union, GH 2000, is aiming to produce a reliable test for hGH in time for the Sydney Olympics. A reliable test for rEPO is closer and was expected to be available for the Atlanta Games in 1996, but there are, at the time of writing, no reports of its application. Once proven tests are available, it is likely that most IFs will add these substances to their list.

Achieving a broad consensus on the substances and practices to be proscribed has been relatively easy: far more problematic has been the achievement of agreement on the procedure to be adopted for administering tests. Among the issues to be addressed as part of the determination of a testing procedure are who to test, when to test, how often to test and how to administer tests. In the early and mid-1980s a number of UK governing bodies willingly adopted an anti-doping policy but made scant effort at successful implementation. Between 1984 and 1988 the Sports Council with the support of the BAAB and the Minister put considerable pressure on governing bodies to respond to the issue of drug abuse by athletes and to introduce drug testing. A variety of inducements and sanctions were applied in order to generate compliance. Inducements came in the form of offers to meet the cost of testing and the provision of advice and guidelines on proce-dure: the sanction was the threatened withdrawal of grant aid, which was crucial for all but a very small number of governing bodies. Despite the efforts of the Sports Council, progress was so slow that the chair of the Sports Council remarked in 1985 that 'even with 100 per cent subsidies from the Sports Council . . . only twenty-five sports have carried out testing since 1979 and some of those on a very, very limited scale' (Sports Council 1986: 1). The revision of policy in 1988 was an attempt to close a number of loopholes and make evasion more difficult. Yet the problems were formidable as many of the more recalcitrant sports were often those that had weaker governing bodies and were among the more commercial. Professional tennis, for example, has a weak governing body with the Association of Tennis Professionals (ATP) and the Women's International Tennis Association (WITA) exercising significant control over the professional competition circuit. Neither the ATP nor the WITA were enthusiastic about drug testing and agreed to limited testing for 'recreational drugs' (marijuana and cocaine) only in 1986. Within the UK the All England Lawn Tennis and Croquet Club, which organises the Wimbledon competition, was criticised for its relaxed attitude to doping. Although it agreed in 1986 to undertake testing, this was only to be for drugs of addiction, with any players testing positive being encouraged to seek counselling. As an illustration of the relative influence of governmental and sports organisations on the attitude of some governing bodies to doping, it is worth noting that the eventual agreement of the ATP and the WITA to allow testing for a broader range of drugs, including steroids, was prompted only by the prospect of tennis being accepted as an Olympic sport. A similarly equivocal and unenthusiastic reaction to Sports Council pressure to undertake testing was also found in weightlifting and in a number of team sports, including soccer, rugby union and rugby league (Houlihan 1991).

The policy shift came in 1988 following the publication in 1987 of a policy review by the Minister, Colin Moynihan, and the international athlete Sebastian Coe (1987). A central change was the establishment by the Council of the Doping Control Service to provide information and education, but most importantly to provide independent testing. Rather than continuing to persuade governing bodies to undertake testing themselves, the Doping Control Unit offered to take responsibility for the technical aspects of testing, such as sample collection and analysis, leaving the governing bodies with the task of identifying those athletes to be tested and the events at which tests would be carried out. The second major policy change was the introduction of out-of-competition testing (see Table 6.6). The introduction of random out-of-competition testing was an acknowledgement that in-competition testing was valuable for only a limited range of drugs, such as amphetamines and to a lesser extent diuretics, but was of little use in attempting to identify athletes who used drugs, such as steroids, that are most effective during the pre-season training period. The action by the Sports Council followed a programme of out-of-competition testing piloted by the BAAB in 1986 and paralleled the decisions by the General Association of International Sports Federations and the IAAF to support the extension of drug testing. The IAAF established its own 'flying squad' of drug testers as a means of bypassing recalcitrant national sports authorities.

By the early 1990s a broad policy consensus was beginning to emerge as was the complex interorganisational framework for implementation, involving governments, domestic and international sports organisations, and international governmental organisations. Yet, just when anti-doping policy in the UK and internationally was reaching a sufficient level of

Table 6.6 UK testing programme, 1988–96

	1988–9	1989–90	1990–1	1991–2	1992–3	1993–4	1994–5	1995–6
Number of sports involved	54	52	53	55	53	49	n.a.	51
Number of sports in OOCT	19	20	24	38	26	27	n.a.	n.a.
Number of samples in-competition	2,610	2,952	3,356	3,782	3,411	2,969	2,976	2,964
Number of samples in OOCT	258	335	476	622	747	965	n.a.	767
Total number of samples	*2,868*	*3,287*	*3,832*	*4,404*	*4,158*	*3,946*	*n.a.*	*3,731*

Note: OOCT denotes out-of-competition testing.
Source: Annual Reports, Sports Council Doping Control Unit.

sophistication of implementation to give some optimism that doping might be effectively challenged, a number of concerns and problems have emerged to prevent complacency. The first was the difficulty of determining the appropriate number of tests and the appropriate balance between out-of-competition and in-competition testing. Currently, the Sports Council will pay for a number of tests which are seen as being in the 'public interest' dependent upon, *inter alia*, the history of positives, the perceived potential for abuse, the calendar of major events and the scale of financial benefits to athletes. In addition to the number of 'public interest' tests paid for by the Sports Council, a number of sports, particularly professional sports such as soccer, cricket, rugby league and speedway, will buy additional tests. One potential problem for the Sports Council is that the leverage it once derived from its threat to withhold grant aid to governing bodies has been undermined by the advent of the National Lottery, which has had the effect of providing a source of funding which is, currently at least, not tied to compliance on anti-doping. As regards the balance between in-competition and out-of-competition testing, the Sports Council, in conjunction with the relevant governing body, will determine an appropriate ratio dependent upon the length of the competition season. Thus, for example, there is only a limited amount of out-of-competition testing in soccer because the season is so long whereas most tests in track and field events are during the out-of-competition period because the season is relatively brief.

A second problem is that the capacity of the Sports Council to undertake tests on foreign athletes participating in events in the UK is often limited by the inadequacy of the regulations of IFs. For example, IFs may require all domestic governing bodies to incorporate anti-doping regulations within their constitution, but these only apply to participants who are members of the national governing body and do not apply to visiting athletes. For foreign athletes to be liable to testing when abroad requires amendment to the constitution of the IF. For example, during the 1995 Five Nations rugby union championship, the members of the four home countries were liable for testing but not those from France. The IF for rugby union has since amended its constitution.

A third, and more significant issue is the speed with which action on a positive test is taken. It is the governing body that decides how to respond to a positive result and most governing bodies will act on all positives. The action taken by the governing body must be reported to the Sports Council but there have been a number of examples of governing bodies delaying action and there is consequently some concern within the Sports Council at the number of actions that are 'pending' for long periods. However, the number of delayed decisions is relatively small and the threat of a withdrawal of the testing service by the Council is sufficient encouragement to most governing bodies to act promptly. A related issue concerns the wide variation between governing bodies at the point at which action is taken. Some will suspend on the discovery of a positive result in the A sample, some suspend after the analysis of the B sample, while others delay suspension until after an appeal has been heard.

The fourth problem is closely linked to the third and concerns the increasing willingness of athletes to challenge positive results in the courts. Following the Diane Modahl case, where the athlete's positive result was overturned on appeal to the BAF and has now led to the BAF being sued for loss of earnings, governing bodies are becoming more cautious in suspending an athlete until after an appeal has been heard. While this is possibly a fairer process, it still allows an unscrupulous athlete to continue to compete and earn income until the appeal. More seriously the scale of damages which an elite athlete could claim is more than sufficient to bankrupt most governing bodies.

Finally, although the process by which tests are conducted is much more rigorous than even ten years ago there are still a number of weaknesses, many of which are similar to those identified in the discussion of Canada. The first weakness is not unique to the UK and involves the process by which sampling officers ensure they have tested the correct person. While the elite athletes in many track events or in soccer are familiar faces, there are many other sports within the Olympic programme where the elite participants are little known. A similar problem of identification arises with the rising stars who are often targeted for testing but are not as yet familiar faces. To overcome this problem the Sports Council is encouraging governing bodies to introduce a more sophisticated membership system, which includes a photograph. A second recurring problem is that of keeping track of the location of athletes, especially during the pre-season period. The degree of laxity in keeping governing bodies informed of their location may be seen, at the very least, as an indication of a lack of commitment to the testing programme. Third, governing bodies are often slow to inform the Sports Council of changes to their national squads. As a result the Council runs the risk of wasting tests on those who are no longer likely to compete at national level.

THE UNITED STATES

As was the case in so many other countries, drug abuse by athletes only became a policy issue for sports organisations in the United States when scandal began to taint the positive public perception of sport and threaten the financial basis of the contemporary sports structure. As explained in an earlier chapter, the US differs from the other countries in this study in a number of important ways, but particularly in the generally peripheral role of the government in shaping elite sport. As a result, the three major sports sectors – college, Olympic, and professional league sport – remain much more autonomous than their equivalents elsewhere. The issue of doping in sport has therefore not emerged as a result of one major crisis, although the death of the University of Maryland athlete, Len Bias, in 1986 did have a considerable impact, but rather rose to prominence on the policy agendas of the major sports sectors as a culmination of a series of events which forced each sector to address the issue of doping and acknowledge the need to interact with related sectors in determining a policy response. At times, the fragmentation of the sports infrastructure has meant that focusing events in one sector have reinforced parallel events in another. However, more commonly, fragmentation has resulted in a dissipation of momentum.

In common with most other countries the Olympic movement plays a central role in defining doping and in providing guidelines for the administration of an anti-doping policy. The USOC, despite its prominence as one of the major Olympic 'powers', has certainly not been at the forefront of the development of anti-doping policy. For much of the 1980s its limited testing programme was designed to fulfil an educational rather than a policing function. Indeed, the primary stimulus to action was the acute embarrassment of watching twelve American athletes withdraw from the 1983 Caracas Pan-American Games because of the unexpected rigour of the testing regime. It must also be added that an important secondary motivation was the growing realisation that athletes were using the current 'educational' programme 'to gauge when to stop taking banned substances in time to clear their systems' (Voy 1991: 89). The response of the USOC was to introduce a testing programme for the Olympic trials held in 1984. In the season prior to the Los Angeles Olympics, eighty-six athletes tested positive, though the results were announced only after the end of the Games, prompting Todd to speculate that '[t]his after-the-fact disclosure was apparently motivated at least in part by a desire on the part of the USOC not to lose face before the Los Angeles Games' (1987: 97). Tests were conducted at subsequent competitions held in the US including the Pan-American Games held in Indiana in 1987, when six athletes tested positive.

The USOC spent $6m. over the four-year period 1992–6, conducting just under 6,000 tests each year. Three categories of testing exist: in-competition testing (approximately 2,500); pre-competition testing (approximately 2,200); and out-of-competition testing (approximately 1,300). It is claimed that pre-competition testing is a further round of testing, but it is much more likely that it is designed to prevent the embarrassment of a positive result at a major competition. Out-of-competition testing was agreed in 1989 but only introduced in 1992 and it is intended that out-of-competition testing will account for the majority of tests conducted over the next few years (Table 6.7). Whereas all Olympic or elite athletes are covered by the USOC competition and pre-competition testing programmes, governing bodies may either conduct their own out-of-competition testing programme or participate in the USOC-administered and funded programme. Currently only eight governing bodies participate in the USOC-funded programme, with the available tests allocated between the eight sports based upon a number of criteria, including the history of drug abuse, the size of the squad, the potential to benefit from drug abuse and the number of tests that the governing body has bid for. There is considerable variation between the number of tests requested by governing bodies, with US weightlifting requesting 500 tests for a squad of 30 by comparison with USA Track and Field (USATF), which also requested 500 tests, but for over 1,500 athletes.

The implementation of the out-of-competition programme depends on close liaison between the USOC and the national sports governing bodies. The pool of athletes to be tested is the product of discussions between the NSO and the USOC and while the selection of athletes for testing is largely random, officials ensure that each NSO has at least one athlete drawn for testing each month and that no athlete is tested more than four times each year. Because many squads use the USOC facilities at Colorado Springs to train, many tests are conducted during these training sessions. However, the USOC employs travelling sampling officers and also has a series of reciprocal agreements with testing authorities in other countries to conduct tests on athletes training abroad. Although the rigour of the testing regime for Olympic athletes has improved considerably since the late 1980s, it is still flawed. Most significantly there remain thirty-one Olympic governing bodies that conduct their own out-of-competition testing and while some have regimes of equivalent rigour to the USOC, most do not, with the most serious weakness being that they generally allow athletes 48 hours, notice prior to a test, ample time to flush out many of the more modern steroids. Indeed, the USOC provided 48 hours notice as recently as 1995. Drug testing is especially problematic for those Olympic sports that draw their athletes from the ranks of professional sport, such as basketball and ice hockey. As will be shown below, professional sports address the problem of drug abuse in a very different way to the major Olympic and 'amateur' sports. Finally, it needs to be borne in mind that the size of USOC grant to Olympic NSOs is determined in part by their level of success in elite competition, a fact which must colour their attitude to anti-doping policy implementation.

Table 6.7 Drug testing by the USOC, 1988–95 (selected years)

Year	In-competition tests	Out-of-competition tests	Total tests
1988	2,700	–	2,700
1992	2,775	246	3,021
1993	3,285	553	3,838
1994	3,178	485	3,663
1995	3,313	n.a.	n.a.

Source: United States Olympic Committee (1995); Drug Control Administration, 1994 Annual Report.

Taking USATF as an example of governing body action, it introduced drug testing at competitions as recently as the mid-1980s. The tardiness of the governing body in establishing an anti-doping policy is emphasised by the rejection of two resolutions from the women's committee recommending the introduction of testing. Far more seriously, Robert Voy, USOC chief medical officer during much of the 1980s, records a number of cases where athletes had tested positive only to avoid a ban due to the repeated willing-ness of The Athletic Congress (forerunner of the USATF) to seek technical loopholes in the procedure of testing or to manipulate the appeals. On one occasion, according to Voy, The Athletic Congress (TAC) helped two promi-nent leading athletes avoid a ban:

> According to former USOC Substance Abuse Committee Chairman Edwin Moses, TAC torpedoed these athletes' drug hearings by providing the drug panels with deliberately insufficient information to counter bio-chemical defenses by the athletes. That way, the athletes were exonerated on legal grounds.
>
> (Voy 1991: 106)

Out-of-competition testing was introduced in 1990, covering a pool of over 750 athletes established by selecting the top fifteen athletes in each discipline. Although an improvement, the regime had a number of weak-nesses including the failure of a large number of athletes to respond to the request to attend the regional testing centres and the provision of 48 hours, notice to athletes which, as mentioned earlier, gave them time to flush steroids out of their system, or artificially to adjust their testosterone–epitestosterone ratio. In addition, testing was limited to those athletes who lived within a 75-mile radius of a testing centre. A surprising number of athletes opted to live just outside the 75-mile limit. In September 1995 the USATF greatly improved the rigour of its testing programme, particularly with regard to the replacement of 48-hour notice tests by random unannounced out-of-competition testing conducted by a mobile sampling team. The number of tests will be drastically reduced from about 600 to approximately 150. The reduction is justified partly on the grounds of the greater impact of unannounced random tests and partly by the increased cost of mobile sampling squads. In addition to the USATF testing programme, there will also be approximately 300 tests conducted by the IAAF in the United States.

The governing body has also adopted a set of penalties that appear to be far more severe than those enforced by other Olympic governing bodies or expected by the IAAF. For a first offence of using steroids or stimulants, there is a four-year ban followed by a life ban for a second offence: for ephedrines, three months for the first offence, four years for the second, and life for the third. It remains to be seen whether the USATF is able to sustain these penalties any more successfully than the German governing body, Deutscher Leichtathletik Verband, which was forced by the German domestic courts to retreat from a four-year ban imposed on the sprinter Katrin Krabbe (Houlihan 1994). The USATF has made significant progress in implementing an anti-doping programme comparable to those in other major Olympic member countries. The problem is whether the USATF can implement the testing regime effectively and especially ensure compliance by athletes and acceptance of the penalties.

The most significant problem facing the USATF is the persistent threat of legal challenge and in particular the prospect of having to defend a case similar to that involving Harry 'Butch' Reynolds. Reynolds tested positive for the steroid nandrolone in 1991 and was duly suspended by the USATF (then called The Athletic Congress) with the support of the international federation, the IAAF. However, Reynolds challenged the decision through a series of arbitration panels and courts and eventually received a supporting ruling by the Supreme Courts that forced the USATF and the IAAF to back down and allow him to participate in the US Olympic trials. Reynolds successfully sued the IAAF and was awarded damages totalling $28m. (see Houlihan 1994 for details). Although the dispute was between Reynolds and the IAAF, the cost of defending the case and the scale of damages awarded has made the USATF and the other Olympic governing bodies extremely cautious in their implementation of anti-doping policy. A further example of an international federation adopting a tougher stance on doping infractions arose in skiing where Kerry Lynch was stripped of his 1987 Nordic Combined World Champions medal and was banned from the 1988 Winter Olympics following an admission of blood doping. This action followed the imposition of only light penalties by the United States Skiing Association (Nafziger 1988).

US Weightlifting (USW) was no more enthusiastic about introducing drug testing than other governing bodies. Up until 1984, following the embarrassment in Caracas the previous year, USW had no anti-doping programme. The 1984 agreement with USOC introduced funded testing, but only at competitions. However, the USW requested extensive competition testing by the USOC ostensibly to 'clean up' the sport, but according to some as a way of bankrupting the USOC drug-testing fund.

The most complex policy-making problems undoubtedly faced, and continue to face, college sport. Any lead that the NCAA might care to give must take account of over 900 individual college sports departments which have to persuade their, often sceptical, college authorities of the need for an anti-doping policy and which, in turn, have to ensure that any policy is secure against challenge within the terms of the legislative framework of their particular state. As early as 1973, through the formation of a Drug Education Committee, the NCAA acknowledged that drug abuse was emerging as a serious problem in college sport and initiated a very modest drug education programme aimed as much, if not more, at the use of recreational drugs as at performance-enhancing drugs. The first, minimalist, phase of NCAA policy was superseded in the mid-1980s by a period of modest activity with a programme of research into the extent of drug abuse and also the first limited administration of tests at NCAA competitions. An important part of the motivation to develop an anti-doping policy came from the publicity surrounding the death of the college star, Bias, from 'crack' cocaine, but a significant prompt to action was 'the economic need to preserve the appearance of fair and equitable competition' (Albrecht *et al.* 1992: 349).

In 1984 the NCAA convention agreed to draft an anti-doping policy which was confirmed at the 1986 convention. The policy included a programme of in-competition testing at any Association championship or post-season match which in the mid- to late 1980s totalled over 3,000 tests each year (Table 6.8). Four years later the policy was revised and the NCAA required its member colleges to undertake year-round out-of-competition testing initially restricted to Division 1 football players, though later extended to include track and field athletes. Out-of-competition testing was also limited to tests for anabolic steroids, diuretics and urine manipulation. Under the current administration the Executive Committee of the NCAA determines the pattern of testing throughout the year and informs tournament directors of the drug-testing plan five days in advance of the day of testing. Subjects for testing in individual events may be selected on the basis of finish position or at random. For team events, participants may be selected for testing randomly or on the basis of playing time or position.

Other elements in the administration of the anti-doping policy follow the guidelines of the IOC fairly closely, particularly regarding the supervision of the provision of the sample, the maintenance of security of the chain of custody and the notification of results and the appeal process. The results of tests are sent from the laboratory to the NCAA, which forwards them to the athlete's college. The NCAA also has the responsibility of determining whether a result is 'positive-ineligible'.

The penalty for a first offence was the suspension of the athlete for a twelve-month period with the loss of all remaining regular-season and post-season eligibility. A distinction is made between recreational (or, to use the NCAA term, 'street') drugs – heroin, marijuana and THC (tetrahydro-cannabinol) – and performance-enhancing drugs. A second offence

Table 6.8 NCAA drug testing between 1986–7 and 1989–90

Year	Total tests	Positive (serious)	Positive (minor)	% positive
1986–7	3,511	34	43	2.2
1987–8	3,900	48	82	3.3
1988–9	3,143	15	90	3.3
1989–90	3,233	15	4	0.6

Source: NCAA Annual Reports.

involving a street drug results in the lesser penalty of the loss of a further season's eligibility in all sports.

The NCAA testing policy is a minimal response to the problem of drug abuse in sport designed more to protect the image of college sport than to eradicate cheating. Because sport, football and basketball in particular, is for many colleges a major source of income and prestige, there is a clear reluctance among college administrations to enquire too deeply into the extent of drug use. In addition, among college athletes, while few can argue that their livelihood depends on sport, many are aware that the continuation of their scholarship depends on high-level sporting performance. However, the force of criticism directed at the NCAA needs to be moderated because of two factors: first, the degree of autonomy of individual colleges and second, the generally unsupportive legal context for an anti-doping policy and the litigious nature of American society. The NCAA has, to its credit, encouraged colleges to adopt an institutional anti-doping policy to complement that of the Association. The NCAA has also provided model rules but does stress the need to 'involve the institution's legal counsel at an early stage' (National Collegiate Athletic Association 1992: 22).

Despite the considerable progress made by individual colleges, it is still only a minority that has developed an anti-doping policy. A recent survey by Fields *et al.* (1994) found that only 29 per cent of the 3,314 colleges in the United States undertook drug testing of student athletes. The most common reason for not instituting a testing programme was opposition from college administration (83 per cent) or anticipated opposition from athletes (53 per cent). Of those that carried out testing, 36 per cent had based their policy on the model provided by the NCAA. Colleges exhibited considerable variation in terms of what they test for, how they select athletes for testing and what action is taken following the identification of a positive result. While 75 per cent of colleges selected athletes on a mandatory random basis, 47 per cent based selection on 'probable or reasonable cause' and 27 per cent operated on the basis of mandatory routine testing. There was also significant variation in the range of drugs tested. Cocaine, amphetamines and marijuana were targeted at 85 per cent, 83 per cent and 77 per cent of colleges respectively. Most significantly, only 56 per cent of colleges tested for other performance-enhancing drugs, including steroids, despite evidence from an NCAA-commissioned survey which indicated that 10 per cent of football players admitted taking steroids in the previous twelve months (Anderson and McKeag 1990). The priority seemed to be the detection of drugs that might interfere with optimal performance rather than for drugs that are designed to enhance performance. Fields *et al.* explain the preference for testing for 'street' drugs by noting that '[s]creening for street drugs has health, safety, and public relations value for these institutions' (1994: 685).

As regards the sanctions imposed following a positive test, there was also wide variation. The most common response (60 per cent) was to refer the abuser to the team physician, with only 45 per cent requiring that the offender accept treatment. Other responses included dismissal from the squad (31 per cent), temporary lay-off (of unspecified duration) (30 per cent), and revocation of scholarship (26 per cent). As with other sports organisations, many colleges had a scale of sanctions with revocation rarely imposed for a first offence. In common with the USOC, the NCAA faces considerable problems in ensuring that its decisions are secure from legal challenge. As Ciccolella noted, 'Inconsistent determinations of the legitimacy of NCAA drug testing have shadowed the program with legal uncertainty' (National Collegiate Athletic Association 1992: 47; see also O'Brien and Overby 1992). In 1989 the Massachusetts Supreme Court rejected an appeal from a student who had been declared ineligible by the NCAA for withdrawing his consent to drug testing: the student had claimed, *inter alia*, that the testing regime infringed his right to privacy. But in the case of *Hill* v. *NCAA* in 1990, there was a successful challenge to the mandatory nature of the NCAA programme on the grounds that it was contrary to the Californian constitution's guarantee of privacy. Similar challenges under the Fourteenth Amendment of the US Constitution were a problem, but were overcome when the Supreme Court ruled that the NCAA was a private organisation and therefore not subject to the Fourteenth Amendment's limitations on the power of the state. However, the Supreme Court also ruled that state universities, while being members of the NCAA, are none the less deemed to be state bodies for legal purposes. Challenges are also possible under the Fifth Amendment, which covers due process of law and protects against self-incrimination (Banks 1992; see also Schaller 1991; Gibbs 1991; and Pernell 1990).

As the Hill case showed, there are state constitutions that protect citizens from intrusion by both public and private bodies. There have also been repeated attempts to challenge the validity of testing under the US Constitution's Fourth Amendment, which prohibits unlawful search and seizure. The interpretation of the Fourth Amendment is still subject to considerable debate, particularly regarding the legality of testing without reasonable suspicion, with courts sending conflicting messages to the NCAA and to college authorities. The overall effect of the continuing legal ambiguity and the fear of punitive damages should a case be lost is that testing regimes are less than whole-hearted. As Ciccolella makes clear, the courts are well aware of the tension between the Constitution and current anti-doping policy. The judge in the case of *Derdyn* v. *the University of Colorado* argued that '[t]he integrity of athletic contests cannot be purchased at the cost of privacy interests protected by the Fourth Amendment' while the Supreme Court pointedly observed that students 'do not shed their constitutional rights . . . at the schoolhouse gate' (both quoted in Ciccolella 1992: 50).

Apart from the intervention of the courts in shaping the content and administration of the anti-doping policies developed in the three main sports sectors, the government has had little public sector involvement in policy development. The legislature has had a general impact through the exertion of pressure on sports organisations to develop and implement anti-doping policy through the conduct of periodic congressional hearings in the late 1980s. More specifically, in 1990 the Congress was persuaded to pass legislation that included anabolic steroids on schedule III of the Federal Controlled Substances Act. This decision followed the passing of similar legislation in a number of states, including Florida and Georgia.

The development of an anti-doping policy in professional sport has been much slower to emerge and is more concerned with the protection of the marketable image of the professional sports than with the eradication of cheating or the promotion of good health among players (Chandler 1991). As Staudohar and Mangan point out:

> The drug control programme worked out between owners and players in basketball, for example, is beneficial to the image of the game because it provides treatment to players who come forward for help and at the same time lets the public know that continued or undisclosed drug abuse will not be tolerated.

> (Staudohar and Mangan 1991: 4)

The mid- to late 1980s was a bad time for the major professional team sports when a number of sportsmen, including Hernell Jackson (basketball, cocaine) and Don Rogers and Larry Gordon (football, cocaine), died from drug overdoses. Positive test results were also returned for baseball players, including Dwight Gooden of the New York Mets, Lamarr Hoyt of the San Diego Padres and for hockey players such as Tony McKegney of the St Louis Blues and Bob Probert of the Detroit Red Wings. The steady stream of positive tests and the deaths of star players made it impossible for the managers of the professional leagues to maintain the facade that drug abuse was a minor problem best seen as a series of isolated episodes.

Yet, even following a number of high-profile doping cases, the response of the governing bodies was weak. In football the NFL testing regime was limited, up to 1990, to an annual round of testing during the pre-season mini-camps, allowing players sufficient advance warning to ensure that they had time to discontinue any doping programme. In July 1990 the NFL Commissioner introduced a far more rigorous testing regime which included random in-competition and out-of-competition testing. However, the NFL's modest attempts to implement a testing regime to tackle steroid abuse were met with a series of legal challenges by the players' union. The players' union took the NFL to court to challenge the imposition of a four-game suspension for a positive test. The union returned to court in an attempt to prevent the NFL publicising the names of the thirteen players who tested positive in the early phase of policy implementation (Weinhold 1991). In addition, there was a series of other potential legal challenges based on possible application of the Fourth and Fourteenth Amendments on very similar grounds to those tested in the courts involving the NCAA (Gregus 1993).

The response of the professional sports organisations is highly equivocal.

The case of Steven Howe, a baseball pitcher, is instructive. Howe had tested positive for drugs six times between 1982 and 1988 and was suspended from baseball for short periods on each occasion. In 1988/89 Howe was under suspension for violating the requirements of his aftercare programme, at which point his case was taken up by the players' union, the Major League Baseball Players Association (MLBPA), which challenged the suspension imposed by the Commissioner's Office which has been responsible for the administration of the policy since 1986. The suspension was lifted, although strict conditions were imposed. Howe was later transferred to the New York Yankees, but breached the sports anti-doping policy again in early in 1991. This episode is illustrative of the problems in enforcing an anti-doping policy in professional sports as a number of competing interests have to be balanced in the determination and implementation of an anti-doping policy: first, there is the Commission's interest in preserving the marketability of league competition; second, there are the interests of the individual franchise holders who, though committed in general to an anti-doping policy, are reluctant to lose players through suspension for drug offences; third, the players themselves and their agents and lawyers, who are concerned to maintain their eligibility; and finally, the players' unions that have to balance the collective interest of members in drug-free sport and the individual member's interest in not having his playing interrupted by suspension.

The strong position of commercial sport in the United States and the fact that the main sports of football and baseball are not Olympic sports has weakened the influence of the IOC and enabled these sports to avoid the pressure arising from the need to satisfy requirements for Olympic participation. In addition, the non-interventionist predisposition of the federal government and the general lack of direct dependence on public funds did little to force the issue up the agenda of commercial sport. The strong links between NCAA college sport and commercial sport also undermined the pro-testing lobby within the NCAA colleges. Moreover, the series of legal challenges from college athletes encouraged an overly cautious approach to policy implementation. However, despite a political culture of individualism and limited government, a constitution that makes policy uniformity difficult to achieve and a relatively open legal system strongly supportive of individual rights, one should not discount the progress that has been made over the past twenty years or so. All major sports – commercial and Olympic – have anti-doping policies. Substantial progress has been made in achieving agreement, based on the IOC policy, on the list of practices and substances to be proscribed. The introduction of unannounced out-of-competition testing has made considerable progress and reflects a greater depth of commitment by NSOs to anti-doping policy.

7   Sport and physical education in schools

The recent intensity of debate about the proper role of sport in schools has proved to be both heated and multi-layered. In most of the countries in this study there are three overlapping themes which provide the context within which school sport policy is shaped. The first theme is the school curriculum and the place of sport within it. The balance of control over the school curriculum between the central government, local/state authorities and the school board varies considerably and affects significantly the pattern of debate over the role of sport. In Ireland and the UK debate over sport has taken place largely at the national level, whereas in Australia, Canada and the US curriculum is a state matter, with variable degrees of school board autonomy, and produces a wider degree of variation in terms of the amount of time allocated to sport and its priority in the curriculum. Whatever the level at which policy debate takes place, there are a number of recurring sub-themes including the relationship between physical education and sport; between health and fitness, and sport; and between curricular and extra-curricular sport. In addition, most countries have a long-running debate over the examination status of sport and PE and also over the appropriate allocation of time to the practice of, and participation in, sport as opposed to the analysis or theory of sport. A third sub-theme which periodically surfaces concerns the type of sport that should be played and whether priority should be given to the traditional as opposed to the new, and to competitive as opposed to non-competitive, sport. The final sub-theme concerned with curriculum issues focuses on the appropriate balance between the development of generic sports skills and the development of sports-specific skills.

A second theme relates to the administrative context within which sport and school sport operate. For example, in the UK sport and school sport policy are the responsibility of two central government departments – the Department of National Heritage and the Department for Education and Employment. A similar division of responsibility is found in Australia. In Canada the federal government plays a key policy role in sport but has little influence on school curriculum matters as this is the prerogative of the provinces. Cultural differences between departments, constitutional protocols between federal and state/provincial administrations and degrees of administrative complexity all combine to affect the pattern and character of debate over policy questions that involve both issues of curriculum and issues of sport development. The final theme relates to the context within which the teachers of sport and PE work. Of particular significance is the status of sport and PE teachers in school. Many of the curriculum issues mentioned above, for example whether sport and PE should be public examination subjects, are closely linked to issues of status. A related issue is the extent to which sport and PE are taught by specialist teachers or as subsidiary subjects by specialists in other subjects.

AUSTRALIA

The dominant analysis of Australian politics in the 1980s emphasised the corporatist features of state activity. Yet corporatism was not limited to the pattern of interest mediation between the state and external interests such as labour and business, but was also evident in non-market domains such as education and training. In addition, Australian corporatism was adapted to federalism: 'Within this concept of corporate federalism, "corporate" serves as a metaphor of the federal government as the policy centre of the "corporation" with implementation devolved to the "branches" (states)' (Lingard *et al.* 1993: 234). The 1980s witnessed a progressive tightening of commonwealth control over the education system which, ostensibly, is a state responsibility. The abolition in 1987 of the Schools Commission and the absorption of the Department of Education within the new Department of Employment, Education and Training were indicative of the ideological shift from 'an earlier more liberal-progressive perspective to a strongly instrumentalist approach designed to "re-form" schooling "in the national interest" ' (Lingard *et al.* 1993: 231–2; see also Lingard 1991).

The publication, in 1988, of the policy statement, *Strengthening Australia's Schools* (Dawson 1988), confirmed the extension of corporate federalism to education (Bartlett 1992). The dual thrust of the policy was to ensure that schools and the curriculum they delivered were more closely attuned to the needs of the economy and that the most effective way of implementing this change in policy direction was to raise the profile of the Commonwealth government. However, the central role played by the Commonwealth government is not new. Keeves, in examining the development of Australian education over the past 150 years, remarks on the degree of uniformity in educational provision and argues that 'it is now possible to consider Australian education largely as a single entity' (1990: 49). In terms of structure there is indeed a marked similarity between the various states and territories, with children required to attend school from the ages of 6 to 15 (16 in Tasmania), although almost all children remain for a tenth year of education and an increasing number staying on to complete years eleven and twelve. There is also very little variation in the curriculum adopted in the different states and territories. Part of the explanation for this relative uniformity lies in the strong lead given by the Commonwealth government in terms of curriculum review and development, but part undoubtedly lies in the increasing dependence of states and territories on Commonwealth funding. In the mid-1960s Commonwealth expenditure contributed only 14 per cent of the cost of education provision: by the mid-1970s the contribution had increased to just under 45 per cent before declining slightly to 38 per cent in the early 1990s. The increase in financial contribution was matched by a growing administrative capacity at federal level. In 1967 the Commonwealth government created the new Department of Education and Science and in 1972 the incoming Labor Government established a Schools Commission, which undertook an assessment of the financial needs of schools.

The increasing financial importance of the federal government in education has paralleled a tendency towards centralisation of curriculum control at state level. The 1970s saw a brief period during which school-based curriculum development was encouraged but for most states there was little of substance to underpin the rhetoric of devolution and the level of real commitment that existed was soon dissipated by the corporatist style of the Hawke Labor government (Bartlett 1992). Watkins, in his study of the move away from the 'advocacy of democratic decision processes towards the more repressive techniques of scientific management' in Victoria, remarks that this trend was not confined to one state but was 'part of a national . . . reassertion of scientific management and economic rationalism' (1992: 241 and 256). An important vehicle for the centralisation of curriculum control was the establishment of the Australian Education Council (AEC) which, with the strong support of the Commonwealth Education Minister, willingly took upon itself the task of developing a national curriculum framework which, as will be explained below, was to have a significant impact on PE and sport.

If the steady increase in federal financing of education and a growing concern with needs of the economy for an appropriately trained workforce has encouraged the federal government to adopt a more interventionist attitude to the curriculum, then the increasing pressure on public expenditure has resulted in a decentralisation of decision making over school budgets. As in many other countries, budget decentralisation to school districts or even to individual schools has been applauded as an example of community control which often disguises a desire by government to distance itself from service cuts. As Kenway (1993) points out, the education service is having to cope with centralising *and* decentralising pressures where the former affect the curriculum and the latter focus on money and management style.

It is within this context of a highly centralised curriculum development process that sport and PE operate. The recent debates about the national curriculum have done much to stimulate discussion about the status and place of sport and PE in the curriculum and particularly about their capacity to compete with the claims of other subjects for space on the modern primary and secondary school timetable. Yet, the current intensity of debate is merely the most recent manifestation of the deeply embedded tension arising from the highly contested nature of the place of sport and PE in the curriculum. Goodson (1983) argues that far from reflecting stable intellectual consensus, school subjects are constantly under pressure from interests within and external to education and that attempts to codify a subject, or even a curriculum, represent a snapshot of the balance of interests at a particular time. In the post-war period and up to the late 1960s, PE often fulfilled a marginal role in the curriculum, relying on the claimed beneficial impact of sport and PE on character and moral development. This perception of the subject was reinforced by the dominance of ex-servicemen among PE teachers and their concern with PE as physical training. PE fared better in the 1970s when, according to Macdonald and Brooker, 'physical educationists usurped support from work in humanistic psychology to declare that of all areas of the curriculum, physical education was most suited to educating of the whole child' (1992: 14). However, the attempt to broaden the basis of PE to include a concern with personal development and a broader range of transferable skills provoked a reaction from those who maintained that the primary focus of PE should be the development of sports-specific skills. In recent decades the claims of PE to a place in the curriculum has had to contend not only with the scepticism of those working in other subjects, but also with the criticism from those who see PE as providing inadequate skills development for participation in organised sport.

To compound the problems facing the teachers of PE, Goodson points to the intense pressure on school teachers to shape their subjects to conform to an academic model of knowledge. 'In the process of establishing a school subject . . . base subject groups tend to move from promoting pedagogic and utilitarian traditions towards academic traditions' (1983: 3). As a means of preserving their status as teachers and also the status of their subject, PE teachers have co-operated in shifting the balance from the practice of PE and sport skills to the intellectual analysis of them and the drift towards credentialism.

By the early 1980s education was being discussed within the discourses of vocationalism and credentialism, both of which stressed the utility of PE as preparation for employment or entry to higher education (Brooker and Macdonald 1995).[1] The practice of sport consequently assumed a lower significance in comparison with the acquisition of theoretical understanding. The priority given to scientific knowledge reinforces credentialism and reflects the attempts of PE teachers to retain their status within the academic community. The emphasis on the study of biomechanics, sports psychology and physiology at the expense of participation in sport and PE emerged in the late 1970s and continue to be strong elements of the secondary school PE curriculum. Other elements of the current ideological context for debates over the future of PE and sport in schools include the discourse on nationalism, which has reinforced the well-established stress on elite success and talent identification at school/junior levels, and the discourse on individualism (or more accurately narcissism) which so frequently elides the concern with a healthy lifestyle with a preoccupation with appearance.

It was within this series of overlapping discourses that the Commonwealth government, working through the AEC, which comprises state and federal education ministers, initiated its review of the Australian curriculum. The starting point for the work of the AEC was an acceptance that a national curriculum was required which would define the 'basic and essential learnings for Australian students' (Marsh 1989: 71). The Hobart Declaration (Australian Education Council 1989) included brief, but vague, references to the importance of the creative use of leisure time and health and fitness. The AEC identified eight key learning areas, one of which, health, included PE. However, of the seven health outcomes identified in the Statement only one mentioned physical activity. According to the Statement, pupils should 'have fun and enjoy themselves through participation through physical activity, acquire knowledge about physical activity and develop confidence and competence in the acquisition of movement skills that will enhance participation in a wide variety of activities' (Australian Education Council 1992: 8). Despite the references to fun and enjoyment (which Taggart *et al.* 1993 feel trivialises PE), Bartlett claims that the general tenor of the curriculum statements is such that a dehumanised and technologised curriculum has been produced. More significantly he notes that one consequence of the corporatist context of curriculum development has been the exclusion of practitioners: 'If they have a presence in the process of development and implementation, this may occur only through an overworked and maintenance-driven national [teacher] union. Teachers, professionals, parents, students and teacher educators generally, however, are excluded' (1992: 235).

According to Brooker and Macdonald there currently exists a series of overlapping and frequently competing representations of PE, where PE as sport is partially complemented by, but also challenged by, PE as health, as an academic study or as science (1995). The intensification of the relationship between PE and health reflects, in part, a response to spiralling health care costs and a view of children as future human capital, and in part the prevailing liberal economic view of the priority of the individual over society or community and the consequent personal responsibility for health. At best the linking of PE to health concerns is a laudable response to the development of a more sedentary lifestyle: at worst it encourages self-absorption and panders to the fetishising of health as an ideal attainable only through dangerous dietary regimes and, for men in particular, steroid abuse. Within the specification of the Health and Physical Education Key Learning Area (KLA) PE teachers had to fight hard to retain a clear statement of the importance of physical activity amid a welter of references to diet and lifestyle activities. In the competition for recognition within the KLA, PE and sport interests, such as the Australian

School Sports Council, had to compete with the increasingly influential health lobby, with the latter arguing that PE's role was as a contributor to health objectives.

It is not just the health lobby that has forced PE advocates on to the defensive – a second source of challenge comes from the well-established sports lobby. The tension between sport and PE has a long history in Australian education. The PE lobby has generally adopted definitions of PE close to that provided by Queensland University of Technology, which sees PE as including 'fitness, skills, movement, dance, recreation, health and sport plus the appropriate values and knowledge in each' (quoted in Crowley 1993: 23) thus placing sport as a sub-set of PE. By contrast, sport has narrower objectives focused on the identification and recruitment of talented children. It is probably the Aussie Sports programme that best characterises the attempt by sport to subordinate the PE curriculum. Aussie Sports was sponsored by the Australian Sport Commission in 1986 and was designed to encourage more children to participate in sport through, for example, the development of modified versions of adult sports. The success of Aussie Sports has come despite serious criticism. However, as Evans makes clear, the criticisms are often contradictory with some berating the scheme for its thinly veiled elitism and others criticising the scheme for being too democratic and teaching children that 'losing is acceptable', and also for being too inclusive and consequently narrowing the opportunities for those who wish to strive for excellence (1990a: 53).

A later innovation was the introduction of Sport Search, a computer software package which provided students with an indication of the sports that they are best suited to on the basis of the entry of data relating to, for example, height, arm span, vertical jump and 40-metre sprint. Unfortunately for some schools, the attractiveness of Aussie Sports has resided in the apparent similarity with PE which has resulted in a number of schools replacing PE with the federally funded Aussie Sports. In the words of Crowley, who chaired the 1992 Senate Inquiry, following the reduction in PE in schools '[m]any schools have assuaged their consciences for removing PE by adopting Aussie Sports' (1993: 23). Aussie Sports is an undoubted success as measured by its adoption in schools and as such represents an example of the influence of the sports lobby, with the Australian Sports Commission at its centre, on the school curriculum. The Australian Sports Commission has also been able to promote successfully the interests of organised sport through the launch of a National Junior Sports Policy in 1994, which links sport to PE and also to health and fitness, yet is clearly aimed at maintaining the traditional role of the school, at least as perceived by sport governing bodies, of talent identification and recruitment.

Traditional PE is also under threat from attempts to promote Sport Education as an alternative conceptualisation of the area of study.[2] For Alexander *et al.* sport education is:

an innovative curriculum model for secondary school PE in which mixed-ability teams are formed at the start of a 20 session competitive season. Students are taught to fulfil a range of roles associated with playing, umpiring, acting as a team coach, manager or captain, serving on a sports management board or on a duty team.

(Alexander *et al.*1993: 18)

In many ways the debate over Sport Education highlights the fissures within the PE profession as there are those who welcome Sport Education as a way of protecting PE from encroachment from health studies and also those, such as Alexander *et al.* (1995), who see it as a vehicle for professional renewal and as a way of relaunching PE while at the same time protecting its traditional core values (see also Evans 1990b). However, the Sport Education programme has been criticised by Brooker and Macdonald on the grounds that it reinforces a masculine sports culture and is consequently far less supportive of female participation. In addition, they suggest that Sport Education overemphasises competitive sport, is uncritical of the role of sport in Australian society and has a significantly narrower focus than PE (Brooker and Macdonald 1995: 106). Finally, Sport Education, like Aussie Sports, represents a rationalist approach to the area of learning as it is based on centralised control over programmes and outcomes.

The current tension between PE, Sport Education and programmes such as Sportsfun and Aussie Sports echoes the ambiguity about their relationship felt by politicians. The influential Senate Report on Physical and Sport Education in Australia, the Crowley Report (Standing Committee on the Environment, Recreation and the Arts, Australia, Senate 1992), in addition to noting that the 'quality and content of physical education . . . has declined' also noted that there was 'a policy and curriculum vacuum surrounding physical education' resulting in 'confusion between what is physical education [and] what is sport education' (ibid. 1992: xiii).[3] In general, the report was strongly supportive of PE as opposed to other programmes, but as Brooker and Macdonald note, 'while the intent of the report has found its way into the rhetoric of national curriculum documents, the position of PE in Australian schools remains underfunded, and consequently unchanged' (1995: 106). Despite the importance of funding, it is likely that the source of inaction on the position of PE lies in the deeply ambiguous attitudes towards the interrelationship of sport and PE held by many PE teachers. The ambiguity is also evident within the government, which was slow to respond to the Crowley Report and, when the response eventually came, it was delivered by the Minister for Sport and not the Minister for Education, suggesting, as Naar observes, that, as far as the government was concerned, 'PE and school sport were a sport issue, not an education issue' (1995: 6). While this choice of ministry might indicate, as Naar suggests, the fact that sports organisations have been at the forefront of the lobby on behalf of PE, it also reflects the muted voice of PE professionals.

In attempting to defend PE against the intrusion of sports-based programmes, PE advocates argue that PE has a much broader focus and is concerned to educate children both about and through physical activity. However, this further pushes PE teachers to increase the academic nature of the subject, a strategy which brings its own problems. Over the past fifteen years or so there has been a steady rise in the academic content of PE programmes, especially at the senior school level. As pressure on the school curriculum has increased, PE has been forced to compete with other subjects that have a far more secure status frequently based on strong and long-established links with higher education and the powerful university lobby. As a result, PE programmes attempt to increase the academic content through the inclusion of sports-related themes from, for example, psychology, science, history and sociology and also through the steady increase in formal assessment. Consequently, pupils spend less time 'doing' sport and PE and more time reflecting on it. Even so, there is little evidence that adopting the norms and aspirations of mainstream school subjects has done PE any significant good. PE is still under considerable pressure to maintain the number of specialist teachers and facilities and the amount of time in the school day. Evans (1990b: 285) talks of school sport being 'under siege' while Brooker and Macdonald, in their study of Queensland, show how the internal reorganisation of the Education Department has resulted in 'the devaluation of PE' (1993: 6) through the drastic reduction in the number of specialist PE advisers, both in absolute terms but also relative to the health area.

In conclusion, PE and its advocates are still fighting a vigorous but frustrating battle to identify and articulate a distinctive set of outcomes for PE as opposed to sport education or health education. The legacy of years of dispute over the definition of PE and the constant threat of erosion from contiguous fields such as health and sport not only exhaust the defenders of PE, but also make it very difficult for policy-makers to provide a decisive lead. It is therefore not surprising that the stimulus that the Crowley Inquiry gave to PE has dissipated rapidly and the initiative has passed more firmly to the health and sports lobbies. Whereas some point to the nature of a federal constitution as a factor inhibiting a strong Commonwealth lead on the promotion of PE, it is much more likely that the primary inhibiting factor is the incoherence of the PE lobby. Where lobbying groups have campaigned on the basis of clear-cut objectives in the school sport area, such as the Australian School Sport Council (ASSC) on the issue of interscholastic sport and the ASC with the Aussie Sports scheme, the Commonwealth government has been willing to provide funding and policy leadership.

As Turnbull (1995) notes, the likely fate of the Crowley Report (1992) should not be unexpected as there have been some nine previous reports dealing with PE and sport, none of which has been able to stop the steady decline in school PE: as Wells comments, '[w]e have had every study and enquiry imaginable and the answer is always the same' (article in *The Australian* entitled 'Sports Debate Falters without Farsighted Policy',

4 March 1993: 12, quoted in Turnbull 1995). Arguably, the continuing inability of the PE profession in Australia to articulate a persuasive rationale for their subject reflects not simply their relative weakness as an interest group in the contest for a share of the curriculum, but also what Crum (1993: 345) refers to as the 'self-reproducing failure of physical education' namely, chronic self-doubt. The consequence of the profession's failure is that on the one hand, PE has been ignored by the framers of the national curriculum and subsumed conceptually within health and fitness, while on the other hand, PE values have been squeezed by the advocates of sport. While ACHPER (Australian Council for Health, Physical Education and Recreation) has been a vociferous campaigner on behalf of the PE profession, the Confederation of Australian Sport, the ASC and the ASSC have been more effective advocates for the interests of the governing bodies.

CANADA

Throughout Canada most children pass through a system of elementary schools from kindergarten to 9 years, then move on to high school until the age of 17 or 18, although junior high schools (for children aged 9 to 13 years) are becoming more common. The most distinctive feature of the administration of education in Canada is the absence of a federal department concerned with education. While education is clearly located at the provincial level, there is significant liaison between provincial education ministers, through the Council of Ministers of Education Canada, which meets two or three times each year and has an administrative support centre and also links to a research centre in Toronto. The broad scope of the Council's discussions and its current particular emphasis on the specification of learning outcomes within the school curriculum partly explain the significant similarity between provincial systems as reflected in school structure, organisation and curriculum. Additional explanations for the high degree of uniformity found in education administration across the country lie, first, in the broadly common financial relationship between the federal government and the provinces, which imposes similar constraints on policy development, and second, in the pressure arising from facing common economic problems and responding to common debates promoted by the existence of national professional organisations within education.

As in many other western industrialised countries, the growing influence of liberal economic policies has dominated much of the recent debate about the funding and purposes of public services in Canada. In a number of provinces education has been at the heart of these debates which, in general, have resulted in a greater degree of provincial control over the curriculum while devolving greater budgetary responsibility to school boards or even to individual schools. However, as with all generalisations there are exceptions. The two provinces that are furthest advanced with the implementation of the liberal economic agenda are Ontario and Alberta.

In 1990 Ontario elected the socialist New Democratic Party (NDP), led by Bob Rae, to government. The NDP survived only one term, losing the 1995 election. However, during its term of office it dismayed many of its socialist supporters by the enthusiasm with which it embraced a liberal economic agenda with regard to public services including education. Although the NDP government campaigned on a policy to *fight recession*, within two years of election its rhetoric had changed to emphasise the need to *fight deficits* in public sector services. Pressure on teachers came from two sources: the negotiation of a 'Social Contract', which worsened the pay and conditions of teachers (and other public sector employees); and the deliberations of a *Royal Commission on Learning*, published in 1995. It is the last source which, in the eyes of many teachers, provided the threat to the established liberal–humanitarian curriculum and their influence over it. The greatest concern is voiced at the shift towards a curriculum defined by learning outcomes derived from the needs of employers. 'Curriculum guidelines should recognize the primacy of certain skills... literacy/communication skills, numeracy/problem-solving skills, group learning and interpersonal skills and values, scientific literacy, and computer literacy' (*Royal Commission on Learning* 1995, vol. 2: 25). While on the one hand, those with an interest in PE and sport in schools may feel that such a definition provides plenty of leeway for interpretation, on the other hand, there are those who consider that the emphasis on skills is at the expense of content. To Martell this suggests a one-dimensional curriculum where, at best, '[t]here are no human purposes here to be considered or complexities of life to be grappled with' and at worst a 'junk-food curriculum' (1995: 255 and 253). Although the business-related skills orientation of the curriculum proposed by the Royal Commission is undoubtedly anathema to some, the Commission did make it clear that there was a place for PE within the curriculum. Indeed, the Commission proposed an enhanced status for PE by requiring pupils to choose courses from either arts or PE rather than selecting between arts, PE and a technical course. What seems to be missing from the debate in Ontario is any significant concern over the effect of the Commission's proposals for the future of PE specifically.

The picture in Alberta is very similar to that in Ontario, if slightly more colourful. If Bob Rae was seen as a socialist who sold out to business, Ralph Klein, who became leader of Alberta's Progressive Conservative Party (PCP) in 1992, was, from the outset, a radical right-wing politician. In the provincial election that followed in 1993, the PCP won 51 out of 83 seats; the Liberals (who also campaigned on a budget-cutting platform) won 32 seats; and the NDP was obliterated. The initial concern of the Klein government was the reduction of the budget, and education expenditure was a key target (Alberta Education 1994). To this end, the number of school boards was reduced with the bulk of their financial responsibilities being transferred to the province and the remaining powers being devolved to 'parent councils'. The curriculum was also modified to place greater emphasis on the needs of business, particularly with regard to a greater emphasis on standardised testing (Robertson and Barlow 1995). As in Ontario, while there is considerable disquiet at the implications for education of a radical right-wing provincial government, there is no significant concern about the impact on PE and school sport. While there are many similarities in the current economic and political context for education generally, and PE and sport in particular, with Australia there are two striking differences. The first is that PE and sport appear to be relatively secure within the junior and high school curricula and the second is that there seems to be a much less acrimonious relationship between sport, PE and health.

As regards the security of PE within the curriculum, there is a generally firm consensus that PE and sport have a role to fulfil. However, on analysis it would seem that the consensus is built around support for sport within schools, with PE perceived either as a synonym for sport or as a sub-set of complementary activities where 'the physical educator is more and more concerned with sport' (Cosentino and Howell 1970: 68; see also Zeigler 1994 for a critique of the current dominance of sport in PE). John goes as far as to suggest that the dominant discourse in the area is one which 'reconstructed physical education and professional preparation around elite sport and served to meet the needs of provincial and federal government sport bodies rather than those of provincial education' (1995: 16–17). Yet, this is a perception that the main lobbying organisation, the Canadian Association for Health, Physical Education, Recreation and Dance (CAHPERD), is content to leave undisturbed and work within. Contrary to the view of Cosentino and Howell in 1970 'that physical education seems to have fragmentized into separate components of health, recreation, sports, and physical education' (1970: 68), the current campaign for Quality Daily Physical Education (QDPE) blurs the distinction between sport, health and PE thereby being able to utilise the additional leverage of both the NSOs and the government programmes such as 'Active Living', devised by Fitness Canada and located within the influential Health Canada department. However, before criticising CAHPERD for colluding in the undermining of PE, it must be borne in mind that its remit goes beyond that of the PE associations found elsewhere, such as those in the UK or Ireland, and specifically includes health and recreation in its title. The current mission of the Association is not to promote PE but rather to help foster an active lifestyle working particularly within educational settings.

The willingness of the PE lobby to work closely with the sports organisations is a product of the development of sport and PE in Canadian schools, which in turn is a reflection of the dual heritage drawn from the English public (fee-paying) school tradition and the priority given to competitive sport prevalent in the US school system. The deep roots of nineteenth-century 'muscular Christianity' in providing a powerful rationale for school and inter-school sport is such that the 'importance of this set of ideas to Canadian sport and physical education cannot be over emphasized'

(Metcalfe 1974: 69). The significance of 'muscular Christianity' in ensuring the acceptance of inter-school sport was complemented by the importance of social Darwinist ideas in securing the place of PE in the curriculum. According to Eastman, the development of athletics and a strong tradition of inter-school athletic competition 'served to actuate the maturation of physical education in Canada' (1989: 49). Martens, quoted in Eastman, argues that the influence of athletics was still strong in the mid-1970s and concludes that 'it is no wonder that the public's image of school physical education is based to such a large extent on the nature and scope of inter-school athletics' (1975: 25). The political centrality of sport by comparison with PE was reinforced more recently by the report of the federal government's Task Force on Sport and the high-profile activity of Minister Campagnola. As in the United States it is still common for PE teachers also to be team coaches, with the latter role being the more important, prompting Saunders to remark that '[p]hysical education slipped into the school curriculum on the coat tails of popular pastime and activity-athletics' (1973, quoted in Eastman 1989).

A crucial role in developing the central place of athletics and inter-scholastic competition was fulfilled by the Canadian School Sport Federation, which had close links and similar concerns to the major sport governing bodies. More importantly, up until the formation of the Canadian Physical Education Association (the forerunner of CAHPERD) in 1933 there was a close alignment between school sport organisations and professional PE bodies, with the latter on occasion being responsible for the organisation of inter-scholastic competition (Eastman 1989). Despite part of the rationale for the formation of CAHPERD lying in the desire to assert the distinctive character and interests of PE and PE teachers, the close organisational relationship with sport continued until relatively recently and the broad mutual sympathy between the two areas remains.

Canadian PE is therefore in a curious position in the school curriculum, comforted by the close association with sport while at the same time weakened by the lack of a clear identity. However, there is a persuasive argument that the pattern of development of school sport and PE has had the beneficial effect of making school sport organisations and sports coaches far less wary of acknowledging the educational aspects of their activities and far less inclined to see PE and educational objectives as attempts to dilute the practice of sport. Given that elite sports success has remained a clear federal objective for so long, it is highly unlikely that the advocates of PE could outmanoeuvre the sports lobby if it came to a serious confrontation over curriculum time or staff appointments. These considerations notwithstanding, Canadian PE is not immune from the pressures evident in the other countries in this study. The general pressure on the curriculum to be more explicitly supportive of the needs of the economy and the ascendancy of radical right-wing economics have put PE under substantial strain. However, the vulnerability of jobs in PE seems no greater than in other subjects outside the Maths, Science, English/French core. There is, though, some concern that the drift towards credentialism in PE is deterring pupils from selecting the subject when it is an option during the later stages of their school career. 'The evaluation process for physical education discourages many students from including this subject in their timetables; it is easier to achieve a 90 per cent average in high school math than a 70 per cent in physical education' (CAHPERD 1995: 5).

The current pressures on school sport and PE need to be seen in the context of developments over the past twenty years or so. At elementary school level PE was accorded very low status until the early 1970s, when substantial progress was made in increasing the quantity and quality of PE in the curriculum. By the early 1980s an increasing number of elementary schools had adopted a programme of daily PE and progress continued to be made throughout most of the 1980s (Broom 1995). Although starting from a much firmer foundation, similar progress was also made in the high school sector where the typical allocation of time was in the region of 2 hours per week. In retrospect, the 1970s was the golden age of school PE. In Manitoba over 90 per cent of schools had daily PE and in British Columbia there was strong political support for the introduction of daily PE (Follatschek 1982). Nevertheless during the 1980s 'physical education requirements have been eroded in almost all provinces and by the middle of the decade most provinces had dropped the requirement in the twelfth grade and in the eleventh grade' (Broom 1995: 161). As the pressure on PE within the curriculum increased, self-doubt began to surface within the PE profession (Verabioff, 1986; see also Johnson 1985 for a trenchant critique of professionalism among PE teachers).

Despite the close relationship between sport and PE organisations, the loose consensus about the nature of the subject, and the fact that there is no specific threat to the subject, it is still under pressure within many schools. According to CAHPERD:

> Physical education is not being perceived in the school system as an essential and unique part of a child's learning [and] only 766 out of more than 15,000 Canadian schools have physical education programs recognized by CAHPERD and Fitness Canada as QDPE [Quality Daily Physical Education] programs.

> (CAHPERD 1995: 4)

CAHPERD also reports that there has been a significant decline of qualified PE specialists. For example, in British Columbia the number of PE consultants (advisers) has been reduced from thirty-three to twelve, with an increasing prevalence of fixed-term appointments (CAHPERD 1994; see also Goodwin *et al.* 1996). More significantly, fewer than half of all PE teachers have a specialist qualification in the subject and one in five has never taken a specialist PE course (CAHPERD 1986). The Association has also highlighted the variability in PE programmes across the country, pointing essentially to the extent to which the profile of PE within a school depends on the lead given by provincial education ministries, the decisions of school boards and the preferences of head teachers. The variation in timetable allocation and the wide range in the quality of facilities tends to affect the opportunities for girls more than boys, with there being fewer female PE teachers and coaches and less opportunity to pursue the activities that are more popular with girls, such as aerobics and fitness training on a year-round basis (DeMarco and Sidney 1989).

In the most recent survey of the state of PE in Canada undertaken by CAHPERD, the overall picture is of PE holding its ground in the curriculum and, in some regions, improving its profile when compared with an earlier Council of Ministers of Education study in the mid-1980s (Johnson and Sinclair 1985) (Table 7.1). Even at the senior high school level, PE is still a prominent option. However, the data need to be interpreted with some care as CAHPERD uses the term 'PE' in a much broader way than is common in the UK or Australia. In a number of provinces it is difficult to

Table 7.1 The status of PE in Canada, 1996 (selected provinces/territories)

	Manitoba	Saskatchewan	Ontario	Quebec	Alberta	British Columbia	Newfoundland
Compulsory?	Yes K–10	Yes K–9	Yes K–9	Yes K–11	Yes K–10	Yes K–10	Yes K–9
Recommended time allocation per week	c. 120 mins	30 mins per day compulsory	Daily (no specific time allocation)	100–120 mins	None	Grades K–3 no set time; grades 4–10 c. 150 mins	120 mins
Actual time allocation per week	Varies widely by school and by year, but c. 80 mins	30 mins per day compulsory	Daily (no specific time allocation)	75–80 mins	150 mins K–6 and 75 hours per year, grades 7–10	Grades K–3 no set time; grades 4–10 c. 150 mins	60–80 mins
Specialist teachers for PE?	High in cities and high schools but as low as 60% in rural areas and rare in junior schools	More common in high schools than junior; few PE consultants	Grade 7 upwards usually taught by specialists	Probably over 80%	High percentage grades 7–10, but far less common at junior level	Only at grades 8–12	80% of teachers; grades 4–12 are specialist
Prospects for PE	Support for specialist teachers from Minister of Education	PE retains a central role in curriculum	Some uncertainty due to the introduction of outcome-based education	Some decrease in time allocation over past 20 years	Good; 25% of schools have QDPE	Pressure on budgets is reducing slightly the use of specialist teachers	PE under no particular threat

Note: K refers to Kindergarten and the numbers to year or grade in a school career.
Source: Adapted from CAHPERD, Provincial/Territorial PE Profile 1995.

identify the time allocation for PE as it is aggregated with health and frequently taught by the same person. Indeed, one of the major changes between the 1985 Council of Ministers of Education survey and the CAHPERD 1995 survey is the reduction in the number of provinces that retain a curriculum for PE that is separate from health. Currently, PE, broadly defined, is compulsory in most provinces and territories and although the time allocation varies, there is no province where the existence of PE is under serious threat. However, a proposal by the Manitoba Minister of Education to remove PE as a core subject in grades 9 to 12 provided a jolt to the complacency of many PE professionals. While the eventual withdrawal of the proposal reflected the lobbying capacity of the PE and sport interests, the grounds for the original proposal are probably a cause for longer-term concern. According to the Minister, 'although tremendous support had been given to physical education, the attitudes of society had not been positively affected by their physical education experience within the school system' (quoted in Janzen 1995: 8). In an era where measurable outputs are increasingly a requirement for continued public funding, PE found itself unable to demonstrate that it 'had paid any positive dividend' (Janzen 1995: 8).

The challenge in Manitoba notwithstanding, PE is, in many respects, in an enviable position in Canada. Yet, much of its apparent security is the consequence of the deliberate cultivation of a low profile in both broader education debates and in debates on that cluster of related and overlapping areas that include health, sport and fitness. The need to raise the profile of PE is acknowledged by CAHPERD's recent campaign 'Physical Education 2000' document, where reference is made to the subject's 'tenuous place on the Canadian school curriculum' (CAHPER 1993). However, the status of PE is also the consequence of what Anderson refers to as 'the present apathy exhibited by physical education specialists toward professional and curriculum concerns' (1995: 283). The promotion of QDPE and involvement in the 'Active Living' programme notwithstanding, Anderson describes the lobbying activity of PE professionals in relation to the curriculum and time allocation for PE as abysmal. The clear implication is that PE prospered within the supportive context of sport in the 1970s and 1980s and is also prospering in the 1990s within the dominant health/fitness framework, but would be extremely vulnerable should either of these frameworks be redefined in a way that marginalised PE activities and values.

IRELAND

In Ireland education is compulsory between the ages of 6 and 15, although most children begin their schooling at the age of 4 and remain in primary school until the age of 12. Secondary education comprises two phases, one of three years (the junior cycle) and the other of two years (the senior cycle). As O'Donovan (1993) notes, the distinctive features of the Irish system are a multiple-subject curriculum, a high participation rate in the senior cycle and the centrality of examinations. The current national PE syllabus, which dates from 1971, is aimed at providing the child with, *inter alia*, a broad range of physical skills, a knowledge of a range of games and other physical activities and self-esteem. At the secondary level the syllabus is designed to introduce the pupil to a range of sports and activities, including gymnastics, dance, athletics, swimming, health education, and outdoor pursuits (Department of Education, no date).

In the early 1990s the Irish government undertook a major review of education which prompted a period of intense reflection on the place of PE and sport in the curriculum and an equally intense round of lobbying in an attempt to protect the status of the subject. This current review of the place of PE in the curriculum is the most recent in a surprisingly brief history of PE in the Irish curriculum. From 1921 to 1939 there were, according to Duffy (1996), a number of broadly unsuccessful attempts to strengthen the position of PE in the curriculum.[4] In an early draft of the Irish constitution, reference was made to the responsibilities of the family and those of the state, which included ensuring minimum levels of education, one element of which was physical education. However, this reference was removed from the final draft, apparently by Eamon De Valera, following a series of discussions with the papal nuncio who was concerned about references to the Church in the constitution and especially about guaranteeing the rights of the family. The 1930s was also a time of considerable concern, particularly within the Church, over the alleged decline in moral standards, as reflected in the increasing popularity of dancing. For the Church, matters 'physical' of whatever kind were best confined to the family and the pulpit rather than the school. The concerns that prompted the Church's opposition to PE in schools and dancing in village halls also led to opposition in the 1940s to the attempt by the government to introduce a public health scheme for mothers and babies (Whyte 1980). For the Church, control over the curriculum was an essential bulwark against moral decline. As one bishop remarked: 'Experience has shown that physical education is closely interwoven with important moral questions on which the Catholic Church has definite teaching' (O'Donoghue 1989, quoted in Darmody 1995: 21). Article 42 of the constitution consequently included a reference to the rights and responsibilities of the family regarding the 'religious and moral, intellectual, physical and social education of their children'. By asserting the rights of the family, the constitution denied the opportunity to include PE as a compulsory element in the school curriculum.

From the 1940s to the 1960s the government made little effort to overcome Church opposition. Although there was some half-hearted discussion in the Department of Education, there was little action (O'Donoghue 1989). Indeed, in some areas there was a diminution in the status of PE. The revision of the primary school curriculum in 1962 relegated PE to an optional subject (Darmody 1995: 21). Ironically, it was a change of attitude within the Catholic Church that revived discussion over the place of PE in schools. The 1951 report of the Commission on Youth Unemployment, chaired by archbishop McQuaid, argued that PE had a positive role to play in ensuring fitness and could profitably be linked with organised sport, a clear reference to the Gaelic Athletic Association (GAA). The report of the Commission gave a considerable boost to PE by recommending that 'physical education be made an integral part of the curriculum of all schools' (Government of Ireland 1951: 47), but progress was extremely slow and it took a further fifteen years for government to adopt a more active role in promoting PE in the curriculum. However, the period from the late 1960s to the 1980s was marked by a significant increase in the role of government in developing the PE curriculum and in providing trained PE teachers and appropriate facilities. The increased interest of the government was not just the result of a changed attitude of the Church and the latter's acceptance that the 'physical' could be associated with health, fitness and sport rather than with dancing and decadence, it was also the result of the growing involvement of the Irish government in international bodies, especially the Council of Europe with its concern with 'Sport for All' and physical education.

The period of sustained expansion of PE within schools peaked during the 1970s and, by the early 1980s, PE was coming under increasing pressure in the face of growing competition for space in the curriculum and public expenditure cutbacks. The variation in the fortunes of PE is evident in the changing pattern of teacher-training provision for PE specialists. In the 1970s approximately 70 students a year were entering the main training college. By 1980 the figure had fallen to 54 and by the end of the decade it had fallen again to 24, reflecting, according to O'Sullivan and McCarthy (1994, not an oversupply of teachers but a decline in commitment to a physical education programme. For John Halbert, education officer to the National Council for Curriculum and Assessment (NCCA) Committee on PE, the 1980s were 'dark times indeed' (1995: 16). The PE profession consequently entered into the period of curriculum review in the early 1990s having to fight tenaciously to retain the hard-won gains of the very recent past. Yet, the gains were modest and never matched the government's protestations of commitment. For example, the recommendation by the Curriculum and Assessments Board in 1985 that PE should form part of the core curriculum was never implemented. Further evidence of government neglect is provided by Deenihan (1991), who carried out a survey of just under 800 post-primary schools. His findings threw into sharp relief the claims that PE was successfully established in Irish schools. Of especial note were his findings that the ratio of pupils to PE teachers in Ireland was, at 534:1, twice that found in Australia, Britain and the United States and that 28 per cent of schools had no qualified PE teacher. In addition, he reported that the amount of time allocated to PE declined steadily throughout the post-primary years from an average of 55 minutes in the first year to an average of 34 minutes in the final year. In addition, over 40 per cent of schools did not offer PE and the record on facilities was also poor with 26 per cent of schools having no indoor facilities, 8 per cent no outdoor facilities and 5 per cent neither indoor nor outdoor facilities. Not surprisingly, Deenihan concluded that 'Physical Education is becoming marginalised' (1991: 12) and provides supporting evidence for Duffy's (1996) later conclusion that there is a discrepancy between the rhetoric of ministerial policy statements on PE and the reality of inadequate provision in schools (p. 13).

The foregoing discussion has shown the importance of the Catholic Church in influencing educational policy in general and the fate of PE in particular. Although not as dominant in the past twenty years as it was in the early years of the Republic, the Church none the less retains an extremely influential position in policy discussions on all educational matters, not least because the overwhelming majority of schools remain denominational.

The task of promoting the interests of PE falls to the Physical Education Association of Ireland (PEAI), founded in 1968. During the early years of the organisation it relied heavily on voluntary officers, but in recent years it has received an annual grant of IR£20,000 from the Department of Education towards the cost of employing full-time staff. The Association's status as a lobby on behalf of PE is precarious in large part because of its continuing dependence on Departmental funding. To compound the reticence that financial dependency might encourage, it is also clear that the government is reluctant for the PEAI to expand its role beyond that of subject-based advocacy and consequently, there is no place for a PEAI representative on the National Sports Council. Even its subject advocacy role is proving difficult to establish: it was not, for example, invited to participate in the convention organised by the government to discuss the recent education White Paper. There have been some moves to overcome the limitations on the role of the PEAI resulting from its resource dependency on government largely through an attempt to develop linkages with other organisations with interests in the sport, health and fitness issues, along similar lines to AHPERD (Association for Health, Physical Education, Recreation and Dance) in the United States. Part of the rationale of building links with related organisations is an attempt to take advantage of their generally closer relationship with government and in part an acknowledgement that debates that affect PE are often subsumed under the heading of sport or health. Reasonably close links have been developed with the National Coaching and Training Centre (NCTC) (also funded by the government) and attempts have also been made to build bridges, via the NCTC, with the major sport governing bodies but with far less success. The GAA is typical in its wariness of the PE lobby believing that there is an overemphasis on fitness in PE which undermines the development of skills for team sports. However, the PEAI is equally wary of the governing bodies and has two predominant concerns: the first is the conventional assertion that there is a need to 'improve the status of physical education at every level', which is readily supported by other bodies; and second that there is an 'over emphasis . . . on school sport from a competitive point of view', a much more problematic assertion (O'Donovan 1993: 709 and 710). The tension between the PEAI and organised sport has been exacerbated by the former's support for the introduction of formal assessment in PE. The evidence from the surveys by Deenihan (1991) and Duffy *et al.* (1992) reported that there was strong support from teachers for the introduction of assessment prior to the publication of the Green Paper. PE teachers had already taken action to enhance the status of PE and their own position in schools by attempting to increase the examination content of the subject through the ASSIST (Assessment in Second Level Teaching) Project. The ASSIST Project was aimed at introducing a more rigorous form of assessment for PE, a framework that would enable the monitoring of a pupil's progress within the seven areas of work in the junior cycle under three broad categories: affective, psycho-motor and cognitive. But the ASSIST materials do not meet the requirements for public examinations and there is a continuing debate over the desirability of attempting to emulate the traditional academic subjects.

It is against this background of a limited capacity on the part of the PEAI to act as an effective advocate for PE and PE teachers and the general lack of cohesion among interest groups that the government launched its recent review of Irish education focused on the publication of a Green Paper in 1992 and the subsequent White Paper in 1995.[5] Prior to the publication of the Green Paper, 'Education for a Changing World', the PEAI had been lobbying for a more prominent place in the curriculum for PE. Much of the Association's activity had focused on the deliberations of the Physical Education Working Party established in 1988 by the NCCA to advise on the role of PE in the post-primary school curriculum. Whereas earlier reports on the curriculum (Department of Education 1984 and 1986) stressed educational reasons for the continued inclusion of PE, the Working Party broadened the rationale by emphasising 'the enormous contribution which physical education can make to personal, social and economic well-being' (Physical Education Working Party 1989: 2). The report painted a picture of a subject under severe pressure and 'in a precarious decline due to the under-supply of personnel, time and facilities' (p. 3). Despite the recommendation of an allocation of two hours per week for PE at second level, a survey commissioned by the Working Party found an average of only 46 minutes. In addition, there was considerable evidence to suggest that the time allocated was frequently poorly used owing to the inadequacy of facilities or the lack of trained staff. The Working Party Report made a series of recommendations, one of which was to pursue the goal of greater assessment of PE. The Working Party also argued for greater clarification of the role of organised games in the school and the role of PE teaching staff in extra-curricular sport.

The review of education in Ireland was prompted by concerns about the escalating cost of the education service and the growing awareness of the importance of education to the success of the government's economic strategy within the European Union. The 1992 Green Paper, 'Education for a Changing World', aimed to locate sport and PE securely within the school curriculum and also provide a context for more broadly defined school sport. However, the document was clearer in establishing policies and procedures for implementation than in articulating the objectives for sport and PE in the curriculum. Part of the reason for this weakness was the parallel work of the Review Body on the Primary Curriculum (established by the NCCA). The Green Paper did note that the Review Body had endorsed the existing principles of school PE established in the 1971 curriculum statement, one of which was to 'enable students to acquire a knowledge of their bodies and a sense of responsibility for their own health and to develop their physical ability through creative activities and sport' (Department of Education 1992: 87–8). The Green Paper omitted to report that the Review Body stressed the lack of training and confidence among teachers, particularly at primary level, to deliver the ambitious 1971 syllabus and the lack of a systematic strategy for in-service training to remedy this situation (National Council for Curriculum and Assessment 1991). However, the section of the Green Paper that dealt with primary education located PE within the context of 'diet, hygiene, posture, flexibility and a healthy lifestyle' (Department of Education 1992: 90). Although less was said regarding the secondary curriculum, the emphasis was much the same where PE was seen as 'a continuation of the initiatives at the primary level and in the particular context of fostering the "Health Promoting School" ' (Department of Education 1992: 96). The emphasis of the policy statement was on health-related fitness rather than on the practice of particular sports. However, the document was often contradictory, arguing, on the one hand, for the delivery of a PE programme from the junior years that would 'promote physical well-being of all students in a non-competitive way' and, on the other hand, asserting the importance of 'enhancing the performance standards by Irish sportspersons . . . as a follow on to the promotion of the physical well-being of children in school' (1992: 130 and 217).

There were few specific references to sport for school-age children in the Green Paper. It was seen as having 'strong links to physical education' but most of the discussion seemed to view sport as an extension of community leisure provision rather than as a complement to PE classes. 'An important feature of physical education and sport within schools is that they should have close links with the sports programme of the community' (Department of Education 1992: 218). The content of the Green Paper suggested that implementation of school sport policy lay significantly, if not largely, with bodies external to the school, including voluntary clubs and community organisations.

> Sport in the community is generally organised by clubs affiliated to national governing bodies, many of which organise competitions for schools. The traditional involvement of teachers in sports organisations

provides the type of dynamic link between them which can benefit both the school and local sports organisations. Such links ensure that the games and recreation activities that are part of community life are integrated, in a suitable form, into the school programme.

(Department of Education 1992: 221)

The publication of the Green Paper was followed by a period of consultation. The document was broadly welcomed by teaching organisations. The PEAI welcomed the statement that PE would form part of the general entitlement of all students from the primary level onwards. It also gave its support to the development of a 'holistic' concept of wellbeing and argued that PE 'was an essential element of the Health Promoting School' (Physical Education Association of Ireland 1993: 6). The preference of the Association for linking PE interests with those of the health lobby was emphasised by its guarded comments about the relationship between the 'in-curricular' PE programme and the extra-curricular (or co-curricular as the PEAI prefers) sports programme. 'Co-curricular activities are complementary to the physical education programme and must not be seen as one and the same thing' (ibid.: 7). Moreover, the PEAI expressed concern at the lack of formal representation of PE specialists via the PEAI on the NCCA Review Body considering the PE Primary Curriculum.

The guarded optimism felt by the PEAI following the publication of the Green Paper was short lived as the subsequent White Paper, published after the 1992 election, was a deep disappointment (Department of Education 1995). Although mentioned, PE was clearly not a priority, being treated as an element in the development of the 'health promoting school' and linked to education on hygiene and diet. More worryingly, sport is mentioned in preference to PE in the summary of the White Paper, fuelling concerns that the government has no real understanding of the distinctive contribution of PE to the curriculum. For Duffy, the retreat from the role advocated for PE in the Green Paper is an indication of the continuing constitutional uncertainty over the proper role of the school, in relation to the family, in matters physical and moral (1996: 18ff.). A further cause for concern within the PEAI related to the preferred method of implementation through regional organisations, fearing that this would further disadvantage PE due to the variability of the Association's regional strength.

Overall, the outcome of the protracted review of the education system in the 1990s was to leave the position of PE largely unchanged. In part, the unsatisfactory outcome for PE was the result of the marginality of the subject to the struggle between the State, Church, parents and the teaching profession over control of Irish education. But the outcome was also the product of the continuing absence of consensus among PE teachers over a series of basic questions within the subject including its primary purpose in schools, its relation with intra- and extra-curricular sport, and the uncertainty over the question of assessment.

As in other countries in this study, one theme that underpins much of the politics of PE is the subject's relationship with organised sport. Within the initial cohort of PE teachers trained in the 1960s there were many who already had strong links with organised sport, particularly through the GAA. Yet, as PE became better established in the curriculum, the GAA and the other major governing bodies became critical of what they considered to be the overemphasis on fitness and strength at the expense of skill. In its response to the Green Paper, the PEAI argued that 'co-curricular activities are not and must not be considered as a substitute for a quality physical education programme' (Physical Education Association of Ireland 1993:2). The different perceptions of the purpose of PE held by governing bodies and the PEAI has led to a growth in mutual suspicion that has made co-operative lobbying problematic.

In conclusion, PE has only a tenuous hold within the Irish school curriculum. In common with other countries advocates of PE have found it difficult to persuade the government that PE can be differentiated from health, fitness and sport with sufficient clarity to warrant separate consideration in curriculum development. The ability of the PEAI to lobby effectively on behalf of PE is undermined by a considerable degree of ambivalence among PE teachers towards the proper location of boundaries between PE, sport and health. Finally, PE advocates have to contend with the deeply entrenched position of the GAA in Irish society and government and the Association's wariness of the implications of PE for the future of Gaelic sports.

UNITED KINGDOM

Education in the UK has been the subject of intense scrutiny for more than ten years. Key political debates have focused on selection of pupils by schools on the basis of ability, local government control over schools, the role of parents in school governance, 'progressive teaching methods' and control over the curriculum. Perhaps the only element of the school system to remain largely intact is the overall pattern of primary and secondary schools. For most children, school starts at the age of 5, when they enter primary school, continues following the transfer to secondary school at the age of 11 until at least the age of 16. In some parts of the country children spend the years between age 9 and age 12 at a middle school. At the secondary level, a mix of schools exist: most are comprehensive (admitting children from the whole ability range); others are selective (requiring children to pass an entrance or selection examination); and a small number are specialist technology schools funded by central government. Most schools are administered by local government, although a small but increasing number are deciding to 'opt out' of local authority control to be funded directly by central government. In Northern Ireland there is no local authority involvement in school administration. All schools are either centrally administered through the Department of Education for Northern Ireland or administered through five Education and Library Boards whose members are nominated by the minister.

Two of the most controversial issues of recent years have been those concerned with parental choice and the imposition of a national curriculum. Parental choice became the watchword of the radical-right critique of schools and the teaching profession which sought to challenge the control exercised by teachers over the content of the curriculum and the methods of delivery. Teachers were seen as part of the problem and an impediment to market-based reform. 'Progressive' teaching methods and a neglect of core skills in literacy and numeracy were identified for especial opprobrium. Both these issues had an impact on debates about the role and importance of PE in the curriculum. Added to these general pressures on schools, there was a set of pressures specific to physical education and while particularly prominent in the 1980s, some remain a source of friction. An especial concern of the governing bodies of sport and of some PE teachers was the perceived drift in the content of the PE curriculum away from the practice of sport and the development of sport-specific skills and towards an overemphasis on the development of generic movement skills (Her Majesty's Inspectorate 1978). A second issue related to the consequences of the protracted dispute between teachers and the government over contracts of employment in 1985. The outcome of the dispute was the imposition on teachers of much more clearly defined contracts which, among other things, specified the number of hours teachers were required to work, and introduced an obligation to participate in staff training, which was often arranged at the end of the school day (Secondary Heads Association 1987). The legacy of the dispute was to dissipate substantially the fund of goodwill among teachers that encouraged them to support extra-curricular activities. PE teachers found it more difficult to persuade non-PE teachers to take responsibility for managing school teams. In addition, PE teachers themselves found that the constraints of their new contracts made the organisation of team training more difficult.

Two further significant issues concerned the policy of selling school playing fields and the introduction of local financial management of schools. In 1981 the government issued regulations designed to encourage local authorities to sell surplus playing fields. Although the main justification for the policy was that many fields were under-used, the policy was a further example of the Thatcher government's enthusiasm for privatisation and its general suspicion of public ownership, especially of land. The introduction of local financial management of schools in the late 1980s was an attempt to reduce the financial control exercised by local authorities over individual schools. Thus, many budget items that were previously met by the local authority education department out of central funds were now devolved to schools. Included in the range of items devolved were the costs associated with sport and PE, such as transport costs to playing fields and swimming pools. As devolved budgets were under constant pressure, some schools reduced their costs by cutting back on transport for sport.

To the series of relatively recent pressures on PE already mentioned must be added the longer-term ambiguity concerning the status of PE and of PE teachers in schools. Despite many recent attempts to strengthen the academic credentials of PE and sport in the curriculum, it has proved extremely difficult to shed the perception of PE that it, in common with art and music, is of a qualitatively different character to other subjects. According to Peters, in one of the most influential statements of the argument, subjects such as Science, Mathematics and History are ' "serious" in that they illuminate other areas of life. . . . They have secondly, a wide-ranging cognitive content which distinguishes them from games.' By contrast 'games' develop a category of skill that 'do not have a wide cognitive content. There is very little to know about riding bicycles, swimming or golf. . . . Furthermore what there is to know throws very little light on much else' (Peters 1966: 159). The impact of Peters' analysis has been to force the advocates of PE on to the defensive, depending on arguments about the instrumental value of PE rather than its intrinsic academic qualities. Consequently, physical educationists rely on the character-forming capacity of PE, its contribution to health and fitness, its place at the heart of national heritage and its value in maintaining a sense of self-esteem.

It is within this generally insecure context that PE teachers had to defend the subject's place in the curriculum during the debate on the content of the national curriculum and the relationship between PE and sport. During much of the 1980s Margaret Thatcher's governments undertook a radical restructuring of many aspects of British society, with schools, along with the trade union movement, being the target for especial legislative attention. In essence, the project of the radical right was to refashion the discourse within which the policy and practice of education was conducted. The long-established frame which prioritised matters associated with equity and individual potential was eroded and replaced by a frame that stressed standards and the pursuit of excellence and which sought policy solutions from the 'logic' of the market. The culmination of the highly ideological debate about the education system was the passing of the Education Reform Act in 1988, a piece of legislation which typified the combination of populist politics and market values. The Act included proposals to introduce a national curriculum, change the admissions process to schools, give greater financial autonomy to schools and provide the opportunity for schools to leave the local government system and receive direct funding from central government. The legislation was designed to weaken the influence of a number of actors in the education policy process, especially local authorities, education advisers and the teaching profession: it was also designed to strengthen the influence of parents and central government.

There were four phases in the planning and implementation of the national curriculum. The first phase was the establishment of the overall framework of the curriculum and was undertaken by politicians and officials within the Department of Education and Science. Once the framework had been agreed working groups were established with broad-based membership to determine the curriculum for specific subject areas. The third phase involved the National Curriculum Council providing a commentary and advice for the Minister on the output of the various working groups. The fourth phase followed the review of the national curriculum undertaken by Sir Ron Dearing, in which he suggested a reduction in the content of the curriculum.

The crucial decision during the first phase was whether or not PE would be included as a foundation subject. Prior to the decision being made, PE had experienced a period of prolonged criticism largely focused on the manufactured polarity between competitive team sport on the one hand, and PE on the other. To the radical right, the former developed the qualities and vocational skills needed for participation in a vigorous market economy, while the latter was damned by its egalitarian rhetoric and preoccupation with the intrinsic value of participation in PE. Given the weight of criticism of PE, where it was 'used by the political right . . . to signify all else that was wrong with state education' (Evans 1992: 234), and the exclusion of PE from the list of core and foundation subjects in the 1987 Consultative Document on the National Curriculum, the eventual decision to include PE as a foundation subject in the national curriculum 'induced an almost audible sigh of relief from PE teachers' (Evans *et al.* 1993: 325). However, as Evans *et al.* were quick to point out, there is a potentially high price to be paid for the security of foundation status.

The Working Group on PE was one of the last to be established and its terms of reference differed from those of most other subjects in so far as it was suggested that PE should be optional for 14–16-year-olds (key stage 4). The attempt to maintain an equivalence of status with other foundation subjects was only one of the challenges facing the group: the other was the overt hostility of the Education Secretary and the Minister for Sport to the group's Interim Report, which was criticised for being too academic and overelaborate, and also for giving too little weight to 'doing sport' (Talbot 1995). The publication of the National Curriculum for PE (NCPE) in 1991 reflected a degree of compromise. The PE curriculum certainly took on board the Minister's criticisms of its interim proposals and gave a greater prominence to sport, and practice as opposed to theory. However, it is also fair to say that the Minister for Sport moderated the force of his criticism in the light of some skilful lobbying by sports organisations and PE bodies.

The NCPE, introduced in 1992, outlined the content for each of the four 'key stages' in a child's school career. At key stages one and two the curriculum includes athletics, games (sports), dance, gymnastics, outdoor and adventurous activities, and swimming. At key stage three swimming ceases to be a requirement and at key stage four pupils should experience at least two activities. Many feared for the status of PE in the 1993 Dearing Review, which was designed, in part, to reduce the volume of material required by law to be taught. Dearing's confirmation of PE's position as a statutory requirement at key stage four calmed many fears, but the review did increase the relative emphasis on games and health-related fitness largely at the expense of outdoor adventurous activities.

The eventual content of the NCPE needs to be seen within the context of the government's broader concern with the alleged decline in competitive sport in UK schools. As well as attempting to determine the content of the PE curriculum, the government was also concerned to develop policy designed to raise the profile of extra-curricular sport. During recent years the government has floated a variety of proposals including the making of additional payments to PE teachers and even amending PE teachers' contracts to require them to supervise extra-curricular core team sport. However, while anecdotes supporting the assertion of a drift away from competitive team sports are common, firm evidence is hard to find. The Secondary Heads Association survey in 1990 found that in state schools the five sports most commonly found in the PE curriculum for boys were cricket, athletics, basketball, cross-country and soccer, and for girls, tennis, netball, athletics, hockey and rounders. A later participation survey in 1994 confirmed the dominance of competitive sport in schools, but did show that traditional team sports were losing their monopoly and were having to vie with newer sports for the commitment of pupils (Mason 1995). The evidence lends weight to the suspicion that a part at least of the lobbying by the major team sports over the design of the curriculum was motivated more by the loss of their privileged position in schools than by a real fear that competitive sport *per se* was under threat.

The process by which the NCPE was determined reflected the government's suspicion of the PE teaching profession. Curriculum design moved through a number of stages, each carefully monitored by the Secretary of State for Education and the Minister for Sport on the one hand, and the School Curriculum and Assessment Authority (SCAA) on the other. The SCAA was given considerable power over the national curriculum project, determining the reviews to be undertaken and the membership and terms of reference of the advisory groups, and also advising the minister on the outcome of the various reviews. It is clear that the membership of the PE advisory group was selected to marginalise those voices that were deemed out of step with the government's right-wing priorities (Evans and Penney 1994).

Attempts to maintain the time allocation for PE and sport have long been a major focus for lobbying by the Secondary Heads Association, the PEA and related PE organisations. In 1987, one year after the end of the teachers' industrial action, the Secondary Heads Association undertook a survey of PE provision in secondary schools and found a marked decrease in extra-curricular sport and an equally sharp decline in the number of non-specialist PE teachers willing to help with school sport. A follow-up survey in 1990 showed that the 'position had further deteriorated to the point where it is clear that pupils in most state schools no longer enjoy the opportunities of their predecessors' (Secondary Heads Association 1990: 1). Among the most significant findings of the survey was that for 41 per cent of 14-year-olds and 26 per cent of 16-year-olds the time allocation for PE had declined with only 8 per cent and 12 per cent, respectively, enjoying an increased allocation. In addition, 70 per cent of state schools suffered a decrease in extra-curricular sport over the two previous years. As recently as 1994 a survey by Harris added to the weight of evidence signalling a decline in provision. Concern at the findings of the Secondary Heads Association and similar surveys was reflected in the government's policy statement *Sport: Raising the Game*, where the government stressed the need to 'reverse [the] decline and put sport back at the heart of school life' (Department of National Heritage 1995: 7). However, the evidence is not clear cut, with Roberts (1996), reviewing a series of recent surveys of participation and facilities, finding little evidence to support the government's concern. In contrast to the surveys by Harris and the Secondary Heads Association, Roberts reported signs of healthy expansion in sport and PE provision with 47 per cent of schools reporting an increase in extra-curricular sport over the previous three years.

However, uncertainty concerning the long-term impact on the allocation of time, finance and staff resources remains. On the one hand, there is concern that despite its foundation status PE will lose out in the intensification of competition for resources as the newly empowered school governors divert resources to the traditional academic subjects. However, a contrary scenario is that schools will realise that sports facilities and sporting success are marketing assets in the sharper competition for pupils. However, what is clear is that the pupils for whom the time allocation has been protected or even increased most successfully are those who are taking PE as an examination subject. Harris found that 64 per cent of schools were offering examinations in PE to 14–16-year-olds and that these pupils received on average 'one hour of PE over and above the core PE time' (1994: 36).

Despite concerns about the long-term position of PE in the curriculum, the general conclusion among PE advocates is that the subject is in a stronger position than many feared when the national curriculum exercise started. However, the relative security of PE is due more to the effectiveness of the sports lobby, especially the Central Council of Physical Recreation (CCPR), than that of the PE lobby. Up until the early 1980s the CCPR, along with most governing bodies of sport, tended to ignore school sport, assuming that the steady flow of talented youngsters would continue from school to club. The sharp downturn in the birth rate and the steady broadening of the PE curriculum to include newer sports, such as basketball, volleyball and fitness activities, prompted a realisation among sports organisations that they faced a more intense competition for a declining pool of talented youth. At the same time a number of governing bodies were expressing concern at the perceived marginalisation of sports-skills development in the PE curriculum (Houlihan 1991). Throughout the 1980s the sports organisations, largely through the CCPR, mounted a sustained lobby aimed at shaping the PE curriculum and protecting the resources allocated to school sport. The strength of influence of the sports lobby is attributable to a range of factors including the receptiveness of the government of John Major, the uncertainty and fragmentation within PE, and the assiduity of the CCPR.

In contrast to the CCPR, the Sports Councils played a peripheral role in the debate on the future of PE for much of the 1980s, inhibited in part by the restrictions imposed by their charters and in part by their location in the machinery of government. Explaining its lack of involvement in school sport, the British Sports Council commented: 'This omission was partly because in the past the Council confined itself to adult and out of school sporting matters, by agreement leaving the national responsibility for school sport with the Department of Education and Science' (Sports Council 1988: 41). During the mid-1980s the Sports Council gradually became more closely involved with the broad issue of sport for school-age children and thus became involved in discussions about sport and PE within schools. A key turning point was the organisation, jointly by the Department of the Environment (the then parent department of the British Sports Council) and the Department of Education and Science, of the School Sport Forum to investigate the 'place of sport in the school curriculum' (Department of the Environment/Department of Education and Science 1986). Although the Forum's report presented an unwieldy set of recommendations, its major effect was to bring together PE and sport interests and more importantly add momentum to the Sports Council's growing involvement in school sport (Houlihan 1991).

In 1993 the Council published a policy document on young people and sport which reflected the organisation's growing involvement in sport for school age children. The Council's shift in policy focus was given additional impetus by the government's policy statement, *Sport: Raising the Game.* While the Council's enthusiasm for school sport has resulted in an improvement in the sports facilities in many schools and the promotion of closer school–club links in many areas, the Council's impact should not be over-estimated. The entry of the Sports Council into curriculum debates has not always been welcomed by all PE teachers, many of whom see the Council as reinforcing the CCPR's lobby in favour of the promotion of traditional team sports and a preoccupation with the interests of elite sport. Despite these reservations, the intervention of the Sports Council and the CCPR has been generally welcomed by the PE lobby, which has been willing to moderate its criticisms of school sport in order to retain a central place in the curriculum. This pragmatism on the part of PE teachers is an acknowledgement of the profession's defensiveness and insecurity derived from being responsible for a largely non-examination subject and one that does not have strong links with university-level study. However, the profession's defensiveness has also been the product of a deeply rooted conservatism and the persistence of a number of divisions within the profession over the defining concerns of the subject (Evans 1990; Kirk 1992).

At best most PE teachers feel a 'wary optimism' at the inclusion of PE as a foundation subject in the curriculum (Kinchin and O'Sullivan 1995: 16) and still remain to be convinced that the current security will persist. Yet PE teachers can take heart from the conclusions drawn by Roberts from the facility survey commissioned by the Sports Council (Hunter 1995). 'It was clear in the Facility Survey that schools considered sport important and were keen to develop community use of their facilities wherever possible' (Roberts 1996: 49). More significantly, Roberts argued that state schools are increasingly viewing their sports facilities as a marketing feature, much in the same way that private schools have traditionally done. However, a bleaker interpretation is one that sees sport reduced to an element in a marketing strategy rather than a component in a curriculum.

Evans and Penney argue persuasively that the government 'intentionally and cynically (albeit mostly indirectly) intervened in the making of the national curriculum for PE for the purposes of promoting its own "restoration interests" ' (1995: 184). Much of the recent political debate on sport has juxtaposed competitive sport with PE, suggesting that the former is a source of positive social and personal outcomes, while the latter is at best well meaning but muddled, and at worst subversive, particularly in the alleged rejection of competition. Furthermore, much of the debate has taken place with PE teachers confined largely to the sidelines through the tight control exercised by the government over their representation on the various working parties and advisory groups. Talbot, in explaining why PE survived in the national curriculum, points to the strength of the sports lobby 'which for the first time was using language complementary with and complimentary to physical education' and the strength of the health lobby which she describes as the 'rugby union mafia in Harley Street' (1995: 27). The overall effect of the sustained right-wing challenge to PE and the dependence of PE professionals on the sponsorship of government and of the sport and health lobbies within the curriculum debate is that PE has been profoundly weakened and the dominant discourse on the PE curriculum reduces PE to sport and has done long-term damage to the broader curriculum and pedagogical ambitions of PE teachers. The price of foundation status has been the loss of an independent voice for PE. As Evans *et al.* sombrely conclude in evaluating the post-Dearing curriculum:

> the remaining text of the NCPE now reinforces a very narrow and 'traditional' definition of PE as comprising a set of separate and distinct areas of activity and openly accords the highest status to that area that has

long dominated the PE curriculum in state schools, namely, competitive team games.

(Evans *et al.* 1996: 7)

THE UNITED STATES

From the early 1980s the US has experienced a sustained period of criticism of the education system in general and the alleged failings of teachers, their teaching methods, and of school management in particular. The 1983 National Commission on Excellence in Education was a seminal report and warned in a statement that captured the American imagination that 'our schools are sinking in a rising tide of mediocrity'. The more moderate policy solutions ranged from curriculum modifications to reforms in the training of teachers, while the more radical focused on the involvement of federal government and especially its funding role. Under the Reagan Presidency in particular, federal involvement in education was heavily criticised for usurping the 'roles traditionally played by state and local governments, private institutions, and families' (Brudemas 1990: 83). Not only was the policy agenda similar to that found in other countries in this survey, but there were also similarities in the policy actors involved. Ranged against an increasingly defensive teaching profession were citizens groups, parents and state politicians (Lawson 1993). The 1980s culminated in the announcement by President Bush of a programme for school reform which would 'literally start from scratch and reinvent the American school. No question should be off limits, no answers automatically assumed' (US Department of Education 1991: 7).

Although the US school system is formally highly decentralised, the weight of Congressional and more recently Presidential concern, particularly when reinforced by federal funding, has tended to undermine the autonomy of school boards. State Education Departments have tended to adopt a more interventionist and regulatory role. The recent 'excellence movement' has led to centralisation of curricular mandates, the introduction of state-wide testing regimes, and uniform teacher certification requirements leading some to complain of the creation of a stultifying and 'overly centralised and homogenised' school system (Raywid 1990: 166; see also Madsen 1994). Superimposed on the decentralised structure is an agenda that is most notable by its uniformity. Formally, each state is accountable for its education system and within most states it is normal for responsibility for school policy to be further decentralised to school boards accountable to their local community. Although generalisation is difficult, a typical state pattern of education would have children: moving from voluntary attendance at pre-school nurseries into the compulsory system at the age of 5; remaining in elementary school until transfer to junior high school at the age of 11; and then moving to senior high school at the age of 14. A high proportion of children move into the higher education sector aged 18. Each state is responsible for accrediting teachers, determining the curriculum and providing buildings and teaching materials. As in the UK there is also a significant private school sector.

Although federal government and Congressional interest in PE has been at best sporadic, there have been a few attempts to stimulate greater support for sport at state and local level. In 1987 Congress passed a resolution encouraging the provision of daily PE programmes for all children up to the twelfth grade. Later, in 1990 as part of the Healthy People 2000 Objectives, the Department of Health and Human Resources outlined a series of goals for PE designed to increase the number of schools offering 'quality daily PE'. Most recently, in 1994, Congress passed Public Law 103–227, Goals 2000: Educate America Act, which included the objective that 'all students will have access to physical education and health education to ensure they are healthy and fit'. To support this Act Congress made available $400m. to fund programmes designed to support implementation. Although this sum is small and has to be spread across all school subjects, there have been a small number of PE-related projects that have received funding.

In general, these policy exhortations have had only a limited impact and the level of provision remains highly variable. The National Association for Sport and Physical Education (NASPE) in a 1993 survey found that there had been a slight increase (from forty-two to forty-six since 1987) in the number of states requiring PE as part of the curriculum, with the majority of states (thirty-three) devolving responsibility for interpreting the requirement to school boards. The survey also found that only four states required PE at all grades from Kindergarten to grade 12 and only one, Illinois, required daily PE. By contrast there were four states that had no PE requirement, six states that required PE only between grades 9 and 12, and twenty-five states that required only one year of PE between grades 9 and 12. It was further revealed that over half of all states allow classroom teachers, untrained in PE, to teach the subject. Finally, evidence from the survey also identified a rise in the number of school districts which were requesting exemptions from the requirement to teach PE owing to increasing financial pressures (NASPE 1993). PE is also experiencing pressure on support services with a number of states reporting that they have lost the services of specialist PE superintendents.

In terms of the PE curriculum, most states are prescriptive, with the curriculum frequently being produced by the board of education, or its appointed superintendent, and often emphasising fitness and skills development. As a result few PE teachers, or indeed schools, have a significant degree of autonomy in relation to the curriculum and its delivery. NASPE is currently attempting to strengthen the PE curriculum and distinguish it more effectively from sport through the production of a model curriculum (NASPE 1992). While the model has proved a useful lobbying tool, there is little evidence of it affecting the pattern of the typical school PE curriculum or challenging the dominance of sport. In most schools the importance of competitive inter-school sport and the prominent role of the coach makes it difficult for broader based definitions of PE, such as those derived from the Dewey tradition with their emphasis on a task-oriented development of movement literacy (Lumpkin 1990). Indeed it is the dominance of inter-scholastic sport that is the most striking aspect of the US school sport structure. In most schools the coaching and PE teaching functions are separate, often taking the form of two distinct contracts, even when both contracts are fulfilled by the same person. Where the coach is not the same person as the PE teacher, there is often competition for curricular and extra-curricular time between the two, with the latter frequently accepting a secondary status. A further indication of the weakness of PE teachers is the fact that they do not have a distinct voice relying mainly on NASPE, which makes it clear that it represents sport as well as PE and furthermore is seeking to broaden its membership by attracting coaches and sports facility managers into its ranks. However, it should be stressed that while many observers identify a tension between sport and PE, as they compete for curriculum time, and suggest a degree of role conflict facing the teacher/coach, the evidence is unclear. While it is true that sport often squeezes the time available to PE, it is doubtful whether this is perceived as a conflict by school administrators or indeed by PE teachers, such is the security of sport in most schools (Massengale 1981; Chu 1981).

The Reagan and Bush governments of the 1980s and early 1990s, characterised by their assault on public expenditure, provided an opportunity to assess the relative security of sport and PE within the school curriculum and budget. One of Reagan's major public expenditure reforms was to cut the scale of federal grant aid to states and to consolidate a large number of service-specific federal financial transfers to states into block grants, thus leaving the states with the responsibility of determining their allocation between services. In many states education suffered severe budget cuts, but in general, sport faired far better than other subjects. For example, in 1991 the Dallas Independent School District laid off 245 teachers, mainly teaching core subjects in high schools, but, initially at least, left the athletic budget untouched. Even when cuts were forced on the athlete budget they were confined to middle schools, and high school budgets were left unaffected (Miracle and Rees 1994: 21). While school sport has been largely protected from the more severe budget cuts, PE has faired less well. A number of states, including California and Illinois, have reduced the time allocated to PE or made the subject optional. Yet the cause of its decline is due more to neglect than to a direct assault on its place in the curriculum. The fact that for many schools PE is synonymous with sport has not only frustrated those who wish to promote PE as distinct from sport, but has led some of the leading advocates of PE to lament that PE teachers are 'an endangered species' in United States high schools (Siedentop 1987a; Griffey 1987).

At a time when there is a general acceptance within national and local politics that the US education system has serious deficiencies, not least of which is chronic underfunding, the relative security of school sport is in marked contrast to the pressures experienced in the other countries in this study. The explanation of the continuing dominance of sport at school level lies in the distinctive history of the development of sport in the US and especially in the power of the college sport model. At first glance, the history of the development of school sport in the US bears a striking resemblance to developments in the UK. The influence of social Darwinism, 'muscular Christianity', and the model of sport in elite schools was clearly evident in late nineteenth-century America. However, where the two countries diverged was in the need of the US to define and assert its national identity and assimilate large numbers of immigrants. According to Miracle and Rees, while the belief that 'sports builds character' became deeply entrenched in England, in the US a variation, 'winning at sport builds character', was adopted (1994: 44). Moreover, whereas nineteenth- and early twentieth-century sport in England was frequently exclusive along class lines, it was generally inclusive in the US. The association between sport, American identity and the education system was firmly established in the early years of the century largely through the rapid institutionalisation of control over school sport by adults. Attitudes and values were rapidly established and reinforced by school and community institutions, especially the Church, which put sport firmly at the centre of school life. Much more so than in British state schools, sport events and rituals form a major element of the US school culture. Sport, or more accurately male sport, defines the school year by seasonal change from basketball to football and the weekly match, and also marks the progress of years through sports-related rituals focused on sport dinners, pep rallies, homecoming and awards presentation events. The significance of sport to the school is frequently reinforced by the significance of school sport to the community or neighbourhood. Miracle and Rees, in describing the senior ceremony, a public sports ritual, note the reciprocal relationship between the school and the community, 'An event as important as this one demanded the presence of community representatives. In turn, the community members added to the perceived importance of the event for the team and the school' (1994: 155; see also Bissinger 1990 and Foley 1990 for further examples of the continuing potency of the symbolism of school sporting success within the community or neighbourhood).

In addition to the important function of socialising immigrants into an idealised American identity, school sport was also very important in socialising participants into a wider set of social values, anticipating a series of adult roles. Sage, analysing the significance of school sport and particularly the pattern of key relationships between coach and athlete, athlete and athlete, and athletes and their sport, comments that:

the structure of social relations in organised sport programs not only introduces the hierarchy and authoritarianism of the larger society to participants, it also nurtures social characteristics, self-images, and class identifications that are important for complaisant transition to adult roles.

(Sage 1990: 199)

At present approximately 5.5m. school children participate in inter-scholastic sport. Although school sport imitates college sport and therefore generally adopts its dominant male ethos, there has been a substantial increase in girls' participation, which is primarily the (inadvertent) result of the passage of Title IX of the 1972 Education Amendment Act. Title IX had the effect of requiring publicly funded educational institutions to meet the sport and PE needs of female pupils and students in proportion to their number in school or college. Although the most public impact was on college sport, the impact on high school sport was equally important. Participation by girls rose from 7 per cent of the total number of participants in 1971 to 34 per cent in 1981, since when the figure has remained largely unchanged, rising only to 37 per cent in 1993.

The growth in the popularity of school sport has continued, but has been surrounded by increasingly sharp controversy. On the one hand there is substantial evidence to suggest that there is a strong correlation between participation in inter-scholastic sport and academic achievement and positive attitudes towards school (National Association for Sport and Physical Education 1994); on the other hand, there are also increasing expressions of concern at the dangers of overtraining (Stone 1988) and the overemphasis on winning (Romaneck 1989). The increasing commercialisation of high school athletics is reflected in the growth of televised matches and competitions, the appointment of professional fund-raisers, and the growth of regional 'all-star' games. School sport is increasingly adopting the attributes of commodification associated with college sport and its overemphasis on winning, entertainment and star status. It is little wonder that inter-scholastic sport is encountering many of the problems found in college sport, including illegal recruiting, eligibility disputes, steroid abuse and the creation of pre- and post-season competitions.

In response to the dominant position of sport in many schools, PE teachers have on occasion sought to build stronger links with the health lobby, arguing that rather than dealing with health education separately it should be integrated into the PE curriculum (Sallis and McKenzie 1991; McGinnis *et al.* 1991). However, NASPE is wary of developing too close an association with the health and fitness lobby, partly because of an appreciation that there are others in the fitness business who could deliver fitness training much cheaper than qualified PE teachers and partly due to a concern identified by Hardman that 'the emphasis on physical fitness will be at the expense of skills development and the attainment of broader affective and cognitive aims of physical education' (1996: 34). Apart from attempting to use links with the health lobby to provide a counterbalance to the coach/sport lobby, PE teachers have also been working to increase the amount of assessment within the PE curriculum as a means of strengthening the academic credentials of the subject. NASPE lobbied hard for the inclusion of assessment requirements for health and physical education in the Elementary and Secondary Education Act when it was debated before Congress.

In conclusion, it is fair to say that PE retains its, admittedly weak, position in the US school curriculum by virtue of its submersion within sport rather than as a result of having successfully established a clear identity of its own. The current vulnerability of PE, as opposed to sport, reflects the long, and largely fruitless, struggle for acceptance faced by advocates of PE. 'As a part of education as a whole, it has been ridiculed, derided, and called inept. . . . School physical education seems especially targeted for cutbacks in budget and personnel and faces a loss of prestige [and] many administrators view it as a low priority in scheduling, or as a frill' (Lumpkin 1990: 212). Lumpkin's bleak conclusion was echoed four years later by O'Sullivan *et al.* who, following a major study of PE teachers, reported that they suffered from 'multiple doses of marginality' (1994: 423).

8 Conclusion

In this final chapter the case studies outlined in Chapters 6 and 7 will be examined, first, in terms of the similarities and differences in the 'life cycle' of the issues, and second, in terms of what they reveal about the existence of a policy community for sport. The case studies provide contrasting perspectives on the policy process. Anti-doping policy has a high international profile whereas school sport and PE is largely a national or local policy issue; anti-doping policy involves a broad range of central and international governmental and non-governmental organisations by comparison with the narrower range of national and local organisations concerned with sport and PE; debate on doping is punctuated by scandal and crisis whereas the debate on school sport and PE is conducted at a lower level of intensity and with less media interest. As such, the two issues allow an element of triangulation in consideration of the hypotheses identified in the opening chapter. The first hypothesis was a simple assertion of an expectation of similarity of policy response to the two issues in the five countries studied. It was further suggested that the source of policy similarity would lie in the characteristics intrinsic to the issue or problem rather than being a consequence of either the particularities of the countries or the result of policy diffusion. The second hypothesis suggested that a policy community was either in operation or emerging. It was also suggested that a series of policy networks were also in operation or emerging to deal with the two issues examined and by implication a wider range of sports-related policy issues.

At the meso level of analysis there are a number of models of the policy process that can be used to identify points of similarity across countries by tracing the progress of the issue through a series of conceptually discrete stages, usually including the following: pre-recognition position; issue recognition, which normally includes the location of an issue within an existing policy area; the formulation of policy options; policy selection; policy implementation; and finally, policy evaluation and refinement or discontinuation. Downs' (1972) issue attention cycle provides a possible ideal type against which to compare the evolution of doping and school sport and PE policy. Using Downs' five stages it is possible to identify similarities, especially in the way in which issues move on to the public policy agenda and identify the key points in policy evolution. However, the model is less useful with issues that are either successful in retaining a significant degree of government commitment or fail to be subject to 'alarmed discovery' or some equally specific catalyst for government response. Downs' model works best with issues that are sharply defined, discrete and dramatic. Although retaining elements of Downs' model, the suggested series of stages is much closer to that outlined by Hogwood and Gunn (1984) namely, deciding to decide, deciding how to decide, issue definition, forecasting, setting objectives, analysing options, implementation, evaluation and policy maintenance, succession or termination.

The issue of doping in sport is one that is easily understood by a variety of non-expert interests, particularly politicians and civil servants; it can also be readily isolated from other related issues such as recreational drug use or match/race-fixing; and its manifestation in the actions of celebrities guarantees wide publicity. As such, doping fits well with the early stages of the Downs model. In each of the countries there were expert lobbyists active at the *pre-recognition stage* and on hand to explain the issue to a wider audience and suggest policy options when the issue moved on to the public agenda. In all five countries there were episodes that promoted the issue on the public policy agenda, normally the positive test result of a major athlete, but in Ireland's case the allegation of drug abuse. It is at this stage that an issue will be taken up by government and change from being a private (or narrow public) concern to being a political problem. However, it is also at this stage that the limitations of Downs' model become apparent. Most obviously, there is the assumption that it is for the government to decide whether to adopt an issue or not. While governments clearly have considerable influence over their agenda, they are also vulnerable to effective lobbying, especially through the media and by professional national and international interest groups. In addition, it is evident from the doping case that the issue took a different policy trajectory from that assumed by Downs. Rather than a realisation of costs leading to a gradual retreat from the issue, a number of governments in the study maintained the policy momentum, often despite a marked lack of enthusiasm on the part of NSOs. It is only in the United States, where federal government involvement has been slight, that there are some (limited) signs of issue fatigue and policy retreat. However, it is true that in Ireland the tentative approach to the issue is partly explained by an acknowledgement that the sum allocated to anti-doping by the Department of Education is substantially less than that needed to launch an effective anti-doping policy.

What neither the Downs model nor that outlined in Table 8.1 does is to provide a basis for explaining the dynamics of the policy process, for example, how issues move from one stage to another, and the relative importance of government and non-governmental interests. Furthermore the issue attention cycle compresses too many key decision points within the first two stages. Similar criticisms have led some to reject the use of models of policy-making that rely on a specification of a set of stages for the analysis of policy-making. However, the value of a sequential model of the policy process is that it not only provides a framework for organising material, but also provides an ideal type against which the actual development of policy can be measured. The weaknesses of the sequential model can be further overcome by combining it with the concepts of policy community and policy network outlined in the opening chapter.

Although the use of the concepts of policy community and policy network provide an opportunity to move away from reliance on the linear models of the policy process, they are also only capable of providing a metaphor for policy-making if they are located within a broader theory of power. Within the varied range of power models, that outlined by Lindblom lays the most persuasive foundation through the combination of elements of elitist and neo-pluralist analyses. The motivation for the exercise of power is the increase or maintenance of sectional advantage. From an initial analysis, in the 1950s, which characterised the policy process as both pluralist and incremental (1959), he revised his analysis over the next twenty years and adopted a position which gave greater weight to the pre-eminent position of business in capitalist societies (Lindblom 1977). In essence Lindblom (and also Dahl 1982) describes a liberal democratic policy process that is biased in favour of business and where business sectors, particularly the media, are able to distort the political agenda. Pluralist competition is considerably constrained, limited in many policy areas to competition between different business sectors. Beyond intra-business competition there is some potential for the state to counterbalance business influence but given the hegemonic position of business in liberal democracies, it is rare for the state to act in a way that is unsupportive. It is not so long ago that professions were seen as a significant counter-weight to business (Dunleavy 1980; Illich 1977). However, professions have been forced on to the defensive for much of the last decade, particularly by radical right-wing governments which viewed professions, most notably those in the public sector, as potent internal lobbies for additional powers and resources. Recent research suggests that professions have lost policy influence in a number of important sectors including education (Barnes and Williams 1993), law and order (Loveday 1993) and health (Flynn 1993). However, while the professions, especially those operating largely in the public sector, have witnessed the undermining of their capacity to determine the policy discourse, they none the less remain a cohesive lobby in a broad range of policy areas and, while having to adopt a less imperious and more negotiative strategy, retain considerable leverage on issues dealt with by policy communities.

Combining the concepts of policy community and policy network with the stages in policy development identified in Table 8.1 provides the context for the analysis of the policy process for drug abuse in sport.

The second stage in the policy process, *issue recognition*, is similar to the stage that Hogwood and Gunn (1984) identify as 'deciding to decide' or, in

Table 8.1 Doping policy: policy evolution

Stage	Australia	Canada	Ireland	United Kingdom	United States of America
Pre-recognition	Early 1980s rumours, among athletes and coaches, of drug abuse at AIS; some pressure from IFs and IOC to address the problem	Rumours, among athletes and coaches, in early 1980s about training methods at some high-performance training centres; some pressure from IFs and IOC to address the problem	Awareness among civil servants and some sports administrators (e.g. OCI) that Ireland out of step with Council of Europe in not having an anti-doping policy	Concern among sports administrators, scientists and some politicians in late 1970s and early 1980s	Small number of sports administrators, doctors and coaches lobbying within sports organisations for action
Issue recognition	Dramatic discovery through the 'Four Corners' television programme, November 1987. The Senate Enquiry, 1989, provided a more systematic feedback on existing policy	Dramatic discovery through Ben Johnson's positive test, Seoul 1988. The Dubin Inquiry, 1989, provided systematic feedback on existing policy	Routine scanning by government through Council of Europe membership, but shock at the allegations of drug taking levelled against Michelle Smith at Atlanta Olympic Games, 1996, also important	Routine scanning as no evidence of a particular episode forcing the issue, but the drama of the two positive tests on British athletes at Seoul Games in 1988 was also important	Dramatic discovery of the issue through the death of star athletes in mid-1980s, particularly Len Bias in 1986
Formulation of policy options	Lead given by IOC but central role for Senate Enquiry, 1989	Lead given by the IOC but central role Dubin Inquiry, 1989	At preliminary stage; modest funds allocated and some consideration of logistics	Lead role by the IOC but Minister (Moynihan) and Sports Council important	Some encouragement given by Congress but policy formulation left to USOC (and IOC)
Policy selection	Dominant role by government, but staying close to IOC lead	Dominant role by government, but staying close to IOC lead	Policy not yet formulated but clear signs that government will determine policy selection	Dominant role by government, but staying close to IOC lead	Central role adopted by the USOC, but federal government/Congress agreed to use its power to ban steroids
Policy implementation	Tightly controlled by government via ASDA	Tightly controlled by government via CCDS	Policy not yet formulated but clear signs that government will determine means of policy implementation	Tightly controlled by government	Responsibility lies with USOC and other major sports bodies, including the NCAA and the NSOs
Policy evaluation, refinement or discontinuation	Controlled by ASDA, but some attempt to involve NSOs	Controlled by CCDS, but some involvement of NSOs	–	Controlled by the Sports Council with increasing involvement of NSOs	Fragmented as USOC, NCAA and NSOs of major commercial team sports all involved

relation to Downs' (1972) model, how issues move out of the pre-problem stage. With respect to doping there were a number of organisations, mainly within sport, which were both aware of and concerned about the issue. At the international level the IOC began to collate information about drug use from 1967 following the establishment of its Medical Commission and produced its first list of banned substances and practices in 1971. One or two other international sports organisations, such as FIFA and the IAAF, were also developing policy positions. Finally, within Europe, the Council of Europe was raising the profile of the issue with governments. While the steady development of policy among international sports organisations and the gradual introduction of testing at international events raised the domestic awareness of the issue, there were few national initiatives until countries were forced to react to a positive test on one of their own high-profile athletes. Using Kingdon's (1994) terminology, the issue became accepted as a problem for most governments following a 'focusing event' whether the result of death, national embarrassment at a positive result, or anger at allegations of doping. Only in the UK and Ireland is it possible to argue that the government's routine scanning of its environment was signifi-cant in leading to pressure to develop a policy on doping. In Australia, Canada and the UK the government was central in the recognition of the issue with sports organisations and any nascent policy network peripheral.

The third stage is the *formulation of policy options*. Analysis of this stage involves identifying the organisations/interests involved in the process which, to a significant extent, is determined by the actions of government in allo-cating the issue to a specific policy area. Only in Ireland has there been a consistent location for sport within the machinery of government in recent years. In Australia, Canada and the UK the location of the sport portfolio was erratic, with responsibility for sport moving through a series of central/federal departments and also experiencing substantial changes in the location in particular departmental hierarchies. One consequence of the frequent transfers of the portfolio is that the early stage of policy develop-ment remained relatively immune from the policy cultures within its successive host departments, with the result that policy options have tended to be formulated with greater reference to an international context than one which was exclusively domestic or departmental. However, as will be discussed below, this institutional instability was not to last.

This stage, the formulation of policy options, is crucial in determining the pace and character of policy development. With regard to doping there was a range of ways in which the issue could be defined, including whether the issue was primarily a domestic or foreign policy concern, and whether it was best defined as a scientific, medical, educational, commercial, sporting or legal issue. The Interim Report of the Black Committee (1989) in Australia encapsulated the variety of ways in which the issue could be defined. Evidence to the Committee suggested variously that the issue was one of health care, foreign policy (due to the possibility of an adverse impact on

Australia's standing in the Olympic movement) and a commercial issue (affecting the marketability of Australian sport). Similarly, in the UK, doping was defined initially as a moral issue for sports organisations and subsequently as a health issue. By contrast, in Ireland the issue was for a long time seen as primarily a matter of foreign policy arising from pressure from Council of Europe membership and increasing involvement in the Olympic Games, with the motive being to demonstrate Ireland's European and international credentials. In all the countries surveyed there is little evidence that a policy community was active in attempting to define the issue and construct a policy network to deal with it. In all countries, apart from the United States, government intervened directly to define the issue of doping, generally as one of morality and health. In the UK the intervention took the form of a policy statement by the Minister which was published by the Sports Council, whereas in Australia and Canada it took the form of government-initiated inquiries. In the UK, Australia and Canada the establishment of specialist anti-doping agencies was both a policy choice and also the creation of a context for further policy formulation. As such, stages three and four, the *formulation of policy options* and the *selection of policies,* blur.

The intervention by governments to establish the Doping Control Unit, ASDA and CCDS (and in the United States to secure the status of the USOC) was not prompted solely by the more familiar motives which led governments to use quangos, such as a desire to depoliticise the issue or to transfer policy development to a more technically expert group. An important motive was the need to manufacture a policy network to 'own' the outputs of the policy process while not owning the process itself. The use of quangos also had the advantage of producing a high degree of institutional stability for the latter stages of policy selection and refinement by insulating anti-doping from the consequences of any future restructuring of the machinery of government. The establishment of a quango to oversee policy development and implementation also enabled a closer link to be developed between domestic policy and the key institutions active at the international level, including the IOC and the major international federations. The preferred institutional arrangements provide a substantial degree of institutional stability and insulation from changing departmental cultures, which has laid the foundation for the long-term involvement of the state in anti-doping policy. The intervention by the government to construct a policy network to legitimise its actions provides further evidence of the absence or the considerable weakness of a policy community in sport. If any semblance of a policy community existed, it was not at the domestic level, but at the international level, where the IOC fulfilled an authoritative role in shaping domestic government debates on objectives and policy options.

The government, through its specialist agencies, fulfilled a determining role in the selection and refinement of policy with generally only minimal consultation with the NSOs but closer liaison with the major international federations and the IOC over issues such as the introduction of out-of-competition testing and the adoption of testing protocols. Once more the role of the domestic sports organisations was, and remains, slight, with them being bypassed by their own government, their international federations and the IOC.

The analysis is much the same when the next two stages are considered. The *implementation* of the particular mix of policy and the *evaluation* of its impact were both determined largely by governments or their agencies. Although decisions about who to select and how to deal with positive results requires substantial involvement of domestic governing bodies, their involvement is very much within parameters determined by government and also by international sports organisations. The obvious weakness of domestic governing bodies is their relative lack of resources. In order to be able to respond to pressure from their international federations and from the IOC for a domestic anti-doping programme, they were forced to accept the offer of public finance to cover the cost of testing. Only in the United States has the testing programme developed without a central role for government, and of the four countries with established programmes, that in the US is the least effective.

Even in the United States, where constitutional and political factors make the development of regulatory policy difficult, the limited progress that there has been in doping policy development is in part a consequence of governmental intervention. The central role given to the USOC by the 1978 Amateur Sport Act has certainly contributed to the, albeit modest, pace and effectiveness of policy development among Olympic sports. Where anti-doping policy has been weakest is, not surprisingly, among the commercial sports such as football and baseball, which see little community of interest on the issue of drug abuse and have consistently prevaricated over policy development. The increasing significance of commercial sports, not just in the United States but globally, makes the reluctance of commercial sports bodies to make more than a minimal effort to address doping a particularly serious threat to policy objectives and also emphasises the deep fissures that prevent the development of a domestic policy network for doping and which also undermine attempts to construct a sport policy community.

Comparing the evolution of anti-doping policy across the five countries suggests a high degree of similarity in problem definition, policy formulation and policy implementation. Canada, Australia and the UK show the clearest similarities, although the United States, despite some important differences in scope and implementation, also displays a number of basic commonalties in policy design. Ireland is probably the most distinctive country, but this is due to the recent arrival of the issue on the Irish political agenda, which in turn is a reflection of the relatively recent involvement of Ireland in sports at international competitive level: the signs are that the trajectory of Irish anti-doping policy will follow closely that found in Canada, Australia and the UK. Except in the US, the primary similarities among the remainder include the heavy reliance on: government funding, legislative support and administrative expertise; the balance within policy between education and deterrence; the use of public funding to ensure NSO compliance in implementation; and the marginal involvement of NSOs in shaping policy.

The primary source of policy similarity lies with the IOC, with the major international federations such as those for track and field, swimming and cycling being secondary sources. The IOC was important in providing the context for policy development through its activity in establishing a defini-tion of doping and introducing initial testing procedures. Although there was some modest policy development at domestic level among governing bodies, governments in most countries adopted the issue only following the series of positive tests on high-profile athletes. It would have been reason-ably easy for governments to ignore the issue of doping on various grounds. Not only were many of the drugs legally available, but governments were also reluctant to criminalise drug taking by athletes when their policies had proved so ineffective with regard to social drug abuse. The willingness of governments to accept doping as a public issue reflects the recognition of the economic, diplomatic and social significance of elite international sport, and also the impact of lobbying by international bodies such as the IOC and the Council of Europe. The latter organisation provided a focus for govern-mental policy-making, not only within Europe, but also globally, with Canada and Australia both using the Council's Charter on Doping as an ingredient in their own policy-making.

Doping in sport is a good illustration of the extent to which the political agenda is becoming international. Although the catalyst for policy-making activity was domestic, the issue had already been defined at an international level, thereby providing a policy framework that was difficult for domestic governments to reject. However, while the activity of international bodies was instrumental in setting the domestic policy agenda, it was generally less successful in achieving uniformity of solutions. It was not just that some countries, such as the former Soviet Union and GDR, sought to subvert the anti-doping policy of the IOC and the international federations. In each country the formulation of a policy response to doping varied according to wealth, constitution and culture. The creation of a common agenda does not in itself lead to common policy solutions: as Harrop observes, 'interdepen-dence does not mean convergence' (1992: 264). Yet, in the examples in this study, the degree of convergence on many aspects of policy is striking. United States sports organisations, which are often portrayed as ambivalent towards the issue, have encountered substantial constitutional problems in implementation. Yet, in common with many other countries, the United States government agreed to add steroids to its list of illegal drugs. In addi-tion, the series of Congressional hearings in the 1980s involving elected members, public officials and interest-group representatives also helped to maintain state pressure on sports organisations while avoiding direct govern-ment intervention.

It should also be noted that in Australia, Canada and the UK the development of policy took a very similar path. The governments' initial response was to expect NSOs to bear the organisational and financial burden of the implementation of doping policy. In each of the countries this strategy represented a wariness of getting involved in the detailed management of an aspect of sport that was considered peripheral to their main policy objective of supporting elite sport and achieving greater international sporting success. However, all three countries rapidly acknowledged the inability (or unwillingness) of sports bodies to implement an effective testing regime and proceeded to adopt a much more interventionist strategy through the establishment of the Doping Control Unit in the UK, ASDA in Australia and the CCDS in Canada. All three bodies have adopted a similar strategy for implementation, including the conception of 'public interest' tests, the centralised training of testing officers, a similar balance and distribution of responsibility between NSOs and the doping agency, and a similar 'arm's-length' relationship with government. The evolution of government policy is partly a response to similar circumstances in each country, most notably the organisational and financial weakness of the NSOs for Olympic sports, and also the public management fashion for semi-independent agencies for service delivery. But the common path of policy development was also due to a learning process in which each country deliberately monitored the experience of the others because of a perceived commonality of approach and intention. Although the similarities between Australia, Canada and the UK are strong, there are also significant similarities between the evolution of policy in these three countries on the one hand and in the United States on the other. The central role given to the USOC, in amateur sport initially, was the consequence of the inability of the NSOs to manage a number of aspects of their sports effectively. Although the 1978 Amateur Sports Act pre-dates the peak of interest in doping in sport, the structure for policy implementation that bypassed the NSOs was already in place.

The most significant aspect of the policy process for doping is the influence of international bodies, particularly the IOC. Part of the explanation for the extent of influence lay in the generally low level of saliency of doping in sport to most governments during the early 1980s when the IOC and the IAAF were establishing definitions of doping and making the initial decisions about testing procedures. Part of the explanation also lies in the reluctance of domestic governing bodies to adopt a policy leadership role on the issue within their own political systems, a factor that emphasises the absence of an effective policy network and the weakness, if not absence, of a policy community. Finally, part of the explanation lies in the capacity of the IOC to retain control over the conduct of the Olympic Games and the rapid increase in the international profile of the Olympic Games over the past twenty years.

The importance of the role of the IOC and the major international federations, and also, for Ireland and the UK, the importance of the Council of Europe suggests that if there is a policy network associated with the issue of doping, it exists at the international, rather than the domestic, level. For the past fifteen years or so the guiding reference for governments in determining policy has been consistency with IOC policy and practice. This is not to ignore the variation in practice between governments (particularly those in former communist countries) and especially between international federations, but rather to emphasise the extent to which the IOC is the acknowledged policy leader.

In none of the countries surveyed is there evidence that domestic policy development was the product of a secure policy network. Furthermore, in all five countries, which are admittedly at varying stages of policy development, there is evidence to suggest that if a policy network is in existence, it is one substantially manufactured by government action. While government agencies play a central role in policy implementation, there is still a number of important functions for the NSOs to fulfil, including tracking athletes, imposing penalties and generally legitimising government involvement. It has therefore been important that NSOs be organised in such a way as to be able to fulfil these functions. Consequently, governments through their agencies have helped to sponsor the emergence of a policy network for doping through consultation mechanisms, conferences and the exchange of information. On a more positive note the sponsoring of a policy network has enabled the refinement of policy such that it is increasingly tailored to the particular characteristics of individual sports. Generally, the consequence of establishing a policy network without the contextualising policy community is that the network is weak and heavily dependent on government, but while this is a clear disadvantage to sports organisations, it is obviously attractive to government. Whether the government sponsorship of a policy network might result in the emergence of a more independent policy network at some future date remains to be seen, but as yet there are few signs of evolution in this direction.

The policy process for school sport and PE stands in sharp contrast to that for doping. Not only is the administrative context more complex owing to a frequent division of responsibility between central/federal departments and between central/federal and local/state government, but the clarity of the issue is also much less sharp. While in all five countries there is an identifiable issue associated with the place of sport and PE in the curriculum, there is little agreement about the precise definition of the issue. Chapter 7 showed how the formulation of the issue varied and included PE or sport, traditional sports or a wider diet of sport, health and fitness or sport, men's sport or women's sport, and sports theory or sports practice. In addition, the debates on sport and PE were frequently merged with, and occasionally submerged by, other issues, including curriculum reform, parental control of schools, budget cuts and teacher (and subject) status. It is not surprising that it is far more difficult to fit the evolution of the issue into a neat series of stages than was the case with doping (see Table 8.2).

However, there is still an interesting and revealing number of similarities

Table 8.2 Sport in schools: policy evolution

	Australia	Canada	Ireland	United Kingdom	United States
Pre-recognition	From the late 1980s school sport a concern of a narrow group of professional PE educationists and some sports bodies, particularly the ASC	Cluster of interest groups with variety of concerns related to school sport and PE, including health, fitness and diet. Most prominent group was CAHPERD, a broad-based lobbying body	Place of sport in schools not problematic: no significant lobby on behalf of PE	Lobbying by CCPR in the mid-1980s supported by PE teachers' bodies	Dominance of sport in schools so great that sport has been insulated from many of the pressures (financial and curriculum reform) on schools: no significant lobby on behalf of PE to challenge dominance of sports culture
Issue recognition	Hobart Declaration signalled the discovery of a range of educational issues, such as academic standards, national curriculum and health and fitness, subsumed debate on sport. The Crowley Inquiry helped, to a limited extent, to distinguish school sport from other educational issues	Key issue is not a threat to school sport, but more the routine maintenance of the resource base. School sport not under special challenge. Marginal to current educational issues, including standards and vocational relevance in the curriculum. Key role for politicians, rather than interest groups, in agenda setting. Marginal role for teachers' interest groups	Pace of development of issue determined primarily by the attitude of the church, with sports and PE interests only becoming active recently. Deenihan Report (1991) significant	Recognition of issue of school sport the product of an accumulation of lobbying and sympathetic Prime Minister. Teachers' strike of the mid-1980s of key importance in highlighting the decline in school sport	No dominant definition of the issue, though gender equity important in recent years: school sport relatively secure: signs of a crystallisation of an issue around the continuing concern with the health and fitness of school children
Formulation of policy options	Took place at two levels, general educational debate where school sport marginalised, and at level of school sport where the Australian Sports Commission was more significant	School sport (and to a lesser extent PE) under no greater threat than other subjects in the curriculum, but rarely considered directly by key policy-makers	Issue of PE and sport in school curriculum subject to government neglect rather than rejection. PEAI weak and too dependent on government. Little interest from NSOs	Level of commitment from key ministers has remained significant; supported by National Lottery funding	Sport and PE relatively well protected from financial pressures on school budgets. Most significant policy has been series of court judgments interpreting Title IX
Policy selection	Central government-led, via the Australian Education Council, but little consideration of sport. ASC more important through the promotion of Aussie Sports. Teachers marginal	Apathy of PE professionals noted, though some lobbying by CAHPERD, but capacity to intervene in major educational issues is weak. Federal government through the Council of Ministers of Education fulfils a leading role in shaping policy selection	Tight control over education by government. Church a key interest group, though influence waning slowly. Interest from the government has rarely been high, with the result that policy for school sport and PE often made by default	Education Minister, supported by the CCPR, of key importance in ensuring the prominence of sport within the National Curriculum for PE. PEA less successful in asserting their view of PE	No evidence of specific federal policies for school sport and PE. But substantial policy impact on school sport and PE arising from decisions in other policy areas, such as equity and, though less significantly, health
Policy implementation	ASC lead organisation in determining character of school sport; provided implementation framework	Potential for some exercise of influence by sport/PE teachers, but profession divided	Tight control by government	Tight control by government. Access by teachers' interests to policy debates also closely controlled	Courts played key role regarding Title IX. Teachers' lobbying groups marginal
Policy evaluation, refinement or discontinuation	Refinement taking place within discourse dominated by ASC, which emphasises participation in sport and elite success. Minor debates on evaluation of health and fitness contribution of school sport	—	Tightly controlled by government	Tight control by government through SCAA	—

when comparisons are drawn across the five countries. At the *pre-recognition* stage the most notable examples of continuity are first, the weakness of the PE profession reflected in its difficulty in establishing a distinctive identity for either PE teachers or PE as a subject. On a number of occasions it was clear that governments and other interested parties to the policy debate failed to acknowledge the definition of physical activity that PE advocates were attempting to promote. More significantly, there is also evidence that among' PE teachers there was, and remains, little consensus regarding the nature of the profession and their subject. In particular, there was considerable uncertainty concerning the relationship of PE to sport, an uncertainty which tended to reinforce the suspicions of the NSOs towards PE lobbyists. In the United States and Canada, the roots of in-school and inter-school sport are so deep that the question of PE's relation to sport is rarely asked outside narrow professional circles, and hardly ever within government. It is therefore of little surprise that in Canada and the United States the advocates of a more broadly based PE curriculum are content to work with school sports interests rather than challenge them directly. In the UK and Australia there is a more vociferous PE lobby but one which is only slightly more successful in promoting a distinctive perspective on the issues surrounding school sport. The PE lobby may be more sharply delineated from other school sports interests, but they are only marginally more successful in sustaining their particular definition of the issues. In Ireland the PE lobby is also weak, but this is less the result of the dominance of the sports interests within policy debates, and more the consequence of government disdain.

The second area where there is notable similarity of context across the five countries is in the relationship of the issue of sport in schools to the broader educational debates that emerged in the 1980s. The uniformity of broad educational agendas in the mid- and late 1980s is substantial, but hardly surprising as all five countries, with the exception of the buoyant Irish economy, were coping with a series of broadly similar economic phenomena including recession, pressure on public expenditure, and increased competition for markets. The move towards the adoption of a populist and liberal economic political agenda led to a marked degree of similarity in the way in which issues in education were defined: parental choice in preference to professional power and the emphasis on vocational relevance as opposed to liberal–humanist objectives for the curriculum were the hallmarks of the period. It is little wonder that the stage of *issue recognition* by government marked the identification of the fundamental questions about the competence of schools, teachers and the curriculum to meet the needs of the late twentieth century rather than the role of sport in schools. Not surprisingly, the issue of sport in schools was swept up on the coat-tails of these grander debates. While the issue of school sport was the subject of focusing events such as the Crowley Inquiry in Australia (Crowley Report 1992), the School Sports Forum in the UK, and, though to a lesser extent, the Deenihan report in Ireland (1991), they were all overwhelmed by higher-profile events which drew attention to the more fundamental questions about the education system such as the Hobart Declaration, the Irish Green Paper, President Bush's 1991 statement, and the decision to introduce a national curriculum in the UK.

Those interests concerned with sport in schools were not able to disentangle their priorities from these larger-scale debates and consequently, at almost every stage of the policy process, school sport and PE interests were struggling to gain recognition for the distinctive nature of their concerns. Yet, it would not be accurate to claim that the interests of sports/PE advocates were ignored or lost in the broader debates in all five countries. In the UK, Australia, Canada and the United States school sport not only survived the uncertainty of educational reform, but often enhanced its position. This success is only partly explained by skilful lobbying by sports organisations. In Canada and the United States the relative security of sport in the school curriculum was a reflection of the long-standing cultural commitment to inter-school sport rather than a reflection of effective contemporary lobbying. In the UK and, to a limited extent, in Australia, it is possible to argue that effective lobbying made an appreciable difference to the policy output. Both the Australian Sports Commission and the CCPR in the UK can claim that their activity was important in the *formulation and selection* of policy options. However, the promotion of Aussie Sports by the ASC as the core element in school sport/PE was against a background of relative indifference by the Australian Education Council and the lack of effective challenge from within the PE profession. The ASC was able to take the initiative in the crucial stages of policy-making by default. In the UK the CCPR, and to an extent the Secondary Heads Association, were consistent and effective in maintaining a profile for the issue of school sport. Yet, while not wishing to detract from their efforts, it was fortuitous that their pressure was being applied at a time when there was significant ministerial (and Prime Ministerial) sympathy for their objectives.

Sport in schools was an identifiable issue in all the countries in this survey, although the nature of the issue varied considerably. However, whether the issue was one of marginalisation of PE or curriculum time for team games, there were a number of common problems facing the policy advocates. The most obvious was the problem of developing a consensus among the various groups with an interest in school sport and PE, due largely to mutual suspicion between teachers, health promoters and coaches. Where a level of consensus was apparent, as in Canada and to a lesser extent in the United States around competitive sport, it was the result of a recognition of the dominance of a particular view of school physical activity. An additional problem faced by the school sport interests was the difficulty in freeing their concerns from the slipstream of larger education policy debates, whether those debates concerned vocational relevance of the curriculum, gender equity or, indeed, a concern with their own professional status.

Overall, the case studies of school sport provide little evidence to support the existence of a policy network for the issue or a more broadly based policy community for sport.

Part of the explanation for the absence of a policy network or community undoubtedly lies in the problems lobbying groups have in a highly fragmented administration as in federal states, with their multiple decision points at federal, state and local levels. Part of the explanation also lies in the disunity of the cluster of interests concerned with school sport mentioned earlier, and especially the disunity within the PE profession. However, part also lies in the lack of interest within government in sponsoring the formation of a policy network due to a belief that the issue was not sufficiently politically significant, that an acceptance of the prevailing balance of interest was adequately reflected in the current policy or finally, for some governments, an acknowledgement that interests critical of existing or preferred policy were insufficiently powerful to warrant incorporation within a policy network. In Canada, for example, the criticism of the prevailing school sport policy emanating from a section of the PE profession was articulate but insufficient to challenge the dominant commitment to the promotion of elite sport and the contribution made by competitive inter-school sport. In Australia, the picture is very similar with the political commitment to elite success making it very difficult for the advocates of a more broadly conceived PE curriculum to challenge the promotional activity of the Australian Sports Commission and the Aussie Sports programme in particular. Irish advocates of school sport and PE were, with the important exception of the GAA, too heavily dependent on government to be in a position to force their policy preferences. It is within the UK that there is the most persuasive evidence of a policy network for school sport. The co-operation between the PEA and the Secondary Heads Association, both representing school interests, and the CCPR, representing NSOs, has in general been mutually supportive and has done much to maintain the profile of the issue of school sport. However, the coalition only existed when the issue was being discussed at a high level of generality and was far less cohesive when the details of the PE national curriculum were being discussed. At this stage the overlap of interest between the CCPR and the government ensured that a curriculum stressing the practice of sport would be preferred. Yet, this policy output flatters the influence of the sports lobby which benefited from a like-minded government rather than the exercise of effective leverage. Finally, in the United States the fragmentation of administrative responsibility for education and the cultural security of inter-school competitive sport left little scope for the successful advocacy of alternative policies and objectives for school-based physical activity.

In both the doping and the school sport case studies, the role of the government was of key importance at almost all stages in the policy process, reflecting not only the weakness of sports interests, but also the highly instrumental attitude of government towards sport. At both central/federal and local levels governments only occasionally viewed sport as inherently valuable; more often it was perceived as a means to a wide range of ends, including international prestige, an element in inter-provincial rivalry, and, increasingly commonly, as an element in an economic strategy for nations, regions and cities. Governmental interest in a range of sporting issues was prompted by the extent to which these broader non-sport objectives were affected.

Governmental interest was also of key importance in determining the development and character of a policy network and policy community. In general, neither secure and clearly defined networks nor communities were evident in the countries studied and, where there were signs of their existence, it was often the product of government sponsorship. As regards the doping issue, the strong intervention by government was partly designed to force reluctant NSOs to take greater responsibility for policing drug abuse among their members. There are clearly a number of policy areas where organised interests are sufficiently powerful and cohesive to make the establishment of a formalised context for policy discussion and, possibly, decision making, a preferred option for government. But as Smith (1993) has argued, in many policy areas the initiative in the formation of policy communities and networks rests with governments and their emergence depends on whether governments have a need for them in terms of legitimating policy choice or co-operation in policy implementation. In relation to the issue of doping, governmental action in Australia, Canada and the UK was discrete and forceful and once the objectives were clearly established and the core machinery of policy delivery was in place, the government began the process of developing a supporting policy network.

The pattern was very different with the case of school sport, not just because of the lower priority given to it by most governments, but also because of the blurred nature of the issue. Less sharply defined issues and those issues dragged along in the wake of major issues do not fit as easily into a multi-stage model of the policy process and are far less readily interpreted in terms of metaphors such as policy network and community. Although on occasion reaching a modest level of public and political debate resulting from lobbying activities, the issue was too often submerged by other political priorities, forcing school sport interests to operate within policy contexts not of their own choosing and over which they had little influence. Consequently, there are many aspects of the issue of school sport that are characterised by debates between a small group of 'experts' and specialists confirming that these aspects remain confined to the pre-recognition stage.

At the end of Chapter 1 mention was made of Wistow's and Rhodes' (1987) observation on the leisure and recreation policy area in the UK that it was better described as an issue network than a policy community. For them an issue network was less integrated, had more participants, and had a lower level of interdependence, stability and continuity than a policy community.

Writing only a relatively short time ago (Houlihan 1991), I suggested that while an effective policy community for sport did not exist in Britain, there were a number of positive signs, including: first, the emergence of a more clearly defined institutional focus for sport policy within government; second, the development of routine contact between government and major organised interests in sport and recreation; third, signs of an emergence of a value consensus; and finally, the emergence of a number of potential policy networks. The institutional focus, through the Department of National Heritage and the restructured Sports Councils, remains intact but the pattern and quality of contact has altered radically. The government still retains the capacity to determine the nature of the pattern of contact within the putative policy community and has dismantled the more collegial and informal pattern of relations, reflected in the broadly based membership of the British Sports Council and the Regional Councils for Sport and Recreation, and replaced it with a more formal and restricted relationship more akin to a contractual relationship between client and contractor than one between partners: the network of links remains intact but the sense of a community founded on a broad-value consensus is weak.

As regards the other countries in the survey, it would be fair to conclude that none has seen the growth in government intervention in sport matched by a counterbalancing growth in the influence and effectiveness of the voluntary sector NSOs. The general pattern is one of growing resource dependence and, in Canada and Australia, the shift away from partnership towards a client–contractor relationship. The apparent buoyancy and health of the NSOs resulting from a dramatic government-funded increase in income and professional staff base is offset by the extent of their dependency on public funding and the erosion of voluntary activity. It is only in the commercial sport sector that a significant capacity to challenge government exists. However, the capacity of commercial sector sports organisations to influence government is based as much on sentiment, for example, in the United States over anti-trust (anti-monopoly) rulings, as on the leverage at their disposal. In general, as government has become more heavily involved in sport and especially elite sport, the sector that has been affected most dramatically is the NSOs for sports that remain substantially non-commercial (a category that includes most Olympic sports). The intervention of government in the direct funding of athletes and coaches, the provision of publicly funded elite training facilities and the public funding and administration of anti-doping policy results in many NSOs fulfilling an increasingly restricted role in sports administration. The erosion of the role of NSOs by domestic governments is exacerbated by the broadening of responsibility of international federations, itself the result of the rapid growth in the importance and quantity of international sport. Finally, where sports have been commercially successful there has often been a period of conflict between the newly rich clubs and/or athletes and the NSO, which often results in a significant loss of control by the latter. A central conclusion from this study is the erosion of influence of NSOs over the development of their individual sports and government sport policy in general. Balancing the weakness of sports organisation in shaping policy is the substantial, and in some cases, determining influence of government. The capacity of the government to determine the institutional context for the discussion and implementation of policy, and often to provide the dynamic for progress in policy-making, is evident in both case studies. In both cases the government, or more broadly the state, demonstrated strong support for elite development. The state sponsorship of anti-doping policy can be seen as important in protecting the long-term utility of international sport as a tool of diplomacy and also as a source of profit for the commercial sector. State sponsorship also allows domestic interests to be protected more effectively as it is better placed to fine-tune policy in response to changes at the international level, for example, in the continuing attempts to harmonise and strengthen anti-doping policy at the global level and particularly with rival countries. Liaison between domestic agencies and the federations and the IOC, as well as through the Council of Europe, is making the formation of an international policy network more plausible.

While school sport was ostensibly a study of a national, if not a local issue, the context within which it was dealt with also reflected the significance of state intervention. Even in Canada and the United States, where political and administrative responsibility for education is so fragmented, the most striking feature was the high degree of commonality both within and between countries in relation to problem definition and policy preference. When governments did intervene directly in issues concerned with school sport, it was generally to promote and protect elite sport objectives. Increasingly governments are acknowledging that the promotion of sport in schools is essential to the achievement of international sporting success. In the UK and Australia government intervened directly to support their preferred models of school sport and also to support the expansion of the responsibilities of quangos to include the promotion of school sport. In Canada and the United States, where the history and depth of cultural commitment to competitive inter-school sport has not required significant intervention, the government has done little to support those advocating a more broadly based and educationally informed sport and PE curriculum.

Finally, and at a normative level, the adoption of sport as an area of public policy has been an important development in post-war liberal democracies. For many countries the interest in sport, and especially elite sport, has been sustained through periods of recession when other services were subject to severe pressure on their budgets, and also through periods dominated by political parties committed to reducing the size of the state. The attention of government was welcomed initially, and continues to be sought by many, but as this study shows, there are two significant aspects of government intervention that are less welcome, the first of which is the admittedly instrumental attitude of government to sport. If governments could achieve their social, economic or diplomatic goals by other cheaper, more efficient means, support for sport would undoubtedly decline sharply. The second aspect that causes concern is that the administrative, financial and personnel infrastructure of sport has been colonised by government. In many cases even the bodies that provide the 'independent' voice for sport depend on public subsidy: thus, policies ostensibly designed to promote autonomy produce even greater dependence. It may seem churlish to complain about the recent dramatic increase in governmental support for sport, but it is hard to suppress the sense of unease at the extent to which so much sport has moved away from its voluntarist roots to largely uncritical dependence on government.

Notes

1 COMPARING POLICY FOR SPORT AND RECREATION

1 On 15 April 1989 ninety-five people died and 174 were injured as a result of being crushed against the perimeter fence and the rear terracing at the soccer FA Cup semi-final between Liverpool and Nottingham Forest, held at Sheffield Wednesday's Hillsborough ground.

2 GOVERNMENT, SPORT AND POLICY-MAKING

1 The correct title of the country is the Republic of Ireland. However, the shorter term 'Ireland' will be used in the text.

4 SUB-NATIONAL GOVERNMENT

1 This section, on New York, draws heavily on Brecher *et al.* 1993. Material relating to other cities is the product of interviews with city officials.
2 An inadvertent consequence of the ending of the Cold War has been to make military installations much keener to share sports facilities (and costs) with their local communities. Examples of effective shared-use agreements can be found in an increasing number of communities, including that between Ratcliffe and Fort Knox in Kentucky (Spencer and Moman 1996).

5 NATIONAL SPORTS ORGANISATIONS

1 The increase in federal funding and involvement in sport stimulated similar proposals at provincial level, although the motive was different. The introduction of the biannual Canada Games in 1967 provided provinces, especially Quebec, with a further opportunity to express their distinctive identity. By the mid-1980s provincial sports organisations were as financially dependent on provincial funds as were their national equivalents. As Broom noted, 'Associations recognize the potential danger of the situation, but very few seem able to reduce the level of dependency' (1986: 82).
2 There are a number of good analyses and histories of the NCAA, including Lawrence 1987; Falla 1981; Thelin 1994; Fleisher *et al.* 1992; and Rooney 1980.
3 See Brower (1976) for a contrary view.
4 See Noll (1991) for a review of the economics of basketball.

6 DOPING AND SPORT

1   The IOC's list of banned substances and practices inludes the following: stimulants, such as amphetamines, caffeine and pseudoephedrine are used to increase alertness, reduce fatigue and also, occasionally, to heighten aggression; narcotic analgesics, such as morphine, are generally used to overcome pain; anabolic steroids, similar to the male hormone testosterone, allow more intensive training as they aid rapid recovery, and also increase muscle bulk; beta-blockers aid relaxation and the control of muscle tremor; diuretics are used either to flush other drugs out of the body or to help fluid loss in weight-related sports. In addition to banning specific substances, the IOC also bans particular practices, such as blood doping, and urine-sample tampering.

7 SPORT AND PHYSICAL EDUCATION IN SCHOOLS

1   This section draws on the work of Brooker and Macdonald (1993; 1995).
2   For an outline of the ideas that underpin the notion of sport education see Siedentop 1982 and 1987b.
3   The conclusions of the Senate Inquiry were reinforced by similar conclusions of two state-level inquiries, both of which highlighted the debilitating effect of the malaise of the PE teaching profession.
4   This section on the historical development of PE in Irish schools draws on Duffy 1996.
5   A Green Paper is a consultative document published by government which usually explores a variety of aspects of a policy issue and outlines a number of policy options without any commitment on the part of the government. A White Paper is a statement of government policy and frequently is published in advance of legislative proposals.

References

Ahearn, T. (1995) Operating a self financing swimming pool – the success factors, paper to ILAM conference, 'Public recreation services . . . planning for the future', 15 June, Dublin.

Aitchison, C. (1993) Internationalisation and leisure research: the role of comparative studies, paper to the 'Leisure Studies Association/VVV', Tilborg, Holland.

Aitkin, D., Jinks, B. and Warhurst, J. (1989) *Australian Political Institutions*, 4th edn, Sydney: Longman Cheshire.

Albemarle Report (1960) *The Youth Service in England and Wales*, London: HMSO.

Alberta Education (1994) *Meeting the Challenge: Three-year Business Plan*, Edmonton: Government of Alberta.

Albrecht, R.R., Anderson, W.A. and McKeag, D.B. (1992) Drug testing of college athletes: the issues, *Sports Medicine*, vol. 14.6, pp. 349–52.

Albritton, R.B. (1994) Comparing policies across nations and over time, in Nagel, S.S. (ed.), *Encyclopaedia of Policy Studies*, New York: Marcel Dekker.

Alexander, K., Taggart, A. and Medland, A. (1993) Sport education in physical education: try before you buy, *ACHPER National Journal*, Summer, pp. 16–23.

Alexander, K., Taggart, A. and Thorpe, S. (1995) Government and school contexts for the development of sport education in Australian schools, *ACHPER Healthy Lifestyles Journal*, Summer, pp. 4–5.

Allison, L. (ed.) (1986) *The Politics of Sport*, Manchester: Manchester University Press.

—— (1993) *The Changing Politics of Sport*, Manchester: Manchester University Press.

Andersen, S.S. and Eliassen, K.A. (eds) (1993) *Making Policy in Europe: The Europeification of National Policy-making*, London: Sage.

Anderson, C.W. (1975) System and strategy in comparative policy analysis: a plea for contextual and experiential knowledge, in Gwyn, W.B. and Edwards, G.C. (eds), *Perspectives on Policy-making*, New Orleans: Tulane University Press, pp. 219–41.

—— (1978) The logic of public problems: evaluation in comparative policy research, in Ashford, D.E. (ed.), *Comparing Public Policies: New Concepts and Methods*, Beverley Hills: Sage.

Anderson, D. (1995) The present and the future, in Anderson, D.F., Broom, E.F., Pooley, J.C., Schrodt, B. and Brown, E. (eds), *Foundations of Canadian Physical Education, Recreation, and Sports Studies*, 2nd edn, Madison: Brown & Benchmark.

Anderson, R.S., Leitch, J.A. and Mittleider, J.F. (1986) Contribution of state parks to state economies, *Parks and Recreation*, October, pp. 62–3.

Anderson, W.A and McKeag, D.B. (1990) *Replication of the National Study of the*

Substance Use and Abuse Habits of College Student-athletes: Final Report, Michigan: Michigan State University.

Andreff, W. (1989) *Economie politique du sport,* Paris: Dalloz.

Andreff, W. and Nys, J.-F. (1994) *Economie du sport,* Paris: Presse Universitaire de France.

Andrew, C. (1983) Local government in Canada, in Bowman, M. and Hampton, W. (eds), *Local Democracies: A Study in Comparative Local Government,* Melbourne: Longman Cheshire.

Antal, A.B., Dierkes, M. and Weiler, H.N. (1987) Cross-national policy research: traditions, achievements and challenges, in Dierkes, M., Weiler, H.N. and Antal, A.B. (eds), *Comparative Policy Research: Learning from Experience,* Aldershot, UK: Gower.

Arbena, J.L. (ed.) (1988) *Sport and Society in Latin America: Diffusion, Dependency, and the Rise of Mass Culture,* New York: Greenwood Press.

Arnold, T. (1989) An international comparison: Australia and Canada, in Department of the Arts, *Sport, the Environment, Tourism and Territories, Ideas for Australian Recreation: Commentaries on the Recreation Participation Surveys,* Canberra: Australian Government Publishing Service.

Asken, M.J. (1988) *Dying to Win: The Athlete's Guide to Safe and Unsafe Drugs in Sports,* Washington DC: Acropolis Books.

Atkinson, M.M. and Coleman, W.D. (1989) *The State, Business and Industrial Change in Canada,* Toronto: University of Toronto Press.

—— (1992) Policy networks, policy communities and the problems of governance, *Governance,* vol. 5.

Audit Commission (1989) *Sport for Whom?* London: HMSO.

Australia (1989) *Drugs in Sport,* Interim Report of the Senate Standing Committee on the Environment, Recreation and the Arts, Canberra: Australian Government Publishing Service.

—— (1990) *Drugs in Sport,* Second Report of the Senate Standing Committee on the Environment, Recreation and the Arts, Canberra: Australian Government Publishing Service.

Australian Education Council (1989) *Hobart Declaration on Schooling,* Canberra: Australian Government Publishing Service.

—— (1992) *National Statement on Health (Final Consultation Draft),* Brisbane: Australian Education Council.

Australian Sports Drug Agency (ASDA) (1991) *Strategic Plan 1992–94,* Canberra: Australian Government Publishing Service.

—— (1994) *Annual Report 1993–94,* Canberra: Australian Government Publishing Service.

Australian Sports Institute Study Group (1975) *Report,* Canberra: Department of Tourism and Recreation.

Baade, R. and Dye, R. (1988) An analysis of the economic rationale for public subsidisation of sports stadiums, *Annals of Regional Research,* vol. 22, pp. 37–47.

Bailey, J. (1989) *Conflicts in Cricket,* London: Kingswood Press.

Bailey, P. (1979) *Leisure and Class in Victorian England,* London: Routledge & Kegan Paul.

Bairner A. (1994) Sportive nationalism and nationalist politics: a comparative analysis, paper to North American Society for the Sociology of Sport (NASSS) conference, Savannah, Georgia, November.

Ballem, C. (1983) Missing from the Canadian sports scene: native athletes, *Canadian Journal of History of Sport,* vol. XIV.2.

Baka, R.S. (1976) Canadian federal government policy and the 1976 summer Olympics, *Journal of the Canadian Association for Health, PE and Recreation,* March–April.

—— (1982) Similarities between Australian and Canadian government involvement in sport, *Proceedings of the 5th Canadian Symposium on the History of Sport and PE*, Toronto: University of Toronto.

Baker, S. (1994) Environment, in Collins, N. (ed.), *Political Issues in Ireland Today*, Manchester: Manchester University Press.

Banks, R. (ed.) (1992) *Substance Abuse in Sport: The Realities*, Dubuque, Iowa: Kendall-Hunt.

Barnes, C. and Williams, K. (1993) Education and consumerism: managing emergent market culture in schools, in Isaac-Henry, K., Parry, C. and Barnes, C. (eds), *Management in the Public Sector: Challenge and Change*, London: Chapman & Hall.

Barrington Committee (1991) *Report of the Advisory Expert Committee on Local Government Reorganisation and Reform*, Dublin: Stationery Office.

Barrington, T. J. (1991) Local government in Ireland, in Batley, R. and Stoker, G. (eds), *Local Government in Europe: Trends and Developments*, London: Macmillan.

Bartlett, L. (1992) National curriculum in Australia: an instrument of corporate federalism, *British Journal of Educational Studies*, vol. XXX.3, pp. 218–38.

Bell, D. (1973) *The Coming of Post-industrial Society*, New York: Basic Books.

Bennet, B. *et al.* (1975) *Comparative Physical Education and Sport*, Baltimore: Lea and Febiger.

Benson, J.K. (1979) Inter organisational networks and policy sectors: notes towards comparative analysis, mimeo, University of Missouri.

Benson J.K. (1982) Networks and policy sectors: a framework for extending intergovernmental analysis, in Roger, D. and Whitten, D. (eds), *Inter Organisational Co-ordination*, Iowa: Iowa State University.

Best Report (1992) *Sport: The Way Ahead*, the report of the Minister's Task Force on Federal Sport Policy, chairman, J.C. Best, Ottawa: Fitness and Amateur Sport.

Birley, D. (1995) *Land of Sport and Glory: Sport and British Society 1887–1910*, Manchester: Manchester University Press.

Bissinger, H.G. (1990) *Friday Night Lights: A Town, a Team, and a Dream*, Reading, Mass.: Addison-Wesley.

Black Committee (1989) Senate Standing Committee on Environment, Recreation and the Arts, Interim Report, *Drugs in Sport*, Canberra: Australian Government Publishing Service.

Boag, A. (1989) Recreation participation survey: activities done away from home, in Department of the Arts, *Sport, the Environment, Tourism and Territories, Ideas for Australian Recreation: Commentaries on the Recreation Participation Surveys*, Canberra: Australian Government Publishing Service.

Brademas, D.J. and Readnour, J.K. (1989) Status of fees and charges in public leisure service agencies, *Journal of Park and Recreation Administration*, vol. 7.4, pp. 42–55.

Bradley, N. (1995) *Integrated Strategy for Recreation at Local Level . . . Opportunities and Threats*, Laois: Laois County Council.

Brailsford, D. (1991) *Sport, Time and Society: The British at Play*, London: Routledge.

Bramham, P., Henry, I., Mommas, H. and van der Poel, H. (eds) (1989) *Leisure and Urban Processes: Critical Studies of Leisure Policy in Western European Cities*, London: Routledge.

—— (1993) *Leisure Policies in Europe*, Wallingford, Oxon.: CAB International.

Brecher, C., Horton, R.D., Cropf, R.A. and Mead, D.M. (1993) *Power Failure: New York City Politics and Policy since 1960*, New York: Oxford University Press.

Breiner, D. (1995) Building a national approach to drugs in sport, *Sport Report*, vol. 15.1, pp. 21–2.

Brooker, R. and Macdonald, D. (1993) Years of turbulence in Queensland Health and Physical Education, 1984–1991: Part 2, *ACHPER National Journal*, Autumn.
—— (1995) Mapping physical education in the reform agenda for Australian education: tensions and contradictions, *European Physical Education Review*, vol. 1.2, pp. 101–10.

Broom, E. F. (1986) The role of Canadian provincial governments in sport, in Redmond, G. (ed.), *Sport and Politics*, Champaign, Ill.: Human Kinetics Press.
—— (1995) The Canadian amateur sport and recreation delivery system, in Anderson, D.F., Broom, E.F., Pooley, J.C., Schrodt, B. and Brown, E. (eds), *Foundations of Canadian Physical Education, Recreation, and Sports Studies*, 2nd edn, Madison: Brown & Benchmark.

Brower, J. (1976) Professional sport team ownership: fun, profit and ideology of the power elite, *Journal of Sport and Social Issues*, vol. 1.1, pp. 16–51.

Brown, D.W. (1984) Imperialism and games on the playing fields of Canada's private schools, in Müller, N. and Rühl, J.K. (eds), Olympic Scientific Congress 1984, Official Report, *Sports History*, Niederhausen, Germany: Schors.

Brudemas, J. (1990) *The Politics of Education: Conflict and Consensus on Capital Hill*, Norman, Ok.: University of Oklahoma Press.

Bryson, L. (1983) Sport and the oppression of women, *Australian and New Zealand Journal of Sociology*, vol. 19.3.
—— (1989) Sport, drugs and the development of modern capitalism, *Sporting Traditions*, vol. 8.1, pp. 135–54.

Buti, A. and Fridman, S. (1994) The intersection of law and policy: drug testing in sport, *Australian Journal of Public Administration*, vol. 53.4, pp. 489–507.

Butler, D., Adonis, A. and Travers, T. (1994) *Failure in British Government: The Politics of the Poll Tax*, Oxford: Oxford University Press.

Butler, G.D. (1975) *Introduction to Community Recreation*, New York: McGraw-Hill.

CAHPER (1993) Physical Education 2000, *CAHPER Journal*, Spring, pp. 15–23.

CAHPERD (1986) *Cross-Canada Survey on Mainstreaming Students with Physical Disabilities*, Ottawa: CAHPERD.

CAHPERD (1994) *Provincial/Territorial PE Profile*, Ottawa: CAHPERD.

CAHPERD (1995) *The Evidence Behind QDPE*, Ottawa: CAHPERD.

Caldwell, G. (1976) Sport and Australian identity, in Jacques, T. and Pavia, G. (eds), *Sport in Australia: Selected Readings*, Sydney: McGraw-Hill.

Canada (1970) *A Proposed Sport Policy for Canadians*, White Paper, Ottawa: Fitness and Amateur Sport.
—— (1981) *A Challenge to the Nation: Fitness and Amateur Sport in the '80s*, White Paper, Ottawa: Fitness and Amateur Sport.
—— (1985) *High Performance Athlete Development in Canada*, Ottawa: Fitness and Amateur Sport.

Canadian Centre for Drug-free Sport (1993) *Canadian Policy on Penalties for Doping in Sport*, Ottawa: CCDS.
—— (1994) *Doping Control Standard Operating Procedures*, Ottawa: CCDS.
—— (1995) *Inadvertent Doping Review: Final Report*, Ottawa: CCDS.

Canadian Heritage (1994) *Athlete-centred Sport: Discussion Paper*, Ottawa: Canadian Heritage.

Carlson, B. (1992) The seduction of amateur sport, *Recreation Canada*, vol. 50.4, pp. 30–1.

Carroll, N. (1979) *Sport in Ireland: Aspects of Ireland 6*, Dublin: Department of Foreign Affairs.

Carson, J. (1965) *Colonial Virginians at Play*, Charlottesville, Va.: Colonial Williamsburg Foundation.

Carswell, L. (1994) Health policy, in Collins, N. (ed.), *Political Issues in Ireland Today*, Manchester: Manchester University Press.

Cashman, R. (1987) A debate in sports history: three views on Saturday afternoon fever, the Australian sporting obsession, *Sporting Traditions*, vol. 4.1, pp. 47–55.

—— (1995) *Paradise of Sport: the Rise of Organised Sport in Australia*, Melbourne: Oxford University Press.

Castells, M. (1976) *The Urban Question*, London: Edward Arnold.

Castles F.G. (1988) Comparative public policy analysis: problems, progress and prospects, in Castles, F.G., Lehner, F. and Schmidt, M.G. (eds), *The Future of Party Government: Managing Mixed Economies*, New York: Walter de Gruyter, pp. 197–223.

Chalip, L. (no date) The framing of policy: explaining the transformation of American sport, unpublished paper.

Chandler, J.M. (1991) Sport as TV product: a case study of 'Monday Night Football', in Staudohar, P. D. and Mangan, J.A. (eds), *The Business of Professional Sports*, Urbana: University of Illinois Press.

Chapman, R.K.J. (1988) The Australian Advisory Council for Inter-governmental Relations as a mediating institution, *Australian Journal of Public Administration*, vol. 47.2, pp.130–6.

Chapman, R.K.J. and Wood, M. (1984) *Australian Local Government: The Federal Dimension*, Sydney: George Allen & Unwin.

Chazaud, P. (1989) *Le sport dans la commune, le départment et la région*, Paris: Berger-Levrault.

Chu, D. (1981) Origins of teacher/coach role conflict: a reaction to Massengale's paper, in Greendorfer, S.L. and Yiannakis, A. (eds), *Sociology of Sport: Perspectives*, West Point, NY: Leisure Press.

Chubb, B. (1992) *The Government and Politics of Ireland*, 3rd edn, London: Longman.

Ciccolella, M.E. (1992) Full court press, *Athletic Business*, January, pp. 47–50.

Clarke, A. (1994) Leisure and the new managerialism, in Clarke, J., Cochrane, A. and McLaughlin, E. (eds), *Managing Social Policy*, London: Sage.

Clements, D.B. (1983) Drug use survey: results and conclusions, *Physician and Sports Medicine*, vol. 11.

Clumpner, R.A. (1984) Pragmatic coercion: the role of government in sport in the United States, in Redmond, G. (ed.), *Sport and Politics*, Champaign, Ill.: Human Kinetic Press.

Coalter, F. (1984) Public policy and leisure, in Tomlinson, A. (ed.), *Planning and People*, plenary papers, vol. 1, Brighton: Leisure Studies Association.

—— (1990) The mixed economy of leisure, in Henry, I. (ed.), *Management and Planning in the Leisure Industries*, London: Macmillan.

Coalter, F., Long, J. and Duffield, B. (eds) (1986) *Rationale for Public Sector Investment in Leisure*, London: Sports Council and Economic and Social Research Council.

Coghlan, J. (1990) *Sport and British Politics since 1960*, London: Falmer Press.

Coleman, W.D. and Skogstad, G. (1990) Policy communities and policy networks: a structural approach, in Coleman, W.D. and Skogstad, G. (eds), *Policy Communities and Public Policy in Canada*, Mississauga, Ontario: Copp Clark Pitman.

Collins, H. (1989) Political ideas and practices, in Meaney, N. (ed.), *Under New Heavens*, Sydney: Heinemann Educational Australia.

Collins, N. (1987) *Local Government Managers at Work*, Dublin: Institute of Public Administration.

Collins, N. and McCann, F. (eds) (1993) *Irish Politics Today*, Manchester: Manchester University Press.

Cooter, G.R. (1980) Amphetamine use, physical activity and sport, *Journal of Drug Use*, vol. 10.

Coper, M. (1987) *Encounters with the Australian Constitution*, Sydney: CCH Australia Limited.

Cosentino, F. (1975) A history of the concept of professionalism in Canadian sport, *Canadian Journal of History of Sport and Physical Education*, vol. VI. 2 December.

Cosentino, F. and Howell, M.L. (1970) *A History of Physical Education in Canada*, Toronto: General Publishing Co.

Cox, A.E., Noonkester, B.N., Howell, M.L. and Howell, R.A. (1985) Sport in Canada 1868–1900, in Howell, M.L. and Howell, R.A. (eds), *History of Sport in Canada*, Champaign, Ill.: Stipes Publishing Co.

Cox, R.H. (1992) After corporatism: a comparison of the role of medical professionals and social workers in the Dutch welfare state, *Comparative Political Studies*, vol. 24.4, pp. 532–51.

Cranz, G. (1982) *The Politics of Park Design: A History of Urban Parks in America*, Cambridge, Mass.: MIT Press.

Crompton, J.L. and Lamb, C.W. (1980) Eliminating community services: the leisure services example, *Community Development Journal*, vol. 15.2, pp. 138–45.

Crompton, J.L. and McGregor, B.P. (1994) Trends in the financing and staffing of local government park and recreation services 1964/65–1990/91, *Journal of Park and Recreation Administration*, vol. 12.3, pp. 19–37.

Crowley Report (1992) Senate Standing Committee on the Environment, Recreation and the Arts, *Physical and Sport Education*, Canberra: Government Publishing Service.

Crowley, F. (ed.) (1974) *A New History of Australia*, Melbourne: Heinemann.

Crowley, R. (1993) The thirteenth Fritz Duras Memorial Lecture: the Senate Enquiry – six months on, *ACHPER National Journal*, Spring.

Crowther Report (1959) *15 to 18*, London: HMSO.

Crum, B. (1993) Conventional thought and practice in physical education: problems of teaching and implications for change, *Quest*, vol. 45. 3, pp. 339–56.

Cumes, J. (1979) *Their Chastity Was Not Too Rigid: Leisure Times in Early Australia*, Longman Cheshire: Melbourne.

Cuneen, C. (1980) 'Hands Off Parks': the provision of parks and playgrounds, in Roe, J. (ed.), *Twentieth Century Sydney: Studies in Urban and Social History*, Sydney: Hale & Iremonger.

Cutright, P. (1969) Political structure, economic development and national social security programs, in Cnudde, C.F. and Neubauer, D.E. (eds), *Empirical Democratic Theory*, Chicago: Markham Publishing Co.

Dabscheck, B. (1991) The Professional Cricketers Association of Australia, *Sporting Traditions*, vol. 8.1, pp. 2–26.

—— (1994) Player associations and sports unions in Australia, in Wilcox, R.C. (ed.), *Sport in The Global Village*, Morgantown, WV: Fitness Information Technology Inc.

Dahl, R. (1982) *Dilemmas of Pluralist Democracy: Autonomy Versus Control*, New Haven, Conn.: Yale University Press.

Daley, J. (1987) *Decisions and Disasters: Alienation of the Adelaide Parklands*, Adelaide: Bland House.

—— (1990) *Quest for Excellence: The Australian Institute of Sport*, Canberra: Australian Government Printing Service.

Daly, J.A. (1972) Sport and society: the role of sport and games in the social development of early Australia, *Australian Journal of Physical Education*, March, no. 55.

Darmody, M. (1995) Assessment in PE, in *Proceedings of the National PE Conference 1994*, Limerick: PEAI.

Davis-Jameson, C. (1990) The politics of creating a recreation service, *Recreation Canada*, vol. 48.7, pp. 22–5.

Dawson, J. (1988) *Strengthening Australia's Schools: A Consideration of the Focus and Content of Schooling*, Canberra: Australian Government Publishing Service.

Deakin, N. (1974) On some perils of imitation, in Rose, R. (ed.), *Lessons from America*, London: Macmillan.

de Búrca, M. (1980) *The GAA: A History of the Gaelic Athletic Association*, Dublin: Cuman Lúthchleas Gael.

Deenihan, J. (1991) Report on PE in Irish secondary schools, unpublished paper, (mimeo).

DeFelice E.G. (1986) Causal inference and comparative methods, *Comparative Political Studies*, vol. 19.3, pp. 415–37.

DeLeon, R.E. (1992) *Left Coast City: Progressive Politics in San Francisco, 1975–1991*, Lawrence, Kan.: University of Kansas Press.

DeMarco, T. and Sidney, K. (1989) Enhancing children's participation in physical activity, *Journal of School Health*, vol. 59.8, pp. 337–40.

Department of Education (no date) *Syllabus in Physical Education*, Dublin: Department of Education.

—— (1938) *Report on Physical Education*, Dublin: Department of Education.

—— (1984) *Issues and Structures in Schools*, Dublin: Department of Education.

—— (1986) *In Our Schools*, Dublin: Department of Education.

—— (1991) *America 2000: An Education Strategy*, Washington: US Government Printing Office.

—— (1992) *Education for a Changing World*, Dublin: The Stationery Office.

—— (1993) *Sports Section, Annual Report 1992*, Dublin: Department of Education.

—— (1994) *Sports Section, Annual Report*, Dublin: Department of Education.

—— (1995) *Charting Our Education Future*, Dublin: The Stationery Office.

Department of the Environment/Department of Education and Science (1986) *Sport in Schools Seminar, Report of Proceedings*, London: DoE/DES.

Department of the Environment (1975) *Sport and Recreation*, Cmnd. 6200, London: HMSO.

Department of the Interior: Australian News and Information Bureau (1962) *Sport: A Reference Paper*, Canberra: Government Printing Office (reproduced in Jaques and Pavia 1976).

Department of National Heritage (1995) *Sport: Raising the Game*, London: DNH.

Department of Sport, Recreation and Tourism (1987) *Annual Report 1986–87*, Canberra, Australia: Australian Government Publishing Service.

de Pencier, J. (1994) Law and athlete drug testing in Canada, *Marquette Sports Law Journal*, vol. 4.2, pp. 259–99.

Dierkes, M., Weiler, H. and Antal, A. (eds) (1987) *Comparative Policy Research*, Aldershot, Hants: Gower.

Doern, G.B. and Toner, G. (1985) *The Politics of Energy: The Development and Implementation of the NEP*, Toronto: Methuen.

Donald, K. (1983) *The Doping Game*, Brisbane: Boolarong Publications.

Donnelly, P. (1986) The paradox of parks: the politics of recreational land use before and after the mass trespass, *Leisure Studies*, vol. 5.2.

Donohoe, T. and Johnson, N. (1986) *Foul Play: Drug Abuse in Sports*, Oxford: Basil Blackwell.

Dooney, S. and O'Toole, J. (1992) *Irish Government Today*, Dublin: Gill & Macmillan.

Dowding, K. (1994) Policy networks: don't stretch a good idea too far, in Dunleavy, P.J. and Stanyer, J. (eds), Contemporary Political Studies 1994, vol. 1, Belfast: The Political Studies Association of the UK.

Downs, A. (1967) *Inside Bureaucracy*, Boston, Mass.: Little, Brown.

Downs, A. (1972) Up and down with ecology: the issue attention cycle, *Public Interest*, vol. 28.1, pp. 38–50.

Dubin Report (1990) *Commission of Inquiry into the Use of Drugs and Banned Practices Intended to Increase Athletic Performance*, Charles Dubin, Commissioner, Ottawa: Ministry of Supply and Services, Canada.

Duffy, P. (1996) From Belmore to the White Paper – how far have we come? in Darmody, M. (ed.), *PE in Europe: The Irish Dimension*, Proceedings of the National Physical Education Conference, Limerick: Physical Education Association of Ireland.

Duffy, P., Leonard, D. and Darmody, M. (1992) PE: Assessment in second level teaching, *Irish Educational Studies*, vol. 11.

Dunleavy, P. (1980) *Urban Political Analysis*, London: Macmillan.

—— (1981) Professions and policy change: notes towards a model of ideological corporatism, *Public Administration Bulletin*, No. 36, August.

Dunleavy, P. and O'Leary, B. (1987) *Theories of the State*, London: Macmillan.

Dunstan, K. (1973) *Sports*, North Melbourne: Cassell Australia.

Eastman, W.D. (1989) School athletic organisation and professional associations for physical educators: a retrospect on interfacing (1900–1986), *Canadian Journal of History of Sport*, vol. XX.2, pp. 49–63.

Easton, D. (1953) *The Political System*, New York: Knopf.

—— (1965) *A Framework for Political Analysis*, Englewood Cliffs, NJ: Prentice-Hall.

Eitzen, D.S. and Sage, G.H. (1986) *Sociology of North American Sport*, 3rd edn, Dubuque, Ia.: W.C. Brown.

Elford, K. (1976) Sport in Australian society: a perspective, in Jaques, T. and Pavia, G. (eds), *Sport in Australia: Selected Readings*, Sydney: McGraw-Hill.

Emy, H.V. (1978) *The Politics of Australian Democracy*, 2nd edn, Sydney: Macmillan.

Emy, H.V. and Hughes, O.E. (1991) *Australian Politics: Realities in Conflict*, 2nd edn, Sydney: Macmillan.

Evans, J. (1990) Defining a subject: the rise of the new PE? *British Journal of Sociology of Education*, vol. 11, pp. 155–69.

—— (1990a) *Sport in Schools*, Sydney: Deakin University Press.

—— (1990b) Sport Education: Is it Physical Education by Another Name? *ACHPER National Journal*, no. 127, pp. 12–18.

—— (1992) A short paper about people, power and educational reform, in Sparkes, A.C. (ed.), *Research in PE and Sport: Exploring Alternative Visions*, London: Falmer Press.

Evans, J. and Penney, D. (1994) The politics of pedagogy: making a national curriculum physical education, in *Journal of Education Policy*, vol. 10, pp. 27–44.

—— (1995) Physical education, restoration and the politics of sport, *Curriculum Studies*, vol. 3, pp. 183–96.

Evans, J., Penney, D. and Bryant, A. (1993) Improving the quality of physical education? The Education Reform Act, 1988, and physical education in Wales, *Quest*, vol. 45, pp. 321–38.

Evans, J., Penney, D. and Davies, B. (1996) Back to the future: education policy and physical education, in Armstrong, N. (ed.), *New Directions in Physical Education: Change and Innovation*, London: Cassell.

Falla, J. (1981) *NCAA: The Voice of College Sports*, Mission, KS: National Collegiate Athletic Association.

Faulkner, J.H. (1982) Pressuring the executive, *Canadian Public Administration*, vol. 25.2, pp. 240–53.

Fields, L., Lange, W.R., Kreiter, N.A. and Fudala, P.J. (1994) A national survey of drug testing policies for college athletes, *Medicine and Science in Sports and Exercise*, vol. 26. 6, pp. 682–6.

Fitness Canada (1991) *Active Living: A Conceptual Overview*, Ottawa: Fitness Canada.

Fleisher, A.A., Goff, B.L. and Tollison, R.D. (1992) *The National Collegiate Athletic Association: A Study in Cartel Behavior*, Chicago: University of Chicago Press.

Fletcher, C. (1993) Competition between regional governments and the federal culture of equalisation, *Australian Journal of Political Science*, vol. 28, pp. 54–73.

Flora, P. and Heidenheimer, A.J. (eds) (1981) *The Development of the Welfare State in Europe and America*, London: Transaction Books.

Flynn, R. (1993) Restructuring health systems: a comparative analysis of England and the Netherlands, in Hill, M.J. (ed.), *New Agendas in the Study of the Policy Process*, Hemel Hempstead: Harvester-Wheatsheaf.

Foley, D.E. (1990) The great American football ritual: reproducing race, class and gender inequality, *Sociology of Sport Journal*, vol. 7.2, pp. 111–35.

Follatschek, J.L. (1982) Daily PE – the result of the French concern, *British Journal of Physical Education*, vol. 18.2.

Franks, C.E.S. and Macintosh, D. (1984) The evolution of federal government policies toward sport and culture in Canada: a comparison, in Theberge, N. and Donnelly, P. (eds), *Sport and the Sociological Imagination*, Fort Worth, Texas: Texas Christian University Press.

Freedman, W. (1987) *Professional Sport and Antitrust*, New York: Quorum Books.

Freeman G.P. (1985) National styles and policy sectors: explaining structured variation, *Journal of Public Policy*, vol. 5.4, pp. 467–96.

Frey, J.H. (1978) The organisation of American Amateur Sport, *American Behavioral Scientist*, vol. 21.3.

Frisken, F. (1988) *City Policy-making in Theory and Practice: The Case of Toronto's Downtown Plan*, Local Government Case Study No. 3, London, Ont.: University of Western Ontario.

Gair, J. (1994) Contracting out: a public service option, *Recreation Canada*, vol. 52.4, pp. 21–2.

Galasso, P.J. (1972) The involvement of the Canadian federal government in sport and fitness, *Canadian Journal of History of Sport and Physical Education*, vol. 3.2, pp. 42–61.

Gerritsen, R. (1986) The necessity of corporatism: the case of the Hawke Government, *Politics*, vol. 21.1, pp. 45–54.

Gibbs, A. (1991) Drug testing and college athletes: conflicts among institutions, students and the NCAA, *West's Education Law Reporter*, vol. 67, pp. 1–11.

Gilmour, R.S. and Halley, A.A. (1994) *Who Makes Public Policy? The Struggle for Control between Congress and the Executive*, Chatham, NJ: Chatham House Publishers.

Glezer, L. (1982) *Tariff Politics*, Melbourne: Melbourne University Press.

Goldberg, L. (1991) *Taxation with Representation: A Citizen's Guide to Reforming Proposition 13*, Sacramento: California Tax Reform Association.

Goldthorpe, J.T. (1984) *Order and Conflict in Contemporary Capitalism*, Oxford: Clarendon Press.

Goodson, I. (1983) *School Subjects and Curriculum Change*, London: Croom Helm.

Goodwin, D.L., Fitzpatrick, D.A. and Craigon, I. (1996) Cut-backs in physical education consulting services: consequences and concerns, *CAHPERD Journal*, Summer, pp. 41–4.

Gordon, H. (1976) The reasons why, in Jaques, T. and Pavia, G. (eds), *Sport in Australia: Selected Readings*, Sydney: McGraw-Hill.

—— (1994) *Australia and the Olympic Games*, St Lucia, Queensland: Queensland University Press.

Gorman, J. and Calhoun, K. (1994) *The Name of the Game: The Business of Sports*, New York: John Wiley.

Gorn, E.J. and Goldstein, W. (1993) *A Brief History of American Sports*, New York: Hill & Wang.

Government of Ireland (1951) *Commission on Youth Unemployment*, Dublin: Government Printing Service.

—— (1991) *Local Government Reorganisation and Reform*, Dublin: Stationery Office.

Greenaway, J., Smith, S. and Street, J. (1992) *Deciding Factors in British Politics: A Case Study Approach*, London: Routledge.

Greenwood, G. (1955) Introduction, in Greenwood, G. (ed.), *Australia – a Social and Political History*, Sydney: Angus & Robertson.

Gregus, D. R. (1993) The NFL's drug-testing policies: are they constitutional? *The Entertainment and Sports Lawyer*, vol. 10.4, pp. 1–4 and 25–8.

Griffey, D.C. (1987) Trouble for sure: a crisis – perhaps, *Journal of Physical Education, Recreation and Dance*, vol. 58.2, pp. 20–1.

Gruneau, R. and Whitson, D. (1993) *Hockey Night in Canada: Sport, Identities and Cultural Politics*, Toronto: Garamond Press.

Haas, P. (1992) Introduction: epistemic communities and international policy co-ordination, *International Organization*, vol. 46.1, pp. 1–35.

Halbert, J. (1995) Physical education at the crossroads: the way forward, in *Proceedings of the National PE Conference 1994*, Limerick: PEAI.

Hamilton-Smith, E. and Robertson, R. (1977) Recreation and government in Australia, in Mercer, D. (ed.), *Leisure and Recreation in Australia*, Malvern, Vic.: Sorrett Publishing.

Hancock, M.D. (1983) Comparative public policy: an assessment, in Finifter, A.W. (ed.), *Political Science: The State of the Discipline*, Washington DC: American Political Sciences Association (APSA).

Hanley, D.F. (1979) *Sports Medicine and Physiology*, Philadelphia: W.B. Saunders.

Hansen, S.B. (1983) Public policy analysis: some recent developments and current problems, in Finifter, A.W. (ed.), *Political Science: the State of the Discipline*, Washington, DC: American Political Sciences Association (APSA).

Hardman, K. (1996) *Comparative Studies in Physical Education and Sport*, Manchester: Centre for Physical Education and Leisure Studies.

Hargreaves, J. (1985) From social democracy to authoritarian populism: state intervention in sport and physical recreation in contemporary Britain, *Leisure Studies*, vol. 4.

Harper, J.A. and Johnson, B.L. (1992) Balancing the scales in public parks and recreation departments, *Recreation Canada*, October, pp. 18–20.

Harris, C.P. (1979) Relationships between federal and state governments in Australia, *Australian Commission on Intergovernmental Relations (ACIR) Information Paper No. 6*, Canberra: Australian Government Publishing Service.

Harris, J. (1994) Physical education in the curriculum: is there enough time to be effective? *British Journal of Physical Education*, Winter, pp. 34–8.

Harrop, M. (1992) Comparison, in Harrop, M. (ed.), *Power and Policy in Liberal Democracies*, Cambridge: Cambridge University Press.

Harte, C. (1993) *A History of Australian Cricket*, London: André Deutsch.

Harvey, J. (1988) Sport policy and the welfare state: an outline of the Canadian case, *Sociology of Sport Journal*, vol. 5.4.

Hechter, M. (1975) Review essay, *Contemporary Sociology*, vol. 4, May, pp. 217–22.

Heclo, H. (1972) Review article: policy analysis, *British Journal of Political Science*, vol. II, pp. 83–108.

—— (1978) Issue networks and the executive establishment, in King, A. (ed.), *The New American Political System*, Washington DC: American Enterprise Institute.

—— (1981) Towards a new welfare state? in Flora, P. and Heidenheimer, A.J. (eds), *The Development of Welfare States in Europe and America*, New Brunswick, NJ: Transaction Books.

Heidenheimer, A.J. (1985) Comparative public policy at the cross-roads, *Journal of Public Policy*, vol. 5.4, pp. 441–65.

—— (1986) Politics, policy and policey as concepts in English and continental languages: an attempt to explain divergences, *The Review of Politics*, vol. 48.1, pp. 3–30.

Heidenheimer, A., Heclo, H. and Teich Adams, C. (1976) *Comparative Public Policy: the Politics of Social Choice in Europe and America*, 1st edn, London: Macmillan.

—— (1983) *Comparative Public Policy: the Politics of Social Choice in Europe and America*, 2nd edn, New York: St Martin's Press.

—— (1990) *Comparative Public Policy: the Politics of Social Choice in America, Europe, and Japan*, 3rd edn, New York: St Martin's Press.

Helmes, R.C. (1981) Ideology and social control in Canadian sport: a theoretical review, in Hart, M. and Birrell, W.C. (eds), *Sport in the Sociocultural Process*, 3rd edn, Dubuque, Iowa: Brown & Co.

Helmstaedt, K. (1994) Time to be fair to the rest, *Swim Canada*, January, p. 16.

Henry, I.P. (1993) *The Politics of Leisure Policy*, Basingstoke: Macmillan.

Her Majesty's Inspectorate of Education (1978) *Physical Education Curriculum (11–16)*, London: HMSO.

Higgins, D.J.H. (1986) *Local and Urban Politics in Canada*, Toronto: Gage.

Higgins, J. (1978) *The Poverty Business: Britain and America*, Oxford: Blackwell.

—— (1981) *States of Welfare: Comparative Analysis in Social Policy*, Oxford: Basil Blackwell.

—— (1986) Comparative social policy, *The Quarterly Journal of Social Affairs*, vol. 2.3, pp. 221–42.

Hill, M. and Bramley, G. (1986) *Analysing Social Policy*, Oxford: Blackwell.

Hillary Commission for Recreation and Sport (1987) *Statement of Intent*, Wellington: Government Printing Office.

Hjelte, G. and Shivers, J.S. (1978) *Public Administration of Recreation Services*, Philadelphia: Lea & Febiger.

Hofferbert, R.I. (1974) *The Study of Public Policy*, Indianapolis: Bobbs-Merrill.

Hogwood, B. (1987) *From Crisis to Complacency*, Oxford: Oxford University Press.

Hogwood, B. and Gunn, L. (1984) *Policy Analysis for the Real World*, Oxford: Oxford University Press.

Holmes, M. (1994) Symbols of national identity and sport: the case of the Irish Football Team, *Irish Political Studies*, vol. 9, pp. 81–98.

Holohan, G. (1995) The state of the nation . . . . Recreation facilities in Ireland, the challenges facing us, paper to ILAM conference, 'Public recreation services . . . planning for the future', 15 June, Dublin.

Holt, R. (1981) *Sport and Society in Modern France*, Basingstoke: Macmillan.

—— (1989) *Sport and the British: A Modern History*, Oxford: Oxford University Press.

Horne, D. (1964) *The Lucky Country*, Sydney: Angus & Robertson.

Houlihan, B. (1991) *The Government and Politics of Sport*, London: Routledge.

—— (1994) *Sport and International Politics*, Hemel Hempstead: Harvester-Wheatsheaf.

—— (1996) Sport in the United Kingdom, in Chalip, L., Johnson, A. and Stachura, L. (eds), *National Sports Policies*, Westport, Conn.: Greenwood Press.

Howard, D.R. and Crompton, J.L. (1980) *Financing, Managing and Marketing Recreation and Park Resources*, Dubuque, Iowa: W.C. Brown.

Howard, J. (1992) Public sector financial facts, *Recreation Canada*, vol. 50.4, pp. 21–2.

Howell, M.L. and Howell, R.A. (1985) Canadian sport in perspective, in Howell, M.L. and Howell, R.A. (eds), *History of Sport in Canada*, Champaign, Ill.: Stipes Publishing Co.

Hulme, D. (1990) *The Political Olympics*, New York; Praeger.

Hunter, P. (1995) *Community Use of School Sports Facilities*, London: OPCS.

Hussey, G. (1995) *Ireland Today: Anatomy of A Changing State*, London: Penguin.

Hyland, D.A. (1990) *Philosophy of Sport*, New York: Paragon House.

Illich, I. (1977) *Medical Nemesis: The Expropriation of Health*, Harmondsworth: Penguin.

Irish, M.D. and Prothro, J.W. (1973) *The Politics of American Democracy*, Englewood Cliffs, NJ: Prentice-Hall.

Janzen, H. (1995) The status of physical education in Canadian public schools, *CAHPERD Journal*, Autumn, pp. 5–9.

Jaques, T.D. and Pavia, G.R. (1976a) The Australian government and sport, in Jaques, T.D. and Pavia, G.R. (eds), *Sport in Australia: Selected Readings in Physical Activity*, Sydney: McGraw-Hill.

—— (1976b) Milk beneath the cream? in Jaques, T.D. and Pavia, G.R. (eds), *Sport in Australia: Selected Readings in Physical Activity*, Sydney: McGraw-Hill.

Jenkins, W.I. (1978) *Policy Analysis: Political and Organisational Perspectives*, London: Martin Robertson.

Jobling, I.F. (1986) The Lion, the Eagle and the Kangaroo: politics and the proposals for a British Empire team at the 1916 Berlin Olympics, in Redmond, G. (ed.), *Sport and Politics*, Champaign, Ill.: Human Kinetics Press Inc.

—— (1991) Sport and the state: the case of Australia and New Zealand, in Landry, F., Landry, M and Yerles, M. (eds), *Sport: The Third Millennium*, Sainte-Foy: Les presses de l'Université de Laval.

John, D. (1995) Moving to the margins: physical education another disposable program? *CAHPERD Journal*, Summer, pp. 15–18.

Johnson, B.A. and Sinclair, J. (1985) *Physical and Health Education: A Survey of Provincial Curricula at the Elementary and Secondary Levels*, Ottawa: Council of Ministers of Education.

Johnson, M.W. (1985) Physical Educators – Fitness or Fraud? *Journal of Physical Education, Recreation and Dance (JOPERD)*, vol. 56.1, pp. 33–5.

Jones, M. (1993) *Transforming Australian Local Government: Making it Work*, St Leonards, NSW: Allen & Unwin.

—— (1987) *British Politics and the Policy Process: An Arena Approach*, London: Unwin Hyman.

Jordan, A.G. and Richardson, J.J. (1982) The British policy style or the logic of negotiation? in Richardson, J.J., *Policy Styles in Western Europe*, London: George Allen & Unwin.

Jordan, G. (1990) Sub-governments, policy communities and networks: refilling old bottles? *Journal of Theoretical Politics*, vol. 2.3, pp. 319–38.

Keatinge, P. and Laffan, B. (1992) Ireland in international affairs, in Coakley, J. and Gallagher, M. (eds), *Politics in the Republic of Ireland*, Galway: Political Studies Association of Ireland.

Keeves, J. P. (1990) The expansion and rationale of Australian education: to the 1990s and beyond, in Saha, L.J. and Keeves, J.P. (eds), *Schooling and Society in Australia: Sociological Perspectives*, Sydney: Australian National University Press.

Kelman, S. (1987) *Making Public Policy: A Hopeful View of American Government*, New York: Basic Books.

Kenway, J. (1993) New education in new times, paper presented to the Australian Curriculum Studies Conference, Brisbane.

Kerr, C. (1983) *The Future of Industrial Societies*, Cambridge, Mass.: Harvard University Press.

Kidd, B. (1981) *The Canadian State and Sport: The Dilemma of Intervention*, annual conference proceedings of the National Association for Physical Education in Higher Education, Champaign, Ill.: Human Kinetics Press Inc.

—— (1983) In defense of Tom Longboat, *Canadian Journal of History of Sport*, vol. XIV.1, May.

Kidd, B. and Macfarlane, J. (1972) *The Death of Hockey*, Toronto: New Press.

Kikulis, L.M., Slack, T. and Hinings, C.R. (1995) Towards an understanding of the role of agency and choice in the changing structure of Canada's national sports organisations, in *Journal of Sport Managment*, vol. 9.2, pp. 135–54.

Kinchin, D. and O'Sullivan, M. (1995) A national curriculum for physical education: a British example, *CAHPERD Journal*, Spring.

Kingdom, J. (1993) Canada, in Chandler, J. A. (ed.), *Local Government in Liberal Democracies: An Introductory Survey*, London: Routledge.

Kingdon, J.W. (1984) *Agendas, Alternatives, and Public Policies*, New York: HarperCollins.

Kirk, D. (1992) *Defining Physical Education*, Brighton: Falmer Press.

Knopff, R. *et al.* (1994) *Parameters of Power: Canada's Political Institutions*, Scarborough, Ontario: Nelson Canada.

Knox, C. (1986) Political symbolism and leisure provision in Northern Ireland local government, *Local Government Studies*, September–October, vol. 12.5.

—— (1987) Territorialism, leisure and community centres in Northern Ireland, *Leisure Studies*, vol. 6.

Knox, C. and Haslem, R. (1994) Local government, in Collins, N. (ed.), *Political Issues in Ireland Today*, Manchester: Manchester University Press.

Komito, L. (1984) Irish clientelism: a reappraisal, *Economic and Social Review*, vol. 15.3, pp. 35–59.

Kraus, R. (1990) *Recreation and Leisure in Modern Society*, 4th edn, New York: HarperCollins.

Laffin, M. (1986) Professional communities and policy communities in central–local government relations, in Goldsmith, M. (ed.), *New Research in Central–Local Government*, Aldershot: Gower.

—— (1989) Public policy making, in Smith, R. and Watson, L. (eds), *Politics in Australia*, Sydney: Allen & Unwin.

Landes, R.G. (1983) *The Canadian Polity: A Comparative Introduction*, Scarborough, Ont.: Prentice-Hall.

Landry, F., Landry, M. and Yerles, M. (1991) (eds) *Sport: The Third Millennium*, Sainte-Foy: Les presses de l'Université de Laval.

Lappage, R. (1985) The Canadian scene and sport 1921–1939, in Howell, M.L. and Howell, R.A. (eds), *History of Sport in Canada*, Champaign, Ill.: Stipes Publishing Co.

Lawrence, G. and Rowe, D. (eds) (1986) *Power Play: Essays in The Sociology of Australian Sport*, Sydney: Hale & Iremonger.

Lawrence, P.R. (1987) *Unsportsmanlike Conduct: The National Collegiate Athletic Association and the Business of College Sports*, New York: Praeger.

Lawson, H.A. (1993) School reform, families, and health in the emergent national agenda for economic and social improvement: implications, *Quest*, vol. 45, pp. 289–307.

Lawson, R. (1973) *Brisbane in the 1890s: A Study of an Australian Urban Society*, Brisbane: University of Brisbane Press.

Le Quesne, L. (1983) *The Bodyline Controversy*, London: Secker & Warburg.

Lewis, G. (1966) The Muscular Christian Movement, *Journal of Health, Physical Education and Recreation*, vol. 5, pp. 27–42.

Lijphart, A. (1971) Comparative politics and the comparative method, *American Political Science Review*, vol. 65, September, pp. 682–93.

Lindblom, C.E. (1959) The science of muddling through, *Public Administration Review*, vol. 19, pp. 78–88.

—— (1977) *Politics and Markets*, New York: Basic Books.

Lingard, R. (1991) Policy-making for Australian schooling: the new corporate federalism, *Journal of Education Policy*, vol. 6.1, pp. 85–90.

Lingard, B., O'Brien, P. and Knight, J. (1993) Strengthening Australia's schools through corporate federalism? *Australian Journal of Education*, vol. 37.3, pp. 231–47.

Ljungqvist, A. (1975) The use of anabolic steroids in top Swedish athletes, *British Journal of Sports Medicine*, vol. 9.

Loveday, B. (1993) Management accountability in public services: a police case study, in Isaac-Henry, K., Parry, C. and Barnes, C. (eds), *Management in the Public Sector: Challenge and Change*, London: Chapman & Hall.

Lovesey, P. (1979) *The Official Centenary History of the Amateur Athletic Association*, London: Guinness Superlatives.

Lowe, B., Kanin, D.B. and Strenk, A. (eds) (1978) *Sport and International Relations*, Champaign, Ill.: Stipes Publishing Co.

Lumpkin, A. (1990) *Physical Education and Sport: A Contemporary Introduction*, St Louis: Times Mirror/Mosby College Publishing.

McCormack, G. (1991) The price of affluence: the political economy of Japanese leisure, *New Left Review*, vol. 189, pp. 121–34.

Macdonald, D. and Brooker, R. (1992) Years of turbulence in Queensland health and physical education, 1984–1991: Part 1, *ACHPER National Journal*, Spring.

McGinnis, J., Kanner, L. and DeGrew, C. (1991) PE's role in achieving national health objectives, *Research Quarterly for Exercise and Sport*, no. 62, pp. 138–42.

McGovern, J.N. (1996) The ADA is a tremendous opportunity, in *Parks and Recreation*, November, pp. 34–5.

MacGregor, R.D. (ed.) (1965) *The Development of Dominion Status 1900–1936*, London: Frank Cass.

Macintosh, D. (1985) The Canadian sports scene since 1976, in Howell, M.L. and Howell, R.A. (eds), *History of Sport in Canada*, Champaign, Ill.: Stipes Publishing Co.

—— (1991) Sport and the state: the case of Canada, in Landry, F., Landry, M. and Yerles, M. (eds), *Sport, . . . The Third Millennium*, Sainte-Foy: Les presses de l'Université de Laval.

—— (1996) Sport and government in Canada, in Chalip, L., Johnson, A. and Stachura, L. (eds), *National Sports Policies*, Westport, Conn.: Greenwood Press.

Macintosh, D. and Hawes, D. (1994) *Sport and Canadian Diplomacy*, Toronto: McGill-Queen's University Press.

Macintosh, D. and Whitson, D. (1990) *The Game Planners: Transforming Canada's Sports System*, Montreal: McGill-Queen's University Press.

Macintosh, D., Bedecki, T. and Franks, C.E.S. (1987) *Sport and Politics in Canada: Federal Government Involvement since 1961*, Montreal: McGill-Queen's University Press.

McIntosh, P. (1987) *Sport in Society*, London: West London Press.

McKay, J. (1986) Hegemony, the state and Australian sport, in Lawrence, G. and Rowe, D. (eds), *Powerplay: Essays in the Sociology of Australian Sport*, Sydney: Hale & Iremonger.

Mcleod, J.M. (1978) The corporatist strain in Canadian politics: the invisible fist, conference paper, *Canadian Political Ideas*, York: University of York.

McManus, M. (1993) The Republic of Ireland, in Chandler, J.A. (ed.), *Local Government in Liberal Democracies: An Introductory Survey*, London: Routledge.

Madsen, J. (1994) *Educational Reform at the State Level: The Politics and Problems of Implementation*, Washington, DC: Falmer Press.

Maidment, R. and McGrew, A. (1991) *The American Political Process*, London: Sage.

Mair, P. (1987) *The Changing Irish Party System*, London: Frances Pinter.

Mandle, W.F. (1976) Cricket and Australian nationalism in the nineteenth century, in Jaques, T. and Pavia, G. (eds), *Sport in Australia: Selected Readings*, Sydney: McGraw-Hill.

—— (1977) The IRB and the beginnings of the Gaelic Athletic Association, *Irish Historical Studies*, vol. XX, no. 80, September.

Marren, D. (1995) Providing public recreation facilities as a business: a case study, paper to ILAM conference, 'Public recreation services . . . planning for the future', 15 June, Dublin.

Marsh, C. (1989) Point and counterpoint: moving towards a national curriculum, *Curriculum Perspectives*, vol. 9.4, pp. 71–2.

Marsh, D. and Rhodes, R.A.W. (eds) (1992) *Policy Networks in British Government*, Oxford: Clarendon Press.

Martell, G. (1995) *A New Education Politics*, Toronto: James Lorimer & Co.

Martens, F.L. (1975) The state of physical education in Canadian schools: a cross country look, *Education Canada*, Fall, pp. 25–30.

Mascarenhas, R.C. (1993) Building an enterprise culture in the public sector: reform of the public sector in Australia, Britain, and New Zealand, *Public Administration Review*, vol. 53.4.

Mason, P. (1985) *Professional Athletics in Australia*, Adelaide: Rigby.

Mason, V. (1995) *Young People and Sport – A National Survey, 1994*, London: OPCS.

Massengale, J. D. (1981) Role conflict and the teacher/coach: some occupational cause and considerations for the sport sociologist, in Greendorefer, S.L. and Yiannakis, A. (eds), *Sociology of Sport: Perspectives*, West Point, NY: Leisure Press.

Matthews, T.V. (1983) Business associations and the state 1850–1979, in Head, B.W. (ed.), *State and Economy in Australia*, Melbourne: Oxford University Press.

—— (1989) Interest groups, in Smith, R. and Watson, L. (eds), *Politics in Australia*, Sydney: Allen & Unwin.

Mercer, D. (1977) Introduction, in Mercer, D. (ed.), *Leisure and Recreation in Australia*, Malvern, Vic.: Sorrett Publishing.

Metcalfe, A, (1974) Some background influences on nineteenth century Canadian sport and physical education, *Canadian Journal of Sport and Physical Education*, vol. V.1, May, pp. 62–73.

Meyer, J.W. and Rowan, W.R. (1977) Institutional organisations: formal structure as myth and ceremony, *American Journal of Sociology*, vol. 80, pp. 340–63.

Mills, M. and Saward, M. (1994) All very well in theory, but what about the practice? A critique of the British idea of policy networks, paper, Political Studies Association Annual Conference, York, 1994.

Milton, J. (1994) Managing services with fewer resources: a study in partnership and innovation, *Recreation Canada*, vol. 52.4, pp. 4–6.

Ministry of State for Fitness and Amateur Sport, Canada (1977) *Towards a National Policy on Amateur Sport, Working Paper*, Ottawa: Ministry of Supply and Services.

—— (1992) *Sport: The Way Ahead*, report of the Minister's Task Force on Federal Sport Policy, Ottawa: Ministry of Supply and Services.

Miracle, A.W. and Rees, C.R. (1994) *Lessons From the Locker Room: The Myth of School Sports*, Amherst, NY: Prometheus Books.

Mirecki, G. (1992) Shaping Canada's future: the essential benefits of recreation, *Recreation Canada*, October, pp. 8–9.

Moore, D. (1994) New minister reveals his plans for sport, *Sport Report*, vol. 14.2, pp. 8–10.

Moriarty, D., Fairall, D. and Galasso, P.J. (1992) The Canadian Commission of Inquiry into the use of drugs and banned practices intended to increase athletic performance, *Journal of Legal Aspects of Sport*, vol. 2.1, pp. 23–31.

Moynihan, C. and Coe, S. (1987) *The Misuse of Drugs in Sport*, London: The Sports Council.

Mugford, S. (1993) *The Value of Sport, Ethics, and The Control of Performance-enhancing Drugs: A Study of Australian Sports Community*, Canberra: ASDA.

Naar, T. (1995) Promises, promises: PE still a major concern, *Sport Report*, vol. 15.2, Winter, pp. 6–8.

Nafziger, J.A.R. (1988) *International Sports Law*, Dobbs Ferry, NY: Transnational Publishers Inc.

Nagel, S. S. (1990) Conflicting evaluations of policy studies, in Lynn, N.B. and Wildavsky, A. (eds), *Public Administration*, Chatham, NJ: Chatham House.

National Aboriginal Sports Foundation (1980) *Annual Report 1979/80*, Canberra: NASF.

National Association for Sport and Physical Education (1992) *Outcomes of Quality Physical Education Programs*, Reston, Va.: NASPE.

—— (1993) *Shape of the Nation 1993*, Reston, Va.: NASPE.

—— (1994) *Sport and Physical Education Advocacy Kit*, Reston, Va.: NASPE.

National Collegiate Athletic Association (1992) *NCAA Drug-testing Education Programme: 1992–93*, Overland Park, Kan.: NCAA.

National Council for Curriculum and Assessment (1991) *Report of the Review Body on the Primary Curriculum*, Dublin: The Stationery Office.

National Recreation and Parks Association (1988) *Indianapolis – A City Reborn*, NRPA Dateline, February, pp.1 and 5.

Nauright, J. (1996) Money, methods, medals: the Australian elite sport system in the 1990s, in Hardman, K. (ed.), *Sport for All: Issues and Perspectives in International Context*, ISCPES Monograph, Manchester: Centre for Physical Education and Leisure Studies.

Nelson, D.N. (1978) Political convergence: an empirical assessment, *World Politics*, vol. 30, pp. 411–31.

Nelson, H. (1989) State politics, in Smith, R. and Watson, L. (eds), *Politics in Australia*, Sydney: Allen & Unwin.

Nicholson, R.H. (1987) Drugs in sport, *National Rifle Association Journal*, vol. LXVI.3.

Nixon, R. (1985) Working together: the role of education and recreation departments, Sports Council Recreation Managment Conference, 'Youth . . . stepping into leisure', London: Sports Council.

Noah, H.J. (1984) The uses and abuses of comparative education, *Comparative Education Review*, vol. 28.4, pp. 550–62.

Noll, R. N. (1991) Professional basketball: economic and business perspectives, in Staudohar, P.D. and Mangan, J.A. (eds), *The Business of Professional Sports*, Urbana: University of Illinois Press.

Norton, A. (1994) *International Handbook of Local and Regional Government: A Comparative Analysis of Advanced Democracies*, London: Edward Elgar.

O'Brien, A. (1993) *Municipal Consolidation in Canada and its Alternatives*, Ottawa: Intergovernmental Committee for Urban and Regional Research.

O'Brien, D. and Overby, J.O. (1992) Drugs and sport: developing a drug policy, *Journal of Legal Aspects of Sport*, vol. 2.1, pp. 32–6.

O'Connor, J. (1973) *The Fiscal Crisis of the State*, New York: St. James Press.

O'Donoghue, T. (1989) *The Physical Education Association of Ireland 1968–1989*, Limerick: PEAI.

O'Donovan, G. (1993) Lichamelijke opvoeding in Ierland, *Lichamelijke Opvoeding*, no. 14, pp. 707–12.

O'Halpin, E. (1992) Policy making, in Coakley, J. and Gallagher, M. (eds), *Politics in the Republic of Ireland*, Galway: Political Studies Association of Ireland.

Olson, M. (1971) *The Logic of Collective Action*, Cambridge, Mass.: Harvard University Press.

O'Sullivan, M. and McCarthy, L. (1994) Physical education in Ireland: a view from the looking glass, in Duffy, P. and Dugdale, L. (eds), *HPER – Moving Towards the 21st. Century*, Champaign, Ill.: Human Kinetics.

O'Sullivan, M., Siedentop, D. and Tannehill, D. (1994) Breaking out: codependency of high school physical education, *Journal of Teaching in Physical Education*, vol. 13, pp. 421–8.

O'Toole, P. (1995) Opportunities for grant aiding in leisure from EU sources, paper to ILAM conference, 'Public recreation services . . . planning for the future', 15 June, Dublin.

Ottawa, City of (1996) *Department of Community Services, Strategic Direction and Organisational Structure*, Ottawa: City of Ottawa.

Pagano, M. (1990) The price of leisure: user fees and recreational facilities, in *The Municipal Yearbook 1990*, Washington, DC: International City Management Association.

Painter, M. (1989) Local government, in Smith, R. and Watson, L. (eds), *Politics in Australia*, Sydney: Allen & Unwin.

Panitch, L. (1977) The role and nature of the Canadian state, in Panitch, L. (ed.), *The Canadian State: Political Economy and Political Power*, Toronto: Toronto University Press.

—— (1979a) Corporatism in Canada? in Schultz, R., Kruhlak, O.M. and Terry, J.C. (eds), *The Canadian Political Process*, Toronto: Holt, Rinehart & Winston of Canada.

—— (1979b) The development of corporatism in liberal democracies, in Schmitter, P.C. and Lehmbruch, G. (eds), *Trends Towards Corporatist Intermediation*, Beverly Hills: Sage.

Panther, N.J. (1995) Commercializing municipal recreation, in *Municipal World*, May.

Paraschak, V. (1989) Native sports history: pitfalls and promise, *Canadian Journal of History of Sport*, vol. XX.1.

Pearson, K. and O'Hara, J. (1977) The flavour of Australian sport, in Mercer, D. (ed.), *Leisure and recreation in Australia*, Malver, Vic.: Sorrett Publishing.

Peppard, V. and Riordan, J. (1993) *Playing Politics: Soviet Sports Diplomacy to 1992*, Greenwich, Conn.: JAI Press Inc.

Pernell, L. (1990) Drug testing of student athletes: some contract and tort implications, *Denver University Law Review*, vol. 67, pp. 279–300.

Peters, B.G. (1986) *American Public Policy: Promise and Performance*, 2nd edn, Basingstoke: Macmillan.

Peters, R.S. (1966) *Ethics in Education*, London: Allen & Unwin.

Peterson, P. (1981) *City Limits*, Chicago: University of Chicago Press.

Petracca, M.P. (1992) *The Politics of Interests*, Boulder, Col.: Westview Press.

Physical Education Association of Ireland (1993) *Response to 'Education for a Changing World'*, Green Paper on Education, PEAI: Limerick.

Physical Education Working Party (1989) Physical education: at a critical crossroads, report to the National Council for Curriculum Assessment, mimeo.

Pigeassou, C. (1991) Sport et économie: l'émergence de nouveaux acteurs en France, les collectivés territoriales, in Landry, F., Landry, M. and Yerles, M. (eds), *Sport: The Third Millennium*, Sainte-Foy: Les presses de l'Université de Laval.

Porter, B. and Cole, J. (1990) *Amateur Sport: Future Challenges*, second report of the Standing Committee on Health and Welfare, Social Affairs, Seniors and the Status of Women, Ottawa: Ministry of State for Fitness and Amateur Sport.

Poujol, G. (1993) Leisure politics and policies in France, in Bramham, P., Henry, I.,

Mommas, H. and van der Poel, H. (eds), *Leisure Policy in Europe*, London: CAB International, pp. 13–39.

Presthus, R. (1973) *Elite Accommodation in Canadian Politics*, Toronto: Toronto University Press.

Pross, A.P. (1986) *Group Politics and Public Policy*, Toronto: Oxford University Press.

Przeworski, A. and Teune, H. (1970) *The Logic of Comparative Social Enquiry*, New York: Wiley.

Ramblers Association (1984) *Keep Out: The Hundred Year Struggle for Public Access to the Hills and Mountains of Britain, 1884–1984*, London: The Ramblers Association.

Ravenhill, J. (1989) Business and politics, in Smith, R. and Watson, L. (eds), *Politics in Australia*, Sydney: Allen & Unwin.

Ravitch, D. (1983) *The Troubled Crusade: American Education, 1945–1980*, New York: Basic Books.

Raywid, M.A. (1990) School governance, in Elmore, R. (ed.), *Restructuring Schools: The Next Generation of Educational Reform*, San Francisco, Calif.: Jossey Bass Publishers, pp. 152–99.

Real, M. (1986) Global ritual: Olympic media coverage and international understanding, unpublished paper, University of Calgary, Canada.

Redmond, G. (1985) Developments in sport from 1939 to 1976, in Howell, M.L. and Howell, R.A. (eds), *History of Sport in Canada*, Champaign, Ill.: Stipes Publishing Co.

—— (1986) *Sport and Politics*, Toronto: Human Kinetics Publishers Inc.

Reiss, S. (1989) *City Games: The Evolution of American Urban Society and the Rise of Sports*, Urbana: University of Illinois Press.

Rhodes, R.A.W. (1985) Power dependence, policy communities and inter-governmental networks, *Public Administration Bulletin*, no. 49.

—— (1986) *The National World of Local Government*, London: Allen & Unwin.

—— (1988) *Beyond Westminster and Whitehall*, London: Unwin Hyman.

—— (1990) Policy networks: a British perspective, *Journal of Theoretical Politics*, vol. 2, pp. 293–317.

Rhodes, R.A.W. and Wistow, G. (1988) *The Core Executive and Policy Networks: Caring for Mentally Handicapped People*, Essex Papers in Policy and Government, No. 49, Colchester: University of Essex.

Richards, S. (1994) State drug testing to be introduced, *Sport Report*, vol. 14.1, pp. 20–1.

Richardson, J.J. (1996) Policy-making in the European Union: interests, ideas and garbage cans of primeval soup, in Richardson, J.J. (ed.), *European Union: Power and Policy-making*, London: Routledge.

Richardson, J.J. and Jordan, A.G. (1979) *Governing Under Pressure*, Oxford: Martin Robertson.

Riordan, J. (1977) *Sport in Soviet Society: Development of Sport and Physical Education in Russia and the USSR*, New York: Cambridge University Press.

Riordan, J. (ed.) (1978) *Sport Under Communism*, London: Hurst.

Ripley, R.B. and Franklin, G.A. (1976) *Congress, the Bureaucracy, and Public Policy*, Homewood, Ill.: The Dorsey Press.

Roberts, G.R. (1991) Professional sports and the Antitrust Laws, in Staudohar, P.D. and Mangan, J. A. (eds), *The Business of Professional Sports*, Urbana: University of Illinois Press.

Roberts, K. (1996) Young people, schools, sport and government policies, *Sport, Education and Society*, vol. 1.1, pp. 47–57.

Roberts, T. (1973) The influence of the British Upper Class on the development of the value claim for sport in the public education system of Upper Canada from

1830 to 1875, *Canadian Journal of History of Sport and Physical Education*, vol. IV.1.

Robertson, H.-J. and Barlow, M. (1995) Restructuring from the right: school reform in Alberta, in Laxer, G. and Harrison, T. (eds), *The Trojan Horse: Alberta and the Future of Canada*, Montreal: Black Rose Books.

Roche, D. (1982) *Local Government in Ireland*, Dublin: Institute of Public Administration.

Rodger, B. (1978) *Sport in its Social Context: International Comparisons*, Strasbourg: Council of Europe.

Romaneck, G. (1989) Teaching and learning – not winning – lie at the heart of high school athletics, *National Federation News*, no. 32.

Rooney, J.F. (1980) *The Recruiting Game: Towards a New System of Intercollegiate Sports*, Lincoln: University of Nebraska Press.

Rose, R. (1973) Comparing public policy: an overview, *European Journal of Political Research*, vol. 1, pp. 67–93.

—— (1988) Comparative policy analysis: the program approach, in Dogan, M. (ed.), *Comparing Pluralist Democracies: Strains on Legitimacy*, Boulder, Col.: Westview Press, pp. 217–41.

Royal Commission on Learning (1995) vols 1–4, Toronto: Queen's Gate Printer.

Sage, G.H. (1990) *Power and Ideology in American Sport: A Critical Perspective*, Champaign, Ill.: Human Kinetics Books.

Sallis, J. and McKenzie, T. (1991) PE's role in public health, *Research Quarterly for Exercise and Sport*, no. 62, pp. 124–37.

Salter, M. (1977) The Indian athlete: exploiting or exploited? *Proceedings of the Society on the History of Physical Education and Sport in Asia and the Pacific Area, 1976*, Natanya, Israel: Wingate Institute for Physical Education and Sport.

Sancton, A. (1992) Provincial–Municipal disentanglement in Ontario: a dissent, *Municipal World*, vol. 102, July, pp. 23–4.

Saunders, J. (1973) A brief on the status of PE in Newfoundland, unpublished paper, Halifax: Government of Newfoundland.

Saunders, P. (1982) *Social Theory and the Urban Question*, London: Hutchinson.

—— (1984) Rethinking local politics, in Boddy, M. and Fudge, C. (eds), *Local Socialism?*, London: Macmillan.

—— (1986) Reflections on the dual state thesis: the argument, its origins and its critics, in Goldsmith, M. and Villadsen, S. (eds), *Urban Political Theory and the Management of Fiscal Stress*, Aldershot: Gower, pp. 1–40.

Schaller, W.L. (1991) Drug testing and the evolution of federal and state regulation of intercollegiate athletics: a chill wind blows, *The Journal of College and University Law*, vol. 18, pp. 131–61.

Scharpf, F. W. (1977) Public organisation and the waning of the welfare state: a research perspective, *European Journal of Political Research*, vol. 5, pp. 329–46.

Schmitter, P.C. (1979) Still the century of corporatism, in Schmitter, P.C. and Lehmbruch, G. (eds), *Trends Towards Corporatist Intermediation*, Beverly Hills: Sage.

Schrodt, B. (1984) Federal programmes of physical recreation and fitness: the contributions of Ian Eisenhardt and BC's Pro-Rec, *Canadian Journal of History of Sport*, vol. 15.2.

Secondary Heads Association (1987) *No Ball*, London: SHA.

—— (1990) *Enquiry into the Provision of Physical Education in Secondary Schools*, London: SHA.

Semotiuk, D.M. (1986) National government involvement in amateur sport in Australia 1972–1981, in Krotee, M.L. and Jaegar, E.M. *Comparative PE and Sport*, vol. 3, Champaign, Ill.: Human Kinetics Press.

—— (1994) Restructuring Canada's national sports system: the legacy of the Dubin

Inquiry, in Wilcox, R.C. (ed.), *Sport in the Global Village*, Morgantown, WV: Fitness Information Technology Inc.

Sharpe, J. (1985) Central co-ordination and the policy network, *Political Studies*, vol. 33.3, pp. 361–81.

Shivers, J.S. (1993) *Introduction to Recreational Service*, Springfield, Ill.: Charles C. Thomas.

Shoard, M. (1987) *This Land is Our Land: The Struggle for Britain's Countryside*, London: Paladin.

Siedentop, D. (1982) Movement and sport education: current reflections and future images, in Howell, M.L. and Saunders, J.E. (eds), *Proceedings of the VII Commonwealth and International Conference on Sport, PE, Recreation and Dance*, vol. 6, St Lucia, Qld.: Department of Human Movement Studies, University of Queensland.

Siedentop, D. (1987a) High school physical education: still an endangered species, *Journal of Physical Education, Recreation and Dance*, vol. 58.2, pp. 24–5.

—— (1987b) The theory and practice of sport education, in Barrete, G.T., Feingold, R.S., Rees, C.R. and Piéron, M. (eds), *Myths, Models, Methods in Sport Pedagogy*, Champaign, Ill.: Human Kinetics Press.

Simeon, R. (1972) *Federal–Provincial Diplomacy: The Making of Recent Policy in Canada*, Toronto: Toronto University Press.

Simri, U. (1979) *Comparative Physical Education and Sport*, Natanya, Israel: Wingate Institute for Physical Education and Sport.

Skogstad, G. and Kopas, P. (1992) Environmental policy in a federal system, in Boardman, R. (ed.), *Canadian Environmental Policy: Ecosystems, Politics and Process*, Toronto: Oxford University Press.

Slack, T., Berrett, T. and Mistry, K. (1994) Rational planning systems as a source of organisational conflict, *International Review for the Sociology of Sport*, vol. 29.3.

Smith, M.J. (1993) *Pressure, Power and Policy: State Autonomy and Policy Networks in Britain and the United States*, Hemel Hempstead: Harvester-Wheatsheaf.

Smith, T.A. (1975) *The Comparative Policy Process*, Santa Barbara: Clio Press.

Smyth, R. (1992) Closing municipal recreational facilities: hard choices in tough times, *Recreation Canada*, May, pp. 8–14.

Soroos, M.S. (1990) A theoretical framework for global policy studies, in Nagel, S.S. (ed.), *Global Policy Studies*, Basingstoke: Macmillan.

Souter, G. (1978) *Lion and Kangaroo-Australia: 1901–1919, the Rise of A Nation*, Sydney: Fontana Books.

Souter, P. (1989) Sports participation in Australia, in *Department of the Arts, Sport, the Environment, Tourism and Territories, Ideas for Australian Recreation: Commentaries on the Recreation Participation Surveys*, Canberra: Australian Government Publishing Service.

Spencer, S. and Moman, S. (1996) A 'Golden' Partnership, *Parks and Recreation*, November, pp. 36–41.

Sperber, M. (1990) *College Sports Inc.: The Athletic Department vs. the University*, New York: Henry Holt & Co.

Sport and Leisure (1985) Opening time, vol. 26, no.2, March/April.

Sport Canada (1983) *Drug Use and Doping Control in Sport – A Sport Canada Policy*, Ottawa: Fitness and Amateur Sport.

—— (1996) *Sport Canada Briefing on Sport Policies and Programs*, Ottawa: Sport Canada.

Sports Council (1986) *Drug Abuse in Sport*, London: Sports Council.

—— (1988) *Sport in the Community: Into the 90s*, London: Sports Council.

—— (1990) The structure of sports administration: international perspectives, mimeo, London: Sports Council.

—— (1993) Compulsory Competitive Tendering Sport and Leisure Management: National Information Survey Report, London: Sports Council.

—— (1995) *Condition and Refurbishment of Public Sector Facilities*, London: Sports Council.

—— (1996) *Valuing Volunteers in UK Sport*, London: Sports Council.

Standing Committee on the Environment, Recreation and the Arts, Australia, Senate (1992) *Physical and Sport Education in Australian Schools*, Chair R.A. Crowley, Canberra: Commonwealth of Australia.

Stanton, P. (1995) Government funding for recreation facilities, paper to ILAM conference, 'Public recreation services . . . planning for the future', 15 June, Dublin.

Staudohar, P. D. and Mangan, J.A. (eds) (1991) *The Business of Professional Sports*, Urbana: University of Illinois Press.

Stewart, B. (1986) Sport as big business, in Lawrence, G. and Rowe, D. (eds), *Power Play: Essays in the Sociology of Australian Sport*, Sydney: Hale & Iremonger.

Stewart, J. (1991) Australian public policy and the problem of fragmentation, *Australian Journal of Public Administration*, vol. 50.3, pp. 361–8.

Stewart, R. (1984) The politics of the accord: does corporatism explain it? *Politics*, vol. 20.1, pp. 26–36.

Stewart, R.G. and Ward, I. (1992) *Politics One: An Introduction to Australian government*, Melbourne: Macmillan.

Stone, M.H. (1988) Implications for connective tissue and bone alterations resulting from resistance exercise training, *Medicine and Science in Sports and Exercise*, no. 20, pp. S162–8.

Stones, R. (1990) Government–finance relations in Britain, 1964–1967, *Economy and Society*, vol. 19.1, pp. 32–5.

Storey, E.H. (1990) The quest for a national policy on recreation: a brief history, *Canadian Parks and Recreation*, vol. 48.2, pp. 7–9.

Stratton, J. (1986) Australia – This Sporting Life, in Lawrence, G. and Rowe, D. (eds), *Power Play: Essays in the Sociology of Australian Sport*, Sydney: Hale & Iremonger.

Sugden, J. and Bairner, A. (1986) Northern Ireland: the politics of leisure in a divided society, *Leisure Studies*, vol. 5.

—— (1993) *Sport, Sectarianism and Society in a Divided Ireland*, Leicester: Leicester University Press.

Swanson, R.A. (1968) The acceptance and influence of play in American Protestantism, *Quest*, vol. 11, pp. 58–70.

Szalai, A. (1972) *The Use of Time*, The Hague: Mouton.

Taggart, A., Alexander, K. and Taggart, J. (1993) Thinking allowed: three teachers comment on the national curriculum, *ACHPER National Journal*, Autumn, pp. 21–5.

Talbot, M. (1995) Physical education and the national curriculum: some political issues, *Leisure Studies Association Newsletter*, no. 41, pp. 20–30.

Teune, H. (1978) A logic of comparative policy analysis, in Ashford, D.E. (ed.), *Comparing Public Policies: New Concepts and Methods*, Beverly Hills: Sage, pp. 43–55.

Thelin, J.R. (1994) *Games Colleges Play: Scandal and Reform in Intercollegiate Athletics*, Chicago: University of Illinois Press.

Thomas, R.H. (1983) *The Politics of Hunting*, Aldershot: Gower.

Thurber, J. (1991) *Divided Democracy: Cooperation and Conflict Between President and Congress*, Washington: CQ Press.

Tindal, C.R. (1995) Measuring results and rewarding success, *Municipal World*, April.

—— (1996) Municipal restructuring: the myth and the reality, *Municipal World*, March, pp. 3–7.

Tindal, C.R. and Tindal, S.N. (1984) *Local Government in Canada*, 2nd edn, Toronto: McGraw-Hill Ryerson.

—— (1995) *Local Government in Canada*, 4th edn, Toronto: McGraw-Hill Ryerson.

Todd, T. (1987) Anabolic steroids: the gremlins of sport, *Journal of Sport History*, vol. 14.1, pp. 87–107.

Travis, A.S. (1979) *The State and Leisure Provision*, London: Sports Council/Social Science Research Council.

Truman, D. (1951) *The Governmental Process*, New York: A.E. Knopf.

Turnbull, J. (1995) The Senate Inquiry and Government Response: Two Years on and 'Little Real Action', *ACHPER Healthy Lifestyle Journal*, Winter, pp. 15–20.

Tygiel, J. (1983) *Baseball's Great Experiment: Jackie Robinson and His Legacy*, New York: Oxford University Press.

United States Olympic Committee (1995) *Drug Control Administration, Annual Report 1994*, Colorado Springs: USOC.

Vail, S. and Roth, T. (1994) Community resource sharing: the Markham story, *Recreation Canada*, vol. 52.2, pp. 10–11.

Vamplew, W., Moore, K., O'Hara, J., Cashman, R. and Jobling, I. (eds) (1994) *The Oxford Companion to Australian Sport*, Melbourne: Oxford University Press.

Veal, A.J. (1989) An international comparison: Australia and the United Kingdom, in *Department of the Arts, Sport, the Environment, Tourism and Territories, Ideas for Australian Recreation: Commentaries on the Recreation Participation Surveys*, Canberra: Australian Government Publishing Service.

Veal, A.J. and Travis, A.S. (1979) Local authority services – the state of play, *Local Government Studies*, vol. 5.4, July/August.

Veblen, T. (1925) *Theory of the Leisure Class*, London: Allen & Unwin.

Verabioff, L.J. (1986) Can we justify daily physical education? *CAHPER Journal*, vol. 52.1, pp. 8–10.

Vig, N.J. and Schier, S.E. (1985) *Political Economy in Western Democracies*, New York: Holmes & Meier.

Voy, R. (1991) *Drugs, Sport and Politics*, Champaign, Ill.: Leisure Press.

Wallerstein, E. (1979) *The Capitalist World Economy*, Cambridge, Mass: Harvard University Press.

—— (1983) *Historical Capitalism*, New York: New Left Books.

Warwick, D. and Osherson, S. (1973) Comparative analysis in the social sciences, in Warwick, D. and Osherson, S. (eds), *Comparative Research Methods*, Englewood Cliffs, NJ: Prentice-Hall.

Watkins, P. (1992) The transformation of educational administration: the hegemony of consent and the hegemony of coercion, *Australian Journal of Education*, vol. 36.3, pp. 237–59.

Weaver, R.K. and Rockman, B.A. (1993) Assessing the effects of institutions, in Weaver, R.K. and Rockman, B.A. (eds), *Do Institutions Matter?: Government Capabilities in the United States and Abroad*, Washington: Brookings Institution.

Weinhold, L.L. (1991) Steroid and drug use by athletes, in Diamont, L. (ed.), *Psychology of Sports, Exercise and Fitness: Social and Personal Issues*, New York: Hemisphere Publishing.

Wellhofer, E.S. (1989) The comparative method and the study of development, diffusion and social change, *Comparative Political Studies*, vol. 22.3, pp. 315–42.

West, D.R. (1973) Physical fitness, sport and the federal government, 1909 to 1954, *Canadian Journal of History of Sport and Physical Education*, December, pp. 26–42.

West, K. (1984) *The Revolution in Australian Politics*, Ringwood: Penguin.

Whyte, J. (1980) *Church and State in Modern Ireland, 1923–1979*, 2nd edn, Dublin: Gill & Macmillan.

Wilks, S. and Wright, M. (eds) (1987) *Comparative Government–Industry Relations*, Oxford: Clarendon Press.

—— (1988) *Comparative Government–Industry Relations*, Oxford: Clarendon Press.

Williams, M.H. (1974) *Drugs and Athletic Performance*, Springfield, Ill.: Thomas.

Wilson, J. (1988) *Sport and Leisure*, London: Unwin-Hyman.

—— (1994) *Playing by the Rules: Sport, Society and the State*, Detroit: Wayne State University Press.

Wilson, J.Q. (1973) *Political Organizations*, Beverly Hills: Sage.

Wiltshire, K. (1992) Australia's new federalism: recipes for marble cake, *Publius: The Journal of Federalism*, vol. 22, Summer, pp. 165–80.

Wistow, G. and Rhodes, R.A.W. (1987) Policy networks and policy process: the case of care in the community, paper, PSA conference, Aberdeen.

Wolfenden Committee on Sport (1960) *Sport and the Community*, London: Central Council for Physical Recreation.

Wolman, H. and Goldsmith, M. (1992) *Urban Politics and Policy: A Comparative Approach*, Oxford: Blackwell.

Woolley, B.H. (1987) Drugs in society and sport in the United States, in Bellotti, P., Benzi, G. and Ljungqvist, A. (eds), *Official Proceedings, International Athletic Foundation World Symposium on Doping in Sport*, Florence: IAF.

Wright, M. (1988) Policy communities, policy networks and comparative industrial policies, *Policy Studies*, 36.4.

Wynne-Thomas, P. and Arnold, P (1984) *Cricket in Conflict: The Story of the Major Crises that have Rocked the Game*, Rushden: Newnes Books.

Zeigler, E.F. (1994) The rise and fall of sport and physical education philosophy: a plea for a renewal of normative approach in the professional curriculum, *Physical Education Review*, vol. 17.2, pp. 133–42.

Index